EAGLE'S PLUME

The Struggle to Preserve

the Life and Haunts

of America's Bald Eagle

Bruce E. Beans

SCRIBNER

SCRIBNER
1230 Avenue of the Americas
New York, NY 10020

Illustration copyright © by Richard Waxberg

Designed by Deborah Kerner
Set in Adobe Caslon and Monotype Castellar

Manufactured in the United States of America

3 5 7 9 10 8 6 4 2

Library of Congress Cataloging-in-Publication Data is available.

ISBN 0-684-80696-7

Permissions for use of copyrighted works:
Acknowledgement is made for permission to publish the following works:

Lines from "The Deserted Nation" on page 85: Reprinted by permission; © 1966, 1994 E. B. White.
Originally in *The New Yorker.* All rights reserved.

Lines from "Big Yellow Taxi" on page 85: "Big Yellow Taxi," words and music by Joni Mitchell.
Copyright © 1970 Siquomb Publishing Corp. All Rights Reserved. Used by permission.
Warner Bros. Publications U.S. Inc., Miami, FL., 33014

Lines from "Seminole Wind" on page 126: Copyright © 1992 Almo Music Corp. & Holmes Creek
Music (ASCAP). All rights reserved. International copyright secured. Used by permission.

For my parents,

for Kathie,

and for Carolyn and Chris,

three generations with whom

I have seen bald eagles

CONTENTS

ACKNOWLEDGMENTS

This book is the result of a collaborative effort by several hundred people who, during the past three years, have graciously given of their time, interest, and expertise to enlighten me—and, by extension, readers like you—about *Hali-aeetus leucocephalus*, the bald eagle. Foremost among them has been zoologist Larry Niles, chief of the New Jersey Endangered and Nongame Species Program. This book began, in essence, during the spring of 1987, when he invited me to accompany him to the state's sole remaining eagle nest in Bear Swamp. His willingness since then to allow me repeatedly to experience bald eagles in the wild, and to spend an inordinate amount of time exploring his knowledge and views, is the foundation of this work.

I also particularly wish to thank ENSP zoologist Kathy Clark, who accompanied Niles and me that first day, and many other days, in the field. Her forbearance in answering my questions has been remarkable. I am indebted also to the entire ENSP staff, including Mike Valent, Eric Stiles, and Doug Ely, as well as New Jersey residents Cynthia Zirkle, Dick Gilbert, and John Healy.

In addition, I wish especially to thank: For assistance with the chapter on Charles Broley, Jean Broley Patric and Jon Gerrard. For the chapters on history, natural history and/or the effects of DDT: Paul Claussen, Sandy Sprunt, Tom Cade, John Turner, John Mathisen, Stan Wiemeyer, Derek Ratcliffe, David Peakall, Robert Risebrough, David Garcelon, Daniel W. Anderson, Daniel Berger, Chuck Sindelar, William Ruckelshaus, and Adam Kushner.

For the Florida chapters: Tony Steffer, Resee Collins, John White, Stephen Nesbitt, Brian Millsap, Don Wood, Paul Schultz, Petra Botha Wood, the late Herbert Kale, James Antista, Grady Caffin, and Joseph Let-telleir, Stephen Fetters, and their law firm, Grimes, Goebel, Grimes and Hawkins.

For the Chesapeake chapter: Mitchell Byrd, Jim Fraser, Cindy Schulz,

Karen Mayne, Dana Bradshaw, Jim Nash, Gibb Chase, George Fenwick, Mike Lipford, Barry Brady, Tony Opperman, Lefty Gregory, George Simmons, Robert Barbera, Henry Parker, Jon Pope, and Mark Di Vincenzo.

For the chapters on Native Americans and black-market trade: in the Upper Midwest, John Cooper, Nando Mauldin, Bob Standish, Bonnie Ulrich, Larry Aitken, and Dwight Dion; in the Pacific Northwest, Joe Sandberg, Robert Ross, Celeste Whitewolf, Paul Randall, Todd Kupferer, Jim Kniffen, Wilson Wewa Jr., Grant Clements, Bill Howland, and Craig Bates.

For the chapter on wool growers in the intermountain West: Doug McKenna, Rex Shaddox, Dan Marshall, John Griest, Gary Mowad, Peter Michaelson, Jeremy Korzenik, Dan Barnhurst, Charles Pelkey, Nancy Thomas, Ron Windingstad, Nancy Zierenberg, Ed Nugent, Nick Theos, Dick Strom, and Santiago Curuchet.

For the chapter on contaminants: Bill Bowerman, Dave Best, Timothy Kubiak, Sergej Postupalsky, Rex Ennis, Glen Fox, Michael Gilbertson, James Sikarskie, Mark Shieldcastle, Linda Birnbaum, William Kelce, Timothy Gross, H. Franklin Percival, Theo Colburn, Joseph Jacobson, Helen Daly, Harold Humphrey, Karen Holtschneider, and Steve Sliver.

For the Alaska chapter: Erv Boeker, Janet Hall Schempf, Phil Schempf, Mike Jacobsen, Ray and Vivian Menaker, Peter Enticknap, Bill Zack, Dave Cline, John Schnabel, Dave Olerud, Dick Folta, David Nanney, Bill Thomas, Lonnie Strong Hotch, and Joe Hotch.

I also wish to thank Peter Nye, Karen Steenhof, Jim Stinebaugh, Georgia Parham, Jody Millar, and Paul Nickerson, as well as numerous employees of the U.S. Fish and Wildlife Service, state wildlife agencies, and nongovernmental organizations. To those with whom I spoke whose names are omitted either here or in the text for reasons of space, I apologize. The book is richer for your contribution.

A special note of thanks is due a number of those already mentioned who generously reviewed portions of the manuscript; their comments and suggestions resulted in important refinements. Many of the historical and natural history details contained in this book would not have been possible were it not for the late Richard "Butch" Olendorff, who compiled the Raptor Information System now housed at the Interior Department's Raptor Research and Technical Assistance Center in Boise, Idaho. My research was also aided immensely by the Bucks County (Pennsylvania) Free Library Center's interlibrary loan staff and by the book department of Kenny's News Agency and Bookstore in Doylestown, Pennsylvania.

To the old friends and new acquaintances who so graciously provided me with lodging, including Joanne and Fran Blinebury, Terry and Carol Porembski Bennett, Jim and Chris Grant Erdahl, Gary Clowers, and Vivian and Ray Menaker, I extend my gratitude.

A number of friends, all ink-stained wretches, offered continual encouragement and advice: John Grossmann, Margaret Kirk, Michael Sokolove, Tim Whitaker, Ben Yagoda, Robin Warshaw, Sandy and Bob Bauers, and W. Lester Trauch. I also wish to acknowledge those teachers and professors who first inspired and encouraged me to read literature and to write—Warren Winterbottom, William Mullen, James Velten, Claude Koch, James Butler, and Jack Seydow—and those editors who have wrestled with my copy, particularly my two long-standing editors at the *Philadelphia Inquirer* Magazine, Bill Eddins and Tom Frail.

The sage guidance and persuasion of my agent, Matt Bialer, secured a contract with Macmillan and adroitly ushered the book through to publication. Hamilton Cain, my editor at Scribner, enthusiastically adopted what easily could have been an orphaned book. His deft hand is evident throughout.

I also wish to recognize my Medicis, Craig Ammerman and Lou Antosh, as well as the support of my in-laws, Cass and Jim Martin. I thank my brothers, Bob and Tom, for their continued interest. My parents, Cecelia and Marvin Beans, first introduced me to the natural world and, throughout my life, selflessly have been a model of parental support and love.

Finally, to my wife Kathie, who was the first to read most of the manuscript, and to my children, Carolyn and Chris: your sacrifice, understanding, and love have been legendary.

I thank you all.

*"The haft of the arrow had been feathered
with one of the eagle's own plumes.
We often give our enemies the means
of our own destruction."*

—AESOP. FL. C. 580 B.C.,
"THE EAGLE AND THE ARROW"

TO SEE AN EAGLE FLY

We who live this plodding life here below never know how many eagles fly over us. They are concealed in the empyrean. I think I have got the worth of my [spy] glass now that it has revealed to me the white-headed eagle.

—HENRY DAVID THOREAU

The road goes west out of the village, past open pine woods and gallberry flats. An eagle's nest is a ragged cluster of sticks in a tall tree, and one of the eagles is usually black and silver against the sky. The other perches near the nest, hunched and proud, like a griffon. There is no magic here except the eagles. Yet the four miles to the Creek are stir-ring, like the bleak, portentous beginning of a good tale.

—MARJORIE KINNAN RAWLINGS, *Cross Creek*

In late spring my children found first a fluffy young mock-ingbird, then a small robin, paralyzed with fear in a birch near our suburban garage. Both birds looked puzzled as to how they had gotten there, and terrified at the thought of leaving.

For bald eagles, despite their tremendous size, first flight is the same frightening roll of the dice.

Since near dawn on this hot June morning, I have been sitting at the edge of a windbreak of tall oaks, peering through a spotting scope across a southern New Jersey field at a young eaglet marooned in a white pine. The nest in which it hatched twelve weeks ago was fifteen feet above its head. But since it had apparently jumped out of the nest two mornings ago—no one had actually seen it—its entire world had encompassed four feet of the branch to which it now clung.

It obviously has been there a good while. Gossamer down festoons the adjacent pine needles. More down floats away on the light breeze as the bird ruffles its feathers and preens its speckled underbelly. One recalcitrant plume sticks to its curved beak like Velcro.

Early this morning one of its parents briefly alighted on the nest, then on the naked arms of a dead tree, or snag, before disappearing as quickly as it had come. An hour later, croaking softly, both parents return from the Cohansey River to perch near the nest tree. When the eaglet was nest-bound, they had delivered a smorgasbord of prey: perch, catfish, and eels from the river, which lies several hundred yards to the north; diamondback terrapins and full-grown muskrats from the salt marsh rimming the river and Delaware Bay; rabbits from the nearby fields; and a black snake captured when the plot out near the road was being hayed. But they offer nothing now. The eaglet expectantly swivels its head nearly 180 degrees to fix their location, but he soon again is abandoned.

Minutes later, he turns around to face a freshening breeze. Extending his wings to their full, astounding reach, he beats them so rapidly the force pulls the branch up. "Fly," I whisper, selfishly wanting to be the only one to witness its first flight. The eaglet is on its own timetable, though. Its yellow feet and dark talons refuse to let go. Neatly tucking one copper-brown wing, then the other, over its back, it resumes its wait . . . for what? Occasionally it spreads its wings and beats them energetically as it lifts one talon, then the other, off the branch. Prelude to a launch? More often than not, the wing beating is merely a halfhearted prologue to a forward lean and a stream of white splash out its backside. A few more wingbeats and it is as still as Buddha again.

As the sun and the humidity climb toward noon, the bird's folded wings droop and the periods of inactivity, of mindless nothingness, draw longer. A bald eagle is a master of energy conservation; even those that can fly spend more than 90 percent of the day simply perching. Picking ticks off my arms and legs, swatting away biting flies erupting from the river marshes, and enveloped by the sweltering heat, I slip into a half daze myself. Forget the supposed romance of wildlife biology; my notes are reduced to occasional "wingbeat, crap, wingbeat" citations.

In observing wildlife, patience is a virtue, consciousness a curse. Our ability to think of the past and the future is what separates us at times from the present—and from the organisms we wish to understand. This dilemma of biologists—the need to record precise data, to make field observations every five minutes—runs counter to the urge to empty the mind in order to try to intuit the essence of the animals they are studying. Yet, as Larry Niles, the chief of New Jersey's Endangered and Nongame Species Program, once told me, the very discipline of sitting there, of forcing yourself to make those regularly scheduled observations, becomes a kind of a mantra itself.

Shortly after noon the bird and I are interrupted from our reveries by the sound of a Jeep rumbling up the driveway that skirts the nest tree. Terry Stites, the farm's affable young caretaker, is returning from his summer job at a local gladiola farm.

A native of Greenwich, the small village across the river settled by Quakers before William Penn founded Philadelphia, Stites worked as a truck and farm equipment mechanic for ten years, but eventually realized no engine was as complex or intriguing as the marshes and woods he had grown up in. At age twenty-six he quit to pursue a degree in environmental sciences and a career as a state conservation officer, or game warden. In order to attend college full time, he and his wife, Stacey, a nurse, answered an advertisement from a northern New Jersey restaurateur, Robert Horseman, offering free lodging in a tenant house in return for watching over more than six hundred acres and more than a mile of riverfront. Stites mows, maintains the out-buildings and equipment, and tries to keep trespassing to a minimum on the property, a former dairy and chicken farm whose main house, a three-story red brick Flemish bond–style home, has the year 1736 inscribed in brick on its gable end. As an added perk, there is the wildlife: deer stealing out of the woodlots, pheasants calling from the underbrush, geese and swans murmuring on the river each winter night, and red-tailed hawks, kestrels, great horned owls and barn owls perched in the trees at dusk.

Then there are the bald eagles, whose nest is clearly visible from his back porch. Stites soon slips through a break in the trees to join me. Now in his late twenties, he has a strong build and an open face framed by short-cropped brown hair and a neatly trimmed mustache. We both study the nest across a field planted in strips of weeping love grass, which arches over to provide excellent cover for rabbits and other rodents.

At first, Stites thinks the young eagle has moved to another branch, but the more he peers the more he believes it is anchored to the same limb it has clung to since sunset two nights before. The bird pulls and nibbles on some pine needles. "That's something new on me," I say, "I had no idea they were herbivores."

"Maybe it's dehydrated," he says. "It's been on the branch since before noon on Wednesday, and this is Friday. The parents could have fed it, but I haven't seen it."

As we watch, the bird sidles farther into the shade to escape the sun. By this time, it is impossible to use the 40-power option on my spotting scope; the heat waves pouring off the field make the image shimmer too much.

An hour later Stites is replaced by Larry Niles, a zoologist who has worked with New Jersey's eagles for the past decade. "Do you think the bird's in trouble from the heat and lack of food?" I wonder.

After peering through the scope, Niles says not to worry: "He's been fed; he's okay. But even if it has been three days without eating, it could be good for him to lose all that fat he's built up in the nest." He also suggests the bird could be slow to take to the wing because it is an only child: "There's no competition factor here."

At least not for the eagle. For Niles this nest, this bird, represented economic development's first significant legal challenge to the recovery of the bald eagle in New Jersey. Two years earlier the upstream city of Bridgeton and Genstar Stone Products, a British-owned mining firm based in Maryland, had proposed sending sand barges nearly as long as a football field up and down the short, serpentine Cohansey River 1,280 to 1,800 times a year. Bridgeton is the seat of Cumberland County, where several decades of glass manufacturing, clothing, and food processing plant closings have resulted in what is often the highest unemployment rate in the state. To counter that, city officials were planning a $9 million port to bring crushed stone to South Jersey and ship out some of the world's finest glass-quality silica sand. But buried under all the hubris about jobs was the fact that the port operation would employ seventeen workers and, initially, far fewer. Typical of the parochial self-interest that in this country too often ignores the overall good, Bridgeton's leaders spoke only of jobs they would bring to their town, not of the seasonal downriver marina and restaurant jobs the barges might threaten, or the farming jobs the sand mines might displace.

To port proponents, the question of whether the river represented suitable habitat for eagles—much less whether the barging operation would have any effect on it and them—was at the very least peripheral, if not a red herring. "To say because an eagle does a flyover of the area, it makes it an eagle habitat, flies in the face of common sense," groused Stephen Carnahan, the director of the port authority. But while issues such as the destruction of wetlands and tidal flats, and increased silt and water turbidity, were key components of the case against the plan, these isolated items represented a much more complex and ephemeral concept, a naturalness, a history, a culture, an emotional response that, when combined, was unique: the Cohansey River. The citizens' group that had dubbed itself the Cohansey Area River Preservation, Inc. (CARP) knew that, in embodying the tranquil wildness they sought to preserve, the bald eagle was a powerful public relations trump card—even if, even in their own minds, the eagle was not at the heart of the case. They savvily slapped an eagle logo on their letterhead and invited a Lenni-Lenape named Dick Quiet Thunder Gilbert to speak at their second meeting.

"We are the endangered species," Gilbert, a mechanic from West Deptford, New Jersey, told more than sixty residents gathered at the Fairfield Township Hall. Beyond Bridgeton, out among the pink peach blossoms and chocolate soybean fields, that message resonated. The village of Greenwich had a long history of protest. During the Revolutionary War, it staged its own tea-burning party. A generation ago it torpedoed a nuclear power plant and an oil tank farm proposed for the nearby tidal flats.

"It's a moral and a spiritual issue," explained Bevyl Prycl, a landscape painter and CARP member from Greenwich. "A lot of people here are not wealthy, and they make their living on the water or off the land. They fish and crab and trap and work in the marinas, and nobody wants to navigate around barges."

For such rural downstream opponents of the port, invoking the bald eagle was an obvious maneuver. Several years earlier, east of the Cohansey, a small population of wintering bald eagles, and the potential for future eagle nests, had saved the equally idyllic Maurice River from both an earlier Genstar barging proposal and, in the watershed of one of the Maurice's tributaries, a state hazardous-waste dump.

But while Niles appreciated CARP's support, his goals and the agendas of such grassroots environmentalists often differ, and he has little time for those who use the birds as a legal hammer for their own purposes and then forget them. Following the Maurice River triumphs, he testified at a hearing to consider designating the stream as a federal Wild and Scenic River. When he began to speak about the negative impact pleasure boating could have on foraging eagles, he was cut off. Don't, he was told, disturb the weekend sailors who support preservation of the river—for themselves. If, as the late Speaker of the House, Tip O'Neill, was fond of saying, all politics is local, so is environmental politics. Everyone favors environmental protection, unless it somehow impinges on them.

After the Maurice rejection, Genstar turned its attention to the Cohansey, which was thought by its consultants to be less favorable for eagles. Their timing, as it turned out, could not have been worse.

Niles has a copy of an old Esso map he found in the Smithsonian Institution archives on which ornithologist Jackson Abbott, in 1955, had marked a nest location on the Cohansey about five miles downstream from Bridgeton, not far from CARP leader Cindy Zirkle's river bluff home. Ed Manners, a longtime New Jersey bird-watcher, recalls a nest as late as the early 1960s even farther downstream, at the very farm where I was now watching the young eagle perched in the tree.

In 1988 bald eagles had first returned to the river at this farm, building a nest in a dead tree along the water. Niles was never contacted before a storm blew away the top of the tree and the nest. The following year, eagle activity along the river accelerated significantly. In late January a farmer complained that eagles were killing his chickens. Sent to investigate, one of Niles's assistants saw an eagle perched nearby. Two weeks later, in mid-February, Niles received a call from Pete McLain, the retired deputy director of the state's Division of Fish, Game and Wildlife and the founder of the state's Endangered and Nongame Species Program. He had been hunting quail with Robert Horseman at Horsemen's farm, and McLain had seen a bald eagle nest—in the same stand of pines where the current nest is located.

Investigating, Niles saw one adult perched on the dead snag, and an enlarged nest that the pair had apparently pirated from red-tailed hawks. Despite the presence of the one bird, though, Niles suspected the eagles had already abandoned the area because Horseman had been working on a pole barn just two hundred yards away as the birds were trying to nest.

No landowner attitude surprises Niles. There were the Weldons, a spry dairy farming couple in their sixties who, despite three years of failed nests in a tree on their property, so treasured the eagles' presence that they awaited their return each winter with an anticipation that approached reverence. From her kitchen window, Libby Weldon kept detailed notes: "April 9, 1992: We think eagles have hatched. . . . April 13: Saw eagles feed young. Both eagles leaving nest unattended for short periods of time but both of them are close by. We are still hoping!"

But on April 14 of that year the eagles abandoned the nest. Reading to me from her notes of a week later, she says, "This is sad; this'll make you cry: 'Both of them sat in the nest,' just sitting there grieving, I guess."

Then there was the property owner who threatened to cut down a nest tree—a tree that the birds, for whatever reason, ultimately left. Bird-watchers, too, have caused problems. One pair of eagles fled their nest after the location of a nearby great horned owl nest posted on a birders' hot line drew flocks of birders to the area. Some birders have also kept nest sites secret. Two years after Niles first began receiving reports of two adults frequenting the Wading River, which drains out of the Pine Barrens into the Atlantic, he got a call from a birder who had long known of a possible nest but had withheld the information in deference to the landowner. "People think we're going to come in, condemn their land, and take it away from them," says Niles, with some exasperation, "but in almost all cases our interests actually converge because the nest is inevitably going to attract attention and they're going to have problems keeping people off the land, which is what we also want [to control] and can help with. But they don't know that."

Scouring the area to see where else the Cohansey birds might have gone after they left the farm nest, five days later Niles searched Back Creek, the next drainage into the Delaware Bay to the southeast. Out on an island in the salt marsh he spotted another empty eagle nest in a dead hardwood, just thirty-five feet off the ground. Possibly the Cohansey pair's first nest attempt, Niles thinks it could have dated back to 1988 or even 1987, but the reason it was now empty was obvious: ringing the island in quarter-mile intervals was a battery of carbide cannons fired repeatedly each winter to scare hordes of migrating snow geese away from the salt hay being farmed there.

Anxious to have the pair solidify their hold on the Cohansey, during the winter of 1989–1990 Niles gambled for a second time on his ability to attract a pair to a nest of his own making. On a cold, clear December day, with his staff and members of CARP supplying him with sticks, he built a nest in a leafless oak just west of Horseman's farm.

At dusk, after Niles had finished, Dick Gilbert, the Lenni-Lenape, lit and puffed on a ceremonial pipe, raised it to the four points of the compass, and, with the pipe in his outstretched arms above him, slowly circled the base of the tree. With his long braids trailing down over his tan parka, Gilbert prayed:

O Great Spirit,
We come here today, in the open,
Indian and non-Indian alike.
We come hoping that you will bless what we are trying to do.
We have abused this gift, this Mother Earth.
We come today to bring the eagle back to the river,
Where their echoes will be up and down this river once more.
Great Spirit, we ask your blessing.
May you smile upon this which we try to do,
The eagle, . . . Wombeleska, . . . the gift, . . . the bird who flies high.

*We may once more send our prayers upon the wings of Wombeleska, up to
you, the Creator, the Creator of all life.
Today we try once more to live in balance,
To follow your original instructions.
May we be worthy of all these gifts you have given us.
Bring the mighty eagle back to the great river.*
Aho!

Listening to Gilbert, watching him reach into a plastic bag to sprinkle
tobacco around the base of the tree, the scientist in Niles knew that all the
prayers in the world would not matter if the eagles did not find the nest suitable. Yet he had spent too much time in the presence of eagles not to intuit
a certain spiritual aura surrounding them.

The birds never did come to the man-made nest. "Why didn't your medicine work?" I gently chided Gilbert later.

"Larry put too much chicken wire in the base of the nest," Gilbert joked.

However, they did return the following breeding season to the river. In
April, Ernie Zirkle, a state veterinary official and the husband of the CARP
president, located the pair in a nest across the river on a small creek just
upstream from Greenwich. It was too late to actually lay eggs, but Niles
observed the two adults there engaged in dry-run housekeeping—all of it a
prelude, he was confident, to successful nesting the following year.

It never happened. Just as the battle over the sand barge proposal was
reaching a zenith, with the state Department of Environmental Protection's
Division of Coastal Resources poised to rule on the barging application, one
of the adult eagles disappeared.

It is the following spring, just before the trees leaf out. Four of us are
crammed into a small single-engine plane, cruising low above the Cohansey,
looking for a bald eagle or nest. "Bruce," Larry Niles says, "you and Paul
[Willey, the pilot] take the left side; Mike [Baytoff, a photographer] and I'll
take the right." Picking up the river upstream at Bridgeton, we skirt a town
in obvious economic stress. Both the Hunt-Wesson food processing plant
and the Owens-Illinois glass plant lie idle. Below Bridgeton, we pass a golf
course and the Zirkles' house sitting defiantly on a bluff at Fairton, then
swing west as the chocolate-colored river beneath us snakes through ever-
widening tidal marsh. Ten miles below Bridgeton, as we near Greenwich,
Niles points to a small finger of woods angling toward the salt marsh.

Banking hard to the right, Willey guides the plane directly above a black gum that still cradles nest remains. "There it is," Niles says. "Nothing in it. They never went back to it. Last year it was a perfect nest, the pair was copulating, everything. Now nothing.

"I personally believe someone shot the other adult."

He could not make his suspicions public because he had no proof. But as he would explain later in court, the mortality rate for adult eagles is very low and they mate for life. If one bird alone is sighted, the other one obviously died—or was killed.

Circling back over the river, Niles looks hard for a bird or nest. Given the size of the nests, it seems odd that aerial reconnaissance is sometimes needed to spot them. But the birds' preference for remote locations in often swampy locales, the urge not to disturb them from the ground, and the sometimes confounding attitudes of both enthusiasts and landowners has forced Niles to log many motion-sick hours aloft—often to no avail. Despite persistent sightings of pairs of adult eagles, his flights along several streams that empty into the Atlantic bays had uncovered no nests. Once he arranged to halt A-10 bombing run drills out of McGuire Air Force Base for thirty minutes so he and a pilot could search the Forked River. "That should save the feds about ten thousand dollars," he joked, "which is what they gave us for endangered species this year."

This time, flying the length of the Cohansey, Niles also came up empty. Not a bird was seen the entire length of the river. Against his better judgment, the Cohansey was becoming a personal issue for him. He felt his scientific credibility was being questioned. He had already been attacked by the Bridgeton Municipal Port Authority when it learned he had built the nest. Accusing him of siding with the environmentalists and implying he was trying to derail the barge project, the authority's executive director, Stephen Carnahan, demanded assurance that successful use of the nest wouldn't preclude use of the river.

In an internal memo discovered and published by a *Philadelphia Inquirer* reporter, Niles in turn ripped into the port authority and sand company's environmental impact statement: "Their understatement of the importance of the river for eagles is negligent, bordering on deceitful." He was irked because some of the eagle sightings he had furnished to the biological consulting firm conducting the environmental impact statement for port proponents had been omitted in a report by Jeffrey Lincer, the biologist handling the eagle portion of the impact statement.

Niles respected Lincer, the founder and former director the National Wildlife Federation's Raptor Information Center, and the former president of the Raptor Research Foundation, the nation's preeminent association of raptor professionals. He suspected the problem was that all of his information had not been passed on to Lincer. (Lincer later testified he had not received all the data.)

Whatever the reason, these omissions didn't surprise Niles. He appreciates the ticklish dilemma many consultants face. While the very nature of the job is a conflict of interest, many with whom he has worked have acquitted themselves well. More than once, however, he has found himself on the opposite side from consultants who deserve to be called "biostitutes"—private professional biologists paid by developers to say what they want to hear and present the biological data they want to see, the true biological impact of the plans be damned. Lincer certainly wasn't in that category. And yet . . . and yet. Niles couldn't understand why Lincer failed to characterize a suite of eagle behaviors that had been observed as breeding related.

Nonetheless, the state Department of Environmental Protection and Energy rejected the barging proposal on twenty-two different environmental and historic preservation grounds. Genstar and the port authority quickly appealed. "It's a question of commerce versus nature and how much each is willing to compromise," explained Neil Yoskin, the port authority's attorney. "The state is not willing to compromise at all. Is it a beautiful river? No question. But the state's made a sentimental decision."

Despite the DEPE rejection, Niles remained pessimistic before the appeal was presented to an administrative law judge. This was no headline-grabbing spotted-owl-versus-logging-jobs controversy. But he knew this was how the majority of the American landscape had been eaten away, one almost imperceptible piece at a time, as a tidal stream slowly erodes its banks.

"There's no smoking gun," Niles conceded. "You can't say this barging thing is going to kill eagles. It's not. But it is going to slowly turn a river hospitable to eagles and what they represent into something that's inhospitable.

"It's an insidious thing."

Two hours north of the Cohansey, the small hearing room of state administrative law judge Naomi Dower-LaBastille is located within a warren of squat blond brick office buildings near the edge of Trenton. On the days Niles and Lincer testified before her, they both exchanged their typical field apparel for understated charcoal gray business suits. Taller and several years older than Niles, with the slightly receding hairline, mustache, and elongated face of Peter Sellers, Lincer testified with the kind of unflappable presence attorneys crave in an expert witness.

But he startled the state with his testimony. Yoskin, the port authority attorney, asked: "You wouldn't say there were no eagles on the Cohansey River?"

"Quite the contrary," Lincer said, "I myself have made three sightings on the Cohansey. Two birds four years ago . . . And Saturday I saw one at the northern end of the river across from the Water Street docking facility. It flew south a thousand feet as it was mobbed by a crow, and a hundred or two hundred feet north of the boundary line of the [sand barge] project it landed in a snag, where an osprey mobbed the bird." It was the closest sighting yet to the proposed docking site.

Niles believed Lincer had just handed the state the smoking gun he hadn't thought existed.

Nonetheless, Lincer insisted the Cohansey offered only "marginal" eagle habitat, less attractive than the nearby Maurice River in terms of perches, human disturbance, and prey availability. Noting that eagles pluck fish only from the water surface, rather than the two- to three-foot deep plunges ospreys take, he believed the increased water turbidity churned up by the barges and tugboats would not hinder the ability of bald eagles to hunt for a meal.

He felt the same way about the fifty acres sandwiched between the river and two creeks, which would become the docking site. To allow the barges to deliver out-of-state stone and take on Jersey sand, a coastal bluff with good perch trees would be destroyed and two bulkhead slips would be thrust into the water. Truck and barge traffic, conveyor belts, the dumping of sand and stone, and workers would all converge on the site.

"In a regional sense," Yoskin asked, "if these wetlands were rendered totally unusable by this project, would that critically impair the bald eagle?"

"I wouldn't think so," concluded Lincer.

A month after Lincer observed an eagle near the site, however, nature further intervened on its behalf. Despite all her hearings, Judge Dower-LaBastille later wrote, "The best testimony was visual, specifically, the site visit and views of the Cohansey's banks as seen from a boat." Standing atop the bluff the Genstar project would destroy, she saw a pair of state-endangered black skimmers fishing directly in front of her. Farther off, an osprey—a threatened species in New Jersey—circled above the water.

"You're aware we saw some skimmers?" the judge, an avid birder who wears her brown-and-pewter hair pulled back in a severe bun, later asked Niles during his testimony. Nodding, he listed other troubled species—including marine turtles, peregrine falcons, ospreys, several hawks, short-eared owls, and great blue herons—that the project could affect. As for bald eagles, he spoke of their history on the river, the many favorable locations for perching and foraging where woodlands ran down to bends in the river, and continued eagle sightings. Disputing Lincer's analysis, Niles claimed that increased turbidity could diminish the eagles' ability to track fish as they dipped and rose in the water. His conclusions: for eagles, the docking site itself was valuable habitat, and any habitat along the river could be considered essential for the bald eagle's survival.

In fact, he said, "In May, two birds were seen again moving in courtship flight at the pond at Fairton, and I suspect next year they'll be nesting."

When Deputy Attorney General Kathe F. Mullally asked him about Lincer's interpretation of the data, Niles's response was unequivocal: "I disagree with his conclusions. He had taken all the sightings and broken them down into characteristics such as flying and perching, and based on that type of analysis he estimated there was no conclusive evidence of nesting.

"But doing that took it all out of context. If you consider them together, they add up to the clear conclusion that [the eagles] are nesting."

In fact, just as the judge closed the record on the case early the following year, the Cohansey pair was copulating. Several days before the Cohansey eaglet was banded, the judge filed her ruling: "DEPE showed that there would assuredly be both direct and secondary adverse affects from the project and its operation, which would create an inhospitable environment for bald eagles for the foreseeable future." She concluded the project was prohibited, in part under state regulations that classify both the site and the surrounding area as a "special area" that must be protected because it is critical to endangered and threatened species.

During her boat ride the previous summer, the judge had also noticed the stark contrast between ports she had seen in Salem, Camden, Newark, and New York and the "port" Bridgeton authorities said existed simply because they had designated it as such.

Of the former, she wrote of "the noise and bustle, loading and unloading, movement of giant cranes, signaling of barge, tug, and container ship traffic and comings and goings of heavy trucks, tractor trailers, and all kinds of commercial and employee vehicles. This picture is in stark contrast to the slow meandering Cohansey with farms, a marina or two, and country houses on its banks, a few pleasure craft and its densest development near Bridgeton City center, which consists of a few dilapidated piers, one smartly kept small oil depot and an old warehouse and offices without a pier, belonging to the Bridgeton Port Authority."

As we sit at the edge of the field watching the Cohansey eaglet, Larry Niles thinks back several years to his nest-building attempt near here and to the prayer of Dick Gilbert, the Lenni-Lenape, beseeching the Great Spirit to allow the eagle to return.

"All animals have spirituality," he says. "We deny it because if we recognized it in all animals or plants, we'd have to reconcile our actions of needlessly killing them and raping the landscape. It's easier to understand the spirituality of the eagle because it's easier to see in some animals like them. One Indian characterization of the eagle is that it is the messenger between God and man. Maybe all nature is in between God and man, but the eagle is just easier to see."

Late in the afternoon Niles observes yet another eagle defecation. "He's shitting so much, he's definitely being fed," he says. Getting up to leave for a conservation awards dinner, he adds, "You still might see him fly."

After walking him back to the house to talk with Stites, I return to my viewing station. The bird is gone! I know it even before I reach for the scope. Panning the nearby branches, the nest, and an adjacent pine only heightens my concern. Had my presence all day, or my movements, caused it to jump prematurely? The understory around the nest tree is thick with raspberry canes and honeysuckle vines. Entangled there, a young downed eagle would be no match for a wild dog. How long, I wonder, should I wait before I go looking for the bird? And if I did find it, what would I do, with little chance of catching it and no way to reach Niles or get it back up into the nest?

Moments later, though, the bird lunges out of the top of a skinny oak and heads toward me with all the confidence of a six-year-old diving into a deep pool. Loping along in an ungainly, labored flight, harried by a tiny bird flying atop it like a remora on a shark, it climbs, circling around a pine at the edge of the field to gain altitude and then takes dead aim for home: its nest. But it miscalculates badly. Coming in far too high, hung up—with indecision and juvenile ignorance—directly above the nest, it tries to drop straight down. Instead, it crashes into a jumble of pine boughs in the tree's crown. *Thwack!* Even from a hundred yards away I can hear the rifle-sharp sound of bone striking wood as its wings slam into the branches. And then . . .

Nothing. For several minutes, no movement at all. Its head obscured by pine needles, the fledgling hangs like a rag snared by a tree in a flood. All I can see is its right wing, extended like an anhinga's wing hung out to dry. Is it dead? Is its wing broken?

I think back to what Niles had told me earlier that day: "One of the main problems in learning how to fly is understanding the wind. They intuitively know how to face the wind to take off because they can hold on to a branch and feel the lift. But eagles have to learn how to use the wind to brake and maneuver. They're like sailboats."

And like sailboats in inexperienced hands, they can veer off course.

After several anxious minutes, though, the bird gingerly pulls its right wing back in. It appears to be only stunned. It still has eight feet to negotiate to the nest, but it is trapped in a maze of slender pine boughs and there is no direct route. As the minutes pass, it becomes obvious the bird is not anxious to undergo another flight ordeal.

Forty minutes after the crash, an adult flies over the field, spots the fledgling, and continues back toward the river—I can hear the gulls calling out there—without so much as a second look. Another fifteen minutes pass before the bird begins to move, first nibbling again on some pine needles, then flaring its wings, trying to figure out how to extend them while encumbered by the branches. More than an hour after the crash landing, the homing instinct and genetic neuro-message that tells a young bird "fly" reaches critical mass. Launching itself out of the tree and veering to the right in the same movement, it flies this time with a prowess beautiful to behold. A few downward wingbeats carry it out over the field, where it throws in a brief plank glide, its wings as flat as a board, then corners 180 degrees back to its left. Ignoring yet another small bird that is hounding it from above, it climbs quickly, taking dead aim on the nest before alighting with the grace of Baryshnikov.

My last view of the eaglet, at sunset, is through the spotting scope from the porch of the tenant house. He is hopping madly from the nest to a slim branch, then back to the nest, over and over again in a declaration of defiant courage. No fear of flying now.

He didn't budge from the nest for another three days.

CHAPTER 2

SHELL GAME

. . . the days upon which we can record: "I saw an Eagle today" are red letter days on our calendar.
—WITMER STONE, *Bird Studies at Old Cape May*, 1937

At the Bear Swamp nest I found the birds had left, quite a shock since I was sure they had a young on the way. . . . All I found [under the tree] were feathers that I collected and brought home. This is all very discouraging.
—JOE JACOBS, NEW JERSEY AUDUBON SOCIETY EAGLE SURVEYOR, IN HIS JOURNAL, APRIL 25, 1965

It was the ultimate shell game. Each spring Larry Niles would climb high into a nest in the crown of a century-old pine to spirit away the eggs of bald eagles.

Once in New Jersey there had been twenty or more nests like it, tucked far up in the trees along the feeder creeks and vast marshes that fed the ocean and rimmed what was once one of the country's richest river estuaries. Now the nest was an anachronism, an almost unknown relic of what had been commonplace on the continent for at least a million years.

For centuries we had shot and trapped the eagles and felled their nest trees, we had electrocuted them and finally poisoned them into near oblivion with the insidious miracle of DDT. Fourteen years after the pesticide had been banned, the female here was still so heavily laced with it that she continued to lay thin-shelled eggs—eggs that she and her mate would soon crush as they hopelessly tried to incubate them. Between 1965 and 1974, they had managed to raise just two young; between then and 1980, none.

Then the state concocted a remarkable ruse. Early each March, shortly after the female lowered her body over her freshly laid eggs like a priest bowing low over an altar, Niles would climb the tree. As the flushed adults wheeled above him in protest, the zoologist would find one or two stained off-white eggs on a cushion of grass and sphagnum moss. In his hand they were still warm, and surprisingly small for such a large bird: about the size of an elongated baseball.

Before lowering the eggs to the ground in a foam-padded case, Niles would dupe the eagles into staying on the nest by leaving behind two plaster egg replicas. The real ones, warmed by a hot-water bottle, he would drive to the U.S. Fish and Wildlife Service research center in Patuxent, Maryland, where Cochin bantam chickens had proved to be even better than machines at incubating eagle eggs. Ten days after they hatched, Niles would complete the sleight of hand, replacing the fake eggs in the nest with two eaglets.

Earlier this morning he had returned from Maryland with the chicks: fifteen ounces each of panting whitish gray fuzz, dark curved beaks, and penetrating dark brown eyes. Their crops full of raw, tweezer-fed chicken, they were down below Niles now, waiting for him to haul them up to the eyrie in a joint compound bucket.

As he considered which overhanging branch he should loop his line over in order to reach the nest, the two adult bald eagles, their white heads and tails flashing in the sun like strobe lights, soared above him.

When Larry Niles was a boy, the most exotic creatures he knew were the ospreys that sometimes appeared as he and his father fished the river near their Bucks County, Pennsylvania, home. Suspended thirty feet in the air, hovering on wings longer than he was tall, the elegant brown-and-white raptors would abruptly drop like rocks deep into the water and emerge from their plunge with the fish he could never seem to catch.

But see an even larger eagle? In Montgomery County, the next county to the west, a young John James Audubon had seen bald eagles wading through a creek, corralling fish and capturing them with their beaks. But like the elk, the wolf, the bison, the mountain lion, and even the Lenni-Lenape who had once roamed these now-broken eastern forests, the bald eagle had long ago vanished from this boy's world. The proud, free bird engraved on the quarters in his pocket, the one with which the country had gone to the polls and gone to war and kept the peace for nearly two centuries, the emblem which in that decade would parachute into the darkness of Vietnam and land on the brightness of the moon, in real life was as fanciful as a unicorn, a ghost from some long-lost Eden doomed to an afterlife frozen in stone monuments, wings uplifted but never flying, brought back from the dead only as a graphic logo, the ubiquitous symbol of the federal government, banks, and billion-dollar breweries.

Just two decades later, though, Niles's life's work had become part of an extraordinary national effort to bring back the bald eagle. Not since a partially drugged bear sow had angrily charged past him in the Okefenokee Swamp had he been so impressed with an animal's unbridled power. The previous year he had been seated in a boat in the middle of a salt marsh, watching young eagles learning how to fly. He had removed them from nests on a wild Canadian lake and brought them to the eastern seaboard, to a "hacking tower" at the edge of a marsh, where large plywood cages were mounted high on utility-pole stilts like some kind of low-rent condominiums. Once released, they would eventually return to this region, when they were four or five years old, to breed.

Fourteen weeks old now, the large brown birds were just discovering how to ride a thermal updraft. Finding one, they circled and began to soar, higher and higher until they were mere specks in the sky. Then they disappeared.

"That's the end of it," he had thought. "We're never going to see them again."

Though they did return briefly, he realized then that at that height they could go fifty miles in any direction by doing little more than simply extending their wings. They had the power to go wherever they wanted. Eagles, he had come to realize, also possessed other powers. Simply because it was thought that bald eagles *might* once again nest on a nearby river, the state was poised to reject that river drainage as the site for a hazardous-waste dump. Tree frogs and the world's largest growth of aptly named sensitive joint-vetch, a rare member of the pea family, would be saved. No one, particularly Larry Niles, thought for a minute that a frog or a weed could have done what the eagle had done. When it came to the animal superstars that biologists had dubbed charismatic megafauna, the bald eagle had few rivals.

Yet eagles are so fragile. Before they could fly, the sight of him in his boat far out in the marsh so disturbed the young ones that they would hide behind the hacking tower poles. After their first tentative flights, some of them had to be rescued because they had become hopelessly trapped in the phragmites, the tall reeds that choked the edge of the marsh. One bird he found there couldn't fly because it had a surprisingly minor hairline fracture of the metatarsal, the equivalent of a finger bone.

They seemed to be so closely engineered that if anything went wrong with them, especially when they were young, they likely would die. Ulti-

mately, what most impressed him was how sensitive they were—to disturbance, to contaminants, to changes in their habitat. Watching them, studying them, he had come to believe they were the perfect indicator: if we could
manage our environment so we could keep eagles, it was likely also to be
healthy for us and the rest of the planet.

If that sounded like environmentally correct cant, the crying-wolf syndrome of researchers trying to rationalize their existence and funding, so be
it. Niles believed it. He also believed the bald eagle had become a powerful
litmus test of another sort: if a country supposedly dedicated to the environment could not or would not bring back its national symbol, what hope
was there for hundreds of other less visible species, or for the nation itself?

Larry Niles had chosen the wrong limb. Swinging away from the
tree trunk to the nest, he heard a sickening crack. The tree was dying, and
the branch to which he had tethered his support line a yard above his head
was breaking. Lunging up, he grabbed the rim of the nest with just his left
arm and hung on, his legs dangling seventy-five feet above the ground. He
didn't shout below to his assistants, who were unaware of what was hap-
pening, because he feared his calls would distress the adult eagles flying
nearby.

A left-hander, he was trying, with his weaker right hand, to loosen the
slipknot he had cinched to the main climbing line. Snugged tight by his
weight, the knot at first would not budge, but he eventually worked it loose.
The line was tied into a safety hook clipped to a ring at his waist. Unclip-
ping it, he unhitched himself from what had become the useless umbilical
cord of the climbing rope and pulled the line off the bad limb. But now
what? Nearly at the top of the tree, he had few options, and his left arm,
clinging to the nest, was weakening. A stifling fear of falling had begun to
overwhelm any professional concerns he had for the eagles. Choosing a
branch he had originally rejected because it looked too weak, he managed
with some difficulty to loop the line over it, snap in the safety hook, and
retie the slipknot. The branch accepted his weight, and his ten-minute
ordeal was over.

Shaken, he rested for a few minutes before hoisting the chicks up into
the nest and removing the plaster eggs. Afterward he rappelled down out
of the tree in the professional quandary of his life. Climbing the dying tree
again in the future to rescue thin eggs was out of the question. But if he
didn't, he knew the chances the pair would successfully fledge young again

were scant. If he didn't do something, though, he knew a storm would eventually blast the nest out of the tree and, he feared, send the state's only pair of bald eagles elsewhere, perhaps even out of state.

Either way, the state's unprecedented recent action—condemning the swamp to protect it from sand-mining development because it harbored endangered bald eagles—would be undermined.

What, he wondered, would become of the bald eagles?

AN EAGLE EYRIE

Skirting the river road, (my forenoon walk, my rest,)
Skyward in air a sudden muffled sound, the dalliance of the eagles,
The rushing amorous contact high in space together,
The clinching interlocking claws, a living, fierce, gyrating wheel,
Four beating wings, two beaks, a swirling mass tight grappling,
In tumbling turning clustering loops, straight downward falling,
Till o'er the river pois'd, the twain yet one, a moment's lull,
A motionless still balance in the air, then parting, talons loosing,
Upward again on slow-firm pinions slanting, their separate diverse flight,
She hers, he his, pursuing.
—WALT WHITMAN, "THE DALLIANCE OF THE EAGLES"

Office Memorandum, United States Government
To: (USFWS) Regional Director, Boston, Mass.
From: U.S. Game Management Agent in Charge, Trenton, N.J.
Subject: Bald Eagle Nesting Populations–New Jersey
There are no nesting bald eagles observed or reported in NJ. One adult bald eagle was
observed at Dennis Creek, Cape May County, during the winter waterfowl survey on
Jan. 9th, 1972.
—HOWARD W. BROWN

 There are no signs, no clearly discernible trails.
Even though he has been there many times, late each spring Larry Niles has to drive slowly along a South Jersey railroad cut, peering into the edge of a sandy, timbered-out woods that seems to reinvent itself each year. Finally, he halts his state-issue Jeep Cherokee at a downed pine that still has the skeleton of a wooden platform, a deer stand used by hunters, tacked to it. "This is it," he says. "I remember the stand."

"You're sure?" I chide. The previous year Niles had kept two dozen television, radio, and newspaper journalists standing in the woods in a steady rain for a quarter of an hour while he thrashed around trying to find the way to New Jersey's oldest bald eagle nest. When he eventually ushered the media to the eyrie, all they saw at the base of the tree was the scattered remains of an eaglet: a dozen dark primary feathers halted in mid-growth as they emerged from their sheaths. Niles suspected that the nestling had been victimized by a great horned owl.

This day, though, based on observers' accounts, he's confident that at least one, and probably two, eaglets await him in Bear Swamp. Shouldering a thick coil of nylon climbing rope, he leads our small group of acolytes in single file down an old logging path that soon gives way to a labyrinth of wild, shoulder-high blueberry bushes. The dispassionate monotone he employs on the phone is hard to square with the figure in front of me. Just under six feet tall, at forty-one Larry Niles is dark complexioned, with a bushy mustache and eyebrows, a resolute jaw, and the well-muscled arms of someone who spent his youth helping his father, a carpenter, build custom homes.

The woodland swamp is a tick mecca, and Niles, who suspects he has contracted Lyme disease at least twice, is like a magnet marching through a pile of iron filings as he plunges through the underbrush. Pausing midway, he picks some twenty ticks off his faded jeans. "I think that's a record for me," he says, bemused.

"That's Larry," zoologist Kathy Clark, his sister-in-law and longtime associate, calls from farther back in the line. "Everything's a competition."

When he first joined the state's fledgling endangered species program, Niles had never climbed higher than the ridge beam of a three-story house. For its egg swaps, the state originally used professional tree climbers and out-of-state biologists. To Niles, however, that seemed inappropriate, an admission on the part of the zoologists that they were not the birds' equal. To command the eagles' respect, to understand them, he would have to experience their nest and the heights at which they lived. To do so, he had to climb nearly eight stories up into a pine that reared up out of Bear Swamp.

It is no accident, he believes, that the bald eagles chose this swamp to make their last stand in New Jersey. The drainage of the nearby Maurice (pronounced "Morris") River once contained about eight bald eagle nests, and even during the birds' nadir eagles wintered in the area. Today the swamp is still the most remote, inaccessible nest site in the state.

"It's thick with blueberries and greenbriers," I was once told by Asa "Ace" Brewster, a concrete burial vault dealer and president of the Mauricetown

Gun Club, which each fall combs Bear Swamp for deer. "We like to say it's so thick sometimes that the only way to get through is to get down on your belly and crawl—and that's tough to do in three feet of water."

Deep in the swamp, Niles briefly veers too far to his left. A good sign, he thinks: unlike previous years, when footprints and the tracks of dirt bikes had wound unmistakably to the tree, there was no indication anyone had penetrated the nest area. Hunching down, Niles dips through a green tunnel of underbrush floored with dripping, boot-sucking sphagnum moss. Emerging, he rips free from the thorny tentacles of greenbrier canes and picks his way through a maze of black gum, red maple, and holly.

We hear the adult bald eagles above us before we see them, their rustling wingbeats followed by high-pitched scolding as they bolt from the nest: "*Kleek kik kik kik kik . . . kik kik kik kik kik.*"

It sounds, as the late New Jersey ornithologist Witmer Stone described it, like chalk scratching a slate. So startlingly weak is the call of the bald eagle that filmmakers often overdub it with the magisterial scream of a red-tailed hawk. The call is also much more posture than legitimate threat. Niles's scalp has been strafed by the talons of a peregrine falcon, but for all the strident alarm calls he has heard, an adult bald eagle has never attacked him. Such incidents are quite rare. Bald eagles elsewhere have swooped down toward trespassers or struck the branches of nest trees to ward off researchers. In Alaska, one defended its nest by driving its talons into the back of a biologist as he began climbing a nest tree. It felt, he later said, as if he had been hit with a moderately swung baseball bat. At this New Jersey nest, volunteer Mark Hedden once saw the larger female come within ten feet of Niles. She flipped over on her back, menacingly presenting her talons to him, but he was so focused on the young birds he never saw or heard her.

As we enter the small clearing around the nest tree, however, the pair is clearly agitated. Above the broken canopy their large, dark forms float, flap, and glide, float, flap, and glide in tight circles against the blue sky, all the while spreading their cries of alarm to each other and to their young. They have been eating well. The white splash of eagle excrement paints the knee-high ferns fiddling their way up through the patchy sunlight.

Like much of South Jersey's flora and fauna, the tree, a relatively unknown pond or marsh pine, is at the northern end of its range. Plated with thick reddish brown bark scales, its trunk so thick a man cannot reach around it, the pine rises out of an organic pedestal it has been building since before Lincoln was president. From the base of the tree the nest, a mass of sticks cradled high in the stout, crooked branches, is barely visible. Seven years earlier, in an act of preservation for both himself and the eagles, Larry Niles built it himself.

It was not as simple as tacking together a bluebird house. As a structure in nature, a bald eagle's nest is rivaled only by the cavernous lodges and half-mile-long dams that beavers construct. Florida homeowners with nests in their backyards talk of perched birds eyeing a suitable dead branch for minutes before launching themselves into the air and driving down onto the branch like a thunderbolt to snap it from the trunk. Built in as little as four days, the typical first-year nest measures two feet high and five feet across, with a slight grass-lined depression in the middle for the eggs. In this great wooden maw you could fit 340 robin nests or nearly 700 sparrow nests. But that is just a first-year nest. Bald eagles, as part of their annual nest maintenance, and perhaps as part of the sequence that triggers breeding, add to their nests each year. Often occupied for decades—a bald eagle nest Lewis and Clark first saw on an island below the Great Falls of the Missouri River in 1805 was still in use more than a half century later—the nests can reach gargantuan dimensions. A thirty-six-year-old Ohio nest toppled by a Lake Erie windstorm in 1925 weighed an estimated two metric tons. The largest nest ever recorded—a St. Petersburg, Florida, eyrie occupied from 1910 to at least 1946—was 9.5 feet wide and 20 feet high.

Niles peers up at the nest. The previous autumn he had done a little repair work to buttress it because it had begun to sag. It looks fine today. Following his near-fall from the original nest tree, Niles was encouraged to build this nest by an Arizona biologist who had successfully lured eagles to his own tripod platforms in the desert.

Searching the swamp by air, Niles soon found another supercanopy tree that, like the original, dwarfed the surrounding hardwoods as the World Trade Center towers dominate lower Manhattan. That December, overcoming his considerable trepidation that he might disturb the eagles, he inched his way up the new tree. Pulling himself up with a safety strap wrapped around the trunk, he found what he was looking for about seventy feet up, fifteen feet from the top of the tree: two branches that spread out in a horizontal V toward the south. Some of the pine boughs above would provide good shade in the heat of late spring and summer, but the branching also was open enough for the adults to be warmed by the late winter sun: the same principles upon which Niles had built his family's passive solar home. There also were good unencumbered perches for both the adults and the young as they first ventured beyond the nest, and it was high enough above the tree canopy so that it offered an unimpeded view of the entire swamp and the gray hint of the Delaware Bay on the southern horizon.

Seventy-five yards to the east he could clearly see the old nest tree. From far across the swamp, in a tall deciduous tree, one of the adult bald eagles clearly saw him. He understood why eagles would select such a spot, with a commanding view of everything around them, yet somehow above it all. But the eagles were not. To the west Niles could see the large sand pile of one silica sand mining company; the view to the northeast was dominated by the plant tower and blue-green dredge pits of another sand company, the Unamin Corporation, whose attempt to mine farther into the swamp had precipitated the state's eminent domain action.

From the air, the lifeless aquamarine water–filled pits that pock Cumberland County look as absurd as would icebergs in Miami. During the Miocene Age twelve to twenty million years ago, a coastal environment similar to the one that exists today laid deposits of silica, or quartz sand, sixty feet deep or more here. What are now the last remaining deposits of glass-quality sand in the Northeast have been drawing glass manufacturers to Millville, seven miles to the north, since 1806.

Sucked up by huge dredges that take advantage of the extremely high water table, the sand is carted to Millville's few remaining glass houses. There, heated to 2,500°F., the sand is transformed into glass laboratory equipment, pharmaceutical containers, Avon cosmetics bottles, and Anheuser-Busch beer bottles, whose labels feature a bald eagle.

In 1982 Unamin, which held a long-term lease, began to cut timber in the swamp to expand its sandpits. Alerted by Clay Sutton, a local biologist, and Dan O'Connor, a Cumberland County conservationist, the state was alarmed. Between 1956 and 1977—three years after another bald eagle pair in the western half of the swamp had vanished—40 percent of the acreage around *their* nest had been altered from woodland to human use, mostly sandpits.

And with the latest threat to Bear Swamp, more than eagles were at stake. The swamp, a lowland hardwood forest more typical of the Carolinas, harbored some trees that were 250 to 300 years old. Nowhere else in New Jersey could you find more state-endangered mistletoe, or state-threatened barred owls and red-shouldered hawks. The swamp sheltered southern songbirds, the first pileated woodpeckers seen in the county in nearly one hundred years, and more kinds of moths and butterflies than one entomologist had found anywhere else on the East Coast.

After two years of negotiations with the sand company and the landowners proved fruitless, the state Department of Environmental Protection invoked eminent domain to condemn 1,500 acres of the swamp around the nest. It had never before taken such action to protect an imminently threatened endangered species. The ultimate cost to the state: $6.5 million.

Which is why Niles was alarmed for more than just his own safety when he realized he could no longer climb the dying nest tree.

To build the new one, he first called down measurements to his assistants for a six-inch-thick cedar pole to span the open mouth of the two branches. They notched it near both ends like a Lincoln Log and hauled it up to Niles with a rope and pulley he had attached to a branch just above him. Lashing the pole across the branches, Niles now had a triangle about three feet on each side. He cupped the opening with chicken wire, and then returned to the ground to help the others gather sticks and limber saplings to form the nest. He wanted sticks about four feet long that ranged in diameter from a half inch to one and a half inches.

The next day, bundle after bundle of sticks was lofted up to Niles's perch, swung out over the nest, and released. Forming a crude basket, he inserted a framework of sticks into the center of the chicken wire, then wove others crisscross around the circumference. By the time the nest was a foot high, the sticks were so intertwined he could not pull any stick out of the tangle.

In Florida a female bald eagle was once observed rearranging one stick twelve different ways before she was satisfied. Like his carpenter father, Larry Niles, too, is a perfectionist. Some sticks were too thick and unpliable, others so thin they broke. "More sticks, more sticks," he kept yelling down to Kathy Clark and another aide. Scouring the swamp for suitable wood, the two quickly began to appreciate the daunting task that eagles carried off with such seeming ease.

Every foot or so Niles threw in some sphagnum moss to bind the sticks. As the nest grew, he borrowed another design concept from the old one: weaving one side of the nest around the trunk of the tree. He figured it would help secure the nest if the Lincoln Log failed, and would prevent preying raccoons from climbing up the bole of the tree directly into the nest. By dusk, the nest was nearly four feet deep and four to five feet across. He finished it off with bunches of wild grass, which he molded in the center to form a soft, shallow cup.

It was growing dark as he reached the ground. Against the sky he saw the silhouettes of the two adult eagles coming into some nearby pines to perch for the night. They were so close he could hear the flap of their wings, and the thought occurred to him that his presence up in the tree might have been keeping them away. He scrambled out of the swamp that night, wondering if he had so violated their territory that they would not again return there to roost.

Had he done nothing, no one could have criticized him if something had gone wrong with the birds. Some, including New Jersey Audubon Society members, believed the less the state managed (read "interfered with") the bald eagle pair, the better. To act, he realized, implied a certain arrogance, a hubris for which he most certainly would pay if the gambit failed.

His concerns were unwarranted. Within a week the pair had abandoned their nest for his. Since then, a dozen young eagles have taken their first flights from it.

There once was a time when Larry Niles liked nothing better than to blast away at wildlife with a gun. He suspects now it was simply part of being a boy, to want to gun down even frogs. At the time it seemed harmless, a Huck Finn diversion.

Leaving early on weekend mornings from their home on the edge of the Philadelphia suburbs, he and his father would hunt squirrels and rabbits in northern Bucks County, or fish the Delaware River or New Jersey Pine Barrens. In southern New Jersey they pulled largemouth bass out of Dennisville Lake, near where Niles and his wife, Kathy, now live with their three boys. Some fall days they would spend their mornings hunting squirrels, their afternoons atop Hawk Mountain's fabled limestone ridge, watching hawks and falcons ride thermals south for the winter.

To him, nature was merely a competition to see who could catch or shoot the biggest and the most. The heft and power of a rifle or shotgun in his hands imbued him with a sense of responsibility. It was a way to stake a claim on adulthood.

Over time, as he started learning the names of the birds and flowers he encountered, his appreciation of the complex natural world deepened. But a life in the service of those who hunt and fish still seemed preordained until his freshman year at Pennsylvania State University, when he stumbled upon Aldo Leopold's *Sand County Almanac*. Here was the father of modern game management questioning the hunt as he laid the foundation for modern-day conservation biology. The idea that Niles had long held, that hunters only kill surplus animals that would otherwise succumb to starvation or disease, he now realized was ridiculous. There *was* no surplus; if there were extra animals, they went to predators like foxes and eagles. It was foolishly egocentric to think otherwise.

This was several years before the first Earth Day, however. Wildlife was viewed as a resource to be managed, the way a farmer would raise a crop. Notwithstanding Rachel Carson's *Silent Spring,* in Niles's circle there was no urgency to bring back any species, much less any sense that any had ever departed. While his friends were specializing in game management—in Pennsylvania, where a million hunters take to the woods on the opening day of deer season, *game* management meant *deer* management—Niles majored in zoology. With state agencies primarily hiring game specialists, it was not an auspicious career move. For his master's thesis, he studied the effect that spraying secondary effluent (treated sewage) on fields would have on mice and meadow voles.

Beginning as a technician, the lowest rung on the wildlife biology ladder, he studied endangered red-cockaded woodpeckers for South Carolina, then moved to southeast Georgia as a state regional biologist. Hot, buggy, and dominated by the timber industry and its sterile pine plantations, the southeast was the Georgia Game and Fish Division's gulag for wayward game managers. No quail. No deer. As far as Niles could tell, every effort to increase the number of game animals, the kind hunters covet, had failed.

Niles loved the work. He captured and put radio-transmitter collars on sixty black bears as part of an effort to end their slaughter by local beekeepers. Under the guise of creating duck habitat, he and a state game manager carved five miles of canoe trail through the Okefenokee Swamp. Later, working with wild turkeys, instead of enhancing access—traditional game management's M.O.—he closed off roads.

It was all in keeping with his growing realization that the experiences he valued most occurred when he was alone outdoors . . . and not killing.

For all this, though, he was still a game biologist, an easterner in a southern backwater yearning both for a good library and for a chance to become involved in the nascent conservation biology wave. Years before, he had been introduced to the fecund coastal marshes and bays of southern New Jersey by his father-in-law, an engineer for whom fishing was an obsession. Entranced by those waters, Niles left his Georgia job in 1983 for a temporary job as the coordinator of research and management for New Jersey's embryonic endangered species program.

He was used to spending his days outdoors on an airboat in search of bears and alligators. His first day, at an isolated office building in Trenton, Niles parked his car in a lot surrounded by barbed wire, passed underneath the probing eye of a security camera and was ushered into a small closet with three desks, no windows, and the overwhelming odor of human beings: one of two rooms that were the headquarters of the New Jersey Department of Environmental Protection, Division of Fish, Game and Wildlife's Endangered and Nongame Species Program.

At thirty-two, he was the oldest of the program's seven zoologists. As the commitment to rescue wildlife embodied in the Endangered Species Act of 1973 gained momentum, the enthusiasm for their work compensated for their meager office. Piping plovers, least terns, and black skimmers were competing for nest sites with bathers on the state's crowded summer beaches. Tree frogs and reclusive corn snakes were disappearing in the Pine Barrens. The largest population of reintroduced peregrine falcons east of the Mississippi needed nurturing. And zoologists were climbing the Bear Swamp tree and flying to Manitoba's remote Lake Winnipegosis for nestlings to repopulate New Jersey with bald eagles. It was a wide open new field. You could find proven techniques for managing traditional game species, such as white-tailed deer, in college textbooks. But little was known about many of these rare species. Making it up as they went along, Niles and his staff conducted research on species as they simultaneously tried to create strategies to save them.

By the time he became the chief of the state's Endangered and Nongame Species Program in the summer of 1992, though, Larry Niles felt that the focus on saving individual species at specific sites was flawed. It left too many prime habitats and wildlife corridors unprotected simply because the animals had not been sighted there. And when environmental impact studies conducted prior to developing a tract uncovered rare species, expensive, time-consuming political and bureaucratic bedlam ensued.

No, like scientists in and out of the government, he now believed that the key to maintaining biodiversity lay in the preservation of entire key ecosystems. The "Landscape Project" he was launching would utilize sophisticated satellite techniques to map soil and vegetation types while biologists systematically surveyed areas for rare species. This would enable Niles's staff to anticipate and identify critical habitats, and areas that were not critical, in order to wrest long-term biological order out of the current chaos on the public and private lands.

"In the areas of greatest conflict with development, we'll be able to make

more sense of the sightings [of rare species] and get into more realistic protection of critical ecosystems," Niles told a group of government land managers gathered at his vastly upgraded Trenton offices. "As the number of
sightings increases, under the current system the conflicts can only get
messier." Given their sprawling nest territories, great mobility, and growing
population, Larry Niles knew that continued conflicts with the bald eagle,
in particular, were inevitable, and would inevitably be messy.

~~ The bald eagle season commences for Niles on a gray, rain-swept day
in early January as he pulls his Jeep onto the shoulder of Interstate 295 where
it arches over Raccoon Creek a mile or so east of the Delaware River. Two
hundred forty-five years earlier, the Swedish naturalist Peter Kalm saw
nothing but a thick fir (presumably Atlantic cedar) forest here. The soil was
so sandy his horse often floundered in the soft powder that passed for a
road. Today a whoosh from a southbound tractor-trailer pushing 70 mph
rips open Niles's door just as Kathy Clark, in the passenger seat, aims her
window-mounted spotting scope a half mile across the creek. "Beautiful,"
she says, focusing on their first bald eagle of the year, an erect, motionless
adult perched in a snag along the creek's edge. Despite the overcast day—or
perhaps because of it—even without binoculars the unmistakable white
head of the bird stands out like a lighthouse beacon.

But Niles's focus is as much on what lies behind the bird: Pureland, a large
industrial park chockablock with two-story buildings sprawling along the
creek nearly to the river. Looking at a topographical map, he locates the bird
and an approximate nest location. The area is mostly wetlands, and he's puzzled. He understands that Pureland's master plan ultimately calls for erect-
ing a building in the vicinity. "How could they develop that?" he wonders.

Pulling off the interstate, he negotiates a maze of industrial park roads
shamelessly named for wild birds until he and Clark spot the nest beyond
an engineering firm's headquarters. Dangling with vines, the nest is high in
a tulip poplar in a wooded peninsula bounded by Raccoon Creek and a
feeder stream that bisects the industrial park. No birds are by the nest, but
across a tilled field they see the same adult in the same dead tree, silhouetted against the plumed incinerator stack of the state's only commercial hazardous-waste incinerator.

"If that's its favorite perch, we're going to have to find some way to rope
off this field," Clark says.

There is also the matter of the nest itself. Anybody could easily disturb the eagles by walking off the parking lot to either the perch tree or the nest tree. They will need signs restricting the area as endangered species habitat, as well as the cooperation of the industrial park.

A Pureland security officer pulls up.

"We didn't know if you guys knew about it," he tells Niles. "We've known about it for a week."

"We just found out about it last week," says Niles, who was alerted by a bird-watcher.

Two years earlier Niles, responding to a phone call, had observed a smaller nest in the same tree, but dismissed it as a red-tailed hawk nest, which it might have been. Eagles, though, have been known to usurp and enlarge hawk nests; this nest is either the work of a new pair of bald eagles or a pair that had been nesting four miles to the north, in Gibbstown, New Jersey.

Gibbstown is the kind of aging blue-collar river town where people still parade up Main Street on the Fourth of July. Between the town and the Delaware River sits what is left of the Repaupo plant, the oldest operating Du Pont chemical plant in the country. Two years earlier, Niles had received a call from the township manager; he had seen two bald eagles fishing for carp in a pond that is primarily fed by secondary effluent from the town's sewage treatment plant. Investigating, Niles found a nest on the pond's far side. It was in one of the pines that Du Pont had planted during World War II to serve as a sound barrier for the explosives it was testing and manufacturing and to produce material for cardboard boxes. Peering through the chain-link fence into the Du Pont property, Niles could see the remains of the overgrown bunkers where World War II dynamite had been stored.

Early that spring Pat Adams, who lives a block and a half away from the pond, looked up from his yard work to see the two adults, their talons locked together, tumbling fifty feet above his head. "It was like watching something on PBS, something you'd expect to see in Alaska," he said. "I found it hard to believe I saw it here." The eagles quickly became a cause célèbre, a proud yet fairly well kept secret. In a town within two miles of two of the highest ranked EPA Superfund hazardous-waste sites in a state replete with them, the bald eagles had validated their environment.

That first year the eagles fledged one young bird, and wowed the people of Gibbstown as they taught the juvenile how to fish in the pond. After strapping a radio transmitter to the eaglet's back, Niles first traced the bird to narrow islands in the river. Then, in September, flying in a single-engine plane about as high as eagles do, he crossed the Delaware Bay and the Delmarva Peninsula to the Chesapeake Bay. He located the Gibbstown bird's signal on the Eastern Shore near the mouth of the Chester River, already seventy miles from its nest. Despite Niles's misgivings, the eagles returned again the following year. But the results were much less satisfactory: the adults abandoned the nest with no trace of eggs or young. It was a mystery. Was contamination to blame, or was it great horned owls?

This year, Niles soon realized, the Gibbstown pair had abandoned their old nest for the new one, several miles south in the industrial complex.

In late March, Niles, who was teaching an environmental science course at Rutgers University's Camden campus, found a note on his classroom door: Don Polec, the whimsical goof on WPVI-TV, the Philadelphia region's top-rated news broadcast, was coming out to do a humorous feature on the eagles nesting in the New Jersey industrial park. For three years Niles's staff had kept the exact location of the pair's nest in Gibbstown a secret. Now, as the pair engaged in the delicate business of incubating their eggs, Pureland had sent out a news release—unauthorized by Niles—that touted the presence of the nest and even specified the expected hatch date.

Niles seethed during the half hour it took him to drive to the industrial park. Television reporters, usually looking for drama that wasn't there, were bad enough. Polec, he knew, would be worse, looking for humor that simply wasn't there. Oh, he understood the gag all too well. He himself had joked about the incongruity of a pair of bald eagles nesting amid the polluted industrial sprawl of Gibbstown, saying—although he could never be positive, since through a spotting scope their leg bands were unreadable—that the birds must have been released in the 1980s from the state's hacking towers. "They have to be our birds," he'd joke. "Only birds raised in New Jersey could pick that site."

But it was that very incongruity, and the challenge it represented, which fascinated him as a zoologist. At the same time, he despised the half-truth stereotype off which the joke fed. Not far from Gibbstown and Pureland there were places of wild beauty as sublime and, in some cases, as unforgiving as anything he could find. In spring he had seen the narrow beaches of Delaware Bay carpeted with shorebirds en route from South America to the Arctic, gorging themselves on horseshoe crab eggs. He had stood in coastal marshes amid thousands of laughing gulls. In the summer, within view of the Atlantic City casinos, he had approached small scrubby islets alive with tricolor and little blue herons, glossy ibises, and the terrible racket that is a heronry.

Then there was winter. Cold, soaking wet, and alone, he once was nearly forced to spend the night on Egg Island, which juts far into Delaware Bay, when strong winds swamped his small aluminum boat while he was checking on a peregrine falcon nesting box. Searching for wintering eagles, he had once knifed his boat up ice-clotted Dennis Creek near his home. The chilled air made his eyes water, and the gray clouds were so low he could neither see nor hear the commercial airliners overhead. The vast marshlands that fed the creek seemed forbidding and deserted—except for the snow geese huddled together in open water. As he approached, they flushed into the air, thousands of them, so many that the cacophony of their calls and wingbeats sounded like the rumble of a jet engine. But he had not raised the geese. Flying above the panicking white maelstrom, hunting for a meal, was a bald eagle.

That, not some perverted joke about the state being one big hazardous-waste dump, was New Jersey to Larry Niles.

Shortly after his arrival at the industrial park, Niles and his assistant, Doug Ely, were met by Mike Hoover, Pureland's young public relations director. To Niles, it seemed as if Hoover resented his presence, as if he were somehow horning in on his publicity gig.

Then Polec and his film crew arrived, and Hoover went into his spiel. "Our main goal is to allow the natural environment to coexist with the built environment," he said, brightening as the video camera rolled. "Hey, we get some surprises, and things happen."

"This," Niles interjected, "is an example of how the two can't live together. If you were going to do this, you should have called us up, and we'd have said wait until we band the birds. This is the most sensitive time, before they're ready to hatch."

Then Niles speculated that perhaps the industrial park, unhappy with the eagles' presence because it wanted to erect another building near the nest, had issued the news release to attract people and disturb the birds so much that they would leave. Already daily gatherings of gawking office workers and truck drivers had trampled the weeds across the narrow creek from the nest. "This is a federally endangered species, and if they abandon this nest we can hold somebody liable for up to $10,000," he warned. Not that any of Niles's Sturm und Drang made Polec's television report. It seemed to Niles that everything Polec said he twisted into some humorous line, then laughed at it himself to see if it would elicit enough yucks to warrant inclusion in his broadcast.

Trying to delay the broadcast until after the birds had hatched, Niles offered Polec the opportunity to take close-up shots of the eaglets when they were banded. Undeterred, Polec aired his brief report several nights later. It was heavy with irony: shots of loading docks and parking lots were spliced together with footage of the incubating female lifting her head above the nest brim to stare down and scream at the entourage. It ended with a lame joke about an anticipated visit—from the stork.

While Polec put his audience to bed with a smile, the nest did not have a happy ending. Days later the female rose up briefly from her incubating posture to look down into the nest, then spent ten days past the expected hatch date further incubating. Concerned, Niles climbed the tree. In the nest he found just one egg, with a piece of shell from another egg stuck to it. Warm and foul-smelling, the egg later exploded with a disgusting methane burst all over Kathy Clark as she tried to prick it. Inside was a well-formed dead eagle embryo.

Niles speculated that the first eaglet must have died shortly after it hatched. That was when the mother rose up, then consumed the chick and tried to finish incubating the other one. While his staff awaited laboratory analysis of the embryo, they suspected that PCBs, or polychlorinated biphenyls, in the eagles' prey had caused embryonic death.

Another new nest, north of Salem, New Jersey, also failed. Niles was hardly surprised. For the past seven years, at four different nest sites, the pair had failed to produce any young. Although New Jersey's most successful bald eagles have maintained the same nests year after year, eagles often construct alternate nests for use in different years. Two or even three nests for each pair are not uncommon in Florida, and as many as five have been attributed to the same pair in Minnesota's Chippewa National Forest.

To Larry Niles, it seemed that the limited available habitat was imposing a trial-and-error modus operandi on the state's newer pairs. This year the Salem area birds had moved from a farm to a small nest overlooking a pond. Old-timers tell of a nest in the same area during the 1950s. Nearby, a farm plot has long been known as Eagle Field. But this year again, no eagles fledged. Yet another nest, in a state forest, crashed to the ground long before any young could be hatched when a mid-March blizzard sheared off one of its support branches.

And on South Jersey's largest freshwater lake, a pair built a new nest on an island adjacent to a state boat launch, but never laid eggs. With the female not fully white in the head and tail—a sign of sexual maturity, which usually occurs between four and six years of age—Niles had expected as much. But before the busy fishing season arrived, he lured the birds away from the water with a nest he constructed in a supercanopy pine, off the water in a more remote section of a state wildlife management area. The eagles were spotted at the nest late in the breeding season, and Niles hoped they would return the following year.

There had been other successes as well. As Administrative Law Judge Naomi Dower-LaBastille was deciding against the sand barge proposal, the new nest along the Cohansey River fledged one young bird. The eaglet arrived just as the scheduled reauthorization of the Endangered Species Act had become a focal point of discontent for the increasingly powerful property rights movement. For those who believed environmental regulations of the past two decades had gone much too far in placing the fate of plants and animals above the fate of humans, their jobs, their property, and their ability—some said their right—to make a profit, the bird was a pox.

On Stow Creek, for the second time in three years, a pair had produced an eagle rarity: three eaglets. Although it was only four years old, from a distant bridge across the creek the nest already looked like an upturned Volkswagen bug or a boat shipwrecked during the Great Flood, a prominent silhouette one hundred feet up in the outspread arms of a sycamore. In mid-February, with a bitter cold wind whipping out of the west, the male was hunkered down low over a newly laid egg or two when the female arrived on a branch above him. With a couple beats of his wings, he soon joined her. After yammering for a moment or two to each other, they quieted with a knowing glance. As the female bowed her head, the male suddenly levitated upward and backward, coming down in contact with her proffered backside. Flapping his wings furiously to maintain his balance on her back, he joined with his mate for a mere ten seconds. Afterward he flew off across the creek, and she dropped down to take his place on the eggs.

The tree itself looms over the broad tidal creek and the rotting remains of a long-forsaken Colonial home on the edge of a soybean field. On the spring morning when Niles climbed the tree to band the triplets, the adult male needed all of that unfettered airspace to gain enough altitude to lug a large channel catfish up into the nest. With his beak, he immediately began to rip the fish into strips for the expectant young to gobble. By the time Niles reached the nest two hours later, only the catfish's head remained.

No bird in North America grows as fast as a young bald eagle. In the twelve weeks it takes an eaglet to fly, it grows from as little as 2 1/2 ounces at birth to anywhere from less than 8 pounds to 14 pounds, with an adult wingspan of seven feet or more. A nestling can gain as much as 6 ounces in a day.

The food demands on the parent eagles, who have been known to deliver five or six prey items a day, and on the area around the nest, are staggering. It's been estimated that in the 120 days between the laying of an egg and first flight, a pair of eagles and just two eaglets need to consume 160,000 calories—nearly half the intake of a 170-pound man.

To keep the nest clean, eagles frequently carry off what's left of their prey after it's consumed. But that day, besides the catfish head, Niles also found: the remains of a menhaden fish; a large dark-winged gull, its feathered wings still attached to a stripped-clean carcass; and three diamondback terrapin shells. Niles surmises that the eagles toss the shells around in the nest like toys. He also found two muskrat carcasses; below, sun-bleached muskrat skulls littered the ground. The marshes around the nest are studded with muskrat lodges, and the adult eagles often sit atop the small grass mounds, awaiting an easy meal.

Years ago in Ontario, the late Charles Broley, a great amateur eagle ornithologist, found sixteen muskrat traps, including several with muskrat bones still intact, in one nest. Lewis Fogg, an octogenarian who for decades farmed and trapped across Stow Creek from the nest, witnessed such heists himself before the eagles declined in New Jersey. "Many times I'd see an eagle go down," he recalled one day, sitting on the tailgate of his pickup truck. "He took not only the rat but the rat and the trap and the stake. Maybe that didn't look funny, but it didn't make us happy, going off with a three-dollar rat."

In visits to hundreds of Florida nests, Broley found other curious items, including a light bulb, a Sunday newspaper supplement, a framed family photograph, a Clorox bottle, a clothespin, a gunnysack, a rubber shoe, a child's dress, a long skirt, a pair of pink lace-trimmed panties, a sugar bag, ears of corn, conch shells, a white rubber ball an eagle had been incubating, and a fish plug, a hook, and seventy feet of fishing line. Researchers in Florida have also found golf rakes, golf balls, and, woven into a nest like sticks, long sandhill crane leg bones.

Far more curious are the fresh sprigs of pine needles that now-retired U.S. Forest Service biologist John Mathisen has found in virtually every nest in northern Minnesota's Chippewa National Forest. The sprigs are always white pine, even though red pine trees outnumber white pine there three to one. Does white pine have a chemical ingredient that repels insects? Does a pine sprig signal to a mate that this nest is the one they'll use?

Mathisen has no idea.

At the base of the Bear Swamp nest tree, Niles straps a climbing harness around his waist and pulls on leather gloves. To the harness he attaches a leather safety climbing strap, and a long-handled aluminum boat hook whose end is swaddled in gray duct tape.

Using a nylon line previously left in the tree, he fishes the climbing rope up to the top of the tree and back down again. Once the other end returns, he clamps a safety clip to his waist and secures the rope's free end with a slipknot to the other end of the line. With his assistant, Eric Stiles, and I tugging on the free end of the line to hold his advance, Niles starts ascending to the nest he knows as well or better than the eagles themselves.

Twenty minutes later, as his head clears the rim, he is startled by the larger of the two nestlings lurking above him. *Hissss!* With her already large wings spread and her dark beak poised open, she lunges menacingly toward him. At this age, she is the most aggressive nestling Niles has ever encountered. "Holy mackerel, we got big birds here!" Niles yells down. Refusing to retreat, she lunges at his hand every time he moves. But he is even more concerned about the smaller male nestling. Every time the female flaps her wings, he backs away, beating his mottled wings and hanging his tail over the far edge of the nest.

Niles had expected the birds to be about seven weeks old. But if they are much older, which he thinks is possible based on their size, the male might jump—a worst-case scenario for zoologists forced to try to locate and recapture a jumper in thick undergrowth. He couldn't tell for sure, though, because he could not get a good look at the length of the male's tail feathers, which are one indicator of age.

Swaying in a stiff breeze, Niles kneels on the nest rim and goes after the larger female first. Crooking the aluminum boat hook behind one of her feet, he subtly nudges her toward him.

As the hooked foot moves forward, so does the other. When she is within reach, he grabs the hooked foot above the talons with his right hand, shoves the other leg into the same hand and encircles the feet in tacky, gauze-like orange veterinarian's wrap, like a rodeo cowboy trussing up a calf.

Niles has been bitten by nestlings, but their beak's grip isn't that strong. It's the talons an eagle kills with, and the four long, curved black ice picks at the business end of each foot have Niles's attention. Once in his hands, the female calms quickly. He has little trouble placing a leather hood over her eyes and tucking her wings into a nylon bag for her descent to the crew below. Meanwhile, as the adults continue to fly directly over the tree voicing their protests, the smaller male fixes Niles with a stare.

Bucking like a bronco inside the zippered gym bag, the female is lowered through the branches to the swamp floor. The action throws off the hood, and after the bag is opened, zoologist Sharon Paul struggles to lock the wings tight and roll the bird onto its back as Kathy Clark replaces the hood.

Once the hood is secured, a peaceful calm comes over the bird. Beneath her full crop, her chest rises and falls quietly as wildlife veterinarian Heidi Stout listens to the bird's heartbeat with a stethoscope. The vet then unfolds the bird's large right wing and inserts a syringe into an artery near the elbow to draw a blood sample. The blood is to be tested for organochlorine pesticides such as DDT, DDE, and dieldrin, as well as dioxin and PCBs.

Clark, using a ruler, then measures the eighth primary feather on the wing to gauge the bird's age. To determine its sex, she uses calipers to record the depth and diagonal length of the bill, the width of the legs, and the length of the hallux, or rear talon (it takes real strength to pry open the clenched talons). The measurements verify what she and Niles had already concluded: the birds are older than they thought, closer to eight weeks, and this large bird is a female. A bird with a bill depth greater than 32 millimeters, or about 1 1/4 inches, is considered female; this one's polished scimitar is 34 millimeters deep. In an unusual ornithological phenomenon called reversed sexual size dimorphism, female bald eagles, like most female raptors, are larger than the males. The reason for the size disparity is somewhat of a mystery. Possibly it enables the males to be more agile hunters.

Moving to the bird's chest, where the short brown feathers have not completely eclipsed the woolly gray down, Clark then plucks three feathers to be tested for such heavy metals as mercury, lead, cadmium, and arsenic. Finally, she uses a rivet gun to attach an aluminum U.S. Fish and Wildlife Service identification band (no. 629-32124) to the left leg, and on the right leg she places a green aluminum band (C4) to indicate it fledged from a New Jersey nest.

Meanwhile, up in the nest the male eaglet refuses to relax. Niles takes his time. He knows he could tear a wing muscle or bone with an ill-timed gesture, but eventually he secures the bird in the gym bag and lowers it, bucking like his sister all the way. Once on the ground, however, he too calms himself.

When the eaglets are hoisted back up to Niles, he removes the tape around their talons, lifts off the hood, and lets them walk out of the bag. For a while they just sit there, unaware that they are free again, until he nudges them. Then they waddle to the other side of the nest and turn, panting in the warm sunshine, as they fix Niles with the unwavering, inscrutable gaze of bald eagles.

When he is finished, he does something he never would have done several years ago. He hauls up a video camera to record footage for a documentary on the struggling comeback the birds have staged in New Jersey. Watching the adults stare at him from a naked branch a hundred yards away, Niles feels confident a slightly longer stay will not cause them to leave.

In the days of just one nest, from an airplane once he had seen them, the male and his previous mate, cartwheeling through the air in an amorous free-fall, their talons locked together in the same foreplay Walt Whitman had described a century earlier. When they broke apart, they flew back here, back to Bear Swamp. They and their predecessors had been here for forty, fifty, sixty years—he had no idea how long—and each winter, even when DDT prevented them from producing any offspring, they had returned. They had come back in 1972, when the U.S. Fish and Wildlife Service and its game management agent in Trenton, Howard Brown, said they didn't exist. They had come back this past winter, after losing their young and a portion of their nest.

They would come back, he knew, soon after he left, back to a once solitary nest that was now one of seven bordering the river and bay. Seven nests, six young. The numbers paled in comparison to Florida, where during this 1993 season more than six hundred occupied nesting territories had produced more than seven hundred young birds. Even closer, along the Chesapeake Bay, nearly three hundred nests had produced more than three hundred eaglets. Still, the two new nests were just two more elements of a comeback so stunning that, throughout most of the country, the U.S. Fish and Wildlife Service was contemplating upgrading the bald eagle's status from endangered to threatened.

Nonetheless, Niles's joy was tempered. Two of his nests were apparently contaminated, as was one more across the bay in Delaware, where the number of nests had stagnated at four for years. Already there was strong evidence that ospreys and peregrine falcons around Delaware Bay were suffering from PCB contamination. Bald eagles here, in Maine, along the Great Lakes, and out west on the Columbia River were being hampered by a persistent stew of chemical contaminants. Even more disturbing, development—the greatest threat to bald eagles ever since Colonial times—in some places was approximating the DDT of the 1990s.

Based on sheer numbers, the case for removing the bald eagle from the national endangered list was probably warranted. But Niles knew it would mean less money, less time spent on the birds' behalf, and psychologically, less concern and more disregard on the part of those who would rather not see a bald eagle appear on their property.

No matter how robust they became, Larry Niles could not imagine a time when bald eagles would not require some sort of special attention. He certainly could not imagine a time when they would fail to command *his* attention.

OMNIPRESENT, OMNIVOROUS

The eagles of the country be of two sorts, one like the eagles that be in England, the other is something bigger with a great white head and white tail. These be commonly called gripes; they prey upon ducks and geese and such fish as are cast upon the seashore. And although an eagle be counted king of that feathered regiment, yet is there a certain black hawk that beats him so that he is constrained to soar so high till heat expel his adversary.
—WILLIAM WOOD, ON GOLDEN EAGLES AND BALD EAGLES IN *New England's Prospect,* 1634

The Eagle, soaring above the clouds, can at will escape the scene of the storm, and in the lofty region of calm, far within the aerial boundary of eternal frost, enjoy a serene sky and a bright sun, while the terrestrial animals remain involved in darkness, and exposed to all the fury of the tempest.
—THOMAS NUTTALL, *A Manual of the Ornithology of the United States and Canada,* 1832

Over the entrance hovers an enormous specimen of the American eagle. . . . With the customary infirmity of temper that characterizes this unhappy fowl, she appears, by the fierceness of her beak and eye, and the general truculency of her attitude, to threaten mischief to the inoffensive community. . . . Nevertheless, vixenly as she looks, many people are seeking, at this very moment, to shelter themselves under the wing of the federal eagle; imagining, I presume, that her bosom has all the softness and snugness of an eider-down pillow. But she has no great tenderness, even in her best of moods, and, sooner or later—oftener soon than late—is apt to fling off her nestlings, with a scratch of her claw, a dab of her beak, or a rankling wound from her barbed arrows."
—NATHANIEL HAWTHORNE, DESCRIBING THE GILDED PINE EAGLE ATOP THE ENTRANCE TO THE U.S. CUSTOM HOUSE IN SALEM, MASSACHUSETTS, IN *The Scarlet Letter,* 1850

"Make sure he ain't a dinge, boys, Make sure he ain't a guinea or a kike, how can you tell a guy's a hundredpercent when all you've got's a gunnysack full of bones, bronze buttons stamped with the screaming eagle and a pair of roll puttees?"
—JOHN DOS PASSOS, *1919*, 1932

Houston, Tranquility Base here. The Eagle has landed.
—NEIL ARMSTRONG, JULY 20, 1969

Prior to the threatened U.S. invasion of Haiti in 1993, strongman Major General Philippe Bimby and his paramilitary troops defiantly marched through the streets of Port-au-Prince wearing T-shirts emblazoned with an American eagle that had a big red "NON" stamped across its wings. No translation, of either the word or the symbol, was needed. A proud American icon, the sine qua non of power, strength, and freedom, the bald eagle's likeness has been reproduced more often and is more recognizable than that of any other bird in the world. So omnipresent is its image in the United States that we have become inured to it, as if an eagle were as commonplace as the dishes on our table or the water pouring out of our faucets.

Stamped on our quarters, half-dollars, dollar bills, and postage stamps, the bald eagle is mounted on homes, storm doors, mailboxes, mud flaps, faux license plates, police badges, and public buildings. It perches atop flagpoles, weather vanes, cheap trophies, and monumental pedestals. It accompanies us from cradle to grave, from the Social Security card we get as infants to the Medicare card we receive upon turning sixty-five, from the U.S. mail to our Internal Revenue Service income tax returns.

It's also an integral part of our language: eagle-eyed, legal eagles, Eagle Scout, a score on a golf hole even better than a birdie. In the mid-1850s, "spread-eagled" denoted both flattening a fowl before broiling it and ridiculous bombast or grandiloquence in praise of the United States. Charles Lindbergh was the "Lone Eagle." Eagles populate the Bible and the works of Shakespeare; they soar through our poetry, paperback book titles, and pop song lyrics. Rock bands, sports teams, school mascots, July Fourth parades, and political campaigns all invoke their glory.

So does the Secret Service in its code name for President Bill Clinton: "Eagle." As the central figure on the presidential seal, the bird is ubiquitous: on the Oval Office carpet and the bas-relief oak modesty panel added to the front of the presidential desk in 1945; on the lecterns from which the president speaks; and on the M&M's that have replaced cigarettes on *Air Force One.* The bald eagle and variations of the nation's Great Seal also figure prominently in the official seals of the vice president, the Speaker of the House of Representatives, the Senate, and the Supreme Court. The bird dominates the logos of the U.S. Navy, Marine Corps, Air Force, Coast Guard, and National Guard Bureau; it is emblazoned on U.S. Army dress hats and on the Congressional Medal of Honor. Federal departments whose logo features the eagle include the State, Defense, and Justice. Ironically the department charged with protecting the bald eagle, Interior, has twice replaced the bird with a bison, which since 1929 has looked westward on the Interior Department seal.

As a standard of quality and excellence, the bald eagle also appears on the logos or in the names of many of the biggest, best, and quintessentially American institutions and businesses, or those that yearn to be: major league baseball's American and National Leagues; the National Wildlife Federation; the National Rifle Association; Anheuser-Busch and Miller breweries; American Airlines; Harley-Davidson motorcycles; Goodyear tires; insurance, investment, and security firms; the electric plug on my clothes dryer; the fishing hooks in my son's tackle box.

The eagle's legacy is also branded into the geography and cartography of the nation: mountains, passes, rivers, creeks, towns, counties, inns, lodges, golf courses, ski resorts, housing developments, and streets are all named for both bald and golden eagles, conjuring up a primordial yearning for an almost mythical wildness that, more often than not, has been tamed and vanquished. Driving near central Florida's Ocala National Forest, I once passed Eagle Nest Baptist Church. "There's a lot of that in Florida," said the woman I was meeting, U.S. Fish and Wildlife Service researcher Petra Bohall Wood. "When you see [something named for eagles], it usually means they're not there anymore."

⌐⌐○ For all the pervasiveness of its image, remarkably few Americans have ever seen a live bald eagle outside a cramped zoo cage. Most wouldn't even know where to look. On the main east-west highway leading into central Florida's Disney World, a southern California woman guesses the best place to search for bald eagles would be Montana. Two young women clerking at a 7-Eleven, one from Massachusetts and another from New York State, suggest Colorado. One man from Michigan and another from Massachusetts have no idea.

All of them are standing just miles away from a bald eagle nest, in a county with ninety active nests, in a state that, outside of Alaska, has the country's greatest concentration of breeding bald eagles. "I talk to tourists about eagles all the time," says Dave Fornicola, a chef at a Disney World restaurant who sees bald eagles regularly en route to work. "Everybody I talk to thinks they're extinct. They don't believe you."

Most Americans picture bald eagles as mountain denizens, magnificent white-headed birds floating over purple mountain majesties. The Rockies do harbor concentrations of nesting bald eagles. Many of Arizona's thirty pairs nest on cliffs. But as North America's representative of the world's eight species of sea eagles, *Haliaeetus leucocephalus* (literally "white-headed sea eagle") depends heavily on fish. Since fish gotta swim, nearly 100 percent of all bald eagles nest within two miles of a body of water—which, for purposes of sustenance, trade, and recreation, is where man also has always wanted to be.

The misconception about mountains is understandable, fueled as it is by centuries of second-rate song lyrics, third-rate art, and confusion over the decidedly different haunts of the bald eagle and its distant, more often mountain- and canyon-dwelling cousin, the golden eagle.

Crass collectors' plates and classic literature have fallen into this trap. In *Moby Dick* Herman Melville wrote of "a Catskill eagle in some souls that can alike dive down into the blackest gorges, and soar out of them again and become invisible in the sunny spaces. And even if he for ever flies within the gorge, that gorge is in the mountains; so that even in his lowest swoop the mountain eagle is still higher than other birds upon the plain, even though they soar." Clearly, Melville either suffered from the common misunderstanding or he was describing the golden eagle, the bird now found predominantly in the high plains and mountainous West as well as in Europe and Asia.

Like the golden eagle, the bald eagle once was just another creature in the teeming Eden of North America. It is thought that when colonists first arrived, anywhere from 25,000 to 75,000 bald eagles patrolled what are now the lower forty-eight states. With a range that currently extends across the continent and northward from Baja California and extreme northern Mexico to as far north as Alaska's Brooks Range and westward out along the Aleutian Islands, estimates of the number of precolonial bald eagles for the entire continent range upward to as many as 250,000 or a half million. But that anonymity—if it could ever be said that a bird of such striking size and beauty was merely a face in the crowd—was forever lifted the day the bald eagle was designated the national symbol in 1782.

The search for a national emblem had begun six years earlier, on July 4,

1776. After adopting the Declaration of Independence, delegates to the Second Continental Congress in Philadelphia appointed Benjamin Franklin, John Adams, and Thomas Jefferson to devise a two-sided pendant seal for the nation's official business.

Six weeks later they weighed in with proposals rife with Old World symbolism and as busy as a Cecil B. DeMille production. The trio was capable of inventing democracy, but not a suitable symbol for it. Franklin's suggestion, ultimately endorsed and embellished by Jefferson, involved a crowded biblical scene: the pharaoh pursuing the Israelites across the parted Red Sea as Moses, empowered by the divine rays of a fiery cloud, commands the waters to envelop the Egyptians. Adams halfheartedly proposed an admittedly unoriginal Hercules being wooed by both Virtue and Sloth.

Assisting these Founding Fathers was Pierre Eugene Du Simitière, an artist and designer from the West Indies. He suggested using a shield emblazoned with the coats of arms of the countries from which Americans had emigrated, and the initials of the thirteen colonies. The shield would be flanked by a soldier in buckskins and Liberty, even then a popular female symbol. Underneath them a banner proclaimed "E Pluribus Unum" (Out of Many, One), the motto of London's *Gentleman's Magazine*. Above the shield and figures was the eye of Providence in a triangle, radiating glory. After replacing the soldier with a goddess representing Justice, the committee adopted Du Simitière's suggestion for the face, or obverse, of the seal, and Franklin's suggestion for the back, or reverse.

But after the Continental Congress tabled their report, it did nothing for nearly four years. In 1780 another congressional committee, chaired by James Lovell of Massachusetts, also failed. Two years later, in May of 1782, the Continental Congress authorized yet a third committee. William Barton, a Philadelphia attorney who served as its consultant, was the first to consider using an eagle. To symbolize both the supreme power and authority of Congress and the sovereignty of the U.S. government, he drew a small, crested white eagle perched on a pillar above a striped shield. It clasped within its talons a sword and a small American flag.

On June 13 Congress turned over Barton's design and those that had preceded it to its Irish-born secretary, Charles Thomson. Teacher, businessman, astute politician, and zealous patriot, Thomson commanded universal respect. The Delaware Indians adopted him with a name that meant "man who tells the truth"; John Adams called him "the Sam Adams of Philadelphia, the life of the cause of liberty."

Synthesizing elements from the previous efforts, Thomson made the "American bald Eagle" his central element. Rising up, preparing to fly with its wings pointed downward, the bird was clutching an olive branch in one talon and arrows in the other. A shield of thirteen red-and-white stripes formed an angled chevron shield on its chest. In its beak it held a banner with the first committee's motto, "E PLURIBUS UNUM," and its head was breaking through distant clouds to a firmament of thirteen stars. The reverse side, which had been suggested by both Du Simitière and Barton, would be the unfinished pyramid topped by the eye of Providence in a triangle surrounded by glory rays.

Reviewing the design on June 19, Barton further modified it: the red-and-white chevron shield was transformed into the now familiar vertical stripes topped by a blue horizontal band; the eagle's wings were upraised into the more majestic and classic display position; and the number of arrows was set at thirteen. Nearly six years after the task was first assigned, on June 20, 1782, the Continental Congress adopted the Thomson-Barton eagle design as the Great Seal of the United States.

Though the bald eagle was unique to North America, at the time it was not a common American symbol. Utilizing a symbolic eagle, however, was far from an original idea. State Department historian Richard S. Patterson speculates Thomson's inspiration for the eagle with a shield on its breast came from Europe. The possible sources: a 1680 German book on European heraldry whose most prominent illustration, labeled "Imperator Augustus," featured a shield borne on the breast of a two-headed eagle; or even more likely, coins with eagle-and-shield designs minted by Russia, Spain, and the Holy Roman Empire, all of which probably were in Du Simitière's coin collection.

Patterson's detective work also uncovered what he believed was the source for Thomson's idea of having the eagle clutch an olive branch and arrows: an illustration in a later edition of Bavarian physician Joachim Camerarius's 1597 book of bird emblems and mottoes, owned by Ben Franklin. Franklin (and possibly Thomson) had consulted Camerarius's work in devising Continental currency seven years earlier. Except for Thomson's substitution of a bundle of arrows for Camerarius's thunderbolts—on ancient coins eagles had grasped thunderbolts ever since the Greeks and Romans associated the birds with Zeus and Jupiter—the similarity between Thomson's design and that of Camerarius is striking. Camerarius's explanation was as follows:

"The left [talon] holds a thunderbolt, but the right an olive branch. That in peace and war I may be mindful of my duty."

Eagles, and man's infatuation with them, far preceded Camerarius, how-ever. The earliest fossils of sea eagles, which evolved from scavenging kites near the tropical coast of what is now southeast Asia, are 25 million years old—much older than man. Bald eagle fossils removed from the Rancho La Brea Tar Pits in Los Angeles date from 11,000 to 38,000 years ago; fossils elsewhere indicate bald eagles have been a part of the North American landscape for at least one million years.

As early as 3500 B.C., Sumerians in the Euphrates River valley were ven-erating the eagles that wintered there as the bearers of men's souls to heaven. According to a Sumerian myth, an eagle stealing eggs was attacked by a snake but saved by a peasant named Etana, who killed the snake. In appre-ciation, the eagle carried Etana on its back into the heavens, but, repelled by the gods, the bird plummeted to its death. Thought to be among the high-est fliers—they are capable of soaring higher than a mile—eagles were viewed by the Babylonians and Assyrians, who succeeded the Sumerians, as well as by the Persians, Romans, some North American natives, and even, at least symbolically, by Christians, as the bearers of souls to heaven.

The eagle's long association with the sun also has led to its depiction as the bird of fire, a close relative, if not the physical representation, of the phoenix and the thunderbird. Both the Babylonians and the Hittites erected temples to eagles, the latter, which contained live eagles, being dedicated to the bird of fire. In Assyria, Ishtar was the royal standard—an eagle with a head of a lion, linked with the sun as a symbol of omnipotence, virility, and immortality.

The constellation Aquila also was considered the eagle god, watching at night over the world. During the day, astrologers in Asia Minor would study the actions of eagles prior to any engagement. The sighting of an eagle feeding on prey or soaring high above was a good omen. To enhance morale, a captive eagle would be released to fly above the troops just prior to the engagement.

In Babylonia, eagles graced walking sticks and seals used to authenticate documents. The Greeks engraved the birds, gripping thunderbolts or prey in their talons, on their coins. Both the eagle and thunderbolts were sym-bols of Zeus. According to Greek myth, Zeus assumed the form of an eagle to carry off Ganymede, a beautiful young man with whom he had fallen in love, to be cupbearer to the Gods.

The word "eagle" is derived from the Latin word for the bird, "aquila"— hence "aquiline nose." Some linguists have traced the word back to the Greek word for hooked or curved, but at least one scholar contended the word root dated back even further to "Huhi," the Egyptian name for God the Father. Crossing cultures to the Bible, in Deuteronomy God is compared to an eagle and repeatedly referred to as the Rock. *Roc,* or *rukh,* was the Arabic word, and *rekh* the Egyptian term, for the giant eagle, or phoenix.

To the Romans, the eagle was the bird of Jupiter, the king of the gods. After Augustus Caesar, who attained the status of a deity during his reign, died in A.D. 14 an eagle was hidden atop his funeral pyre. As the flames intensified, the bird was released skyward, signifying the apotheosis, or ascent, of the emperor's soul. With some modification, the custom was continued for Roman rulers for more than 250 years. As the messenger of Jupiter, the eagle was also the favorite deity of the Roman army. According to Pliny, beginning in 104 B.C. each Roman legion marched into battle behind a spear or staff topped with a silver (later gold) eagle, its wings uplifted and holding a thunderbolt. Used earlier in this manner by the Persians, the eagle—either one- or two-headed—was embraced as an imperial and/or imperious emblem by Charlemagne and the Holy Roman Empire, Otto the Great, the Byzantine Empire, the Poles, Russian czars, Napoleon (whose son was dubbed L'Aiglon, or the Eaglet), German city-states, Prussia, and Hitler. Video news footage from Baghdad shows proud bas-relief eagles hovering on the walls above Iraqi dictator Saddam Hussein.

Depictions of double-headed eagles have been found among ancient artifacts unearthed in both Asia Minor and the mounds left in Ross County, Ohio, between 200 B.C. and A.D. 300 by people of the Hopewell culture. During the Crusades, one of the classic symbols of heraldry was the one- or two-headed eagle emblazoned on shields. By then the eagle had become a Christian symbol of the Resurrection and of Saint John the Evangelist. American wood-carvers would later carve eagles atop a wooden Book of Revelation in an apparent evocation of John.

Although Native Americans were totally removed from this European culture, they too were transfixed by the birds. A number of tribes regarded eagles, both bald and golden, as deities. Many clans and religious fraternities took the eagle's name. Medicine men used eagle wing bones to suck disease out of the body, eagle talons were worn as amulets, and highly prized feathers were worn in ceremonies and as badges of honor. From the Southeast to the Pacific Northwest, the bird or its feathers symbolized peace. Even today most tribes throughout the country continue to view the eagle as a messenger between the Creator and themselves. "One feather held in the hand is like a telephone line which carries our small voice farther than we could ever send it any other way," a Commanche–Lakota Sioux woman now living in Oregon once told me. "If we have one feather, the spirit of the eagle is with us as a warrior beside us, and when we die he carries our spirit on his wings into the spirit world."

Despite its universal appeal and symbolism, Benjamin Franklin denounced the 1782 selection of the bald eagle for the Great Seal. Two years later Franklin, who since 1776 had been this country's minister to France, met Pierre Charles L'Enfant near Paris. An officer in the Continental Army, L'Enfant would later lay out the grand plan for Washington, D.C. This time, however, he had come to show Franklin his design for the insignia for the Society of the Cincinnati. It featured an eagle that resembled the Great Seal's bird—which, with its scrawny, fowl-like legs and small head, somewhat resembled a turkey.

Membership in the society, which today is still is based in Washington, D.C., was open to officers of the Continental Army, who could pass on their membership to their eldest male heirs, much as British titles and property ownership were handed down. Franklin found the concept of hereditary knights absurd in the egalitarian society America yearned to be. His disgust might have helped color his now-famous attack on bald eagles, which appeared in a January 26, 1784, letter he wrote to his daughter, Sarah Bache, in Philadelphia.

Referring to the propensity of eagles to steal fish caught by the smaller osprey, or fish hawk, he wrote:

> I wish the Bald Eagle had not been chosen as the Representative of our Country. He is a Bird of bad moral Character. He does not get his Living honestly. You may have seen him perch'd on some dead Tree near the River, where, too lazy to fish for himself, he watches the Labour of the Fishing Hawk; and, when that diligent Bird has at length taken a Fish, and is bearing it to his Nest for the Support of his Mate and young Ones, the Bald Eagle pursues him and takes it from him. With all this Injustice, he is never in good Case but like those among Men who live by Sharping and Robbing he is generally poor and often very lousy. Besides, he is a rank Coward: The little *King Bird* no bigger than a Sparrow attacks him boldly and drives him out of the District. He is therefore by no means a proper Emblem for the brave and honest Cincinnati of America, who have driven all the *King birds* from our Country. . . .

I am on this account not displeas'd that the Figure is not known as a Bald Eagle, but looks more like a Turkey. For in Truth the Turkey is in Comparison a much more respectable Bird, and withal a true original Native of America. Eagles have been found in all other Countries, but the Turkey was peculiar to ours; the first of the Species seen in Europe being brought to France by the Jesuits from Canada, and serv'd up at the Wedding Table of Charles the ninth. He is, besides (tho' a little vain and silly, 'tis true, but not the worse emblem for that) a Bird of Courage, and would not hesitate to attack a Grenadier of the British Guards who should presume to invade his Farmyard with a red Coat on.

Franklin's history was a bit muddled, since the first North American turkeys to cross the Atlantic were domesticated birds from Mexico. They quickly became so popular that they were brought back by English colonists to the Atlantic coast. Today hunters sitting motionless for hours in a spring snow praise the wild turkey's cunning. A handful of immense toms exploding out of a spruce stand can startle the stoutest of hearts. But there is also something unseemly about a supposed national emblem which has been so domesticated that each year more than a quarter-billion turkeys are sold and consumed.

Eminent ornithologists, however, would later agree with Franklin's harsh assessment. They found little to recommend in a bird with a pathetically weak voice unwilling to protect its nest, one that steals fish from others and lazily bellies up next to vultures to pick through garbage or shamelessly dine on the latest roadkill.

Foremost among the detractors was John James Audubon, whose personal correspondence seal featured a wild turkey surrounded by the motto: "America My Country." Of the bald or white-headed eagle, he wrote, "Suffer me to say how much I grieve that it should have been selected as the emblem of my Country." Audubon had a much higher opinion of a species he christened the Bird of Washington, or the Washington Sea Eagle, and painted the proud bird for his classic 1827 folio, *The Birds of America*.

Comparing it to its namesake, George Washington, he wrote: "He was brave, so is the Eagle; like it, too, he was the terror of his foes; and his fame, extending from pole to pole, resembles the majestic soarings of the mightiest of the feathered tribe. If America has reason to be proud of her Washington, so has she to be proud of her great Eagle."

Audubon unknowingly was exalting the juvenile version of the adult bird he found so ignoble: the bald eagle. His description matches that of a young bald eagle but for one important difference—its supposed wingspan of 10 feet 2 inches is 3 feet greater than that of most of the bald eagles he saw. Describing the bird primarily from memory, Audubon could have been confounded because the wing and tail feathers of first-year eagles are significantly longer than adult plumage. Combined with the fact that young eagles weigh slightly less than adults, this greater wing surface makes it easier for them to first fly, since they can fly more slowly and rise up more easily in smaller or weaker updrafts.

As for the thievery perpetrated against ospreys, it was rationalized in a Delaware trapper's folktale recounted by ornithologist Witmer Stone: "The Eagle years ago agreed to show the Fishing Hawk how to build a nest if the hawk would keep him supplied with fish. After receiving the desired information, however, the hawk failed to keep his end of the bargain, so henceforth the Eagle made a practice of worrying and robbing the Fish Hawk every time he found him carrying fish."

Apparently more than ospreys have failed to keep this pact. Seagulls, loons, herons, and many waterfowl; vultures, harriers, and peregrine falcons; ferruginous, red-tailed, and rough-legged hawks; and golden eagles, among others, have all been relieved of their food by bald eagles. Floating on its back, more than one sea otter has had an eagle surprise it from behind to pluck a tasty morsel from its paws. Eagles have even attempted to steal just-shot waterfowl from hunters. And at least one small pack of coyotes was frightened off a dead cow by a single bald eagle.

Nothing better illustrates a bald eagle's pirating instincts than a tale told by Audubon. On the Mississippi River near Natchez, he saw a bald eagle flush a flock of vultures off the carcass of a dead horse and give aerial chase to one of them that had a yard-long rope of entrails dangling from its mouth. Grabbing hold of the viscera, which the vulture was unable to disgorge, the eagle pulled the innards and the vulture along for twenty or thirty yards until they both fell to the ground. Then, after striking the vulture dead, the eagle devoured its hard-won prize.

As biologist Mark Stalmaster notes, the eagle preferred to steal from the vulture rather than eat the unattended horse carcass and, after killing the vulture, preferred to eat the entrails rather than the vulture itself. To view this as rank laziness, however, is to anthropomorphize; this kleptoparasitism, as biologists call it, is primarily an energy-saving expedient, the act of an ingenious opportunist adapting to whatever the environment offers. It is not a one-way street, either. Golden eagles and coyotes have moved bald eagles off of carcasses. Michigan researcher Bill Bowerman on three occasions observed herring gulls and a raven either pirate a fish from an eagle or force it to lose its prey before the eagle could deliver the fish to its nest.

These questionable characteristics aside, the bald eagle is an outstanding American symbol, a raptor wrought on the grand scale. It is a bird of keen sight, whose large, penetrating yellow orbs are probably capable of vision about two-and-a-half times better than ours (but certainly not eight to ten times greater, as is commonly thought). The stunning white head and tail of the adult is thought to be an indicator to other birds, including other bald eagles, that they have entered the occupied, defended breeding territory of a pair of bald eagles. Should they survive their first year, bald eagles are also long-lived—up to nearly fifty years in captivity, perhaps as long as twenty-five to thirty-five years in the wild. Presumably faithful to their mates for life, like many birds, bald eagles also are devoted parents. Adults spend half of each year involved in building and repairing nests, courting, incubating their eggs, and raising their young.

Among those who believe the eagle was a brilliant choice is John Turner, the Bush administration's director of the U.S. Fish and Wildlife Service. As a young biologist, the Wyoming native surveyed the intermountain West for bald eagles during the birds' nadir in the 1960s. He has also guided many raft trips down the Snake River through Grand Teton National Park, and for tourists the unquestionable highlight of most trips is their first sighting of a bald eagle.

"They're a perfect wild symbol of strength and beauty," Turner says. "It's strictly a North American bird, and I don't know of any other bird that can take prey from all three mediums—the water, air, and land." Only bald eagles and ospreys, Turner notes, can pluck a fish out of the water while in flight. While they cannot match a peregrine falcon's 200 mph dive, bald eagles—along with only falcons and accipiters, or woodland hawks—have the speed and maneuverability to occasionally capture birds, including those as large as geese, on the wing. Swooping underneath their prey, they roll upside down and bury a talon in the other bird's breast. Like golden eagles, bald eagles also attack prey on land.

One February morning, fifteen miles away from Disney World's Magic Kingdom, I arrived on the shores of Florida's Lake Tohopekaliga just as an adult eagle rounded the point to my left. The bird was well below radar.

Closing quickly with a few measured, effortless wingbeats—picture Carl Lewis's long, easy stride—it reached down with its right talon to snatch a gallinule (a henlike waterfowl) out of the water.

It was easier than a child filching a Fig Newton from a jar. Silent. Clean, quick, efficient. Then, lifting up over the marsh grass, the eagle wheeled twenty feet overhead. I could hear the gallinule's brief, weak pleas, and I saw it twist its head completely around to look up at this looming predator that was carrying it away, back over acres of orange groves, to be eaten.

After they disappeared, I looked back to the water. The other gallinules appeared not to have noticed the sudden absence. Or perhaps they simply were stunned, as was I, into silence.

In its universal appetite, the bald eagle is also a true American. When the birds are tending a nest, in some areas fish make up as much as 90 to 100 percent of their diet. After a fish kill, Charles Broley once found twenty-three fish in one Florida nest. The eagle's menu from the water includes salmon, trout, herring, eulachon, eel, cod, chub, sculpin, mullet, ocean catfish, catfish, dogfish, rockfish, sunfish, whitefish, red snapper, striped bass, mackerel, menhaden, yellow perch, brown bullhead, sucker, pickerel, northern pike, trout, sheepshead, blue pike, carp, shiner, and gizzard shad, abalone, octopus, squid, snails, crabs, and freshwater mussels.

This preoccupation with fish can be seasonal, however. At certain times of the year, such as during the winter when migrating waterfowl concentrate, eagles' tastes can turn to birds. Often haunting areas where hunters may have left crippled and dead birds, eagles have been known to consume more than seventy-five different species of birds. These include a slew of different ducks, geese, brant, mergansers, grebes, storm petrels, American coot, gallinules, sora, at least seven different kinds of gulls, at least six different herons (including great blues), anhingas, cormorants, pelicans, auklets, puffins, murrelets, guillemots, fulmars, terns, oystercatchers, grouse, ptarmigan, sandhill cranes, wild turkeys, ravens, flickers, longspurs, finches, and sparrows.

Even the remains of a few raptors, including hawks and ospreys, have been found in nests. Before their passing, passenger pigeons were on the menu of eagles that haunted the pigeon roosts. Since carrion is an important winter food source, some biologists have speculated that the demise of the great buffalo herds and the huge flocks of birds that once darkened the sky contributed to the bald eagles' decline in the late nineteenth century.

Among reptiles, bald eagle prey comprises turtles, terrapins, and snakes, including rattlesnakes. Its mammalian diet is much more diverse: muskrats, nutria, brown rats, mice, voles, tree and ground squirrels, prairie dogs, porcupines (an obvious mistake), raccoons, opossums, skunks, weasels, martens, foxes, rabbits, jackrabbits, Arctic hares, sea otter pups, occasionally young lambs and pigs, and rarely chickens and domestic ducks, cats, and dogs. Opportunists that take what is most readily available, they also scavenge on the carcasses of sheep, cows, deer, elk, bison and even sperm whales. Lacking a discerning sense of smell, they pick through landfills and garbage dumps in Florida and Alaska. Eagles are also fond of sea lion dung and vulture vomit. During the summer of 1969, two bald eagles were flushed from a half-submerged object they had been feeding upon on the shores of the Yukon's Lake Laberge. The man had been dead for a month.

Franklin's objections aside, the side of the seal featuring the eagle in 1782 was cut into a die that authenticated the official documents of the United States. (Despite the years of debate, the other side of the design was never used as part of the Great Seal). Pressed into a white paper wafer embedded in red wax, the seal was first used on a document that authorized General George Washington to negotiate with the British for the exchange of prisoners. Our fixation with eagles, however, did not take hold until Washington's April 30, 1789, inauguration. As he was sworn in on the balcony of New York City's Federal Hall, the most ostentatious items on Washington's plain suit were metal buttons stamped with an American eagle. Above him, in one of the first architectural uses of the eagle, L'Enfant had rendered the new nation's Great Seal on the building's pediment.

Throughout the country Americans celebrated that day with fans, handkerchiefs, and coat buttons bearing the American eagle insignia. That October Washington left New York for a victorious tour of New England. Backlit by candles, starched and whitewashed eagle designs stenciled on windows greeted Washington along his route.

Three years later the bald eagle was stamped on buttons and badges exhorting a reticent Washington to seek a second term. By then, the eagle had become as synonymous with the country as Washington himself. In an effort to placate native leaders, the president gave out scores of George Washington Indian Peace Medals—so many that, by 1800, the large medals imprinted with bald eagles had become an indispensable part of native diplomacy. The birds were equally at home in the kitchen—on stoves, butter molds, cider jugs, and whiskey flasks—and in the parlor—on coverlets and Duncan Phyfe, Sheraton, and Hepplewhite chairs, Chippendale desks, silver tea services, Chinese porcelain, mirrors, and clocks. They were affixed to houses, taverns, inns, courthouses, post offices, and wooden ships, and found on quilts and wedding lace, playing cards, canteens, powder buckets, military caps, and volunteer fire company regalia.

The nation's most famous live eagle also appeared during the nineteenth century: "Old Abe," a nasty, contentious bird caught by a Chippewa and traded in Eau Claire, Wisconsin, for a bushel of corn. Tethered to a platform at the head of what became known as the Eagle Regiment, the bird saw Civil War action at Vicksburg and Corinth. Returning home with full military honors, Old Abe represented Wisconsin at the Centennial Exposition in Philadelphia before suffocating to death during a brief fire in the basement of the Wisconsin Capitol. He was then stuffed and put on display.

In 1869, shortly after Old Abe became a celebrity, bald eagles appeared on ten-cent and thirty-cent stamps—among the first postal issues not to feature one of the country's early leaders. American eagle coins date back much earlier. One numismatic legend claims an eagle first appeared on American coinage in 1776 on a Massachusetts copper (or cent). It apparently never existed. Two New York coppers in 1787 and a Massachusetts half-cent in 1787 and 1788 were the first true eagle coins in this country. Nationally, a 1791 Washington cent featured an eagle, as did the first silver dollar struck in 1794 and the first American gold pieces in 1795, which were called "eagles": ten- and five-dollar coins. Quarter-eagles worth $2.50 first appeared in 1796, twenty-dollar double eagles and gold dollars in 1849, the year of the California gold rush. Today bald eagles appear on the quarter, the Kennedy half-dollar, the Susan B. Anthony dollar, and all U.S. gold and silver bullion investment coins, which feature a family of eagles—as usual, on the "tails" side.

As with our coinage, over time the eagle on the Great Seal has matured into a much more robust and accurate representation of a bald eagle. The second principal die, cut in 1841 after the first had worn out, was illegally used for more than four decades. While removing the crest from the eagle's head was an improvement, the engraver reduced the number of arrows to six and made the red pales in the shield twice as wide as the white. It took James Horton Whitehouse, the chief designer for Tiffany's, to achieve near perfection in 1885. In addition to correcting the 1841 errors, he made everything about the eagle—its fierce talons, its large wings, its feathered upper legs, its imposing head—more grandly eagle-like and more in keeping with a country poised to assume world leadership.

Through two world wars and the Great Depression, through Korea and Vietnam, this bird and its more stylized cousins have been with us, a big, bold bird of prey equally capable of winning the Cold War and soaring across insipid inspirational posters and smoke-eating ashtrays. I once saw an elderly couple sweeping metal detectors across a grade school playground in search of lost nickels and dimes. Their van's spare tire cover was imprinted with the logo of an organization I have never been able to track down. The legend around the rim touted something like the North American Association of Metal Detectors and Archaeologists. In the center, a bald eagle flew high above the earth. Its extended right talons were brandishing a metal detector.

Only a bird whose image has been so pumped up by centuries of public relations jabberwocky would be considered capable of the legendary feats that have been attributed to eagles. A country long enamored of its own manifest destiny could have nothing less than an omnipotent conqueror for its national emblem.

Concerning eagles, National Audubon Society ornithologist W. Bryant Tyrrell said in the mid-1930s, "Newspapers will print anything as long as it is sensational." Among the earliest accounts of an eagle attempting to carry away a child is a story related in 1811 by Alexander Wilson, the father of American ornithology. He said the following supposedly occurred near Great Egg Harbor, New Jersey. A woman was weeding her garden with her infant nearby when "a sudden and extraordinary rushing sound, and a scream from her child alarmed her, and starting up she beheld the infant thrown down, and dragged some few feet, and a large Bald Eagle bearing off a fragment of its frock, which being the only part seized, and giving way, providentially saved the life of the infant."

In the 1830s ornithologist Thomas Nuttall claimed to have heard of an incident at Petersburg, Georgia, near the Savannah River, in which an infant dozing outside its house was seized by an eagle and carried five miles away to its nest, where the child was soon found dead. Yet another account credits an eagle with flying five miles across the mouth of North Carolina's Neuse River with a small lamb gripped in its talons. One of the most pervasive, influential examples of this mythmaking was disseminated by McGuffey's *Readers,* the grade school series whose dramatic, highly moralistic tales heavily influenced the teaching of reading in this country between 1840 and 1920. Among the stories read by millions of American children was "The Eagle's Nest," which involved an evil golden eagle spiriting away a young child to its eyrie atop a steep mountain in Scotland. With a crowd of a thousand amassed below, the girl's mother does what no man would dare—she scales the cliff. As in many of these tales (and a good indication that they are indeed fiction), when she reaches her daughter the child is completely unharmed and unmarked by piercing talon wounds.

But as Americans continued to shoot down eagles and other birds of prey for their crimes, real and imagined, of carrying out their role in the food chain, the mythologizing persisted. One of Thomas Edison's primitive turn-of-the-century films included a patently bogus scene of an eagle hoisting a terrified infant high above a mountainous lake. In 1937, a Hollywood producer perpetrated a similar hoax, rigging up his petrified eighteen-month-old daughter and a semi-tame golden eagle with wires and a pulley to make it look as if his daughter was being pirated away.

Not to be outdone by early cinematic special effects, the print press churned out tales of attacks on children and adults by fifty-pound eagles with ten-foot wingspans. Consider this 1929 article from the *New York Herald Tribune:*

> Somerset, Ky., Sept. 22—George Meece, eight years old, today narrowly escaped death from an attack of a bald eagle which swooped down to the hill on which he and four companions were playing, seized him by his overalls and took him about twenty feet into the air before dropping him. In falling, the boy, who weighs fifty pounds, landed on his head and was stunned. According to the boys, the eagle had about a ten-foot spread of wings. It is thought the shouts of Meece's playmates frightened the bird and caused it to drop the lad.

To demonstrate how error-prone these accounts can be, the *Literary Digest,* quoting from the *St. Louis Post-Dispatch,* claimed it was actually George's 35-pound brother, Jimmy, who was lifted 75 feet in the air before the eagle flew lower and dropped the boy 200 feet from where he had been seized. Around Bald Mountain, wrote Danville Mayor W. O. McIntyre, "The men have loaded their guns and sworn vengeance against all eagles. Legends of babies carried away and never seen again have been revived. . . . There is, of course, reason for fear. . . . If [Jim] had been a little lighter, the eagle might have succeeded in carrying him away."

These figments of the imagination are not the exclusive purview of the past, either. The cover of the August 3, 1993, issue of the *Weekly World News* (the same supermarket tabloid that last year featured exclusive pictures of a wheelchair-bound JFK visiting his mother, Rose, before her death) screamed: "EAGLE FLIES AWAY WITH 2-YR.-OLD BOY! Toddler found safe on the ground—four miles away!" The headlines and a two-page inside story were accompanied by "the most amazing photos ever taken!"

According to the paper, a harpy eagle, which is capable of carrying off monkeys and sloths, carted the boy away from his mother as she tended sheep in a mountainous region of Argentina. The paper claimed the boy was flown four miles before he was dropped in a meadow near the eagle's nest. "They found the little guy among the boulders, miraculously unhurt," the reputed photographer, Hector de Varas, was quoted as saying.

Virginia Tech wildlife professor Jim Fraser, who, like a lot of eagle experts, taped the article to his office door, agrees they were the most incredible photographs ever taken. Harpy eagles frequent the high canopy of the Amazonian rain forest, not sheep-grazing country. Checking out the plumage in the photographs, Fraser said, "To me, it looks like an immature golden eagle"—which could not begin to lift the boy, much less transport him four miles.

Were they not so wary of humans, bald eagles probably would be capable of killing a young child. Since the time of Genghis Khan, eagles in Mongolia have been used to hunt prey that includes wolves. But to make off with a child, a pig, or a lamb for great distances? Testing such claims, one falconer who had trained a 12-pound bald eagle in captivity found the bird was unable to lift off from the ground with a doll that weighed more than 4 pounds. If the 4-pound doll was placed on a slope, the eagle could fly 30 yards with her burden; with a 6-pound doll, all she could do was drag it. Finally, if an 8-pound doll was set on the edge of a steep bank, the eagle was able to snatch it and glide with it for just about 40 yards.

His recommendation: don't leave an infant on the edge of a cliff near hungry eagles. Other than that, we are safe from our national symbol—but it has hardly been safe from us.

"IN AT THE DEATH"

Scarcely does an eagle come into our State now and get away alive, if he tarry more than a day or two.
—BARTON EVERMANN, "BIRDS OF CARROLL COUNTY, INDIANA," *The Auk*, OCTOBER 1988

Eagles are becoming more scarce in all parts of the state, due partly to the settling up of the country, but mainly due to the fact that every man's hand is against this grand bird. . . . I have known of several instances where the farmer has waited until the nest contained young, cut the tree and destroy [ed] the young and at that time [shot] the parents who are so solicitous for the young that they lose their usual caution.
—OSCAR E. BAYNARD, "THE BALD EAGLE IN FLORIDA," *Oölogist* FEBRUARY 15, 1916

 How about getting someone to band some bald eagles while you are in Florida?" Richard Pough, a National Audubon Society official, asked Charles Broley late in 1938. "Couldn't you find some boy who might do it under your supervision?"

Nearly fifty-nine years old, Broley had recently retired as a bank branch manager in Winnipeg. With his bald head and aquiline nose, the Canadian even resembled an eagle. During the previous sixteen years Broley and his second wife, Myrtle, a writer and poet, had transformed themselves into talented amateur ornithologists. Prowling the marshes and grasslands of Manitoba and the lakes of Broley's native Ontario, where the couple had a summer cottage, Broley had long since become more birder than banker. With the bank windows always spotless and binoculars tucked into his drawer along with checks and withdrawal slips, not even work stood between Broley and the sighting of migrating red-tailed hawks. Meticulous, as one would expect of a banker, Broley had a careful eye for ornithological detail and rare birds. He was diligent as well, collecting and recording from nests so many duck down feathers that he often identified particular duck species simply from their fluffy down.

Pough and Broley had been corresponding with each other for some time, but their conversation, during a meeting of the American Ornithologists' Union, in Washington, D.C., marked the first time they had met. The Broleys, along with their nine-year-old daughter, Jeanne, had stopped at the AOU meeting en route to Florida, where they intended to winter for the first time. A trim, wiry man about five feet nine inches tall, Broley had seen other Florida snowbirds on a previous trip south: elderly men, so many of them with glazed looks on their faces, rapidly deteriorating as they quickly lost interest in everything around them. A peripatetic man of prodigious energy and perseverance, particularly when an activity involved birds, Broley wanted nothing of that sort of life. But he had some doubts about Pough's proposal.

"Are there many bald eagles in Florida?" he wondered. There were indeed, but none had ever been banded there, and only about seventy had ever been banded in all of North America.

"Too many of these fine birds are being shot," Pough told him. "We'd like to stop that." The naturalist also wanted to learn much more about the behavior of the eagles. He handed Broley four large aluminum rings, or bands, to secure around the legs of young eagles. The practice dated back to young John James Audubon, who tied thread around the legs of phoebes to identify spring migrants returning to caves near his Pennsylvania home. The bands Broley received bore identifying numbers and instructions to notify the Bureau of Biological Survey, the forerunner of the U.S. Fish and Wildlife Service, when a bird wearing one was found.

Neither Pough nor Broley had any idea where these bands would soon reappear.

After his arrival in Tampa, the first nest Broley found was so conveniently located that he erected an observation blind on the ground to gauge when the young would be the optimum size for banding. Broley quickly discovered, however, that at least some Floridians were highly protective of the eagle nests. Many, through either ignorance or cunning, suggested he search in the mountains. "Lots of buzzards, but no eagles [here]," they'd say. Early in his banding endeavors, he was arrested three times in one month when alarmed Floridians called police about a man robbing eagle nests. He was also mistaken for a "revenue man" in search of moonshine; twice his car was nearly burned by deliberately set grass fires.

Gradually, that first year, he found quite a few other nests along the Gulf Coast—in swamps, in suburbs, in game preserves, on a golf course, and on the grounds of a veterans' hospital. Most of the recorded eagle nests then were located on Florida's east coast. Broley, though, had serendipitously stumbled upon a Tampa Bay region that once harbored a plethora of eagle eyries—so many that the birds apparently formed one of the world's densest concentrations of large, breeding raptors.

Following Pough's advice, Charles Broley recruited a couple of fifteen-year-old boys to climb the nest trees. They had evidenced their interest by informing him they wanted to remove a great horned owlet from a nest for a pet. For practice, Broley agreed to accompany the boys to the owl nest. Climbing first, he was gashed near his eyes by the mother. When it was the boys' turn, he cautioned one of them to ward her off but not to harm her.

"I'll kill her if she bothers me," the boy replied. Although the boy did reach the nest, at Broley's urging he left the owlets. But the youth climbed poorly, and on the drive home he repeated that he'd kill any adult bird that bothered him. He also vowed to capture owlets, and perhaps a young eagle, as pets.

Hearing that, Broley knew he would have to climb the trees himself—no small feat when you consider his age and the fact that the first limb of most of the pines was at least 40 feet off the ground. Eschewing the climbing irons, safety belts, and lines most eagle banders use today, Broley fashioned a 40-foot rope ladder with wooden rungs as well as another 40-foot length he'd tie to the first for particularly high limbs. To secure the ladder on a limb, he first would toss some lead fishing weights attached to a light cord over the branch. Later, after throwing his arm out one windy day trying to loop the cord over, the former lacrosse player attached a large, bent kitchen spoon to the end of a long stick in order to flip the lead weights up over the branch. Years later he employed a slingshot and nylon fishing line.

With that line he pulled up a clothesline, then used that to haul up a heavy rope to which he had fastened his ladder. With pliers and bird bands tucked into his pockets, Broley was ready. On his first climb, his feet immediately swung so far forward on the wooden rung that his arms were supporting most of his weight. Later he would learn to scale the supple ladder differently, climbing it from one side, like a circus aerialist, in order to keep the swaying ladder more perpendicular.

On his initial climb, however, up a tree near Sarasota, his arms were trembling by the time he reached the first branch. It was 50 feet above the ground. He still had another 50 feet to scale. From there, he climbed up from limb to limb; if the branches were too far apart, he'd toss a rope he was carrying over a limb and pull himself up. Once underneath the nest, the six-foot-wide and -high nest flared out above him like a bowl. Eventually for such cases Broley would carry a light "nest ladder," a 12-foot rope ladder he secured by tossing a rope right over the nest itself. Once up there, the only other tool he might use was a poulter's stick similar to the boat hook New Jersey's Larry Niles uses today, to nudge the legs of the larger eaglets toward him.

The first time, however, he managed to scramble up around the nest by hand. As he did so, a large eaglet poised on the rim panicked and sailed off some 400 feet into palmetto scrub. The bird wasn't quite ready to fly, but it could glide. Up in the nest, the remaining eaglet embedded a talon in one of Broley's inexperienced hands; he had to remove it with pliers. After banding the bird, he descended to track down the escapee. After scaling the tall tree yet again, Broley hauled the eaglet back up bundled in a piece of canvas: the first of some seventy such "jumpers" he returned to their nests.

Broley used all four bands in a matter of days. Pough sent him a dozen more; they were gone in a week. Pough then sent him a hundred more bands with this written caution: "Don't let those boys take any unnecessary risks."

"Boys!" Broley wrote back. "I'm climbing trees myself."

To reach the nests he often had to slash through palmetto, catclaw vines, and marshes, occasionally sidestepping and killing poisonous rattlesnakes and cottonmouths. He was attacked by great horned owls, which, he later figured, had taken over about 13 percent of the eagle nests he visited. One owl tore off the right shoulder of his shirt and planted all eight talons in his back and arm. But the more he climbed, the stronger and more fit he became. His lack of acrophobia was remarkable. Soon he was relishing difficult trees with 80-foot-high first limbs.

In three months, Broley banded forty-four eaglets. By the time he left Florida for his island home on a lake in Delta, Ontario, he had no definite plans to return. But the astonishing results of those first banded birds soon would be bringing him back to Florida nearly every winter for the rest of his life.

Ornithologists believed that the southern bald eagle, *Haliaeetus leucocephalus leucocephalus*—then considered a smaller, separate subspecies from its northern cousin, *Haliaeetus leucocephalus alaskanus*, but now considered a smaller member of the same species—did not migrate. Of the six banded birds that were recovered that first year, four were found in Florida. Then one of the first eagles Broley banded, in St. Petersburg late in January 1939, was found shot more than 1,000 miles to the north in Columbiaville, New York, on May 8. Three weeks later a bird he had banded in Largo was found shot in Virginia. The following year one of Broley's birds appeared in Quebec. On June 1, 1941, another of his birds was found on Prince Edward Island, 1,600 miles north of where he had banded it less than four months earlier. In 1947 one of Broley's first-year birds was caught 2,500 miles from home in a leghold fox trap, 200 miles north of Broley's former Winnipeg, Manitoba, home.

Riding the prevailing winds, young bald eagles were leaving Florida shortly after they learned how to fly, then returning again in September or October. Since some of his Florida sources told him the adults also seemed to disappear during the summer—in mid-May of 1994, one Sarasota couple saw about fifty adults and first-year birds soaring northward—Broley assumed the adults he was unable to band were making the same journey. (Recent research indicates many adults do remain in Florida during the hot summers, but it is also apparent that some wander at least as far north as the Chesapeake Bay.)

Between 1939 and early 1946, forty-eight of the 814 bald eagles banded by Broley were recovered. Where they were found, and why, is a testament to their mobility, a lesson in how perilous the first year of an eagle's life can be, and a sobering commentary on the war on wildlife then being waged. Culled from the banding records he fastidiously kept on index cards, Broley's list of reported recoveries reads like the script for a contemporary urban television newscast:

FLORIDA: Found dead, shot, found dead, found wounded, shot, found
    injured, found dead, killed, found dying, shot
GEORGIA: Shot, shot, found dead, shot, captured, shot
MISSISSIPPI: unknown
SOUTH CAROLINA: Shot, found dead, found dead
NORTH CAROLINA: Captured, captured, killed, killed
VIRGINIA: Band found, shot
PENNSYLVANIA: Found dead, found dead, found wounded
INDIANA: Shot
ILLINOIS: Shot, shot
CONNECTICUT: Shot
NEW YORK: Found dead, shot, shot
MICHIGAN: Shot
MAINE: Found dead
QUEBEC: Found wounded

NEW BRUNSWICK: Shot, found dead, shot
NOVA SCOTIA: Found dead, shot, shot, shot
PRINCE EDWARD ISLAND: Shot

Of the forty-eight birds recovered, more than half were shot or killed.

Between 1917 and 1954, the territory of Alaska paid bounties on 128,000 slain eagles. Over the past few centuries, far more were shot in the lower forty-eight. Broley eventually estimated that 90 percent of his birds that were found had been gunned down. One Bradenton, Florida, woman told Broley she sensed the young from the nest near her home were saying good-bye to her as they chattered away on a dead tree in mid-May one year. She was right, Broley told her: one of the two was shot dead just two days later in North Carolina. Broley was learning firsthand one of the major reasons that bald eagles had become more myth than reality for most Americans.

Three years before Broley first arrived in Florida, the National Audubon Society had commissioned W. Bryant Tyrrell to survey the bald eagles in the Chesapeake Bay area. In his report, he summed up human attitudes toward the birds as follows:

> General: The majority of the local people are ignorant of the existence of the Eagle about them.
> Sportsmen and gunners: Erroneously believes [sic] the Eagle does considerable damage to game, and usually desires to kill them. Though one sportsman does more damage to the game than many Eagles. . . .
> Trappers: Claim that the Eagle destroys the animals in their traps, and therefore kills them. One trapper on the James River in Virginia who had a line of about 1,000 traps told of the Eagle's [sic] destroying as many as 10 rats a week in his traps, which represented a loss of possibly $15 to him. It is no wonder he was anxious to kill them.
> Lumbermen: Have no regard for them. One tree cut down last winter which had an Eagle's nest in it, had a saw log 56 ft. long. Five nests destroyed in the winter of 1935–1936. . . .
> Game Wardens: Usually ignorant of the existence of nests in their territory.

While oologists, or egg collectors, played a much more minor role than gunmen in the decline of the bald eagle, their impact, at least locally, could be significant. That certainly was true in Delaware and New Jersey, where

Tyrrell heard of one collector who paid five dollars for every nest shown to him. Persisting in coveting eagle eggs long after any scientific usefulness had waned, oologists in 1935 robbed three of the five known bald eagle nests in Cape May County, New Jersey. One Salem County nest visited by ornithologists seven times in fifteen years in the 1920s and 1930s never held any young, thanks to egg raids. A bird such as the bald eagle, with a relatively long sexual maturation period and relatively low reproductive rate—an average of two eggs a year, with often the first hatched the only survivor—could not long endure such thievery.

Consider the turn-of-the-century exploits of southeast Alaska's George C. Cantwell. To reach his initial eagle nest 100 feet up a tree, he first climbed a smaller nearby tree and precariously crossed over to his target on an outstretched limb. Finding no eggs, he moved on to another nest where an incubating female objected to his rap on the trunk. "I needed another Eagle," Cantwell, who was armed with a rifle, proudly recounted, "and soon had her plugged with cotton."

He took her two eggs; flushed another mother off her nest and blasted her with his gun; killed a Pacific loon as it rode the crest of a swell; and clambered up into the second eagle's nest to claim two more eggs. Sitting atop that eyrie, he greatly admired the view: a flotilla of green islands marching up the Alaskan archipelago to the north, "while on the entire south and west rolled by the great Pacific, where the red sun was sinking beneath the waves. Who would not be an eagle on such an island—monarch of all he surveyed." Cantwell illustrated his account in an 1899 edition of *The Osprey* journal with a picture of himself holding the dead birds. The caption: "A Good Day For Eagles."

But it was Florida that had long represented the nirvana for oologists who craved eagle eggs. In the late 1880s, during just two winter seasons along the Indian River on Florida's Atlantic coast, one physician from Utica, New York, collected twenty-six sets totaling forty-seven eggs. Several years later, in December 1891, Willard Eliot of Tampa accompanied a friend on a horse-and-buggy egging expedition to the edge of Tampa Bay.

"What oölogist has not wished to find an eagle's nest, and dreamed of climbing some huge tree or scaling a steep cliff in quest of one," he asked in *The Oölogist* journal. No doubt the answer was a null set. After a difficult climb with tree spikes seventy feet up to the first eagle nest he had ever seen, Eliot reported that "the sight that met my gaze sent a shade of disappointment over my face for there sat two young eagles."

Too late to get any eggs, Eliot remained resourceful: "Taking the young eagles for mounting I soon descended and we started on. In about two hours we had found two more nests, and obtained two fine sets of eggs. As it was now getting late we packed the eggs safely in our dinner basket (an indispensible [*sic*] article on eggin' trips) and started homeward. To say that we were happy would not express it. I had found what I had been looking for for several years and my joy kept bubbling over at times."

Nearly a half century later, when Broley first arrived in Florida, oologists there were still active. A set of two bald eagle eggs was worth ten dollars. Broley heard of one man who had collected a bushel basket full of eagle eggs around Merritt Island on the east coast. In Tampa, one federally licensed collector, whom Broley eventually stopped, had pounded cleats into the nest trees he visited every year. Broley, in error, did not believe the many collectors who claimed the eagles would lay a second set of eggs if the first set was taken. But the collector's timing had to be perfect in order for a double (or second) clutch to occur. The following year, Florida's refusal to issue egg collecting permits and the enactment of the federal Bald Eagle Protection Act curtailed the practice and sent the remaining egg collectors underground.

Broley, though, still had to deal with ranchers and farmers. Willing to believe any story of poultry predation, farmers were toppling every nest tree they could find, Witmer wrote in his 1937 classic, *Bird Studies at Old Cape May*. But of the first eight hundred nests Broley climbed in Florida and Canada, he found the feet or heads of poultry in only two—and they were probably discards from butchered fowl.

One Florida rancher shot a banded immature eagle because, he said, it was taking his pigs.

"Did you see the bird make off with a pig?" Broley asked the rancher.

"Well, no. But he was flying around, and the pigs acted frightened. They ran all about, squealing—"

"Have you missed any of your pigs?"

"Well, I'm not sure, haven't counted them lately, but there's likely some gone."

"Did you ever know positively of an eagle taking a pig?"

"Perhaps not, but my grandfather said eagles took pigs."

It must have been so.

Broley was also an eyewitness to the greatest and longest-lived threat to the bald eagle: the destruction of its habitat. During World War II, he noticed that the army's demand for timber was exacting a tremendous toll on Florida's pines, forcing some eagles inland. After the war, that demand never flagged. By 1949 most of the large pines on Pine Island, near Fort Myers, had been felled, reducing the number of active nests from twelve to just four. Two winters later, Broley was shocked to see that in less than a year two sawmills had leveled what he considered the last remaining haven for nesting bald eagles on Florida's Gulf Coast, a 3,000-acre stand of immense pines that stretched for five miles along the Gulf above Sarasota. "Three eagle nest trees were left standing," he wrote, "but the eagles were so disturbed by the timber cutting they did not nest."

In just a decade in Florida, Charles Broley had seen tremendous changes. Thousands of acres had been cleared for market gardening and lumber, with few trees remaining large enough to support a nest. In addition, "Housing construction all along the coast is crowding the big birds from their favorite nesting territory along the waterfront," he wrote in a 1950 *Audubon* magazine article, "and I am wondering, where in another ten years these eagles will find a place to nest."

It was, he said, a case of too many people, too much building. It was also nothing new for the bald eagle, which had been shot, trapped, poisoned, and displaced by humans. The decline of the bald eagle was preordained from the time of Columbus, as inevitable and inexorable as the manifest destiny that pushed Americans across the continent. When Europeans first arrived on the eastern shores of North America, bald eagles nested from Labrador to just below the Arctic tundra in Alaska and along the entire length of the Aleutian Islands, and from Florida to Baja California. Along the coastlines, major rivers, and lakes, it nested in every state but West Virginia and Rhode Island. There was such an "infinite number" wintering in Casco Bay, Maine, in 1668 that many were shot to feed hogs. Even as late as the mid-1800s bald eagles were a common sight in New York. In the winter, they were "extremely abundant" floating on ice in the Hudson River, bringing the fish they captured into Manhattan parks to devour. During the winter of 1844, sixty to seventy eagles were shot on Long Island.

Among the first to detect the impending decline was Audubon, who had seen hundreds of eagles as he traveled down the Mississippi from the Ohio to New Orleans before the advent of steamboats. By 1834, however, their numbers along the heartland's rivers had markedly declined. Audubon theorized that the game animals the eagles preyed upon had fled deeper into the wilderness to avoid persecution by man.

But there was no safe haven farther west. In California a nest occupied in 1849 four miles from Sacramento was abandoned by 1857, disturbed either by constant steamer traffic or by gunmen. By the end of World War I, stockmen in the San Joaquin Valley were destroying eagles, golden and bald, by indiscriminately poisoning the carcasses of cattle and sheep to kill coyotes, mountain lions, and other predators. Ever the trendsetter, California developed a new way of dispatching eagles in the mid-1930s. According to one estimate, two hundred eagles, mostly balds, were shot from planes in the Sacramento Valley in 1936. One rancher paid $700 in bounties to his employees that year for killing eagles.

While the members of the Emergency Conservation Committee based in New York City might have been guilty of hyperbole, in 1935 its alarming "Save the Bald Eagle!" pamphlet claimed that you could drive each summer for hundreds of miles along the fish-rich coasts and rivers of the Pacific Northwest without seeing an eagle. Lobbying to end the eagle bounty in Alaska, the committee concluded: "The Bald Eagle is now so far on the road to extermination in the United States proper that its case there is probably already hopeless."

Whether you kill an eagle or level the trees in which it nests and roosts, the ultimate effect is the same: a world with fewer, or no, eagles. Nothing underscores the low regard most Americans had for bald eagles, or the sense that they, like everything else in this New World, were limitless, than the following journal passage:

St. John's River, East Florida, 7th February 1832. . . . On approaching the nearest nest, we saw two young birds standing erect on its edge, while their parents were perched on the branches above them. As we went nearer, the old ones flew off silently, while the young did not seem to pay the least attention to us, this being a part of the woods where probably no white man had ever before put his foot, and the Eaglets having as yet had no experience of the barbarity of the race. The captain took the first shot: one of the birds was severely wounded, and tumbled half way from the nest towards the ground, when it recovered, flapped its wings, and suddenly sailed away until we lost sight of it. . . . One of the sailors was told to shoot the other, which had not moved from its position; he missed it; and as I saw it make movements indicative of its surprise and fear, I fired, but wounded it so slightly in one pinion, that it was enabled to fly off in an irregular manner towards the river. This I judged was the first attempt it had ever made to fly. . . . After some time I reached our boat, and at the same instant was surprised to see the wounded bird perched on a low stump within half gun shot. I fired, and the bird fell, but before I reached the spot, it flew off again and tumbled into the river, where, in this to it new and wonderful element, it flapped its wings, and made way so fast, that I took to the water and brought it ashore. . . . After all, it was necessary to knock the bird on the head, which done I returned to the party, none of whom had yet found their prey. . . . [A]fter a few hundred yards walking among palmettoes, Spanish bayonets, sword-grass, and other disagreeable undergrowth, we discovered the poor bird gasping its last agonies. On examining their bodies we found both well supplied with shot, and I became more assured than ever of the hardiness of the species.

On the same river, 8th February. We visited another nest, on which, by the aid of a telescope, we saw three young ones in the posture described above. The bird first shot fell back in the nest and there remained: it was struck by a bullet. The next was so severely wounded that it clung outside the nest, until fired at a second time, when it fell. The third was killed, as it was preparing to fly off. . . . [I]n a few hours these young birds were skinned, cooked, and eaten, by those who had been "in at the death." They proved good eating, the flesh resembling veal in taste and tenderness.

—John James Audubon

Of the ninety-two nests Broley observed in 1950, only twenty-three produced young. Sixty-nine, or 75 percent, failed. His list included these items:

Birds around but did not lay eggs	30
Nested but eggs did not hatch	19
Trees with nests, cut	4
Young disappeared from nest (or shot)	3
Great horned owls took nests	7
No. old birds returned to claim nests	6

Broley speculated that the extremely hot and dry weather of 1949 and 1950 had caused the eggs to addle. "Surely it cannot be possible that all these birds are becoming old and sterile," he wrote. "Young birds must be replacing them continually." Of the thirty pairs that did not nest, Broley observed: "Many of these birds are continually disturbed by building, lumbering, and farming activities, but some nests are inactive for no apparent reason." In the March-April 1951 issue of *Audubon* magazine, Broley continued to report on an increasingly grim situation. "Nesting is late this year and in my four-day trip I banded only four birds, the first for the year," he wrote. "Also, many birds are not nesting."

In both 1951 and 1952, in the 100 miles from Tampa south to Englewood he could find only two active nests, with thirty to forty inactive ones. "Also," he reported in his 1951 letter, "in this four-day trip, I did not see one immature [more than a year old] eagle. In 1946 and 1947, I saw as many as twelve standing in one small area."

The number of young birds he was banding was falling precipitously:

1946:   150 birds banded
1947:   113
1948:   85
1949:   60
1950:   24
1951:   24
1952:   15

By 1955 his nests were experiencing an 84 percent failure rate, and the situation continued to worsen. In 1957, he found just forty-three nests attended by adults, but only seven had any young. The next year Broley had to drive 100 miles down the coast before he found the one bird he would band that season. Two other nests had juveniles that were too old to risk banding. In all of his once prolific territory, he found just ten nests with adults.

In 1940 there were an estimated five hundred active nests in Florida. Eighteen years later, Broley doubted there were eighty. It had been four years since he had received a report of any of the record 1,240 birds he had banded. Elsewhere, eagles were dwindling along the Chesapeake and Delaware bays. Between 1956 and 1958 all the known nests in a four-county New Jersey area failed to produce a single eaglet. Along the frontal ridge of the Appalachians in eastern Pennsylvania, immature bald eagles were now one of the rarest of fall migrants. In 1957 just one out of every thirty-three bald eagles passing south over the Hawk Mountain Sanctuary was immature. From his home along the banks of the Mississippi in East Moline, Illinois, Elton Fawks wrote to Broley that in his last count of fifty-nine wintering bald eagles, only one was immature—clearly a sign of a dying race.

In 1934 Charles Broley had canoed into a Manitoba marsh expecting to see nearly twenty thousand nesting Franklin's gulls. He found instead hundreds of dead gulls, their carcasses twisted and distorted by convulsions, their nests filled with dead chicks and rotting eggs. The bellies of the gulls, young and old alike, were fat with grasshoppers—grasshoppers, he concluded, that had been poisoned and, in turn, had fatally poisoned the gulls.

A quarter century later Broley reached a somewhat similar conclusion regarding bald eagles. He articulated his theory in a startling, landmark article that appeared in the July-August 1958 issue of *Audubon* magazine: "*I am firmly convinced that about 80 percent of the Florida bald eagles are sterile.*

"This is the only conclusion I can reach after watching nests in which the eggs have failed to hatch in seven consecutive years."

What was the cause? Broley speculated that heavy spraying of insecticides, particularly DDT, was to blame. Noting the eagles' heavy reliance on fish, he recalled a fish kill in the early 1950s in Tampa Bay in which the dead fish had large residues of DDT. "An eagle is naturally going to catch the most sluggish fish and is it not possible," Broley wondered, "that a cumulative amount of DDT in eagles has caused sterility?"

He pointed out that James B. DeWitt, chief of the Chemical Control Section of the U.S. Fish and Wildlife Service's research center in Patuxent, Maryland, had found that feeding DDT to breeding quail caused almost all of their offspring to die quickly, either during the embryonic stage in the egg or shortly after hatching. Among conservationists there was a growing belief that the cumulative effect of insecticide spraying was killing wildlife and had the potential to cause sterility. Conceding he was not a trained biologist, Broley concluded with a plea for immediate scientific study of Florida's nonproductive bald eagles: "Our American bald eagle—national emblem of this country—is a very sick bird."

CHAPTER 6

"THE DDT MAN IS COMING"

Ill fares the land, to hastening ills a prey,
Where wealth accumulates, along with spray.
Chemists and farmers flourish at their peril:
The bird of freedom, thanks to them, is sterile.
—E. B. WHITE, "THE DESERTED NATION," *The New Yorker,* OCT. 8, 1966

Hey, farmer, farmer, put away that DDT now,
Give me spots on my apples but leave me birds and the bees.
Please!
—JONI MITCHELL, "BIG YELLOW TAXI," 1970

Let's not be members of the silent majority . . . while the militant minority destroys the
technology that man has developed for his own survival and health, as well as for the
protection of wildlife. With 2.8 billion people in the world of 1972, all having a need for
housing and food, there might not be enough caves to go around if we are forced to
return to the "balance of nature" culture of our prehistoric ancestors; and the few eagles
that remain would surely end up in stew pots in those circumstances, anyway.
—ANDREW J. ROGERS, "EAGLES, AFFLUENCE AND PESTICIDES,"
PRESIDENTIAL ADDRESS TO THE AMERICAN MOSQUITO CONTROL
ASSOCIATION, APRIL 24, 1972

 Charles Broley was right about DDT. He was also, in one sense, wrong. Initially, his suspicion that rampant pesticide use was extirpating bald eagles did not meet with universal acceptance. As he conceded, he had no real proof. He, like others, had considered another possibility: the nuclear rain of strontium-90 isotopes—the radioactive fallout from above-ground nuclear testing in the Nevada desert and on Pacific atolls—that had worked its way into

America's pasture grass, the milk of its dairy cows, and the bones of its children.

Among those who doubted Broley's pesticide hypothesis was Joseph C. Howell, a University of Tennessee zoology professor who had been studying bald eagles in east central Florida for thirty years. Howell conceded in 1958 that the number of birds was decreasing, but he attributed a 50 percent drop in the nests he had been surveying since 1935 to rapid residential and agricultural development. There were still many bald eagles in the area, however, and each year Howell visited, he found new nests.

However, by 1965, only five of the two dozen nests he had visited since the Depression remained. The Merritt Island region, which had more than one hundred nests in 1886, harbored just a dozen. Spurred on by Broley, in 1961 the National Audubon Society launched its Continental Bald Eagle Survey. While the survey's initial numbers were not completely comprehensive, the counts were sobering. With the percentage of immature birds continuing to decline, fewer than four thousand birds were known to be wintering in the contiguous states. The Midwest, including the Mississippi and Missouri valleys, was harboring more than half of them, with most of the rest concentrated in Florida, the Pacific Northwest, and the Mid-Atlantic states.

Even more abysmal were the spring nesting results. In the two decades following World War II, the number of breeding bald eagles in many areas of the country had declined by more than half—as much as 90 percent to 100 percent in some regions. And of the active nests that did remain, the breeding failure rates ranged from 55 percent to 96 percent. The initial Audubon counts were not inclusive. But outside of Washington's San Juan Islands, in the lower forty-eight states the Audubon survey in 1963 tallied a mere 417 bald eagle pairs. That year, 89 of Florida's 190 nests fledged a total of 122 young—half the known total for all of the lower forty-eight states. Two years later those Florida numbers had slumped further. Outside of the Pacific Northwest, about which little was known in terms of numbers, the other major concentration of eagle nests was found inland, around the western Great Lakes. Fewer than half of the 148 active nests in Michigan, Wisconsin, and Minnesota were fledging young eagles. The lakeshores themselves, where it was thought there once had been one nest for every ten miles of shoreline, were moribund. Of the nineteen known nests, only one pair produced any young.

Elsewhere, fewer than a fifth of Maine's meager thirty nests fledged young. The rest of New England had no known nests. On the Chesapeake

Bay, which claimed two hundred nests in 1936, just fifty-one nests could be found, and only 15 percent of those were successful. While a dwindling number of northern bald eagles might continue to winter in the contiguous U.S., by the mid-1960s some biologists feared it was likely that resident nesting bald eagles would soon disappear. At the very least, America's national symbol was perilously close to becoming an irrelevant curiosity, a magnificent anachronism ill-suited to the modern age. "I didn't think we would lose all of them, but something was very seriously wrong," says Alexander "Sandy" Sprunt IV, the National Audubon Society's research director. "When we started in 1960 the suspicion was that it was DDT, but no one really knew."

DDT was so pervasive in the wild that, of fifty-eight bald eagles found dead or incapacitated in twenty states and two Canadian provinces, all but one Alaskan bird analyzed in 1963 had traces of the pesticide. The year before, three failed eggs collected from southern New Jersey nests by Joe Jacobs, an amateur eagle enthusiast, contained 11.4, 24.3, and 36.9 parts per million of DDE, a metabolite, or slightly altered form, of DDT—levels that, we know now, clearly were high enough to cause reproductive failure. Significantly, the New Jersey counties where the eggs had been collected, the counties where bald eagles were staging their final, feeble stand, were the last in the state to have established mosquito extermination commissions, the last counties where aerial spraying and fogging had blanketed the salt meadows and freshwater marshes where the eagles fed with thousands of gallons of DDT-laced fuel oil.

While the Audubon Society was assessing eagle populations, the Bureau of Sports Fisheries and Wildlife, an arm of the U.S. Fish and Wildlife Service, undertook a series of experiments to determine the effects of DDT. It was known that DDT, in high enough doses, lethally poisoned the central nervous system. Late in 1961, eleven eagles were captured along the eagle-rich Chilkat River in southeast Alaska and taken to the federal-state experimental fur station in Petersburg, Alaska. Fed fish impregnated with DDT, all of the eagles on the higher doses died. The three consuming the highest doses died within two to three weeks. Even one of the two that consumed 80 parts per million DDT—25 times less than the highest doses—perished, with pronounced tremors, in three months. These results mirrored the outcome of similar studies with other birds and mammals, and generally the fish and other prey that eagles were eating contained far less DDT than what the dead eagles had been fed.

The following year, fourteen more eagles were trapped along the Chilkat and brought to Petersburg, where they were fed lower doses of DDT that approximated levels found in some eagle prey. The result: ingesting low levels of DDT over two to four months was not fatal. Once the eagles stopped eating food laced with the pesticide, the amount of DDT and DDD (another slightly altered form of DDT) in their bodies decreased.

One nagging problem remained: after the eagles resumed a clean diet, residues of DDE—a less toxic but much more stable metabolite of DDT produced by many living organisms that ingest DDT—did not diminish in the eagles' tissues. In fact, the DDE levels in the eagles' livers increased two months after they stopped eating DDT. Apparently the livers were still transforming the ingested DDT into DDE; but it was also possible that the DDT within the fish had metabolized into DDE before the eagles consumed the fish. The researchers frankly did not understand the significance, if any, of the lingering DDE residues.

These studies, however, did disprove Charles Broley's theory in at least one respect: DDT was not making bald eagles sterile. After being fed low levels of DDT, the sperm activity in the testes of male bald eagles was completely normal.

But something was clearly awry. At the base of a nest tree near Salem, New Jersey, one spring Joe Jacobs found the fluffy white head of an eagle chick so young it still had the egg tooth on its beak. His conclusion: "the young bird died and . . . the adult bird or birds tore the head off and ate the body."

DDT is the familiar acronym for the chemical dichlorodiphenyltrichloroethane. Although it was first synthesized in 1873 by an Austrian student, it was not until 1939 that its insecticidal properties were discovered by Paul Hermann Müller, a Swiss chemist with the J. R. Geigy Corporation in Basel, Switzerland. Looking for a stable compound that would kill insects on contact, as opposed to when they ingested it, Müller began to investigate variations of chloroform, an anesthetic poison favored by insect collectors. Chloroform is a classic chlorinated hydrocarbon—a molecule with a central carbon atom whose surrounding hydrogen atoms have been replaced in part by chlorine atoms. The extraordinary ability of carbon atoms to bond with each other and with other types of atoms, in an almost infinite variety of complex configurations, helps explain why there exists such an incredible diversity of life—and why, in the hands of an organic chemist like Paul Hermann Müller, chlorinated hydrocarbons held such promise.

To gauge the effectiveness of his compounds, Müller introduced flies into a large glass chamber after first coating the inside of it with a fine spray of whatever analog he was testing. The reaction of the flies to the DDT he concocted was remarkable. So toxic was the compound that, even after the chamber had been well cleaned, flies that entered it died on contact. Müller's research group soon learned it was equally effective on potato beetles and clothes moths. Cheap, easy to apply, and odorless, DDT was far more persistent and lethal to the nervous systems of insects than any previously known insecticide. And yet it was supposedly so safe for plants and animals that it could even be applied, in powder form, to human skin with no ill effects.

After being successfully tested on both insects and humans in the United States in 1942 and 1943, the synthetic compound was first hailed as a miracle early in 1944. Used to dust the clothes and hair of lice-exposed persons, DDT powder was credited with halting a typhus epidemic in Naples, Italy—even though authorities were close to controlling the epidemic with other means before they utilized the DDT. At the onset of World War II, no insecticide existed to protect Allied troops in the South Pacific from such mosquito-borne diseases as malaria and yellow fever. But diluted in kerosene or fuel oil, only one-fifth or one-fourth of a pound of DDT effectively treated an acre. Ahead of Allied troops, entire islands were blanketed with aerial sprays of DDT. Malaria rates dropped tremendously, with no apparent ill effects to heavily exposed servicemen.

By the time the War Production Board first released surplus DDT for civilian use in the United States on August 1, 1945, it was being touted as the atomic bomb of pesticides, making the world as safe from bugs as Little Boy and Fat Man several days later would make it safe from Japanese despotism. Its discovery and, shortly afterward, the creation of even more toxic chlorinated hydrocarbon compounds such as chlordane, aldrin, dieldrin and heptachlor (all since banned) raised widespread hopes that insect-borne disease soon would be vanquished.

Such utopian hubris, such blind faith in science and technology, was as understandable as it was naive. Müller's discovery, which earned him the 1948 Nobel Prize for medicine, would spare hundreds of millions of people around the world from the threat of malaria. In the United States, DDT played no real role in eliminating the disease. Part of the wonder, though, of DDT was its wide applicability: across America, swarms of Colorado potato beetles, cotton boll weevils, and nuisance mosquitoes quickly succumbed to Müuller's magical spray.

Embracing this wonderful new chemical world in the 1950s and 1960s, millions of American children ran behind army-surplus Jeeps retrofitted with tanks and nozzles as they crawled down urban and suburban streets, enveloping the kids' neighborhoods in a sweet fog of DDT. Dr. Nancy Thomas, who now necropsies hundreds of dead eagles each year at the National Wildlife Health Research Center in Madison, Wisconsin, ran through clouds of DDT in her Chicago rowhouse neighborhood. My wife did likewise in a Philadelphia suburb. Larry Niles's wife, Kathy, did it at her family's summer home along the New Jersey shore. The whoosh of the spray nozzle was as tantalizing as the bell of an ice-cream truck. "He's coming, he's coming," the children would chant to each other, "The DDT man is coming." They would run or pedal their bicycles into the fog, trying to keep up, as Kathy Niles remembers, entranced by the fact that you could lose each other in the great billowing cloud.

What harm could it do? Insecticides impregnated kitchen shelf paper. Public health officials sprayed some children with DDT in schools and swimming pools in a wrong-headed attempt to ward off polio, which is transmitted by a virus. But no one ever told our parents how quickly DDT could move up the food chain. The first report of DDT in animal milk was published in 1945, the same year the pesticide was released for civilian use. Three years later the first evidence of DDT in human fat and breast milk was reported. Tests conducted during World War II had shown that long-time high exposure to DDT caused "fatty degeneration of the liver and kidney" in rats, and in 1945 two reports by British researchers who had exposed themselves to DDT—several by touching walls painted with a 2 percent DDT solution, another by applying it to his skin in an acetone solution—concluded that humans exposed to DDT suffered central nervous system problems, including body tremors, painfully aching joints, muscular weakness, fatigue, insomnia, acute anxiety, and depression.

By 1950 Food and Drug Administration researchers had determined that the typical American diet contained about 0.05 parts per million of DDT and the average American's body fat contained 5.3 ppm DDT. Complaining that it was increasingly difficult to find enough vegetables free of pesticides, the Beech-Nut Packing Company regrettably allowed limited residues of DDT in its baby food. Every restaurant meal the U.S. Public Health Service sampled contained DDT. Echoing a refrain occasionally heard today, both the American Medical Association and Beech-Nut protested that the government had permitted DDT and related pesticides to be marketed without adequate knowledge of the long-term effects of ingesting foods containing DDT.

Chemical manufacturers, farmers, and the U.S. Department of Agriculture countered that the Food and Drug Administration's provisional tolerance levels for DDT—zero for milk, 7 ppm for fruit—were adequate, particularly since, despite higher levels of DDT in their blood and fat, there had been no reports of DDT-related deaths or injury among the persons most heavily exposed to it: those who applied it. Buttressed in part by Dr. Wayland J. Hayes, a U.S. Public Health Service toxicologist who had studied volunteer convicts who had ingested DDT daily for as much as a year, supporters successfully reiterated this position for the next two decades.

To certain entomologists, however, the unintended effects DDT was having on insects were more distressing than any vague human health concerns. In some cases DDT was killing off predators and parasites that preyed on the target insects more effectively than it was eliminating the insects themselves, opening the door for the targets or even lesser insect pests to explode out of control. Given the mind-boggling genetic diversity and lightning-quick reproductive capabilities of insects, it also was inevitable that DDT-resistant strains soon evolved. (Even if only a small percentage of insects survived the DDT, these highly resistant individuals could rapidly reproduce entire resistant populations—an ability denied to higher organisms such as eagles, with their fewer numbers, longer life spans, and four- to five-year sexual maturation.) By 1947 house flies in Italy had developed such genetic resistance. DDT-resistant lice appeared during the Korean War, and resistant mosquitoes also rapidly evolved.

Nonetheless, DDT quickly superseded arsenic-based pesticides to become, by far, the world's most widely used pesticide. More expensive and less effective than DDT, these predecessors had been restricted to farm fields and fruit orchards. But because DDT was more potent and economical to use, because it was not acutely toxic to mammals, and because it could be sprayed from the air, it swiftly invaded ecosystems and areas that the arsenic pesticides had never infiltrated: wetlands, woodlands, urban and suburban shade trees. It was sold as an emulsifiable spray, a dust, a wettable powder, and in a granular form. Its use peaked in the late 1950s at nearly 79 million pounds—almost half a pound per year for every man, woman, and child living in the United States. By then, the country was exporting even more DDT than it consumed.

Among its most prominent targets: gypsy moths in the Northeast, fire ants in the Southeast, and the bark beetles that were spreading Dutch elm disease throughout the East and Midwest. The long-lasting compound, though, was not so much a targeted pesticide as a biocide, an indiscriminate poisoner of myriad life-forms. The term "organochlorine"—"organo" because the formulations are based upon carbon and hydrogen, two of the principal building blocks of life—had become an oxymoron. As early as 1946 government biologists were reporting that heavy applications of DDT could kill birds and fish. A decade and a half before Rachel Carson warned the nation of an impending silent spring, it arrived in Princeton, New Jersey, in 1947, courtesy of the federal Bureau of Entomology and Plant Quarantine. As soon as the bureau launched its experimental program to spray the town's elms twice a year with DDT, dead birds began to litter manicured lawns, and far fewer nestlings than usual survived. Though the water-based sprays were only 1 or 2 percent DDT, each tree annually was being drenched in four and a half pounds of DDT—a far greater concentration than was used in any other DDT spray program. The following year, as the spraying continued, Princeton residents picked up dead birds of nearly thirty different species.

As Dutch elm disease and the saturation spraying spread across the Midwest, so did avian deaths. Initially the protests of housewives and local conservationists did little to overcome the blanket endorsement of the U.S. Department of Agriculture and many entomologists, some of whom were connected with agriculturally oriented land-grant universities. They viewed the wildlife deaths—if they considered them at all—as an inevitable, insignificant price to pay for progress, for greater crop yields and improved public health. Although many scientists loathe engaging in public advocacy, some began to openly question the spraying.

Among them was Michigan State University ornithology professor George J. Wallace, who noticed that the East Lansing campus transformed itself into a robin graveyard after the state Department of Agriculture initiated DDT spraying there. First the birds lost their balance; then they suffered tremors, convulsions, and death. Nearly two-thirds of the other bird species that used to summer in East Lansing also either vanished or dramatically declined in number. The tale was similar, Wallace learned, throughout the state wherever elms had been sprayed. Often the brains of the dead birds contained lethal amounts of DDT, and Wallace found high contaminant levels in embryos and abandoned eggs.

In Urbana, Illinois, Dr. Roy Barker, of the Illinois Natural History Survey, discovered why. Finding concentrations of DDT and DDE in the brains of dead robins and in the bodies of the earthworms they ate, he established that the earthworms, as they mulched fallen elm leaves, were recycling the DDT. "Any program," Wallace complained, "which destroys eighty or more species of birds and unknown numbers of beneficial predatory and parasitic insects needs further study."

Yet as these million-dollar spraying campaigns continued to kill wildlife, they failed abysmally in their objective—to stamp out Dutch elm disease. The only apparently effective control was a decidedly low-tech solution that had been known for years: the prompt removal and destruction of wood that was diseased or infected with the bark beetles. This labor-intensive approach required a long-term commitment to vigilance and prompt sanitation. To an agricultural industry long addicted to the quick fix from a drum of pesticide, and to an agri-chemical industry addicted to its wildly growing market—between 1951 and 1966 pesticide use increased nine times faster than food production—it increasingly was the chemical way or no way. If it's not working anymore, increase the dosage. If that doesn't work, find something more toxic. The cost—in terms of money, damage to the environment, and possible human health hazards—be damned.

This approach ignored what Rachel Carson called "the other road," dismissing long-known principles of pest control such as crop rotation—or, in the case of urban elms, planting a variety of trees—to avoid creating a monoculture ripe for devastation by a single insect species. It neglected the tendency of insect populations to rise and fall cyclically. It ignored the fact that the sprayings were often killing the birds and other insects that were the primary predators of the target insects. It was blind to the then-nascent concept of integrated pest management, which carefully monitors the populations of both target species and their natural enemies, orchestrating a symphony of shifting measures that range from marshaling biological controls such as pathogens, parasites, and predators to applying, only when and where needed, specific, targeted pesticides. In retrospect, automatic, preemptive organochlorine use seems to be much more primitive than utilizing sterilized male insects, parasitic wasps, or bacterial spores to control insects.

Nonetheless, the Dutch elm disease tragicomedy replayed itself in the Midwest with an all-out assault on seemingly innocuous Japanese beetles. Both dieldrin and aldrin, which are, respectively, 50 times to between 100 and 300 times more toxic to quail than DDT, were employed. Songbirds, squirrels, rabbits, muskrats, and domestic cats died. The Japanese beetles inched westward.

In the South, the U.S. Department of Agriculture's eradication mania elevated the fire ant from an extremely minor agricultural pest with a painful but rarely fatal bite into a major public enemy. Though its mounds are easily identified, the USDA elected to spray tens of millions of acres with dieldrin pellets and heptachlor. Wild fish and birds, game birds, domestic livestock and poultry, crabs, and shrimp all perished. Several species of snakes, lizards, and frogs disappeared locally. The fire ants lived on.

Though gypsy moths primarily infest woodlands, to supposedly eradicate them millions of acres of farms and suburbs of Long Island and eastern New York were cloaked with DDT. It killed fish, wiped out thousands of colonies of pollinating honeybees, tainted dairy herds, and rendered vegetable crops unsalable. Trout in Lake George failed to reproduce. Two days after balsam firs along the New Brunswick's Miramichi River were sprayed with DDT to combat spruce budworms, many of the river's fabled young salmon were dead. Stone fly nymphs, the larvae of caddis flies and black flies, the aquatic soup upon which the young salmon feed, were destroyed. With nothing to eat, by August none of the remaining salmon fry spawned the previous autumn had survived. Only a sixth of the year-old salmon were still alive. A similar budworm campaign around Yellowstone National Park sentenced brown trout, and the aquatic insects that nourished them, to a similar fate.

The result of such assaults: in many American towns one of the continent's most prolific birds and one of the first signs of spring, the robin, never appeared. Chickadees and cardinals no longer brightened a winter's day. Bird feeders remained untouched for weeks. Dawn arrived unaccompanied by the trill of warblers, the soothing lament of mourning doves. Those were the sounds of silence to which Rachel Carson gave such eloquent voice, the images that, more than three decades after the 1962 publication of her book *Silent Spring,* are still burned into the American consciousness. She contended that in attempting to destroy a relatively few "pests," we were, Borgia-like, risking our own systematic destruction.

"How could intelligent beings seek to control a few unwanted species by a method that contaminated the entire environment and brought the threat of disease and death even to their own kind?" wondered Carson, who was suffering from breast cancer, which ended her life two years later. "[W]e have put poisonous and biologically potent chemicals indiscriminately into the hands of persons largely or wholly ignorant of their potentials for harm. We have subjected enormous numbers of people to contact with these poisons, without their consent and often without their knowledge. . . .

"I contend, furthermore, that we have allowed these chemicals to be used with little or no advance investigation of their effect on soil, water, wildlife, and man himself."

Although it was derided by some critics as too hysterical and emotional, as a work unworthy of a former staff biologist for the U.S. Fish and Wildlife Service, the book became an overnight best-seller. In the wake of the mounting public pressure generated by *Silent Spring*'s popularity, the USDA continued phasing out its aerial spray programs. President John F. Kennedy's Science Advisory Committee was the first of several government committees to call for the orderly phase-out of persistent pesticides. Little changed immediately, though, regarding the regulation and use of pesticides.

But to a public whose faith in modern science was already shaken by fallout from nuclear weapons testing, the publication of *Silent Spring* triggered a shift of tectonic proportions. Carson's book illuminated the terrible power we had unleashed in our seemingly benign control of nature, a control over which we ourselves ultimately had no control. *Silent Spring* irrevocably set in motion a sequence of events that, ten years later, led to an event the budding environmental movement at that time had found unthinkable—the banning of DDT.

It is one thing to find a dead or dying robin on your lawn, its muscles twitching uncontrollably because its brain has been short-circuited by organochlorines. Ferreting out the extraordinarily more subtle, time-delayed impact that DDT and its offspring were having on bald eagles and other birds, and its modus operandi, was a far more complex challenge.

The detective work began in Great Britain in 1961, when the Nature Conservancy, an agency of the British government, assigned naturalist Derek Ratcliffe to survey peregrine falcons. Pigeon fanciers in the mining valleys of south Wales were complaining that a population explosion of peregrines, the sleek 200 mph raptor rockets, was decimating their birds. After a few months of springtime fieldwork, Ratcliffe returned with a totally different saga: nesting peregrine falcons had nearly disappeared from southern England, and elsewhere throughout Great Britain their numbers had decreased significantly. For the first time in memory, many of the known nest sites were empty. Ratcliffe found others with a solitary adult, or with pairs of birds that inexplicably seemed uninterested in each other or did not fledge young because, in some cases, the eggs broke. Some didn't even lay eggs. The peregrines fared even worse the following year.

What was causing their unprecedented demise? Ratcliffe was aware of the mass killings of wild birds—including seedeaters, and sparrowhawks, kestrels, and owls that might have fed upon such birds—that had occurred from the mid-1950s to the early 1960s, after British farmers applied dieldrin, aldrin, and heptachlor organochlorines as seed dressings to their grain crops. He also was familiar with the U.S. Fish and Wildlife Service's research indicating that quail suffer reproductive failure after being fed DDT—the same study Charles Broley had cited. Also, during his first field season, Ratcliffe had recovered an addled peregrine egg from an eyrie in the Scottish hill country. Even though it was found some distance from any agricultural area, the egg contained small, sublethal amounts of dieldrin, DDE, heptachlor, and lindane. Two years later, thirteen more recovered eggs had similar, and sometimes substantial, residues, as did an adult tiercel, or male peregrine (so called because it is a third smaller than the female), found dead in its eyrie on an island off the Devon coast.

That year Ratcliffe suggested the peregrines were dwindling and failing to reproduce because they were victims of secondary poisoning: they were being poisoned by eating pesticide-tainted prey.

One American ornithologist intrigued by Ratcliffe's theory was Joseph J. Hickey. In the late 1950s Hickey, a professor at the University of Wisconsin in Madison, initially had been unfazed by reports of songbird holocausts. It couldn't be helped: widely sprayed pesticides would understandably kill some birds. Besides, he later told author Thomas R. Dunlap, housewives, who were among the most vocal opponents, were not scientists. But after being struck by the bizarre sight of a ripe Illinois mulberry tree without a bird in it, he examined the effects of DDT more closely. Comparing three Wisconsin towns whose elms had been sprayed for three years with three towns whose elms had not been treated, Hickey concluded in 1959 that robin populations had collapsed as much as 98 percent. On his own university campus in Madison, spraying the elms that year killed at least 86 percent of the nesting birds.

A year before Ratcliffe's falcon report surfaced, Hickey had heard rumors of a peregrine falcon crash in this country. After learning of Ratcliffe's assertions, during the spring of 1964 Hickey recruited Daniel Berger, a thirty-three-year-old Milwaukee laundermat operator with a passion for peregrines, and Chuck Sindelar, a senior biology-conservation major at the University of Wisconsin–Stevens Point, to check more than a hundred East Coast peregrine falcon nesting sites. (Sindelar would spend the next twenty-five years nearly tripling Charles Broley's record by banding 3,500 Wisconsin eagles.) Hickey had compiled a survey of many of the same eyries in 1939–1940. Not expecting much—none of Hickey's local contacts were seeing falcons—Berger and Sindelar visited 133 peregrine falcon nest sites from Georgia to Nova Scotia. Three months and 14,000 miles later, the two had failed to find a single fledgling. There were no adults. Every eyrie, some of which were known to have been active for at least a hundred years, was deserted. Although bald eagles were in desperate shape, in less than a quarter century peregrine falcons had disappeared from the eastern United States.

The following year a National Audubon Society conference in Port Clinton, Ohio, explored the bald eagle dilemma; Hickey gathered sixty researchers in Madison, Wisconsin, to pool information on peregrine falcons; and NATO drew eighty more European and American scientists to a pesticide conference in Britain. In Madison, Derek Ratcliffe and a colleague pinned the worldwide peregrine falcon population crash on extraordinary reproductive failure. Ratcliffe described watching peregrine parents breaking and eating their own eggs—a phenomenon never before reported in the annals of ornithology.

Those present at the Madison conference were already well aware of how DDT and other organochlorines could bioaccumulate, or build up exponentially, in the bodies of wildlife, as the synthetic compounds climbed up the food chain. They needed to look no farther than Clear Lake, a large recreational lake eighty miles north of San Francisco. In order to control nuisance gnats, between 1949 and 1957 DDD, a closely related metabolite of DDT, had been applied three times to the lake waters. After the first application, none of the lake's one thousand pairs of western grebes expired. That year, though, none of the elegant fish-eating birds bred. After the second and third applications, grebes died by the score. By 1959, only twenty-five pairs could be located, and no nests or young grebes were discovered. Greatly diluted, the total DDD applied amounted to just .143 parts per million in the water. Shortly after the last application, no trace of the pesticide could be found in the lake water itself. In water, organochlorines dissolve poorly; yet they are readily absorbed by organic matter, and they concentrate in the adipose tissue, or fat, of organisms, including birds—and man. In this case, the body fat of the dead grebes contained DDD residues of 1,600 parts per million—11,000 times the concentration in the water. It was a classic case of bioaccumulation: plankton in the water—even plankton several generations removed from the last application of DDD—had built up 5 parts per million DDD; plant-eating fish contained 40 to 300 parts per million. At the top of the food chain were the meat eaters such as grebes and California gulls, which contained concentrations of 2,000 ppm; Brown bullhead fish carried 2,500 ppm, an amount 85,000 times greater than the seemingly innocuous levels applied to the lake itself.

Given the persistence of organochlorines in the environment and their concentration in higher organisms, some of the researchers in Madison questioned whether any level of organochlorine pesticides was safe, whether any use could be considered discriminate. As Senator Abraham Ribicoff noted in the wake of *Silent Spring,* the basic premise of pesticide regulation—that pesticides stay where they are first applied—was false. Once Paul Hermann Müuller's genie was released into a food chain, it seemed impossible to put it back into its 55-gallon drum.

Tom Cade, a Syracuse and Cornell ornithologist who later spearheaded efforts to reintroduce peregrine falcons in the East, was among those in Madison calling for an experimental ban on pesticide use along the Atlantic coast. The data, he believed, were persuasive enough to at least warrant exploratory action. Never before had the ornithological world seen anything like this. Peregrine falcons were disappearing across two continents. Around the Baltic Sea, the white-tailed sea eagle, the bald eagle's closest relative, was as troubled as the American bald eagle. Even though pesticides were a prime suspect, the agri-chemical interests scoffed at Cade's suggestion. Most ornithologists conceded there wasn't enough known, in terms of either field studies or laboratory research, to definitively indict DDT.

Back in Britain, though, Derek Ratcliffe soon tightened the evidence noose. In a manuscript he sent Hickey the following year, Ratcliffe speculated the egg breakage could be the result of thinner shells. Hickey suggested testing the hypothesis by measuring the eggshell thicknesses of a handful of pre- and post-1950 eggs. A friend of Ratcliffe, Desmond Nethersole-Thompson, had an even better idea: weigh a large number of old and recent eggshells. Thinner shells would weigh less. Prowling through the British Museum and private collections that included their share of modern illegally gotten eggs, Ratcliffe put together a series of peregrine falcon eggshells dating from the mid-nineteenth century. Starting with the year 1947, the year DDT first was widely used in Britain, Ratcliffe detected a pronounced drop of nearly 20 percent in the shell weights. The results were similar for the eggs of sparrow hawks and golden eagles from western Scotland. These birds had also been breaking their eggs and suffering serious population declines. The shells of eight unaffected species showed no change in weight.

Again attempting to duplicate Ratcliffe's results here, Hickey dispatched Daniel Anderson, one of his graduate students, to scour U.S. egg collections. Visiting more than a hundred U.S. and Canadian museums and collectors, Anderson measured or gathered data on 35,000 eggshells from twenty-five different species. A consummate schmoozer, Anderson befriended enough collectors to weigh seventy-three eagle eggs taken illegally after the 1940 enactment of the Bald Eagle Protection Act, including forty-five eggs oologists had gathered after the advent of DDT. Most of those eggs had been pilfered illegally in Florida. Hickey and Anderson concluded that Charles Broley had been prescient. From the late 1800s to the introduction of DDT, hundreds of Florida eggs showed no significant change. But the shells of six eggs from 1947–1948 were 15 percent thinner, and that average rose to 22 percent in 1958–1959, the last breeding season that Charles Broley banded a bald eagle.

Besides bald eagles, North American birds that had experienced major eggshell thinning included peregrine falcons and ospreys. On Gardiners Island off Long Island, the number of osprey fledglings dropped from about six hundred in 1948 to just four in both 1965 and 1966. The eggshells of prairie falcons, red-tailed hawks, merlins, white pelicans, brown pelicans, double-crested cormorants, common egrets, great blue herons, murres, herring gulls, and ashy petrels—all generally fish eaters, bird eaters, or other flesh-eating birds that tended to be at the top of the food chain—had all suffered thinning. Populations of several were waning.

The decrease in eggshell thickness invariably first occurred between 1946 and 1952, particularly in 1947. The close time correlation to the first widespread use of DDT and the lack of any other pervasive environmental change proved to be compelling evidence against the pesticide.

California brown pelicans sustained the greatest eggshell thinning: 34 percent to 53 percent. Many of their eggs were so thin they were crushed by the weight of their parents almost immediately after they were laid. Sprayed by crop dusters, spread by trade winds and ocean currents, the DDT fog America's children wrapped themselves in had enshrouded the living world. DDT had embedded itself in bacteria and in plankton in both the Gulf of Mexico and the cold waters north of Scotland. It didn't matter whether phytoplankton cells were alive or dead; both absorbed DDT at the same tremendous rate. British and Australian bats carried it. It had infiltrated birds, impalas, and elephants in Rhodesia, penguins on the Ross Ice Shelf in Antarctica, and auks in the Arctic.

Researchers at the U.S. Fish and Wildlife Service's Patuxent Wildlife Research Center in Laurel, Maryland, meanwhile, attempted to replicate the thin-shelled eggs found in the wild. Mallard ducks that had been fed DDE produced fewer than half as many ducklings as the untainted ducks, and nearly a quarter of their eggs cracked.

Captive bald eagles and peregrine falcons, however, were considered too rare, too valuable, and too difficult to breed to serve as the subjects of a study on the effect of organochlorines on raptors. Instead, Patuxent researchers chose to study American kestrels, or sparrow hawks, a relatively abundant falcon about the size of a jay that had successfully been bred in captivity. They divided thirty-six pairs of kestrels captured in the Northeast and Florida into a control group and several other groups; they would feed the latter food that contained either low or high doses of DDT and dieldrin, another commonly used organochlorine pesticide. The low dose mirrored residues often found in the prey taken by raptors in the wild; the high dose, just below lethal amounts, equaled prey levels found in some areas.

The toxicologists studied the kestrels' reproduction in 1967 and again in 1968, when an additional twenty-four pairs of first-year kestrels—the offspring of the original specimens—were fed organochlorines and allowed to breed. The results: in 1968 the eggshells produced by the adults fed organochlorines were 8 to 10 percent thinner than those of the untainted control group; even more significantly, the eggshells produced by the first-year birds were 15 to 17 percent thinner—approaching the eggshell reductions Ratcliffe and Anderson had found after 1947 in peregrine falcons and bald eagles.

The birds exposed to the DDT and dieldrin, particularly the first-year birds, also produced fewer young. Once laid, eggs would disappear. The Patuxent researchers, Richard Porter and Stan Wiemeyer, assumed the thin-shelled eggs were breaking and then the eggs or newly hatched birds were being eaten by the parents—the same phenomena Ratcliffe had observed among wild peregrine falcons in Britain. Ratcliffe believed the adults' exposure to organochlorines was affecting their ability to parent. He observed peregrine pairs prematurely halt nest construction, be inattentive incubators once the eggs were laid, destroy eggs, eat their young, and on at least one occasion evict sparrow hawks from their nest and raise the sparrow hawk chicks. In Canada, affected merlins defended their nests less often and less aggressively, and other ornithologists observed apparently abnormal courtship behavior.

Organochlorines, it is now known, might have caused such conduct by triggering enzymes that alter hormone levels. But this aberrant behavior is difficult to sort out from a natural parental reaction to eggs breaking. Wiemeyer, now a U.S. Fish and Wildlife Service contaminant specialist in Nevada, believes that "More likely the eggs started to crack and leak and the birds, seeing that, probably threw them out or ate the contents."

In conjunction with their DDT-dieldrin experiments, Porter and Wiemeyer also fed food laced with just DDE to another group of kestrels. Again the birds laid thin-shelled eggs. Another researcher, Jeffrey Lincer (subsequently the consultant in New Jersey's defeated sand barge plan), later found that the greater the levels of DDE fed to kestrels, the thinner their eggshells—mimicking correlations found in the wild between DDE levels in kestrel and peregrine falcon eggs and the thickness of their shells.

Wiemeyer's later analysis of contaminants in bald eagle eggs concluded that reproductive failure occurred when levels of DDE in eggs were as low as 3.6 to 6.3 parts per million. With bald eagles in particular, that failure to produce off-spring involved more than producing thin-shelled eggs. The actual structure and strength of the shell, more so than mere thinning, may have been dramatically altered. Embryonic death also probably took place, as did failure to thrive by chicks that somehow managed to hatch in a highly contaminated area. It is not diffi-cult to imagine an adult eagle devouring such an ill-fated eaglet. Wiemeyer recalls that several still-viable eggs taken from the wild for artificial incubation at Patux-ent resulted in eaglets that were in poor condition. "We had real problems keep-ing them going," he says. "In some cases we lost them."

So much of one or more organochlorines could have been stored in the yolk sacs that when the embryo rapidly absorbed it, the pesticide was either lethal or, if it did hatch, so toxic that the bird couldn't adequately compete or survive. When stressed, a bird will call upon its stores of fat, where the DDT-DDE is stored. Once mobilized, it travels through the bloodstream to the brain and central nervous system, where even a fraction of the organochlorine benignly stored in the fat tissues can prove fatal, often as a result of dehydration.

Any sort of stress—hunger, cold, injury, disease, migration, egg laying, or, in the case of an eagle embryo, the extraordinary act of developing and hatching—could activate this pesticide cocktail.

By the late 1960s the link between DDE and reproductive failure in bald eagles and other birds was firmly established. Just how DDE was thinning eggshells was unclear, however. Researchers considered several mechanisms that could have disrupted calcium metabolism. The theory most readily accepted up to the present: DDE inhibits calcium ATPase, the enzyme that acts as a calcium pump, transporting calcite ions from the bloodstream through the muscular walls of the uterus or shell gland. Once inside the gland, the calcite binds with carbon to form a shell around the shell membranes encasing the fertilized yolk and albumen, or egg white. In 1975 three researchers in Maine, David Miller, William Kinker, and David Peakall, determined that in the shell gland of Pekin ducks, a species susceptible to shell thinning, as little as .2 ppm of DDE depressed calcium ATPase enzyme levels. In other words, DDE wasn't reducing calcium levels in the eagles' and falcons' blood; it was preventing the calcium that was in the female's bloodstream from penetrating the shell gland to make thick, strong eggshells. To buttress this theory, the trio repeated the same experiment with chickens, which, like other so-called gallinaceous birds, never underwent eggshell thinning. As suspected, the DDE did not lower the chickens' calcium ATPase enzyme levels. No one yet knows why chickens, but not bald eagles or peregrine falcons, were immune to DDT.

By the early 1970s the tide had irrevocably turned against DDT. In 1969 the nation's growing environmental consciousness resulted in the passage of the National Environmental Policy Act, which required environmental impact statements for all major federal projects. A year later we celebrated the first Earth Day. Between 1967 and 1970 the U.S. Department of Agriculture had banned the use of DDT for a myriad of purposes: for flies and roaches; on cabbage, lettuce, and more than sixty-seven other crops, including tobacco; on elm and other shade trees; on beef cattle, goats, sheep, and pigs; on seasoned lumber, finished wood products, and buildings; around commercial, industrial, and institutional establishments; in aquatic areas; and around the home and garden on flowers and lawns. And it had ordered a review of remaining uses.

After grabbing national headlines by laying out its case against DDT during a lengthy series of administrative hearings in Wisconsin, in October of 1969 the emboldened Environmental Defense Fund led a coalition of environmental groups in petitioning the USDA to halt the use of "economic poisons containing DDT." Little more than a year later, major responsibility for federal regulation of pesticides was transferred from the lax Department of Agriculture to the new Environmental Protection Agency. Under a court order resulting from the EDF suit, early in 1971 the EPA initiated a formal administrative review of DDT by officially canceling its approval of all the remaining DDT products and uses. The resulting hearings pitted the old DDT guard—the U.S. Department of Agriculture, growers, and chemical manufacturers—against the new wave EPA and Environmental Defense Fund, which had been founded in 1967 for the express purpose of eliminating DDT. After seven months of hearings, 125 witnesses, and 8,900 pages of testimony, the hearing examiner, a former Penn Central attorney and Bureau of Mines examiner named Edmund M. Sweeney, recommended that all essential uses of DDT be retained. DDT, Sweeney asserted, represented no health risk for man. Demonstrating the obvious bias he had exhibited against many of the EDF witnesses, Sweeney also concluded that DDT did not "have a deleterious effect on freshwater fish, estuarine organisms, wild birds, or other wildlife."

The decision now rested with EPA administrator William D. Ruckelshaus. The question had stirred such animosity that, during a briefing, Ruckelshaus feared it was difficult for the opposing attorneys to constrain themselves from physically assaulting each other. From New Jersey to California, a few entomologists so believed in the worth of DDT and its human safety that they were claiming they ate it daily. For years after his decision Ruckelshaus monthly received a photograph of a healthy-looking man, sans shirt, who contended that DDT was so harmless he was sprinkling it on his cereal. More than two decades later, letters to the editor occasionally still vilified him for his "political" decision.

Yet at the time, the usefulness of DDT as a public health weapon in the United States was a moot point: it hadn't been used in that manner for at least twenty years. Domestic use had declined to just 12 to 14 million pounds a year. About 86 percent of that DDT was being applied to cotton, with soybean and peanut applications accounting for most of the rest. But the four largest cotton-growing states had already either banned or discouraged the use of the pesticide. Ruckelshaus concluded that DDT's risks to society, at least by then in the United States, far outweighed its benefits.

In a decision that was more responsible for the bald eagle's recovery than passage of the Endangered Species Act, Ruckelshaus, on June 14, 1972, overruled Sweeney and canceled virtually all domestic use of DDT by the end of the year. He cited the pesticides' impact on lower organisms, including raptors. But the possible long-term implications for man, who, like the bald eagle, fed at the top of the food chain, was the crucial factor. "Even though we couldn't describe the risk to man in terms of any demonstrable impact, including cancer, the risk was nevertheless quite broad," Ruckelshaus, the current chairman and chief executive officer of Browning-Ferris Industries, Inc., said recently. "Not only was it showing up, but it was also increasing in the fatty tissues of man."

That situation, Ruckelshaus believed, could only be exacerbated by continued use. Those persons still applying DDT were doing so in increasing amounts in order to achieve the same effect. "If we guessed wrong," he said, "or, on the basis of knowledge at the time, decided there was no risk to man, the risk if we were wrong was quite high."

Ruckelshaus concluded that no label instructions or directions for the proper use of DDT, even if followed, could eliminate the risk to man and the environment, but he stopped short of banning the compound's manufacture and export. In Third World countries, where mosquito-borne diseases still persisted, he reasoned, the compound's benefits in suppressing malaria might outweigh its other risks. In the factual findings of his opinion and order, he concluded:

II. CHEMICAL PROPERTIES OF DDT
A. *Basic findings:*
1. DDT can persist in soils for years and even decades.
2. DDT can persist in aquatic ecosystems.
3. Because of persistence, DDT is subject to transport from sites of application.
    a. DDT can be transported by drift during aerial application.
    b. DDT can vaporize from crops and soils.
    c. DDT can be attached to eroding soil particles.
4. DDT is a contaminant of fresh waters, estuaries, and the open ocean; and it is difficult or impossible to prevent DDT from reaching aquatic areas and topography nonadjacent and remote from the site of application.

B. *Ultimate finding:*
The above factors constitute a risk to the environment.

III. ACTIVITY IN FOOD CHAIN AND IMPACT ON ORGANISMS
A. *Basic findings:*
1. DDT is concentrated in organisms and transferred through food webs.
    a. DDT can be concentrated in and transferred through terrestrial invertebrates, mammals, amphibians, reptiles, and birds.

   b. DDT can be concentrated and transferred in freshwater and marine plankton, insects, mollusks, other invertebrates, and fish.

2. The accumulation in the food chain and crop residues results in human exposure.
3. Human beings store DDT.

B. *Ultimate finding:*

The above factors constitute an unknown, unquantifiable risk to man and lower organisms.

IV. Toxicological Effects

A. *Basic findings:*

1. DDT affects phytoplankton species' composition and the natural balance in aquatic ecosystems.
2. DDT is lethal to many beneficial agricultural insects.
3. DDT can have lethal and sublethal effects on useful aquatic freshwater invertebrates, arthopods, and mollusks.
4. DDT is toxic to fish.
5. DDT can affect the reproductive success of fish.
6. DDT can have a variety of sublethal physiological and behavioral effects on fish.
7. Birds can mobilize lethal amounts of DDT residues.
8. DDT can cause thinning of bird eggshells and thus impair reproductive success.
9. DDT is a potential human carcinogen.
      a. Experiments demonstrate that DDT causes tumors in laboratory animals.
      b. There is some indication of metastasis of tumors attributed to exposure of animals to DDT in the laboratory.
      c. Responsible scientists believe tumor induction in mice is a valid warning of possible carcinogenic properties.
      d. There are no adequate negative experimental studies in other mammalian species.
      e. There is no adequate human epidemiological data on the carcinogenicity of DDT, nor is it likely that it can be obtained.
      f. Not all chemicals show the same tumorigenic properties in laboratory tests on animals.

B. *Ultimate finding:*

DDT presents a carcinogenic risk.

Myrtle Broley, Charles's wife, died suddenly of a heart attack in March 1958 in Florida. The following bald eagle breeding season, Charles Broley returned to Florida by himself. Checking about sixty nests, the man who had banded far more bald eagles than anyone in the world found just two young.

That April he left Florida for his family's longtime summer retreat, a lovely white cottage with a veranda overlooking a lake in Delta, Ontario. After burning some leaves there the following month, he was rowing across the lake toward town when he noticed the leaf fire had reignited. Racing back, he began to haul water from the lake to put out the spreading blaze, to no avail. Broley collapsed, apparently of a heart attack, and was overtaken by the flames, which also consumed his cottage.

Seventy-nine years old, he died never knowing he had correctly identified DDT as the culprit that had decimated his bald eagles.

Six years ago, in the largest chemical dumping lawsuit in U.S. history, the Department of Justice sued Montrose Chemical Corporation of California and its six successor companies for dumping millions of pounds of DDT into the Pacific Ocean. Between 1947 and 1982, the Montrose plant in Torrance, Los Angeles County, was the nation's largest producer of DDT. For a decade after the pesticide's use was banned in this country, Montrose continued to produce DDT for export. The billion-dollar federal suit alleges that between 1947 and 1971, Montrose dumped DDT-contaminated wastewater into public sewage lines, which ultimately discharged the DDT through an offshore subsurface pipe into the Pacific Ocean off the Palos Verdes Peninsula just north of Los Angeles Harbor. It's thought that between 1953 and 1970 Montrose pumped about 1,800 metric tons of DDT into the Pacific.

Between 1947 and 1961 Montrose allegedly also dumped another 700 metric tons of DDT into the San Pedro Channel between the coast and Santa Catalina Island and the other Channel Islands. Records indicate that in 1957 and 1958, for example, between 2,000 and 3,000 barrels of DDT-contaminated wastes were dumped at sea. According to the Justice Department, the barrels were punctured before they were heaved overboard.

DDT was also blown from the site and from landfills where Montrose waste was taken, and DDT-contaminated runoff and groundwater apparently found its way from the plant site to the sediment underneath Los Angeles Harbor. Since the late 1960s and early 1970s, the coastal environment of southern California has had the world's highest levels of DDT contamination. Since then, concentrations of DDT in fish caught in the affected areas have exceeded the safe "action levels" established by the Food and Drug Administration. Due to the high DDT and PCB levels in the fish, for the past ten years California has issued a fish consumption health advisory for the area and banned commercial fishing of white croaker.

The Justice Department lawsuit, which was filed on behalf of the National Oceanic and Atmospheric Administration and the Interior Department, sought damages from Montrose to fund both a cleanup of seventeen square kilometers of tainted ocean sediment and the restoration of the area's natural resources, including its bald eagle population. Historically, twenty-four to forty bald eagle pairs nested in the short oaks and on the cliffs of the eight Channel Islands that lie off the southern California coast. After brown pelicans quickly rebounded in the wake of the ban on DDT, one of the islands, Santa Catalina, was chosen as the major release site in southern California for transplanted bald eagles. Between 1980 and 1986, thirty-three young eagles obtained as nestlings from British Columbia, Washington State, and northern California were hacked—raised—and released on Santa Catalina. Three years ago construction workers found a completely emaciated eagle on the island. A resident there since her release twelve years earlier, her feathers were erect, her body was trembling, her eyes were twitching, and her coordination was so poor she was using her wings to try to stand upright—all symptoms of severe DDE poisoning. After the bird's death the next day, a necropsy detected DDE brain levels that were higher than those found in all but one of the more than seven hundred bald eagles the U.S. Fish and Wildlife Service had analyzed between 1964 and 1981.

The first pair of hacked eagles to attempt nest-building on Santa Catalina did so in 1984. Apparently not until 1987 were any eggs laid, and those eggs were broken during incubation, as were the eggs laid by another pair the following year. Since 1989 all eggs laid by the two to three surviving active pairs of adult bald eagles have been replaced by fake eggs and artificially incubated. Of those eggs, only two of the embryos have actually hatched and survived long enough to be placed back in their nests. The yolk lipids of the eggs that have failed have contained some of the highest concentrations of DDE ever found in bald eagle eggs.

As a bird develops within an egg, water vapor naturally escapes through pores in the shell. Two decades ago, thin-shelled eggs of several species appeared to be losing water at a reduced rate, apparently because organochlorines had significantly reduced the number of shell pores. So reduced were the number of pores in the shells laid by contaminated common terns that the embryos suffocated. In yet another organochlorine anomaly, the structure of the bald eagle eggs now being laid on Santa Catalina Island appears to be altered in a significantly different way. The shells are so thin in places that the embryos are losing water at a rate so rapid that there is not enough volume to support the shell. Inevitably, incubating parents would crush them. Even after the Santa Catalina eggs were rescued, the embryos would die during artificial incubation if humidity wasn't enhanced to counter the dehydration.

Robert Risebrough, a molecular biologist in Berkeley who has studied DDT since the 1960s, and David Garcelon, the ornithologist responsible for the Santa Catalina eagle hackings, now believe that in bald eagles, this deleterious effect is produced even before the DDE-thinned shell is formed. Above the shell gland, or uterus, in the isthmus of the oviduct tube, the developing egg is encased in keratin shell membranes. Risebrough and Garcelon theorize that DDE causes this membrane to have fewer sites upon which the calcium can later crystallize.

The result: like a bald eagle egg recovered along the shores of Lake Superior more than a quarter century ago, sections of the Santa Catalina eggs are so bereft of calcium you can practically see through the shell.

In March of 1995, after the federal government spent nearly $24 million in scientific research to make its case against Montrose and the other defendants, the federal judge who had presided over the case since it was filed in 1990 dismissed the lawsuit on the grounds that the federal government had waited too long to file it. During his ruling, U.S. District Judge A. Andrew Hauk dismissed environmentalists as "do-gooders and pointy-heads running around snooping." The Justice Department is appealing.

CHAPTER 7

TAKING CARE
OF AN EAGLE'S NEST

First of all, we read about eagles who are renewed.
—PETER MARTYR D'ANGHIERA, 1457–1526, "DE ORBE NOVA DECADES,"
1516, CONCERNING REPORTS OF PONCE DE LEON'S SEARCH FOR THE
MYTHICAL FOUNTAIN OF YOUTH

*There are just too many people moving into Florida—the [Gulf] coast is soon going to
be one long village.*
—CHARLES BROLEY, JANUARY 22, 1951

 Late in the afternoon of December 28, 1987, Sergeant Grady Caffin, a Florida wildlife law enforcement officer, received an anonymous tip: a bald eagle nest at a new housing development had been disturbed. With an annual population growth rate in Florida during the 1980s that exceeded that of many Third World countries—even today more than five hundred new people move daily to the Sunshine State—the only real news for Caffin was that someone actually had reported it. Like its human population, Florida's eagle population, which has rebounded to approximately two-thirds of its pre–World War II numbers, is booming. Last year more than eight hundred active nests—more than could be found in any state other than Alaska—produced nearly a thousand young eagles.

Conflict between these two burgeoning populations, human and eagle, is inevitable. More Florida residents (in excess of 13.6 million at the latest estimate) and 40 million tourists a year mean more road-killed animals. More Florida eagles feeding on this carrion has resulted in more *eagle* road-kills than anywhere else in the country. Several years ago one central Florida cattle rancher picked up seven dead bald eagles in just three months along a fourteen-mile stretch of highway near Lake Kissimmee. At the National Wildlife Health Research Center in Madison, Wisconsin, about 20 percent of the dead bald eagles examined died as a result of collisions with vehicles and stationary objects such as wires and towers. Of the birds submitted from Florida, nearly half have been struck by cars and trucks.

As development impinges on suitable nesting territories, raptor rehabilitators also have noticed a marked increase in the number of birds they treat for talon puncture wounds, the apparent losers in eagle-eagle territorial battles. One adult female killed by other eagles at a state park north of Palm Beach had her skull fractured. Multiple talon thrusts had pierced her breast, neck, head, and left eye, and her breast, abdomen, and part of her head were stripped of feathers.

Yet for all its pave-Paradise, put-up-a-parking-lot mentality, a shrinking but still sizable chunk of Florida is still timberland, cattle ranches, and wild swamp—prime habitat for generally reclusive eagles. If a nest tree falls in the forest and nobody hears it, or doesn't want to hear it because his construction job depends on the nest vanishing, well . . . In his eight years with the Florida Game and Fresh Water Fish Commission, Sergeant Caffin had learned that nest disturbances were harder to prove than arson. Within the next six months he would also investigate a nest tree pushed over on a developer's own ten-acre waterfront homesite and a nest tree killed by an herbicide in another area earmarked for development. Those investigations led nowhere. But that was not the case with this complaint.

Caffin, who was in his early thirties, had been named for his uncle, a federal judge who helped oversee the eminent domain condemnation that created the Big Cypress National Preserve in south Florida. Caffin himself had spent much of his youth camping, fishing for bass, and hunting ducks in a large uninhabited stretch of pine flatwoods, ponds, and lakes. Now called Deltona, this area can be found on any state map: houses, condominiums, shopping centers, and golf courses. In Florida, population growth and development are unstoppable. His job, Caffin felt, was somehow to help manage that growth in order to preserve some of the real Florida he had known as a boy, and to ensure that humans and wildlife could coexist.

Working hard on a chaw of tobacco, he pointed his state-issue Dodge Ram utility truck down Interstate 75 toward the far eastern edge of Bradenton, on the Gulf Coast south of Tampa Bay. Caffin arrived at the new development along the east bank of the Braden River shortly before dusk.

Today, off to one side of the obligatory shopping center fronting the main highway, an American flag and red-white-and-blue pennants touting "MODELS" flap at the entrance to the housing development called Braden

River Lakes. Popular starter homes, the $80,000 to $115,000 stucco ranch houses have comfortable interiors. Yet, like many of the new homes constructed in Florida, they sit on ground intentionally poisoned as a five-year guarantee against termites. As for the idyllic-sounding Braden River "Lakes," they are nothing more than backyard holes, herbicide-laced storm water retention basins guarded by "No Swimming or Fishing" signs.

None of this, however, existed when Caffin arrived nine years ago. No houses had yet been built, and the main road that cut through a former cattle pasture to the river was not completely paved. Following it, Caffin met another state wildlife officer, Adolphe Rogers. East of the road, in an open field not far from the river, they discovered the remains of a large nest at the base of a solitary pine tree. Amid the stick and grass debris, they noticed eagle feathers and down. A slash had been cut across the trunk of the tree, pine resin oozed from even fresher spike marks marching up the trunk—and two white-headed eagles were flying into the tree with more sticks to rebuild.

As it grew dark, two surveyors, the only workmen still present, told the officers they had no idea how the nest had been toppled. The following morning Caffin and Rogers continued their investigation with Brian Millsap, a state nongame wildlife biologist who previously had handled the National Wildlife Federation's nationwide midwinter bald eagle survey. Based on the large volume of sticks and Spanish moss (usually the nest cup's finishing touch), Millsap concluded the eagles had just completed building. Finding no eggs or eggshell fragments, he turned his attention to the oozing sap marks that climbed up the tree to the nest crotch. One of his own climbing spikes fit well into the holes.

When a bald eagle approached with a long stick to arrange it in the tree crotch, the trio retreated. Over the next hour the two adults made several trips to the tree with sticks and grass. Millsap noticed that the birds appeared to be disturbed by human activity along the main road about 300 feet from the nest. Accordingly, he and Caffin recommended to the handful of surveyors and construction workers completing the road that they discontinue activities within 750 feet of the nest—the minimum buffer zone generally recommended by the U.S. Fish and Wildlife Service's bald eagle habitat management guidelines for the southeastern United States.

This 750-foot primary buffer zone—about 40 acres—provided what one state biologist would later call a "comfort zone" for developers. Outside the zone, they generally could continue their activities without being concerned if eagles abandoned their nest. But if the developer entered the buffer zone and the birds left, they risked criminal prosecution.

In this case, however, state and federal law, including the federal Bald and Golden Eagle Protection Act and the Endangered Species Act, already had been violated. Later that day Millsap and Caffin outraged the developer of the $9 million development by wrapping both the tree and a radius of 50 feet around it in yellow crime-scene tape. The construction project itself soon ground to a halt. While denying responsibility for the nest itself, a little more than a year later the St. Petersburg developer of the project, Flotilla, Inc., and its president pleaded guilty in federal court to violating the Bald and Golden Eagle Protection Act.

Despite that plea, however, in 1990 Flotilla sued the state and the city of Bradenton in an inverse condemnation action that underscored the high stakes involved when eagles and man covet the same land. Flotilla's multi-million-dollar suit claimed that the city, the state, and the state Game and Fresh Water Fish Commission had unlawfully seized its land by insisting upon preservation zones around the nest and another partially built, unoccupied nest found a week later.

The case went to the heart of almost every endangered species conflict in this country. If society says buildings should be accessible to disabled persons, who should pay for the cost of a wheelchair ramp—society or the building owner? If society dictates improved pollution controls, should private businesses and individuals be forced to spend additional funds in order to comply? Should individuals bear the cost of setting aside land for open space or storm runoff? If it is determined that houses should not be built on a flood plain, should we as a society pay someone whose investment in land is rendered useless as a result of that zoning?

Some of these questions are easy. Some are not, particularly given what Supreme Court Justice John Paul Stevens calls the "increasingly complex problems in land-use and environmental regulation." Government laws and regulations follow Newton's third principle: to every action, there is an equal and opposite reaction. Nearly every government action—the supposed collective will of society—costs certain individuals money or enhances or devalues their property and investments. If a pair of eagles builds a nest on a property earmarked for development, who should bear the cost of protecting them—the property owner or you and I?

When Flotilla vice president Joe Lettelleir first saw the cattle pasture adjacent to the Braden River in 1984, it was one of the most perfect development sites he had ever seen. The land was dry, with high banks along the river. With no flooding problems, fill dirt, an expensive item in Florida, would be unnecessary. Except for a drainage system of interlocking ponds, little clearing or excavation was necessary, since the pastureland had been mowed down like a lawn by the cattle. It was so clean, Lettelleir often said, that on all of the 176 acres, there were less than thirty trees.

Five years earlier the area had been rural and remote. But by 1984 a 1,000-unit apartment complex sat just across State Road 64, and Interstate 75, west Florida's main north-south artery, had opened just two miles to the east. For Lettelleir and his partner, Stephen Fetters, it seemed ideal. As associates at the Florida Federal Savings and Loan Association in St. Petersburg, the two had talked for years about, in Lettelleir's words, "wanting to get out and do our own thing."

In terms of personality, Lettelleir and Fetters presented a striking contrast. Tanned and well dressed, with a sonorous voice, black-tasseled loafers and a gold chain bracelet, Lettelleir had been an executive vice president at the S&L. Of medium height, when challenged he could turn into an opinionated, flippant, confrontational pit bull with the righteousness of a man who believed he'd been wronged. As he neared forty, he had long been a fixture in St. Petersburg, the town where he was raised. A past president of the St. Petersburg Chamber of Commerce, he served as chairman of the board of the Pinellas Marine Institute, a rehabilitation program for youthful offenders. He was also a member of the Kiwanis Club and a number of other civic organizations and committees. News of his appearance at social events, of his daughter's debut and selection to the Sun Goddess Court and of his son's college graduation, was reported in the *St. Petersburg Times,* the liberal paper he despised.

Lettelleir had been a strong proponent of individual property rights long before eagles began nesting on his property. In the early 1970s he resigned as chairman of the St. Petersburg Planning Commission in protest over an environmental movement that preserved open space and achieved zoning changes that reduced the city's permitted construction and dwelling-unit densities.

Lettelleir had first met his partner after the Jacksonville savings and loan association for which Fetters worked merged with Lettelleir's S&L in 1975. Fetters, a high-ranking lending officer, moved to St. Petersburg and ran one of Florida Federal's subsidiaries under Lettelleir. Tall, lanky, and graying, Fetters was much more reserved and low-profile. An avid camper, he and his wife contributed to a considerable number of environmental organizations, including the Wilderness Society, the Sierra Club, the National and Florida wildlife federations and the World Wildlife Fund.

In 1983, at the height of the deregulated, go-go 1980s in Florida, the two left the savings and loan to establish a number of so-called shelf corporations with which they hoped to launch various development projects. One of these, with Fetters as president and Lettelleir as vice president, was Flotilla. With it, the following year they began what was to be their major project with the purchase of what they decided to call Braden River Lakes.

By the fall of 1987, a Flotilla appraiser was touting Manatee and Sarasota counties as one of the fastest-growing areas in Florida and in the country: "This constant immigration fuels the housing and construction industries . . . [and] brings with it the demand for services, and the increase of professional and retailing populations dictates a need for office and commercial spaces." The future growth of the county, the appraiser concluded, would be in the area near I-75, which was becoming "a more desirous area providing a need for continued development of land zoned for multifamily, single-family, and commercial use."

That's Florida. That's Braden River Lakes. Under Bradenton's zoning regulations, all three such uses, if the city approved, were allowed on the property, and Lettelleir and Fetters had plans envisioning all of it. In 1984, for $6 million, they and various corporations they owned purchased 60 acres fronting the highway for commercial development and 176 acres behind it for 793 single-family homes and multifamily villas.

To finance the purchase, the interest payments, and the cost of developing and marketing the tract, they obtained mortgages from Park Bank and Edwards that totaled more than $7 million. Lettelleir already owned, by his estimate, $25,000 to $30,000 worth of shares in the St. Petersburg bank. Two months later their Bay Development Group, Inc., purchased additional bank shares worth $150,000. Lettelleir insists there was no quid pro quo. Less than two years later the Federal Deposit Insurance Corporation took over Park Bank in what, at the time, was the largest bank failure in Florida. (Subsequently a number of mid-level bank executives were convicted of fraud, and a shareholders' suit alleged that bank officials had broken the law by lending money in return for the purchase of bank shares.)

After the FDIC assumed control of Park Bank, Flotilla was forced to find another lender. Though the partners had already sold $3.4 million worth of the commercial real estate along the road, they increased their new mortgage-development loan with Royal Palm Savings and Loan Association of West Palm Beach to $9 million in order to finance the property and construction costs. Flotilla projected a profit of nearly $1.7 million, while Royal Palm, which had taken a profit interest in the project, expected to earn $965,000 in addition to its interest earnings on the loan.

But in less than four years, Royal Palm would be closed by the Resolution Trust Corporation, at a cost to taxpayers of $470 million, and Lettelleir and Fetters, who had another development project in Fort Myers that foreclosed in 1989, would be liable for millions of dollars for just this project. They blamed their ill fortune on two bald eagles.

Eagles were no strangers to the shallow, oyster-reefed Braden River. When Raleigh Edwards purchased the Flotilla property near the end of World War II, a pair of eagles were nesting in a pine tree near the river. According to an affidavit he signed before his 1990 death, the nest tree died about 1970, but the eagles continued to nest in it for several more years. "I observed the eagles using my property as long as I owned it," wrote Edwards, who first grew tomatoes, then raised dairy cows and finally beef cattle before selling the property to Flotilla in 1984.

When the nest was torn down late in 1987, however, the Florida Game and Fresh Water Fish Commission had no record of an eagle nest in the area. Several golfers at River Isles, the adjacent retirement community that lies along the river to the northwest, had observed eagles in the vicinity long before that, however. Among them was retired teacher Wayne A. Hammond, a longtime bird-watcher from the Cleveland suburbs. He saw an eagle along River Isles' sixth hole, which abuts the Flotilla property, as early as 1985. During the next two years he saw two adults soaring and circling around each other in what he assumed was courtship flight. It must have been, for in April of 1987, with a spotting scope he observed two juveniles being fed by an adult in a nest on an island somewhat west of what is now the Braden River Lakes recreation center.

That summer and fall more golfers, including two members of the Bradenton Planning Commission, saw bald eagles carry grass from the golf course toward three pine trees on the Flotilla property near the river. (One of the golfers remembered seeing eagles flying to a nest in those same trees for several years after River Isles opened in 1973.) Those flights appeared to stop, according to planning commission member Guy Arthur, after a weed-clearing mower was parked underneath the trees sometime that fall.

Construction workers, though, continued to see the birds. From the day they purchased the property in 1984 until late 1987, however, both Lettelleir and Fetter say they never saw an eagle during their periodic visits. After someone noticed a large nest in a dead tree on an island in the river shortly after the 1984 purchase, Larson Engineering, the developers' engineering firm, had recommended that all the trees on the property be cut down to avoid potential eagle-nesting conflicts. They decided against leveling the trees, Lettelleir said, because the island nest turned out to be have been built by osprey.

By November of 1987 the bald eagles' presence could not be ignored: they were building a nest in the heart of the planned residential development, 300 feet from the main road then under construction. Incongruously, the eagles had situated their nest near two diesel generators that were running twenty-four hours a day to pump out a deep drainage excavation hole. Alerted by their engineers, Fetters and Lettelleir visited the site themselves. They knew immediately it meant trouble. Years earlier, when Lettelleir was working with Florida Federal Savings and Loan, he had handled the S&L's joint venture in the Landings, a residential development along the Gulf Coast in Sarasota. Confronted with an eagle's nest there, the developer dedicated the nest area (now abandoned) as a small sanctuary, and used the eagle nest as a marketing tool. Lettelleir learned then that an eagle's nest required a certain setback, within which no development could occur. He thought the radius was a couple hundred feet.

After viewing the eagles and their nest, Fetters and Lettelleir understood the implications, if not the legal chapter and verse. Their mind-set: you jump through all the regulatory hoops while the interest clock keeps ticking on a $9 million loan; you're under construction for seven months and $38,000 away from completing a $1.1 million road and drainage infrastructure when, of all the rotten luck, a pair of eagles starts erecting a nest in one of those few trees. Centex Homes, now the nation's largest home builder, already had bought one phase of the development and had an option to buy another, with the contractual understanding that Flotilla would complete the drainage system, the main road, and a small recreation center where the road terminated at the Braden River.

The eagles, Lettelleir and Fetters knew, would cost them money, so they made a conscious decision. Continue to work just as you have since May, they told their contractors and subcontractors. If you make noise day and night, that's fine. If in the normal course of work, you come by the tree, if you bump it, that's fine, too. They fervently hoped the birds would go elsewhere, especially after their engineers informed them the recommended setback is generally 750 feet, or approximately 40 acres.

"I had no idea," Lettelleir would later testify, "if the birds were to leave the area that that was a federal offense."

During a joint federal-state investigation spearheaded by the state, Sergeant Grady Caffin, Officer Adolphe Rogers, and Lieutenant David Stermen of the Florida Game and Fresh Water Fish Commission determined that a federal offense indeed had occurred. Interviews and sworn statements they collected disclosed the following:

Joe Vickers, a subcontractor hired to keep the tract clear of underbrush, was plowing near the nest some time in the fall of 1987 when he was approached by Fetters. Vickers recalled later that Fetters told him he had a problem with the eagles and wanted to know if Vickers could do anything about it. "He told me he'd give me a hundred dollars cash if I could just knock the tree down . . .

"Well, you know, I'm working there, that would be all right," Vickers said. He recalled that after Fetters left, "I went over and put the dozer against it. If I would've let the clutch up, the tree would've been down."

But with the blade of the bulldozer cutting into the tree, Vickers decided against it. "I just got more respect for them," he said. "I just couldn't do it. I got morals to me, I love the wildlife. I move out in it, I live in it, I don't kill it, I don't like nobody else messing with it."

The week before Christmas John Henslick, a consulting biologist who had seen an eagle fly over the property the previous September while he was mapping the wetlands on the site, visited the Bradenton offices of Larson Engineering. He was told by Jim Farr, the firm's land planner assigned to the development, and Bill Wilson, the firm's construction supervisor, that eagles were building a nest on the Flotilla property. The discussion, as Henslick remembered it, surged back and forth: Well, we can't take it down now. Too many people are aware of it. If we do take it down, how are we gonna do it? Sometimes the wind blows real hard out there and that could knock the nest out.

It seemed to Henslick the conversation focused more on why the nest could not be taken down than on destroying it. Asked about the situation, Henslick said a corridor would be required to protect the birds and the nest. "If the thing is cut down and it's reported, then you've got serious problems," he warned.

Two days before Christmas, Farr met Fetters at a Bradenton City Council meeting. According to Farr, Fetters was aware of the eagles' nest, grumbled about the birds, and said they "would be taken care of." Farr, who cautioned against disturbing the eagles, did not know specifically what Fetters had in mind. But he assumed it would be legal.

On Saturday morning, December 26, Henslick stopped by the site briefly and verified that eagles, not ospreys, were indeed constructing a very large nest. The following Monday morning, interested in obtaining additional consulting work regarding the eagles, Henslick called Farr at Larson Engineering. Farr told him what Fetters had said.

"What do you mean, 'taken care of'?" Henslick asked.

Farr told him it was going to be a "positive action."

"I assume that means we're going to follow the rules and everything?"

"Yeah, that's what we're going to do."

That was 8:00 A.M. At noon, eager to try out a camera his wife had given him for Christmas, and for her to see her first eagle nest, Henslick took his wife to the site. Once out there, though, he couldn't locate the nest. He began to think he was looking at the wrong tree—until he walked over to it. The nest was on the ground, along with some feathers and fish skeletons. The eagles were gone.

Henslick called Farr, who in turn phoned Fetters, the developer. Farr was incredulous at what he says was Fetters's response, which to him sounded like a thinly veiled admission: "The nest must have been blown out by the wind." Whatever knocked it down, Henslick and Farr knew it hadn't been the wind: that morning hardly a breeze was blowing, and over the weekend the maximum wind velocity recorded at the Sarasota-Bradenton Airport had been 12 knots, or 13.8 miles per hour.

In federal court Fetters's attorney later admitted his client had spoken with a workman about bumping the tree to see if the birds would move. Today, though, Fetters, now a district vice president of a Tampa mortgage corporation, is circumspect about the allegations tied directly to him: the $100 offer to Vickers and his supposed statement about the wind blowing the nest out of the tree. "Those are the allegations," he says, shaking his head dolefully. "I can't comment on hearsay."

Neither he nor Lettelleir, though, waffles about the destruction of the nest itself. Despite the obvious conclusion most people would draw, Lettelleir says, "I do not know to this day, and Steve Fetters to this day does not know who went up that tree. A lot of people don't believe us, but it's a true story."

⟨⟩ The following month, during a meeting in the Lakeland regional offices of the Florida Game and Fresh Water Fish Commission, and in a follow-up phone call and letter, state biologist Brian Millsap explained to Lettelleir that U.S. Fish and Wildlife Service guidelines for the southeastern U.S. recommend a primary buffer zone of 750 feet to 1,500 feet outward from the nest. Such activities as development, construction, logging, and the use of chemicals toxic to wildlife are banned within this zone year-round, and unauthorized human entry and low-level aerial flights are highly discouraged during the October 1 through May 15 nesting season. The guidelines also recommend a secondary zone extending another 750 feet to a mile, depending upon the feeding habits of the particular birds. While such low-impact activities as hiking, camping, and hunting are permitted within this area at any time, the guidelines for this secondary buffer zone frown heavily upon: commercial and industrial development; the construction of multistory buildings and high-density housing developments between the nest and feeding areas; and the construction of roads, trails, or canals that would make it easier for people to reach the nest.

Lettelleir wondered if the fact that the eagles had chosen the site with all the construction activity surrounding them was a factor in mitigating the size of the preservation zone. In his unorthodox view of eagle ecology, "The more construction you do, the more you bring up the little critters and the mice and so forth and make it a better feeding ground for the eagles to come in and land in the middle of your road. . . . For whatever reason, they like the activity."

The behavior of particular eagles *is* a factor in determining the ultimate buffer zone. In Florida, a small minority of so-called urban eagles are so tolerant they have built their nests in backyards. One pair still nesting on a lake northeast of Orlando keeps house in the middle of a condominium complex that was under construction when the eagles first arrived. Construction was halted, until after their first young fledged.

In the case of the Flotilla development, however, Millsap felt the birds were disturbed by the activity on the road 300 feet from the nest.

"That's because their nest was thrown out," Lettelleir retorted.

Because these eagles had shown some tolerance to human activity, Millsap determined only a 750-foot primary buffer zone would be needed. But he judged that cushion was necessary around the disturbed nest tree *and* around the tree with the partially completed nest, the one to which the River Isles golfers had first seen the birds flying. While Millsap was reluctant to endorse home construction within those zones, he said the state would consider a proposal to complete the road during the non-nesting season.

Portions of four of Braden River Lakes' six building phases fell within the primary zones. Development activity in the affected areas would be frozen as long as the eagles used the nest or nests and, if they were abandoned, up to five years afterward, in case the birds, which often use alternate nests, chose to return. Millsap told Lettelleir that if workers violated the buffer zone and the eagles did leave the nest they seemed to be rebuilding, they and Flotilla risked criminal prosecution.

That January the Bradenton City Council put on hold its prior approval of all plans within the buffer areas and shelved Flotilla's application for an unaffected section. Construction ceased and did not resume until after the nesting season, in August, after a Flotilla attorney had negotiated with the state to reduce the buffer zone around the active nest from 40 acres to 24.5 acres. That enabled the road and a scaled-back recreation area to be completed.

It is difficult not to wonder if the conflict would have been resolved more smoothly had Flotilla promptly reported the presence of the nest. Lettelleir thinks not. In his view, nothing illustrates the state's attitude better than the reaction to one of his early proposals.

Shortly after the destruction of the nest was reported, Lettelleir says he got a call from the late Margaret Busch, a good friend who was the wife of Gussie Busch, the late Anheuser-Busch beer baron. The St. Louis Cardinals, which Anheuser-Busch also owned, trained in St. Petersburg. Lettelleir says that Mrs. Busch had already arranged with wildlife biologists at Busch Gardens for the eagles to be transferred to the amusement park–animal safari attraction in Tampa.

Lettelleir excitedly called Millsap. "We're in luck," he recalls telling the state biologist. "You get to save the eagles and I get my land back." The response from Millsap, who routinely received requests from property owners wanting to move bald eagle nests, was unequivocal: you can't put eagles into captivity. The habitat guidelines, Millsap knew, were intended to preserve suitable eagle habitat as much as they were designed to preserve particular birds.

"It wouldn't be true captivity, high in a tree in Busch Gardens," Lettelleir's wife, Becky, protested during a break in the subsequent civil trial. "Although they could certainly fly off, they'd be fed."

"I can't imagine," Lettelleir said, "better protection."

What, I asked later, was Busch Gardens going to take? The birds? The nest? The tree?

"I have no idea how you do it," Lettelleir said, "but I assumed they did know how because it's pretty important to their logo."

❧ Convinced that prosecutors were intent on making an example of them merely to placate environmentalists, Lettelleir wanted to fight the criminal case that was mounting against Flotilla. He and Fetters felt they hadn't done a thing to destroy the nest. But by the fall of 1988 Fetters, the president of Flotilla, was under so much stress as a result of the case that he agreed to a plea-bargain with federal prosecutors.

Two months later, on behalf of himself and Flotilla, in federal court in Tampa, Fetters admitted encouraging workers to disturb the nesting bald eagles. For violating the Bald and Golden Eagle Protection Act, the corporation was fined $20,000. Fetters's sentence included a $4,000 fine, a year's probation, and one hundred hours of community service, which he fulfilled by working with youthful offenders at the Pinellas Marine Institute.

❧ The last clause of the Fifth Amendment to the Constitution states: "nor shall private property be taken for public use, without just compensation." The government occasionally moves people off land to flood it for a hydroelectric or flood-control dam project, runs an interstate highway through someone's backyard, or invokes eminent domain on farmland in order to erect a new high school. Clearly these are physical takings for which the government must compensate property owners.

But what if legitimate environmental concerns merely affect the allowable uses of a landowner's property? Several years ago, the U.S. Supreme Court considered the case of South Carolina developer David Lucas, who in 1986 bought two oceanfront lots on the Isle of Palms for $975,000. Homes worth hundreds of thousands of dollars grace that beach, and Lucas intended to erect two more—until South Carolina in 1988 enacted the Beachfront Management Act. Declaring that houses built too close to the shoreline posed a threat to life, property, and the environment, the act banned home construction on Lucas's lots. Unfair, or were such plans folly to begin with? In an area of constantly shifting shorelines, Lucas's lots had been completely underwater as recently as 1969.

Supreme Court Justice Antonin Scalia, writing for the 6–3 majority, wrote that "when the owner of real property has been called upon to sacrifice *all* economically beneficial uses in the name of the common good, that is, to leave his property economically idle, he has suffered a taking"—

whether or not the regulation serves a valid governmental purpose. (Stopping short of declaring a taking in Lucas's case, the court returned the case to state court for further review. To settle, South Carolina paid Lucas $1.575 million and, ironically, sold the property for building lots.)

After pleading guilty in federal court, Flotilla sued the state and city of Bradenton for illegally taking the preservation zones around both the nest and the partial nest. "Our constitutional mandate is to protect the wildlife of Florida," responded Steve Nesbitt, Florida's chief eagle biologist. "It's not our job to ensure somebody makes a profit on their investment."

During the course of a three-day civil trial in Bradenton in January of 1993, attorneys for the Florida Game and Fresh Water Fish Commission argued that the federal habitat guidelines the state had recommended were simply that: *guidelines,* which Flotilla was free to follow or ignore, although the firm would ignore them at its peril should the eagles abandon the nest. The state also contended that a taking had not occurred—in part because Flotilla's entire property had not been rendered useless.

In fact, two years earlier the state had dissolved the preservation zone around the partially completed nest, and Flotilla had sold that land to Centex for single-family homes. Just prior to the trial, the state had informed Flotilla it was dissolving the main nest preservation zone because the eagles had abandoned the area and the nest had fallen apart. "I'm not challenging whether the state of Florida is right or wrong giving the birds forty acres," Lettelleir, who by now had gotten out of the development business, testified. "I think I'm saying that you took my forty acres, here's what it costs. We had no societal cross to carry."

Flotilla's attorneys contended that state and federal laws, including the Bald and Golden Eagle Protection Act and the Endangered Species Act, made the U.S. Fish and Wildlife Service's guidelines anything but voluntary: if you engage in activity within the ultimately agreed upon preservation zone and the eagles leave, you will be prosecuted.

Circuit Court Judge Scott M. Brownell agreed, ruling that the state must pay Flotilla full compensation—$4 million, Flotilla's attorneys estimated, plus interest and attorneys' fees, which Lettelleir said would double that figure. The city of Bradenton, which Flotilla had also sued, was cleared.

The judge declared the state responsible for what he called an "environmental taking." The state's criminal penalties and the U.S. Fish and Wildlife Service's guidelines were two parts of the recipe. "The last prong," he wrote, "the element that is usually supplied by a governmental body in a regulatory taking, namely the passage of some legislative action which destroys the owners' use of the property, was, in this instance, supplied by the birds, not the legislature. That was the selection of the land on which to nest. By Administrative Regulation and Criminal Statute, together with the Guidelines, the State effectively created a habitat for the eagles, and empowered the eagles to decide which land would be taken."

The state immediately appealed.

Lettelleir, who now runs Environmental Review Incorporated, a St. Petersburg consulting firm that advises prospective real estate buyers regarding the presence of pollutants, views himself as a foot soldier in the wise use movement. But during the appeal he rejected the assistance of wise use advocates, who claim that environmental regulations have deprived private property owners of the lawful use of their own land. "We're taking the posture that this is a condemnation suit, not an environmental suit," he said. "They took my land, pay me. I don't have anything against the birds. If the state declares they want to buy this land or, for the protection of whatever, or to set up a park, or build a road, they've gotta pay."

In the wake of Brownell's ruling, state biologists were told by their own lawyers to avoid advising developers regarding the federal nest disturbance guidelines. The message to any developers inquiring about what they could or could not do in the vicinity of an eagle's nest: You're on your own. If the eagles are disturbed, you'll be prosecuted. For further guidance, they referred the developers to the overworked and understaffed U.S. Fish and Wildlife Service.

James Antista, the Florida Game and Fresh Water Fish Commission's legal counsel, feared Florida had been victimized by its success in bringing back the bald eagle. He believed the birds, which were considered threatened by the state, had increased because of protective federal and state laws and the habitat guidelines. As the eagle population increased while its pristine habitat decreased, more eagles were being driven into areas inhabited by man. Antista wondered if eagles that enter a property after development has commenced should be any less protected than those living in undeveloped wilderness. Do we say eagles in developed areas are not entitled to protection, or are entitled to less protection? If so, they will be pushed back into shrinking wilderness areas.

If the national policy is to protect eagles so that they will reproduce, Antista concluded, we must protect them wherever they go. To him, the judge was saying: That might be a fine objective, but wherever the eagles land, if they cause some loss, delay, or inconvenience to property owners, the state must pay.

A year later, though, Florida's Second District Court of Appeal overturned Brownell's decision. Citing both state and federal legal precedents, the appeals court stated there is no constitutional right to exploit or to profit from anticipated development of your property. Although some of the Braden River Lakes sections were sold to contractors for less than what Flotilla had hoped, the court noted that Flotilla was able to sell almost all of its land—another key point in takings law (and to sell it for more than it had paid for it).

The appeals court also cited a number of other wildlife cases, including one in which a Montana sheep rancher appealed his $3,000 fine for shooting a marauding grizzly bear to protect his sheep. In others, Wyoming ranchers had claimed the grazing of wild horses and burros devalued their private lands; a California landowner complained about not being allowed to disturb tule elk on his property; timber interests balked at a protective zone imposed on Maine woods to protect a deer herd; and a Louisiana farmer sought compensation after deer devoured his sweet potato crop. In all of these cases, which were denied, federal or state courts agreed that the government could protect animals whose unwanted occupation of private land had arguably diminished that land's market or production value.

In a decision subsequently upheld by the Florida Supreme Court, the Florida appeals court, ruling against Flotilla, concluded: "The government neither owns nor controls the migration of the wildlife species it protects. Rather, the government merely employs its police power 'to protect these [endangered and threatened species] as a natural resource.'"

⌒ Two years after they rebuilt their destroyed nest and attempted to raise young (it's uncertain whether any young fledged), the bald eagles fled the Flotilla property for a large timbered island thick with rattlesnakes in the middle of the river. Following the civil trial in January of 1993, Lieutenant David Stermen, Sergeant Grady Caffin and I searched for them one morning in a game commission airboat. The Braden River is so shallow that the dorsal fins of mullet cut V-shaped wakes through the surface—easy pickings for bald eagles. Winding through braided channels, we circled a large remote island studded with cabbage palms and dead lighter knot pine, the source of a handsome wood that Floridians over the years have harvested for use in paneling their homes.

After spotting the nest several hundred yards inland, high in the crotch of a magnificent longleaf pine, Sterman edged us toward a shore bristling with oyster beds and red mangrove, then cut his raucous engine. With her back to a southern breeze, the female was in her brooding posture: head erect, but hunched over slightly to shelter her young out-of-view offspring. In profile, she turned her head to the left to peer at us. Safely ensconced in her eyrie, she appeared calm, but for the quarter hour we watched, her eyes never left us.

To reduce the Resolution Trust Corporation's judgment against Flotilla, in late 1992 Lettelleir deeded the former nest preservation zone to the RTC. Three years ago Centex Homes, the principal builder in Braden River Lakes, bought the tract from the RTC for $472,000. Surveyors and grading equipment set to work. The cattle pasture that once surrounded the nest tree is now dotted with single-family homes. The tree itself was quickly cut down and replaced with a backyard storm water retention basin—one of the artificial Braden River Lakes.

SEMINOLE WIND

Ever since the days of old
Men would search for wealth untold
They dig for silver and for gold
And leave the empty holes.
And way down south in the Everglades,
Where the black water rolls and the sawgrass sways
The eagles fly and the otters play
In the land of the Seminoles.
—JOHN ANDERSON, "SEMINOLE WIND"

Like Faulkner's Dilsey, the eagles of Florida's Pinellas County endure. Surrounded by a burgeoning population of 850,000, they've abandoned the nests Charles Broley knew in the 1940s and 1950s. They're gone from a golf course, gone from the grounds of a veterans' hospital. Yet in one of Florida's most densely populated counties, more than a dozen bald eagle pairs have still managed to find their niche. None, though, have proved more enduring than the pair—and their offspring—that nest a few miles northwest of St. Petersburg, on Lake Seminole. During the 1992–1993 breeding season, theirs was the most-watched eagle eyrie in Florida. For at least fifteen years the birds had nested on the lake's eastern shore, a county park oasis of tall cattails and taller green pines.

When county officials, anxious to relieve east-west traffic congestion, proposed spanning the middle of the lake with a concrete bridge, environmentalists balked. Too near the bald eagle nest, they protested. State biologists disagreed. The nest was 1,500 feet south of the proposed bridge, they reasoned, protected by the county park. To ensure that the eagles weren't disturbed during the bridge construction, however, in 1992 the county hired a consulting firm, Biological Research Associates of Tampa, to monitor the nest.

The assignment fell to Tony Steffer, a burly forty-year-old ecologist from Red Bank, New Jersey, who had spent nine years with the National Wildlife Federation, banding eagles on the Chesapeake Bay, but was now a St. Petersburg resident. When engaged in eagle work he preferred a denim jacket and jeans, with a compass hung on his back and straps rigged to the back of his belt to keep the weight of his Leica binoculars off his neck. Having done consulting work on a number of nest sites, he knew the eagles of Pinellas County better than anyone. Few spent more time observing them.

Initially, the judgment of the state biologists appeared to be correct. In September—about the time adult bald eagles begin returning to their nesting territories—bridge construction workers first noticed the eagles fishing in the lake, particularly in the morning. The first time the workers saw them, the birds seemed quite curious, flying about thirty feet above their heads. Once, as the men drove pilings into a canal, one of the eagles swooped down nearby to pluck a fish from the water. Suddenly, though, they were gone from their old nest. Dave McDonald, a Pinellas County bridge inspector who knew little about eagles until the bridge project began, made the crucial observation. From a smaller bridge he noticed the birds carrying sticks to what he presumed was a new nest. Steffer located it, about three wing flaps and a glide from the old nest, a half mile to the east along a narrow canal that served as a flood-control outlet for the lake.

Bridge or no bridge, Steffer wasn't surprised the birds had moved. The previous year they had fledged two young from their old nest, but that tree had been dead and bereft of bark since the spring of 1985. Two years before that, their nest had blown out. Except for one year since then, the eagles had continued to suspend their nest there, literally out on a limb. Each year the nest would blow away, but the female continued to rebuild. Despite their persistence, most eagles—unlike ospreys—vastly prefer live trees for nesting. Years ago the tree and others around it had been tapped for turpentine. On their trunks, Steffer found chevron-shaped scars. He suspected that the topping had killed the nest tree. But it had also stunted the crown of the tree and made it ideal for an eagle nest.

To reach the new nest, which actually was an alternative they had used six years earlier, the pair had to fly over community baseball fields and the parking lot and football field of Osceola High School. "When they originally established the alternative nest, the high school wasn't here," Steffer explained, "but with the level of fragmentation that's occurred, they are willing to put up with it." The nest was about forty-five feet high in another slash pine. It wasn't very big, perhaps a couple feet deep, but the eyrie they had abandoned also had been rather insubstantial. The last time Steffer saw the female on the nest, she was crouched low over it, her tail sullied by constant contact with oxides in the decomposing nest material. As she had been for nearly a month, she was incubating eggs.

⁓ Wildlife biologists, whether they are government employees or private consultants, depend mightily on volunteers to make the daily observations that time or circumstance prevent them from making themselves. In this case, Tony Steffer was relying on Jay Jones, a crusty unemployed writer in her early fifties who for the past sixteen years had lived in a small cabin within the county park.

One late December afternoon, Jones approached the nest from across the flood-control canal, just past a house that was under construction. Despite the hammering, the male eagle was sitting calmly on the eggs. Shortly after Jones made the five-minute trip back to her cabin, the female alighted on a snag in front of her house. Before she disappeared, the eagle spent fifteen minutes there devouring a fish. "I was happy, and everything was right with the world," Jones recalled. "Except for one guy . . ."

The following morning, four days after Christmas, Jones and another eagle aficionado, Dr. Phillip LeRoyer, arrived on the bank of the canal at about ten-thirty.

"Oh, there's a bird flying!" said the doctor, spotting one of the adults overhead.

"Yeah, but there's no tree," Jones said sickly. It had vanished behind a fringe of Brazilian peppers along the canal. Airborne, both adults were at treetop level circling around and around their downed nest, mewing to each other in a very low monotone. Jones assumed they'd been doing that ever since the tree went down.

Rushing back to her cabin, she phoned Steffer in his Tampa office.

"Tony, the tree's gone."

"Are you joking?"

"There was no wind, no lighting bolts, no tornadoes. But the tree is gone."

That was the first day the eagle eggs could have hatched.

After notifying a state biologist, Steffer sped across Tampa Bay on Interstate 75, picked up Jones, and followed a dirt road back to an abandoned

In most regions, fish are the preferred food of bald eagles.
Copyright © Tom and Pat Leeson.

The evolution of the Great Seal of the United States: the original (*left*) 1782 Thomson-Barton eagle design approved by the Continental Congress in 1782; the illegal 1841 design (*center*); and an impression from the 1904 die based on James Horton Whitehouse's classic 1885 design that has been with us for more than a century. *Photographs from the National Archive.*

A still from an early Thomas Edison film featuring an obviously staged scene of an eagle carrying a baby high aloft above a lake. *Reproduced from the Collections of the Library of Congress.*

A World War I recruiting poster by Charles Livingston Bull. *Reproduced from the Collections of the Library of Congress.*

Charles Broley in a Florida nest with two of the 1,240 eaglets he banded. *Photograph courtesy of Jean Broley Patric.*

New Jersey zoologist Larry Niles prepares to capture one of three eaglets high in a sycamore at the Stow Creek nest. *Photograph by Clay Myers.*

Prairie, an injured captive eagle, feeding Seminole Wind, the foster chick she incubated after the egg survived a five-story fall. The egg's nest tree was illegally felled near St. Petersburg, Florida. *Photograph courtesy of Tom Scasia.*

At about four to five weeks of age, the sheaths of feathers begin to replace eaglet's gray down. *Photograph by John F. Turner.*

Four eagle chicks hatched at the U.S. Fish and Wildlife Service's Patuxent (Maryland) Wildlife Research Center awaiting transfer to nests in the wild. *Photograph by James Carpenter, U.S. Fish and Wildlife Service.*

Bald eagles reach adult size in twelve weeks or less, but do not attain an adult's white head and tail plumage until they are four to five years old. *Photograph by Craig Koppie, U.S. Fish and Wildlife Service.*

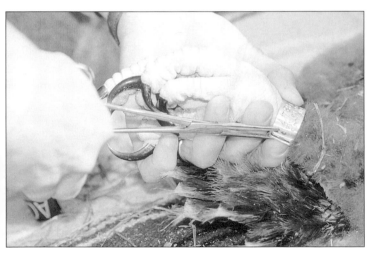

The foot and talons of a six- to seven-week-old bald eagle fill the hand of New Jersey zoologist Kathy Clark as she bands the bird. *Photograph by Clay Myers.*

Bald eagles normally hatch two eggs, and often only raise one eaglet, but New Jersey's Stow Creek nest fledged triplets four out of five years. *Photograph courtesy of Larry Niles.*

Bald and golden eagles poisoned with thallium along the Utah-Colorado border, spring 1990. *Photograph courtesy of the U.S. Fish and Wildlife Service.*

A bald eagle fatally poisoned after eating a nearby mule dear carcass laced with the pesticide aldicarb in East Canyon, Utah, spring 1992. *Photograph courtesy of the U.S. Fish and Wildlife Service.*

A cross-billed eaglet discovered in a nest on Michigan's Woodtick Peninsula in 1993. PCBs are suspected of causing such birth defects. *Photograph courtesy of James Sikarskie.*

One bald eagle displaces another on a salmon carcass at the Chilkat River's bald eagle council grounds. *Copyright © E. Woody Bausch.*

Bald eagles and gulls hover around a salmon spawning channel on the Chilkat, downstream from the ancient Tlingit village of Klukwan. *Copyright © E. Woody Bausch.*

Spread across the gravel bars and perched in the cottonwoods, as may as 3,500 bald eagles gather at one time for a late-season salmon run along the Chilkat River in southeast Alaska. *Copyright © E. Woody Bausch.*

A bald eagle descends. *Copyright © Tom and Pat Leeson.*

Mollie Beattie, director of the U.S. Fish and Wildlife Service, releases a rehabilitated bald eagle dubbed "Hope" on June 30, 1994, the day the service proposed upgrading the bald eagle's status to "threatened" throughout the contiguous United States. *Washington Post photograph by James Thresher.*

mobile home. About seventy feet beyond that they found the tree, its two-foot-thick trunk severed, from two sides, by a chain saw. Felled toward the canal, the tree was a jumbled mass of broken branches. Sap oozed out of every limb. Scrambling toward the top of the tree, they were surprised to find the bottom half of the nest still lodged in the crotch where it had been built. The nest lining, however, had been ejected two feet forward. Gingerly spreading out the limbs that covered it, Steffer found one bald eagle egg amid a cushion of Spanish moss, fine grasses, and eagle down. Uncracked, the egg had survived a five-story plunge.

He left it lying there until Eric Hansberry, a game commission law enforcement officer, arrived to secure what was apparently a crime scene. As soon as Hansberry viewed the egg, Steffer scooped it up and gave it to Jay Jones, who warmed it in her hands inside her down vest. The night before had been chilly, but the egg seemed to warm up rapidly. Steffer then wrapped it in a paper towel, placed it in a Styrofoam 7-Eleven coffee cup, and gave it to Hansberry. With an instant heat pack wrapped in a towel atop the egg to emulate normal incubation, Hansberry drove more than halfway across the state to the Florida Audubon Society's Madalyn Baldwin Center for Birds of Prey, the Southeast's largest raptor rehabilitation center.

Some wildlife biologists view wildlife rehabilitation as little more than a public relations sideshow, an often doomed attempt to save individual specimens that, due to illness, injury, or stupidity, were otherwise destined to die. Critics deem it a foolish intervention, a deus ex machina in the Darwinian scheme of life. And, they argue, even if rehabilitators do succeed, the impact of any released animal on a species' entire population is inconsequential.

Obviously the center's curator, Resee Collins—a woman, like so many in her nurturing field—disagrees. Because many of the raptors are injured as a result of human activity, she believes we have a moral obligation to rehabilitate them. There's also an educational value, she believes, in the public attention these birds attract. The number of birds released by Florida Audubon has assumed a certain weight as well. Since the center opened in Maitland, an Orlando suburb, in 1979, it has released about 150 bald eagles back into the wild. The year before Collins received the call about the recovered egg, sixteen of the thirty-seven eagles admitted to the center were ultimately liberated, one of them five months later, after veterinarians applied innovative corneal eye shields for damaged corneas. Had local veterinarians not volunteered much of their time and services, the medical rehabilitation costs for that bird alone would have exceeded $1,700.

In her mid-thirties, Collins had first worked at the raptor center as a volunteer shortly after it opened. A journalism and public relations student, she had been the director of the children's zoo at the nearby Central Florida Zoo when she volunteered to work with the zoo's birds of prey. A one-winged red-tailed hawk and two starving young ospreys propelled her into this seven-day-a-week life. Located on the edge of a small lake, the Florida Audubon center includes an old house that has been converted into a veterinary lab, offices, and a small gift shop; an enclosed flight shed; and a circular aviary with separate enclosures radiating from a central service access like spokes from a wheel to house hawks, owls, vultures, ospreys, and eagles. Unable to be released into the wild because they are permanently disabled physically or developmentally, the birds are kept for public exhibit and educational programs.

Once Hansberry delivered the egg, Dr. Leslie Powers, a Winter Park veterinarian, candled it—viewed it, backlit by a strong light, to determine if it was fertile. Had it been opaque, there would have been no developing embryo. But the silhouette Powers lit was dark, with a small air cell visible inside that indicated the embryo was far along in its thirty-three- to thirty-five-day development. Putting a stethoscope up against the egg, Powers detected a faint heartbeat and heard scratching noises. Although it had plunged more than forty feet, although it had been chilled for more than twelve hours, the embryo somehow was still alive.

After her staff had observed the egg for twenty-four hours in an incubator, Collins received state and federal clearance to have two of the eagles in the aviary attempt to incubate it. Residents of the center since shortly after they fledged in 1980, Prairie and T.J. had tried each of the past four years, unsuccessfully, to breed. All the eggs Prairie had laid were infertile. Missing his left wing ever since he flew into a power line northeast of Orlando, T.J. was incapable of fertilizing Prairie; he couldn't align himself properly during copulation. Prairie was also missing her right wing. She had been found with an arrow through it in Osceola County, south of Orlando. The wing had to be amputated.

Undeterred, Prairie had dutifully been sitting on one of her infertile eggs for several weeks when Collins slipped the new egg into the nest that she and her mate had built of sticks, grass, and pine needles supplied by the staff. One of Collins's assistants, Dianna Flynt, kept Prairie at bay with a net while Collins inserted the egg next to the infertile one.

"*Kleek kik ik ik ik . . . kleek kik ik ik ik,*" the female railed in a high-pitched territorial warning as Collins closed a plywood door. Then, waddling over to the nest, Prairie bent her head low to examine the new addition. Quickly accepting it, she tucked some pine needles around it, and settled over it. Plucking some feathers from her lower abdomen, she expanded her brood patch, the patch of bare skin both adults have to increase warmth to the egg through direct skin contact; the feathers also line the nest. Rocking down low over her eggs into the nest cup, Prairie pulled more nest material up around her and began to incubate both eggs. To provide consistent warmth, occasionally she turned the egg with her beak.

To reduce disturbance, Collins closed the aviary to visitors. Tom Scala, a center volunteer, connected the video camera trained on the nest to a closed-circuit television monitor in the center's gift shop. It permitted the staff to monitor the egg's progress and provided as many as fifty visitors a day with the unique opportunity to view an eagle in the making.

Three days later, faint peeps, like the trill of a muffled flute, could clearly be heard: pipping, the first sign of hatching, had commenced. The embryo was now breathing with its lungs. Rotating inside, the chick was beating on the shell with its egg tooth, the protuberance on the tip of its beak. The adults, confused by this unprecedented event, chattered a lot to each other and brought food to the pipping egg. By the following evening, the egg was completely cracked. About a quarter after seven the next morning, nearly a week after it had plummeted to the cold ground, the eagle chick from Pinellas County first appeared on the video monitor. A ball of gray and white down, with large dark eyes and a black, cheeping beak, it seemed unharmed by its ordeal. Again, the adults were bewildered. Initially they were more solicitous of the infertile egg, incubating it while ignoring the live chick. By midmorning, Prairie had eaten the eggshell, both for its calcium and, were she not in an enclosed aviary, to remove a potential lure for predators. The hatchling, with a bit of eggshell still stuck to its right wing, waddled unsupervised about the nest. T.J. nearly stepped on it while offering a large stick to his incubating mate.

Finally, though, shortly before four o'clock in the afternoon, Prairie dripped some nasal fluid onto a shred of fish and offered it to the open-mouthed eaglet. Soon the foster parents were taking turns brooding the eaglet to keep it warm. As it was fed bits of fish, quail, and rodents during the ensuing days, its crop, the pocket below its neck where food is stored, bulged constantly. No other bird in North America, as Collins points out, grows so rapidly, and this eaglet was gaining as much as a quarter pound a day. Its head, its eyes, and especially its large, ungainly talons, were all writ large. At two weeks of age the eaglet could thermoregulate its own temperature, so its foster parents no longer needed to brood it; they also lost interest in their other egg.

The public's fascination with the chick, however, escalated. The story of the miracle hatching had been broadcast on the CBS Evening News, CNN Headline News, and Paul Harvey's syndicated radio commentary. The Associated Press and United Press International transmitted the story nationwide to newspapers and radio stations. In a video on the eaglet later produced by the raptor center as a fund-raiser, Collins asked rhetorically, "Is one of anything significant?" For many Americans who heard of the little chick, the answer was a resounding yes. Each day about fifty people crowded into the center's gift shop to watch the live video of the eagle chick. In two weeks, more than thirteen hundred people from as far away as California, Connecticut, and Wisconsin also had called to suggest more than seven hundred names for the eaglet. "Miracle" was proposed in English, Spanish (Milagro) and Latin (Mirus), as well as Miracules and Miracle Aquila. Others suggested Hindonbird, Egg Flew Young, Eagle Knievel, Bungee, and Timberrrrr. HaChaTaLomeHaFaNome, which in Seminole means "Eagle Falling," was another suggestion.

While some zoos and wildlife biologists refrain from naming particular animals—they're not pet dogs or parakeets, they're wild animals—the rehabilitation center frequently assigns both an identifying number and a name to birds in its care. It helps the staff to identify individual birds, and in this case, the media and public were clamoring for a name. In mid-January the center's name selection committee chose Seminole Wind. The name was suggested by Barbara Tafelski of Clearwater, Florida, the town just north of the nest tree site. Seminole is the name of the lake and the town nearest to where the nest tree was felled. Seminoles, of course, are Florida's Native Americans, and Collins's staff hoped the eaglet would soon be flying in that wind. Tafelski was also a fan of John Anderson, the country musician from the central Florida town of Apopka whose recent "Seminole Wind" recording decried the rape of Florida's priceless, unique environment.

The bird, though, didn't think much of its celebrity. A day after its name was announced, the eaglet turned its punk-rock head and back toward the video camera, leaned forward, and aimed a jet stream of white splash at the lens. The white splash, in fact, became another measuring stick for the bird's growth. Higher and higher, as if Tom Sawyer's duped friends were growing taller by the day, the eaglet painted the aviary's gray plywood enclosure walls with vertical sprays of white.

By February 1, shafts of dark feathers had begun to supplant the bird's woolly gray down. Nine days later, these feathers were much more pronounced when Resee Collins removed Seminole Wind from the aviary. The bird, now nearly five weeks old, was definitely a female. Her wingspan was already 42 inches, and she weighed 6 pounds, more than T.J., her foster father. She was transported back to Pinellas County, more than 100 miles away, and hoisted 85 feet in a padded nylon duffel bag into an active nest that already contained two other eaglets. After the eaglet was released, all three young birds stared intently at Tony Steffer, the biologist who six weeks earlier had found Seminole Wind's egg. The three were as still as a Rodin sculpture. "She's right in between [the other two eaglets in size and age]," Steffer reported to Collins after he rappelled down out of the treetop. "They look just like a set of triplets."

The investigation of the nest destruction that began the day Steffer rescued the egg, however, had quickly grown cold. The nest tree had been about a hundred feet south of the mobile home of Don Deal, a masonry contractor in his late fifties originally from Indiana, and his wife, Pat. The couple had lived there, in a small rural pocket along the canal, for about fifteen years. During this time, eagles had roosted in a big pine in their backyard. The birds used to raid the food bowl of their Doberman pinscher. Occasionally, Pat would look up while swimming in her pool to see an eagle perched above her. The Deals also remembered when the pair had nested in the tree that had been cut down six years earlier. Like their constructions at the dead nest tree, that nest, too, had blown out.

The night the tree was felled, Pat was inside her home about nine o'clock when she heard a heavy thud.

"What was that?" she asked Don, who was just walking back from another mobile home on their property that they were renting to their daughter and son-in-law.

"I don't know, but I heard it too," her husband told her. Although he'd heard dead trees fall before, he went back out to investigate, flashlight in hand. Elongated taillights—a pickup truck, he assumed—were retreating from a mobile home just to the south that had been abandoned for three or four years.

Deal and his wife had no idea what had happened until the following morning, when their yard filled with Florida Game and Fresh Water Fish Commission vehicles. A V-shaped cut carved by a chain saw had dropped the tree toward the bank of the canal. On its way down, it had crashed into and sheared off the top of another large pine. The following day, using his chain saw to rip through the maze of broken limbs, Deal helped investigators locate bits of broken eggshell, the remnants of a second egg twenty feet away from where the still-viable egg was found.

The dirt road that led to the abandoned mobile home yielded no clues; there were too many indistinguishable tire tracks. Interviews with all the owners of property within 1,500 feet of the nest tree also proved fruitless. Deal bristled at unsupported implications that he somehow had been involved. He also doubted that the woman who owned the abandoned mobile home and the property where the tree had stood was aware that eagles were nesting there. South of her lived a physician. East of the Deals' property, a nursing home had been proposed for another five-acre tract, but construction there would not have disturbed the nest, particularly in the off-season.

Deal remains puzzled as to why he and his wife did not hear a chain saw. He speculates the tree could have been cut with an electric chain saw. Game commission investigators determined that an electrical outlet at the mobile home had been used recently.

Outraged environmentalists and Pinellas County soon pledged a reward that grew to $10,000 for information leading to the arrest and conviction of those responsible for felling the nest tree. "U.S.A. AMERICAN EAGLE," proclaimed a billboard erected near Lake Seminole to publicize the reward and a toll-free number. "HOME DESTROYED BY CHAIN SAW."

Two weeks after the tree was felled, Tony Steffer is still trying to discover where the pair is building its new nest. Time, he knows, is running out on them for this breeding season. From a construction pontoon boat captained by Dave McDonald, the bridge inspector, at midday Steffer and I spot the two adults perched in a snag near their old nest on the lake's east shore. From behind us, a cacophony of construction noise—gas generators, whining power saws, trucks beeping as they moved in reverse, men pounding together wooden forms for concrete—reverberates toward the eagles. They appear to be inured to the din. The eagles share the lake with several colonies of great blue herons, who roost like tufts of gray cotton candy in the crowns of pines. One heron alights on a lower snag, but quickly takes off again after spotting the eagles above it.

"In the morning they're most active fishing and with the nest stuff," says McDonald, a stout man who wears his short-trimmed hair underneath a hard hat. "And to me there's good fishing here: bass, speckled or Nile perch, and a lot of catfish—big ones."

But the eagles had already had their day's fill. "This is what it is in the afternoons," says Steffer, peering through his binoculars at the motionless birds. "In the evening they might do some territorial flights, but they don't have to work hard for their food. We're just happy they haven't abandoned their territory."

Afterward Steffer drives me to one possible location for the pair's new nest site, a pine on the edge of a baseball field not far from the pair's original nest. "I saw her putting sticks in that tree," he says. "If they nest there, we'll have a chain-link fence up and people here all the time; we'll have a stakeout.

"People are pissed off somebody chopped the tree down. If they ever catch 'em they're gonna throw the book at 'em."

A few minutes later we stop by to see Jay Jones, Steffer's volunteer observer. She's not home, but arrives a few minutes later on Rollerblades, lathered in sweat from a half-hour roll through the park. Once she has a cup of coffee and lights up a cigarillo, she's ready to talk as we sit underneath a paddle fan on her screened-in porch. As Tony discusses nests that might be good candidates for returning the chick to the wild, Jay pops up from her chair. At first she thinks she's spotted a great blue heron, but, "No," she says, "It's Big Bird," the dispossessed female eagle, reconnoitering as she flies along the lakeshore.

The day after the felled nest tree was discovered, Jay and Tony had seen the eagles copulating again on one of those snags near their old nest. Concerned as they were that the birds would abandon their territory, it was a reassuring sight. By the third day the birds seemed completely calm. "They took the whole thing better than we did," says Jones.

She admires the female's persistence, continuing to rebuild her blown-out nest year after year. And she marvels at the male's uncharacteristic unwillingness to help. "He sits there and watches her," reports Jay. "He can do nothing for longer than any creature I've ever seen."

But he can hunt. Jay once saw him pluck a gull out of the air. To avoid the eagle, the gull wheeled 180 degrees and veered down, but it was no match for the eagle, which reached down and snared it with a single talon. Both crashed into the reeds, but the eagle lifted up again with the gull still firmly in its grasp. "The gull still had the temerity to try to wriggle free," she recalls, "so the eagle reached down with the other talon and broke its neck."

~~ Training his spotting scope across an arm of Lake Tarpon, Pinellas County's largest lake, Tony Steffer peers at the nest in which, more than a month ago, he placed Seminole Wind. She is now ten and a half weeks old, nearly ready to fly. All brown with some gray-white mottling, all three eaglets have their backs to us, facing into a strong March wind. The one in the middle, possibly Seminole Wind, is beating its wings, levitating above the branch and nest. "They're branching out, doing all kinds of crazy things in this wind," Steffer says as the bird lifts up and levitates backward to the edge of the slightly swaying nest. "They're scaring the hell out of me." He had felt the same way this past week when he visited the nest after the so-called storm of the century blew through. The following morning, Steffer hadn't seen the adults, but one of the eaglets had been confidently holding on to a branch and, like one of the eaglets today, beating its wings in the high winds.

"See how sleek he is," Steffer says of the most active eaglet. "I wouldn't be surprised if he's been doing some flying." We're viewing the nest from an empty lot at the edge of Eagle Watch, a new private, gated housing development of $200,000 brick-and-stucco homes that sits across a narrow arm of the lake from the nest. Next door, landscapers are planting a palm tree. Inside the red tile–roofed house, a large industrial vacuum cleaner roars. A few doors away, men slap rolls of tar paper down onto another roof. Whether they like it or not, these Lake Tarpon birds rapidly are being transformed into urban eagles.

Searching for an appropriate nest in which to place the foster chick, Steffer checked Pinellas County's other dozen nests from the ground and by plane. He had several primary considerations: age compatibility with the other eaglets, a good prey base that could support an additional eaglet, a protected location, and easy access to observe the bird.

He quickly narrowed the possibilities down to two. At one site, he couldn't see clearly into the nest. But here our vantage point was only about 100 yards away. When Steffer peered through his 25-power spotting scope, he felt as if the birds were sitting next to him in his living room. And the nest was hung 85 feet high in a longleaf pine standing within another protected county park. He also knew that the other two eaglets had hatched about the same time as Seminole Wind. One was four or five days older than the other, and when he climbed the nest tree to verify their age, it had slapped him in his face with its wings. A week later, when he hoisted Seminole Wind up into the nest, the younger one—which, at approximately five and a half weeks, was about Seminole Wind's age—was just as feisty.

Though triplets are rare, after spending fifteen hours observing the nest, Steffer also had no doubt the parents could provide for an extra eaglet. The nest was as well provisioned as a New York deli. From Lake Tarpon the adults were hauling back every type of fish and waterfowl imaginable, including tilapia, bass, coot, and gallinule, and they were making deliveries not just in the morning but throughout the day. On one climb to the nest Steffer found the remains of a little blue heron. He spoke with Alfred D. Boyd, the former owner of the large Boot Ranch tract where the houses were being built. Boyd, who still lived near the base of the nest tree, told Steffer the eagles took occasional armadillo that he killed and left out for them. Boyd recalled having had to beat them off a newborn calf when they attempted to devour the afterbirth.

"When mom and pop came back to the nest with a huge bass and a duck at the same time, I knew they could feed an extra mouth," Steffer says.

A few minutes later, one of the adults soars across the face of the wind to perch several hundred yards to the west, in a cypress in which the pair had once nested. Back into the nest moments later, it lifts itself onto a branch just above the largest eaglet. After disappearing for a while, both adults fly over the cypress and out toward the lake. The eaglets are on their own. Though the wind blows harder, one of them persists in branching—riding the wind, its rapidly beating wings fully extended. As the wind strengthens, the bird inches closer to the nest, its only concession. For a moment, as it lifts up, I think it is flying. The other two, though, remain hunkered down.

As we are leaving, the wind calms, and so does the aerialist.

Soon, though, all three were airborne. On April 11, more than two months after she was placed in the nest, Tony Steffer saw Seminole Wind and her two siblings in the air, flying. By May they were gone from Lake Tarpon.

After he had placed Seminole Wind in the nest, Steffer thought he should have put the U.S. Fish and Wildlife Service bands on the left legs of her foster siblings. Since she was banded at the raptor center on her right leg, he could have differentiated her, with his spotting scope, from the other two eaglets. But he had banded their right legs as well. Which meant that, as soon as he placed her in the nest, she ceased being the celebrated Seminole Wind and became just another of Florida's bald eagles—something, he thought, that was altogether better and more appropriate.

~⁓ Though they failed to lay another set of eggs after their nest tree was toppled, the following year Seminole Wind's parents were successful. First they erected a nest in the county park, in one of the trees they were tending after their nest was felled. They were copulating and doing a lot of what Tony Steffer calls sky-dancing. But a great horned owl perching nearby dissuaded them from that site, and they hastily constructed another nest in a fine pine across the lake. There, rather uneventfully, they fledged two young eagles two years in a row.

The publicity and the $10,000 reward for information about the perpetrators who felled their nest tree generated just one call to the law enforcement division of the Florida Game and Fresh Water Fish Commission. It was a misguided tip from an inmate phoning from the Pinellas County jail. The case has never been solved.

Seminole Wind and her leg band—USFWS no. 62938954—so far have not been found. This coming winter or next, she will be ready to breed.

AS THICK AS FLIES

We had a great many complaints from farmers, especially in the tidewater sections of the state, that eagles were destroying their lambs and as we had an abundance of eagles in Virginia, especially along the large rivers entering into the Chesapeake Bay and in some of our mountainous sections, we acceded to the desires of the agricultural interests and lifted the protection. We believe if you were to come to Virginia and make an investigation, you would find that there is no scarcity of eagles down this way.
—M. D. HART, EXECUTIVE SECRETARY, VIRGINIA'S COMMISSION OF GAME AND INLAND FISHERIES, EXPLAINING IN 1932 WHY VIRGINIA WAS AMONG FOUR STATES, INCLUDING MARYLAND, WHICH HAD REMOVED BANS AGAINST KILLING EAGLES

In the stillness of a mid-July afternoon, they are gone. Their presence, though, is palpable: around the base of any of their great roost trees remain the unmistakable signs—enormous amounts of shit and feathers—of bald eagles. Scores of them come in off the hot, humid river in the late afternoon, winging a couple hundred yards inland to the tall pines and oaks thrusting above spindly upland hardwoods. Always they demand clear flight lines, an unimpeded view. Here they perch, preening away their molting feathers and spraying the forest below with white splash, till darkness and sleep envelop them.

Odorless, the liquid excrement splatters and dries on the fallen leaves and underbrush like ceiling paint spun off a roller. Lying atop dry leaves, propped upright and sheathed by cobwebs, the feathers are an endless palette of browns and whites. There are dark primary feathers—the eighteen-inch-long "fingers" at the edge of an outstretched wing—their shafts curved like airfoils, their worn leading edges radically tapered, their quills thicker than pencils. With one poised in your fingertips, it's easy to imagine an eagle quill being used nearly two centuries ago to record entries in the journals of Lewis and Clark. Extending your arm and slicing it forward through the air, you feel the lift that kept the feather and its eagle aloft, that carried them here, to the Virginia Tidewater, from Florida or Massachusetts or South Carolina.

Beneath the trees, the dark brown secondary flight feathers, with some of their bases trimmed in shimmering white plumes, are more symmetrical. There are also soiled off-white tail feathers; fourth-year tail feathers marbled brown and white, hinting at the promise of what will replace them, the pure white tail rudders of a bird ready to breed; small light brown chest feathers; short undertail coverts and underwing linings; and lighter-than-air dandelion puffs of dancing white eagle down. Arrested in their slow, pendulous descent by twigs and greenbrier thorns, the gossamer down and plumes drape the woods like Spanish moss.

Seven thousand one hundred eighty-two: that is the total number of contour feathers, excluding down, that a researcher once plucked from a dead year-old female. Of her nine pounds total weight, those feathers and the down weighed about one and a half pounds—two and a half times as much as the entire skeleton, and slightly more than the massive pectoral muscles that power the wings themselves.

At the faintest suggestion of light, an hour before the summer sunrise, the roost along the James River stirs. One bald eagle, then two, then three at a time, rarely more, call to each other in their high-pitched, rising voices: "*kik kik kik kik kik.*" Then, silent but for the muffled downbeat of their large wings, they move out, again two or three at a time, barely perceptible in the predawn darkness. Silence, more calls, then more large birds airborne toward the wide, languid river. By the time the sun lifts out of the Chesapeake Bay fifty miles to the east, a hundred bald eagles have poured out of their sanctuary within the James River National Wildlife Refuge to feed.

Upstream, Mitchell A. Byrd launches his College of William and Mary boat out onto the high tide to meet them. At the wheel of the flat-bottomed Boston Whaler, he barely stands five and a half feet tall. Part droll leprechaun, part cantankerous gadfly, for decades the recently retired biology professor has been the conscience of wildlife conservation in Virginia. He is dressed in a purple mesh shirt, putty-colored jeans, and worn sneakers, his pale face shaded by the brim of a canvas work cap. Draped around his neck is a pair of twenty-five-year-old Leitz binoculars, their rubber eye cushions eaten away by the sunblock he slathers on his pale face to ward off a fourth reoccurrence of skin cancer.

Stay out of the sun as much as possible, his doctors told him. But here, on the water, is where he belongs. By stressing the natural history and ecology of organisms, wildlife management, and conservation, he assiduously built the William and Mary biology department into the largest on campus. After his retirement several years ago, though, the department was hijacked by molecular and cell biologists. To him, the laboratory work they find glamorous was sheer drudgery. If his reputation wasn't as large as others felt it should be, it was because he had focused more on observing wildlife and lobbying for its preservation than on publishing statistic-laden academic papers about it.

He also never ceased to be amazed by how oblivious most human beings were to the natural world around them. In his view, few people noticed or even cared about bald eagles anymore. "The bald eagle is no longer an important species," the leader of the U.S. Fish and Wildlife Service's advisory Chesapeake Bay Bald Eagle Recovery Team will tell you in a soft Tidewater drawl. "It's doing well." Move on to the next basket case or, worse yet, simply move on.

In the boat with Byrd and me this morning are Scott King, an undergraduate armed with a clipboard and photocopies of a topographic map to record the location of each bird we find; and Larry Niles, the New Jersey eagle zoologist intrigued by the phenomenon of scores of eagles gathering together in the summertime. Leaving a small marina, Byrd turns his back on the pulp mill–chemical plant complex that dominates the Hopewell, Virginia, shoreline and points the boat downstream. Just risen, the sun bathes the river in soft light. Mist and croaking great blue herons rise along the water's wooded edge. Fish break the calm surface—a year earlier a menhaden vaulted the high gunwales into Byrd's boat—and terns plunge into the water after them.

Almost immediately bald eagles appear. An adult perches on a snag in the river. Three dark immatures hitch a ride on a floating log. Byrd ignores Tar Bay, off to his right, where new mansions dominate a bluff stripped naked of trees.

We spot several more adult eagles, but Byrd's survey does not commence until we reach Powell Creek, a freshwater stream that marks the western boundary of the wildlife refuge. Clad in lush green hardwoods—tulip poplars, oaks, maples, hickories, and gum trees—the bluff at Maycocks Point looms beyond the creek entrance. With the approach of Byrd's boat, two immature bald eagles, silhouetted against the morning sky, lift up from the point.

As we round it, another immature flashes out over the water before retreating back over the trees. Quickly two more young birds, like parachutists leaping from a plane, bail out of the trees along the river's edge. There are three in the air at one time, then two more, and another and another, then two adults. "Look at this," says Byrd, "they're like flies up there." Later in the day, when it is hotter and they've already fed, the eagles won't bolt as readily from their perches. But this early in the morning they are easily agitated, and most flush as the boat intrudes within a hundred yards of them. One adult, its proud head thrust forward in profile like the figurehead of a great sailing ship, ventures out across the broad river. The rest beat toward a slight cove ahead of us where even more birds, four adults and three immatures, are perched.

This is the greatest density of eagles we will encounter all morning. In little more than half a mile, seventeen bald eagles have revealed themselves. Mitchell Byrd, though, who has been surveying these eagles for more than a decade, quickly tempers his enthusiasm. "All of this," he says with evident disgust, sweeping his right hand along the cove's dense hardwoods toward a small downstream dock, "will be demolished for a half-billion dollar project by the Q Corporation."

He says "Q" as if it's a poison he's been trying, unsuccessfully, to spit out. Earlier in 1994, just three years after the refuge was established to protect the roosts and foraging areas of the East Coast's largest summer congregation of bald eagles, Byrd had learned that a new, extremely secretive high-tech security firm, the Q Corporation, was planning to develop two in-holdings, consisting of five privately owned tracts, within the refuge. Like wedges driven through the heart of the refuge, the two in-holdings all but cut off the prime shoreline of Maycocks Point from the rest of the preserve. One of the in-holdings was a former sand-and-gravel operation up Powell Creek. The other is the 130-acre Parker tract, the wall of green trees before us that is dripping with eagles. Just a quarter-mile away lies the roost from which a hundred eagles exited within the past hour.

If the sales to Q Corporation were consummated and its initial plans were approved, Byrd understood that a deep-water docking facility and boathouse—a "water vessel staging building," in company parlance—would extend into the water here. From the docks a road would cut through the tall hardwoods to two helicopter landing pads, satellite dishes, microwave towers, security fences, surveillance cameras, emergency floodlights, and eight buildings totaling 715,000 square feet, or nearly 15 football fields of floor space. These buildings would include a three- or four-story corporate headquarters of 135,000 square feet with no windows on the lower floors; a windowless one-story, 300,000-square-foot operations building; and a hotel and visitors center for clients, many of whom would arrive by helicopter to maximize security. Among these visitors, company officials suggested at one closed briefing, would be federal officials of the absolute highest rank, since the White House and national security agencies were supposedly among its clients. The sand-and-gravel tract would serve as a test site for crashing vehicles into security gates. Working in three or four shifts seven days a week, 1,200 employees would drive through the refuge on what now is a narrow gravel road.

Surveying the refuge area two weeks after the U.S. Fish and Wildlife Service had announced its proposal to upgrade the status of the bald eagle from endangered to threatened, Byrd believed the case represented a formidable test of the embattled habitat-protection provisions of the Endangered Species Act. The three nests on the refuge were protected by that act, the Migratory Bird Treaty Act, and the Bald and Golden Eagle Protection Act. But with as many as a thousand different eagles thought to be utilizing the area between May and September, their roosts and foraging areas, which traditionally have received far less attention, were far more important than a trio of nests.

The Q Corporation, or Q International Group ("Q" was the code name of the agent who equipped James Bond with his clever weaponry), claimed to have spent four years scouring the entire East Coast until it determined this was the only property that met all its requirements. Among them: a site with close proximity to Washington, D.C., navigable water access, total isolation from commercial and residential areas, and a wide buffer of property around the site that could not be developed.

The U.S. Congress had guaranteed that last prerequisite when it authorized the expenditure of nearly $7 million to establish the 4,100-acre James River National Wildlife Refuge. It did so with the understanding that the primary purpose of the refuge would be to protect the roosts and foraging perches of the largest known summer concentration of bald eagles in the East—not to protect the proprietary interests of a private corporation. From Q Corporation's perspective, though, the site was ideal. Its only neighbors would be non-talking bald eagles. But, Byrd wondered, once the company moved in, how many bald eagles would still be its neighbors?

"I think what they are doing is using a taxpayer-financed refuge to satisfy their mania for secrecy," said Byrd. "I think it's obscene. If they had any thoughtfulness at all they'd realize it was obscene, but that's the reason for their selection of the property."

⌁ Bald eagles have long been known to congregate during the winter. They gather on the upper Mississippi and Missouri rivers, on Washington State's Skagit River, in the Klamath Basin along the Oregon-California border, even in the sagebrush country of Utah and western Colorado, where they feed upon jackrabbits. These are primarily birds from Canada and the northern states, pushed south by ice in search of open water and available food. One startling measure of how much we have altered the landscape is that, along the Mississippi and Missouri, the eagles mainly gather just below locks and dams, where open water and stunned fish are most readily found. Bald eagles also roost together during the winter on the Chesapeake Bay. More than a hundred spend the harshest months on the Potomac; there are 150 each on the Rappahannock and James rivers.

But in 1977, when Mitchell Byrd was first asked to come to the Potomac River by a gentleman farmer named Jim Nash, summer gatherings of bald eagles were little known. Heading north that late spring morning from Williamsburg, Byrd expected to see a few bald eagles. After all, according to Nash, there had been two to four bald eagle nests on his family's antebellum plantation for as long as anyone could remember. Byrd saw thirty eagles that first day, and since then by boat he has counted more than fifty along the bluffs and in the tall hardwoods and marshes that rim the Potomac shoreline just forty miles downstream from Washington. In part due to the efforts of Byrd and Nash, an estate adjacent to Nash's farm that was once earmarked to become a full-blown recreational state park is now the Caledon State Natural Area, a limited-access preserve set aside for summering eagles.

Byrd later discovered that the Rappahannock, the next finger of water below the Potomac sluicing out of the Virginia Piedmont, harbors even more eagles each summer than the Potomac. A stretch of the James River midway between Richmond and Williamsburg, though, has turned out to be Byrd's mother lode. In 1970, while studying ospreys below Hopewell, he once saw forty bald eagles along the river. He wrote that off, however, as an anomaly; perhaps they were drawn by a freak fish kill. Several years after Jim Nash summoned him to the Potomac, however, Byrd got a call from Joe

Hamilton, a forester for Continental Forest Industries. The company owned a 3,500-acre loblolly pine plantation along the James River several miles downstream of its Hopewell paper mill. After harvesting 300 acres of pine some distance from the river, Hamilton's crew had herbicided and then torched the remaining hardwoods and brush prior to replanting. Among the casualties were some large oaks. That summer, Hamilton told Byrd, the large leafless trees filled with bald eagles—forty to sixty of them at a time.

"You mean turkey vultures, don't you?" Byrd asked. "What color are they—brown?"

"Most of them, but not all," Hamilton said. "Some of them have got white heads and tails. A mature bald eagle—it's hard not to recognize it."

Unconvinced, Byrd came out late one morning to investigate. "There's two now," the forester told him, gesturing toward a tall leafless oak. Hamilton, Byrd realized, had indeed spotted two immature bald eagles. Returning before dawn one morning, Byrd watched as seventy bald eagles poured out of fifteen to twenty trees. Gradually his sporadic trips onto the river to determine where the eagles were feeding evolved into nearly weekly summer surveys. Even on slow days, in a couple hours Mitchell Byrd likely sees more bald eagles than anyone outside of southeast Alaska. The sight of a dozen bald eagles in the air simultaneously is not uncommon. At low tide he once inched past an exposed sand spit in the middle of the river; the spit was cloaked with bald eagles. Thick as gulls, there were twenty-six of them.

"Why here?" Larry Niles wonders as the boat plows along the south shore of the James.

Mitchell Byrd shrugs. Even after more than a decade of studying and pondering these eagles, he cannot say with scientific certitude. It's an equation too complex to be reduced to a formula or replicated in a laboratory test tube. "I think it's the undisturbed nature of the place," he finally offers, "the shallow water, the good food supply, and lots of perching trees to forage from." Byrd and his colleagues at the Center for Conservation Biology on the William and Mary campus have developed sophisticated eagle habitat analysis maps for both the James River and the Rappahannock. Among the factors that appear to be critical in attracting bald eagles to roost or nest are close proximity to wide stretches of the rivers or their tributaries; mature forests; and distance from paved roads, piers, and areas of high housing or building density. Oddly enough, a lot of optimum or at least usable habitat—it's green and yellow on the center's computer-generated maps—is unoccupied. On both the James and the Rappahannock, that's true of both nesting bald eagles and those that congregate in roots along the rivers during the long, hot summer. "As the population has expanded, they've been clumping themselves together," he says.

Along the Rappahannock, for example, in three different places there are now two pairs of bald eagles nesting within two hundred yards of each other—far closer proximity than most other breeding eagles would tolerate. "In this area," Byrd says, passing his hand over a mapped area of the Rappahannock about eight miles long, "there are twenty nests. And then for ten miles of what looks like good habitat, there's nothing. I think they're packing themselves together for the best feeding opportunities."

The same is true along the James River. Including the three nests on the James River refuge, ten of the river's thirty nests are concentrated along Byrd's eight-mile-long survey route. Though under the influence of four-foot tides, the five-parts-per-thousand salinity of the water here is so low that the plantations pump water directly out of the river to irrigate their cornfields. Up Powell Creek this nearly fresh water nurtures Virginia's largest population of the globally rare prairie senna, a yellow-flowered marsh plant. Rare sensitive joint-vetch and Long's bittercress grow nearby. These slightly brackish waters are also productive nurseries for shad and herring, which spawn along the refuge up Powell and Flowerdew Hundred creeks, and for rockfish, or striped bass.

Ironically, at least on the James, the tremendous industrial development upstream of the refuge could also, perversely, be enhancing the number of easily available dead or dying fish. Several miles above the refuge, in the mid-1970s an Allied Chemical subsidiary in Hopewell, Virginia, spewed Kepone pesticide into a creek that feeds the river. Fish were killed and contaminated, and the river was closed to fishing. The effect on birds was never studied, but today Byrd believes it was not a coincidence that the James was the only one of Virginia's rivers from which nesting eagles and ospreys disappeared completely. In 1976, when there were only eighteen active eagle pairs in the entire state, none resided on the James River. Byrd spent four years flying the length of the James and its tributaries before he found his first nest, not far down river from where we are today.

In the twenty miles between Richmond and Hopewell, seven miles upstream from the refuge, there are, according to a U.S. Fish and Wildlife Service report, two large municipal sewage treatment plants and nearly ten major industrial wastewater discharge sites, including the plants of Du Pont, American Tobacco, and Philip Morris in Richmond and the Allied

Chemical (now Allied Signal) Corporation in Hopewell. These discharges, the FWS claims, have created extensive sludge deposits "which will degrade river water quality for many years to come and probably account for the numerous fish kills in the area." More dead fish, mostly gizzard shad and white catfish, are found floating in this section of the river than anywhere else along the James. The river here is plagued with high fecal coliform counts and low oxygen levels. That's particularly true in the summer when the James heats up to what feels like tepid bathwater and oxygen-starved fish literally suffocate.

"Most dead fish you see are gizzard shad," a fisherman told me as he sorted his day's catch at a marina above the refuge. "They're real sensitive to oxygen and temperature. They'll die in a heartbeat."

⌁ Downstream from the refuge, Mitchell Byrd patrols the edge of Flowerdew Hundred Plantation, whose nearly five-mile-long shoreline seems to span two time zones. When he reads, Byrd suffers from a slight astigmatism, but his practiced vision is twenty-twenty when it comes to picking camouflaged bald eagles out of the trees. Following the flight of two adults, he spots the dark form of an immature eagle obscured within the shade of a bald cypress. Nearby, the two adults and yet another immature perch atop cypress boughs, the adults' white heads set off like diamonds nestled atop soft green pillows. "We've counted the two adults," he says. "The immature's a new one. Look at them—a bunch of chickens."

Just then, above the clamor of Byrd's outboard engine a sweet song echoes sharply out of thin band of wooded marshland.

"Oh," he says, "a prothonotary warbler singing. It's pretty late [in the season] for that."

When Mitchell Byrd was thirteen, his father had a cypress boat built for twenty dollars, and Byrd began to haunt the cypress swamp bottomlands of the Blackwater River in Franklin, Virginia, near the North Carolina line, prime habitat for the prothonotary warbler. After wintering each year from Mexico to Colombia, the males would brighten the somber swamps each spring with their deep yellow, almost orange head and breast—they're not called *Protonotaria citrea* for nothing—and their sweet "zweet zweet zweet zweet zweet zweet" breeding calls. What gorgeous creatures they seemed to the Tidewater youth.

After completing his doctorate at Virginia Tech in 1954, Byrd spent two years, not by choice, "figuring out better ways to kill people in the army's biological warfare program." Discharged in 1956, he launched his long teaching career at the College of William and Mary in Williamsburg. The classroom Byrd most preferred was outdoors; the lecture he most frequently gave preached the need for conservation. Initially, he focused his studies on colonial nesting birds, particularly terns and herons. Byrd first worked with birds of prey in the early 1970s, surveying decimated osprey populations. Under contract with the state, he later added bald eagles, and then Virginia's flourishing peregrine falcon reintroduction program, to his purview. His creed was summed up by renowned ornithologist Frank Chapman, who once said, "Don't be an ornithologist if you can help it. But if you can't help it, go ahead."

Flowerdew Hundred Creek drains into the James near a sharp, narrow bend in the river. As we pass the creek's mouth, a white-headed adult eagle swoops low before us to pluck a small fish out of the golden water. These dead, dying, and slow-moving fish, however, are only a part of the eagle equation here. A few minutes later, an hour into the survey, we enter the cypress-fringed mouth of Wards Creek. Two immature bald eagles—the fifty-eighth and fifty-ninth eagles of the morning—perch in a snag to the east.

"That's Willow Hill Plantation over there," says Byrd, referring to one of many early English plantations. "Down below here is Upper Brandon and Brandon Plantations, and across the river are Weyanoke Plantation, Sherwood Forest, Westover, Berkeley, and Shirley Plantation. That's why I think this river is so attractive; it's just so undeveloped," even though it was first settled nearly four centuries ago.

It was along this river in the early 1600s that the struggling Virginia Company of London finally found the prosperity it craved, with the cultivation of tobacco in 1612. To tend to that labor-intensive plant, the New World's first African-American indentured servants arrived here on Dutch slave ships. Flowerdew Hundred Plantation, abutting the refuge to the east, was established in 1619. Upstream and across the river, Berkeley Plantation was the birthplace of both President William Henry Harrison and "taps," which was composed on a bugle there in 1862. That was when Lincoln steamed up the river to review McClellan's Union troops after the reluctant general had backed away from Richmond and Robert E. Lee. The Confederate general also was intimately familiar with the area. His mother was born and married at Shirley Plantation, where he was taught for a while in a converted laundry house.

Two years after McClellan's encampment, Union engineers in just eight hours built what is thought to have been the longest pontoon bridge in military history, a 2,100-foot span across the river to Flowerdew Hundred. It took four days for Ulysses S. Grant's entire Army of the Potomac to march across it, to the beat of drums and marching bands. Continuing on, they marched across what is now the wildlife refuge en route to the pivotal ten-month siege of Petersburg that ended the Civil War. After journeying up the river to inspect Petersburg mere hours after Lee's forces had fled, Lincoln told Admiral David D. Porter, "Thank God I have lived to see this." Eleven days later he was assassinated.

But long before the North and South clashed here, long before the native uprising of 1622 claimed the lives of a third of the English colonists, including Robert Maycock, the point on the wildlife refuge that bears his name was inhabited by Native Americans. Between A.D. 200 and A.D. 900, during the period that marked the transition between roaming hunter-gatherers and sedentary village agriculturalists, natives frequented Maycock's Point. If not year-round residents, they certainly lived here during the summer. Several hundred of them, perhaps, gathered to harvest freshwater mussels, discarding the shells in middens that now run as much as three feet deep for 2,000 feet along the point. They also came for the fish. Later nicknamed James River bacon, sturgeon as thick as logs migrated up the river to spawn. And archaeologist Tony Opperman suggests that the people also harvested the "tuckahoe," an Algonquin word for the bitter aquatic tubers, such as pickleweed, which still thrive today in the creeks and marshes.

Farther up Powell Creek on the refuge lie the buried remains of Weyanoke Old Town, the site of a short-lived colonial settlement that superseded what, for centuries, had been a native trading center. Here and at Maycocks Point, pieces of chert, jasper, and flint from as far away as Georgia, the Carolinas, the mountains of Virginia, and possibly Pennsylvania and Ohio indicate that humans were here as much as 8,000 to 9,000 years ago, during the late Paleolithic epoch. A Clovis spearpoint, stone flakes, and a scraper found next door at Flowerdew Hundred are approximately 11,000 years old.

Before the refuge was established, archaeologists excavating the site up Powell Creek also uncovered more than three hundred dog skeletons dating from between A.D. 1400 and 1600, the largest such find in the East. Among them were two dogs lying on their backs with their feet upright. Next to both skeletons lay the severed right arm and hand of a human body. Lefty Gregory, the archaeologist who unearthed them, suggests that perhaps the ritual was performed to prevent the spirit of the human victim from returning to haunt his killers, or to render him powerless in a fight if his killers met him in the afterlife.

Bald eagles witnessed all of this. Before the seventeenth and eighteenth centuries, before deforestation and maniacal persecution reduced the numbers of all predators, the density of nesting bald eagles on the Chesapeake Bay could have rivaled that of southeast Alaska today: about one pair for every 2.4 miles of shoreline. With 7,800 miles of coastline, there could have been more than three thousand pairs—two-thirds of the current total for the entire lower forty-eight states—nesting on the Chesapeake when the English first sailed up the James River.

⁓ In the spring of 1986, Kiewit Industries of Omaha, Nebraska, the parent company of Continental Forest Industries, decided to jettison its timber and paper business by liquidating more than a million acres of timberland, including Continental's 3,500-acre loblolly pine plantation along the James River. When Mitchell Byrd learned the property was for sale, he quickly changed from an intrigued ornithologist to a conservation activist. Among the organizations he alerted were the state Department of Game and Inland Fisheries and the Nature Conservancy.

Most environmental groups function primarily as advocates for nature, lobbying and litigating for government regulation and for the protection of finite natural resources—but not the Nature Conservancy. In 1992, when most environmental groups were struggling, it earned a profit of $59 million on $278 million of revenue. That year its $144 million worth of donations nearly equaled the combined total of the donations received by the other nine largest environmental groups. Its assets of $855 million, including nearly a quarter-billion dollars' worth of securities, were five times larger than the combined assets of the other nine groups. Backed by such financial muscle, the Nature Conservancy has made its reputation by taking a radically different environmental approach. To preserve habitats it considers biologically rich and rare, the organization that only half kiddingly refers to itself as "Mother Nature's real estate agent" simply purchases conservation easements, or buys the tracts outright.

As a result, the Conservancy's offices are inundated with calls from people demanding swift action. In Virginia, however, often it's a case of mistaken identity. Plants that concerned citizens believe are rare small whorled pogonias inevitably are just common Indian cucumber root. Homeowners also call, upset that a proposed development will mar their pastoral view. A shame, to be sure, but the Conservancy is not in business to protect hay-fields.

The response to such pleas by George Fenwick, then the Nature Conservancy's state director in Charlottesville, was the same as his initial response to the calls he got about the eagles congregating on the James River tract: not interested. He employed a Noah's ark approach: make sure you've protected at least two of everything before you go on to save fifty or a hundred. And by the late 1980s bald eagles were recovering so well on the Chesapeake Bay that even the U.S. Fish and Wildlife Service gave them a lower priority.

Fenwick hoped somebody would protect the area, but a loblolly pine tree farm didn't much interest him. The entreaties, however, kept coming: from the state's Natural Heritage Program, which the Conservancy had launched, and the Virginia Department of Game and Inland Fisheries; from the U.S. Fish & Wildlife Service; from the Lower James River Association; from garden clubs, local property owners, and antebellum plantations; and from Mitchell A. Byrd. Fenwick was vexed trying to explain to newspaper and radio reporters why the Nature Conservancy wasn't interested in protecting bald eagles. The drumbeat of support, the opportunity represented by Continental's desire to sell, and the U.S. Fish and Wildlife Service's interest in placing the tract on a refuge-acquisition priority list if the Conservancy would expedite the purchase, ultimately convinced Fenwick to open negotiations. There was another factor as well: Fenwick's interest in cultivating the influential support of Mitchell Byrd.

It took Fenwick about a year to cobble together enough loans, gifts, and funds from the Conservancy's revolving land-preservation fund to engineer the largest transaction its Virginia chapter had ever undertaken: the May 1988 purchase of the original 3,515-acre tract from Continental Land Sales for $1.85 million. But as congressional inaction delayed the hoped-for federal acquisition, the Nature Conservancy's interest costs soared so high that the Virginia chapter's ability to preserve other worthy parcels was compromised. However, support from individuals, corporations such as Newport News Shipyard–Tenneco and Mobil, and foundations such as North Shore, Best Products, the Bailey Wildlife Trust, and the Chesapeake Bay Foundation enabled the Conservancy to hold on to the property until Congress, two and a half years later, finally appropriated $2.4 million to cover the Conservancy's costs.

The establishment of the James River National Wildlife Refuge, however, did not completely eliminate the threat to bald eagles. The same year the Nature Conservancy bought the Continental tract, Michael J. Bogese Jr., a Hopewell developer, had spent $2.1 million to buy Maycocks Point, one of the birds' prime riverfront foraging areas. Until sewage disposal requirements apparently proved too costly, he planned to erect eighty-three large estate homes along the river.

Again the Nature Conservancy successfully intervened, obtaining an option on the 635-acre property until the federal government paid Bogese $4.5 million in January 1992 to purchase the tract, which was then added to the refuge. Although the Bogese Tract was only about one-fifth as large as the refuge's original acreage, it cost nearly twice as much because much more river frontage was involved and because it had already been approved for development.

Mitchell Byrd remembers a time when, flying along the Potomac River in search of eagles' nests, he could see that development ceased not far below Washington. But as the then-scant nests have multiplied—there are now five nests on or near the Mason Neck National Wildlife Refuge, approximately eighteen miles below Washington—so has the development pressure. Now the great engine of federal government has pushed housing, traffic, and an eight-lane interstate south of Mason Neck, with more development advancing toward Fredericksburg, just west of the Caledon State Natural Area. Two years ago advertisements first appeared for Eagle Bay, a sixty-eight-home development along the sandy beaches directly upstream from Caledon.

Throughout the Chesapeake Bay basin, only 10 to 15 percent of bald eagle nests are located on property controlled by government agencies or environmental groups. The rest are on private land, and each year more of these territories are affected by logging or new housing. But even good habitat apparently preserved for posterity on public land is not inviolate. Ecosystems rarely mirror artificial property lines. Even a preserve as large as Yellowstone National Park—with its controversies regarding bison roaming beyond park boundaries and the reintroduction of timber wolves, and proposals to tap geothermal springs and set up a gold-leaching operation just outside the park—illustrates the impact humans can exert from outside of these man-made islands.

In the spring of 1994, just three years after the James River National Wildlife Refuge was established, Mitchell Byrd first heard of the Q Corporation's plans to develop the two tracts sandwiched within the refuge. He learned of the proposal following a briefing in late April attended by local, state, and federal officials and representatives of private industry. Many of them had been asked to sign nondisclosure agreements in which they vowed not to divulge information they learned about Q Corporation for at least five years. Some federal officials refused to sign. Local government officials who had helped lure Q Corporation to the rural corner of Prince George County were not talking, however. "As far as comments from me about bald eagles and the Q Corporation," said Harold H. Owen, executive director of the county Industrial Development Authority, "our comment is absolutely nothing."

Shrouded in secrecy, the proposal, like the company itself, seemed to have materialized out of the ether. Interviewed by phone by Mark Di Vincenzo, the *Newport Daily Press* reporter who first broke the story, company president Robert T. Barbera said he was speaking from his Staten Island home, where he worked part of the time. Checking a computer database of business credit reports, DiVincenzo found a Staten Island address but no telephone listing for a Q Corporation. Although Barbera told government officials the company wanted to consolidate its operations in New York, New Jersey, and Connecticut, none of the three states had incorporation records for the Q Corporation or Q International Group.

In mid-May, the Q Corporation disseminated a press release claiming the Prince George facility would be the world's most advanced single-source facility dedicated to developing high-security equipment and services. Its customers would include the United States, foreign governments, multinational corporations, and wealthy individuals. Replete with high-tech security jargon—Communications security (COMSEC) and computer security (COMPUSEC) systems, "encryption algorithm," "TEMPEST engineering," "specialized information facilities," "classified and sensitive disintegrators," "specialized containers and vaults," "information security analysis," "assessment and audits"—the release promised an impressive variety of services and products ranging from intelligence and counterintelligence support services to head-of-state and diplomatic vehicles and aircraft, command and control systems, advanced armor, and specialized security equipment for military and intelligence facilities, embassies, and diplomats' residences.

Yet the release's Q International letterhead divulged no address or phone number for the company. Interested journalists were to contact Harold Owen, the executive director of the county industrial development authority—one of the officials who had been refusing to comment. Despite the apparently tenuous nature of the Q Corporation, Byrd was hardly surprised when the owners of the properties within the refuge failed to respond to a U.S. Fish and Wildlife Service overture indicating its willingness to discuss a possible purchase. Most outsiders—particularly conservationists, whether they were federal bureaucrats or meddling biology professors from Williamsburg, a scant twenty-five miles away—were viewed with distrust.

A few years earlier Byrd was using a radio receiver to try to locate a recently fledged eagle when he heard a pickup truck heading his way. When it stopped with its bumper just shy of the back of Byrd's legs, he suspected he was in for an interesting conversation. Two local men in their fifties— deer hunters scoping out the area, Byrd presumed—got out.

"You lose something around here, buddy?"

Byrd said he was looking for eagles.

"Ain't no eagles around here," came the reply. "The Nature Conservancy bought it and the eagles ate all the rabbits, ate all the foxes and the turkeys here so there was no food and they left."

"I saw eighty-five eagles from my boat on the river yesterday," Byrd informed them.

"You ain't seen no eighty-five eagles. We used to hear of an old fool from William and Mary come out, a Dr. Byrd, who always saw lots of eagles, but we never believed him. We hear he's too old to be in these parts anymore."

⌒ In particular, Byrd was not surprised that Henry D. Parker Jr., the owner of the waterfront tract Q Corporation coveted, wanted nothing to do with the federal government. A member of the Prince George County Board of Supervisors, Parker had often expressed his disdain for federal and state mandates and had opposed the refuge since it was first proposed. "The only government Henry Parker likes," one local reporter confided, "is the government he controls. He's anti–any other government."

A barrel-chested man now in his mid-fifties, Parker operates a grocery on Route 10 just up the hill from the entrance road to the refuge and his property. His store is a state-licensed checking station for bear, deer, and turkey hunters. You can also fill up with gas, buy mulch or firewood, and pick up bait, ice, cold cuts, a six-pack of beer, and American Eagle brand bullets and shotgun shells. Prince George, the county seat of the like-named county (pop. 27,000), is about eight miles from the grocery. One of the roads Parker travels to reach the courthouse complex is named in honor of plantation owner Edward Ruffin. An unreconstructed secessionist who gladly fired the opening volley on Fort Sumter, Ruffin took the news of Lee's surrender at Appomattox four years later rather badly: he blew his head off.

Reached by phone at his store, Parker confirmed that his as-yet unsigned sales agreement with Q Corporation contained a clause requiring the corporation to return the land to him if it did not use it, and another barring the transfer of the property to any environmental group. In part, Parker favored the jobs and economic development the project would generate. As for federal acquisitions to protect bald eagles, he said: "The land that they purchase, whatever amount it is or wherever it may be in the United States, has no effect on the net gain for the bald eagle. John Q. Citizen could own it and the same results would come about. When I see a nation in debt as we are in debt, I see it as a waste of funds."

It was common knowledge: any guy walking into his store could tell you it was foolish for the government to buy land for eagles. "Are they gonna buy Claremont, Brandon, and all of the plantations across the river?" Parker wondered with a laugh. "I've been here all my life and ain't ever seen any change." Besides, he added, "All of that land on the river has been zoned industrial for many, many years and has been worked as that [upstream], and there's been no effect on the eagle.

"The last thing I'll tell you is that the U.S. government is to blame for the diminishment of the eagle. They approved DDT and it's a proven fact that it just about wiped them out, so now who blames who?"

Robert T. Barbera, Q Corporation's president, spoke with me by phone in late July. He said he was returning my call from one of several offices on Staten Island that would soon be closed. Based on background noises, I inferred that he was speaking from his home. Responding to concerns raised by federal and state agencies, Barbera had recently announced alterations in Q Corporation's plans that would cost at least $20 million. A newly formed team, he said, of more than twenty environmental engineers, wetlands specialists, wildlife experts, and attorneys had recommended moving the closest buildings 1,000 feet back from the riverfront, rather than 500 feet. To minimize noise, buildings where testing would occur would be soundproofed, silencers would be placed on ventilation units, and all parking facilities and parts of some buildings would be situated underground.

Barbera exuded complete confidence that the environmental hurdles could be overcome. Referring to the narrow gravel road that leads to the properties, I asked, "Are there any problems with the right-of-way through the refuge?"

"The right-of-way road needs to be expanded," he conceded, "but it's not critical whether we work it out with the Fish and Wildlife Service. The worst-case scenario will not stop the project."

How, I wondered, could a several-year search that canvassed the entire East Coast have settled upon a property with so much potentially troublesome environmental baggage?

"When we first located the property in 1993," Barbera said, "we were well aware of the eagle situation, and we were prepared for the eventuality that someone would not want the project there. We'd done eight months of research on those properties [when opposition was first raised] and were aware of all the circumstances around it, so there was no surprise on our part when opposition started to occur.

"We're very confident the hurdles can be overcome."

I wondered if it wasn't unseemly to use a taxpayer-funded wildlife refuge as a security buffer.

"According to all the research, the concentration of bald eagles is on the edge of the James River," he countered. "I can't figure the purpose of buying 5.5 square miles of property [it was actually 6.4 square miles] that cannot be developed. The county and state loses money on that property, and I think Prince George [County] needs a project like this. It's a small rural county, but this is a big economic boost to its people, with revenues and employment."

As for the identity of the Q Corporation's backers, he maintained the corporation was not registered anywhere because it was being formed by a consortium of other security firms, Fortune 50 companies and investment banking firms. Eleven of the firms, he said, were incorporated in New York State under their own names. At that moment, he said, 160 consultants and 220 employees were working full-time for the Q Corporation. Further information concerning the principals would be provided in a matter of weeks, he said, with the filing of corporation papers in Virginia and the distribution of what he grandiosely called "an international press release."

Given the corporation's apparent mania for secrecy, I told Barbera some opponents of the project had speculated Q was a clandestine front for the CIA or some other undercover federal agency operation.

"That's not the first time I've heard that," he said. "I've heard everything from a terrorist operation to an illicit drug operation, but we ignore it. . . . The average person can[not] come in and do business with us. It's just impossible. The fact we keep a lot of information private or confidential is what leads people to make up rumors or start stories."

As Barbera spoke, I could hear a dog barking.

⌇⌇◗ When I next spoke with Byrd, the ornithologist was underwhelmed. "I think they're whistling Dixie," he said. "I've looked at the topo maps, and I don't know how they can fit all that into the property if they set it back 1,000 feet. It's my understanding they haven't even delineated their wetlands yet." Byrd found the affair increasingly bizarre. Having canceled a June meeting with the U.S. Fish and Wildlife Service and the U.S. Army Corps of Engineers at the last minute, and unable or unwilling to meet in July or August, Q Corporation seemed to be waging a public relations campaign solely through the press, dangling the prospect of hundreds of jobs and millions of dollars in tax revenues before local citizens to keep Prince George County in lockstep behind its plans.

What kind of company, Byrd wondered, announces it is hiring six hundred people before it even purchases land and gets regulatory approval for its plans? Who or what, he wondered, *was* the Q Corporation? By all accounts Barbera was a young man, yet Barbera had told me he and the other unnamed founders had been incubating the concept since the mid-1980s. He told the *Richmond Times-Dispatch* that he had worked for eight years as an operations director for a "large security company that handled classified government contracts." He also claimed to have freelanced as a facilities engineer for a major television network and to have designed security modifications for diplomatic vehicles for a European automobile firm. However, he refused to identify any of his former employers.

By August, Barbera was saying the company had decided to eliminate the pier and the boat-renovation facility along the river—one of its original prerequisites. Barbera was also saying the company would temporarily operate for several years in space it planned to rent in Richmond. If the corporation could function there, Byrd reasoned, perhaps it did not need the solitude and protection of the James River National Wildlife Refuge.

He also was astounded by Barbera's supposed $20 million worth of plan alterations. Few established corporations, much less an upstart, could afford what amounted to $20 million worth of environmental mitigation costs. That was twice what Q Corporation was supposedly paying for the land, and at $10 million, or about $25,000 per acre, the acquisition costs were more than three times the high per-acre price the USFWS had paid for the Maycocks Point section of the refuge. With that kind of money in a county where an average acre cost just $1,500, the Q Corporation could have purchased thousands of less sensitive acres elsewhere.

As it was, Byrd believed his entire eight-mile survey area, from Maycocks Point and Parker's property to Flowerdew Hundred and Wards Creek, were all critical pieces to the bald eagle puzzle. The main roost was essential because of its close proximity to the best, most heavily used foraging area, which most certainly included Henry Parker's shoreline. He was concerned about the fragmentation of the eagles' habitat. He was concerned about them colliding with microwave towers. He was concerned about noise, particularly night noise, disturbing the eagles.

He doubted traffic would have much of an impact, but he believed the greatest threat was the cumulative impact of all these factors. "It's difficult to measure," he conceded. "A lot of times with a biological system the only way to measure an impact is to have it happen. Then it's too late."

Indeed, he believed the impact would be felt immediately. Despite the company's supposed noise-abatement modifications, Byrd questioned how Q could engage in major land clearing, excavation, and construction without producing noise. Why bother mitigating noise problems, he wondered, if the noise generated by the construction of soundproof buildings so scared away the eagles that there would be none left later to be disturbed?

Byrd also looked at the issue in its historical and aesthetic context, although he knew that such arguments carried no weight. The portion of the James River in question currently has no industrial development. There was no uglier sight in North America, he believed, than the view one saw if one stood on the Benjamin Harrison Memorial Bridge below Hopewell and looked upstream at the Stone Container Corporation pulp mill and the Allied Signal chemical plant. "Let's keep the crap up there," he thought.

Mitchell Byrd finally met Robert Barbera in late September at a meeting between corporation officials and government environmental agencies. Several days later, Barbera again laid out his latest vision of the Q Corporation headquarters complex in a press briefing that had the tenor of an adversarial congressional hearing. At the press conference Barbera, a young man in his late twenties or early thirties with an impeccably trimmed black beard, an exquisitely cut dark blue pinstripe suit, and designer tortoiseshell glasses, refused to be photographed. "I've got a director of security who said absolutely, 100 percent no," Barbera told *Richmond Times-Dispatch* reporter Jon Pope.

At both meetings, Barbera said he believed the project could be developed without federal permits, even though the USFWS had said it would "continue to deny any access through our refuge that we determine to be incompatible with refuge purposes" and had informed Barbera that it would not grant him a transportation or utility right-of-way to one of the parcels. If federal permits were required and they were denied, Barbera countered, his corporation would sue the federal government.

To minimize the impact on eagles, Barbera said exterior construction could be accomplished when the eagles were not present. He spoke of using employee car pools to reduce traffic. And he unveiled a new proposal to further lessen disturbances—digging a thousand-foot-long tunnel under the wildlife refuge to link the two inholdings. Byrd found the cost of such a venture and the practicality of boring through a high water table mind-boggling. In response to a question from Byrd, Barbera said private consultants whom he refused to identify had delineated the wetlands on the property. That was not the understanding of the FWS and the Army Corps of Engineers.

Barbera, though, seemed unfazed by the hard questions. He asserted that Q Corporation had access to $800 million worth of capital. Thirty thousand people, more than the entire population of Prince George County, had supposedly applied for jobs. And of the seven thousand letters the Q Corporation claimed to have received, Barbera said all but twenty-two supported the project. With money and public sentiment on his side, he was confident he would prevail.

By late November of 1994 the Q corporation still had not bought the 406 acres within the James River National Wildlife Refuge. The corporation's articles of incorporation—papers Q said would be filed in Richmond as early as June—had yet to materialize. After months of talk and press scrutiny, no one other than Robert T. Barbera—not Mitchell Byrd, not U.S. Fish and Wildlife Service officials, not Prince George County officials, not county supervisor and inholding owner Henry D. Parker—could say with absolute certainty that the Q Corporation and its proposal were legitimate.

Then, the week after Thanksgiving, FWS biologist Cindy Schulz received a one-minute phone call from Barbera. The Q Corporation, he told her, was abandoning its plans for the property within the refuge and was considering other sites in Prince George County. Barbera later told reporters the refuge location had become too costly. Since then, though state officials have assured Byrd that the Q Corporation is legitimate, Barbera has not reappeared.

After Q abandoned its plans, the FWS immediately renewed its efforts to acquire the two properties within the refuge. Byrd shared the agency's concern. There was some hope that several of the owners of the former sand-and-gravel tract might be willing to sell. But Henry Parker, at least, was not interested.

"No, no," he said during a brief phone call. "I have other parties interested already."

To complete Mitchell Byrd's eagle survey, we cross to the north side of the James River at Weyanoke Point. The river is extremely narrow here. As it curves sharply around the point, the scouring motion of the current dredges a channel ninety feet deep. Not far off the channel, though, toward the shoreline, Byrd's outboard engine scrapes a mud flat. Great blue herons levitate out of the cypress-shaded shallows, but here bald eagles are few. One reason: sections of the northern shoreline are dotted with homes. We glide by a low, mean ranch house featuring a Confederate flag, a barking dog, and a shirtless potbellied man heading toward his car.

"You know how you tell a redneck, don't you?" Byrd asks.

"No, how?" I wonder.

"Ask him for his ID and he shows you his belt buckle."

Our eagle sightings are more sporadic, more spread out. A study by a Virginia Tech graduate student, David Buehler, concluded that fewer than 1 percent of more than 1,100 radio telemetry sightings of Chesapeake Bay bald eagles occurred on developed shorelines. As the demand for waterfront property increases, so will conflicts with eagles. The Chesapeake Bay Executive Council projects an increase in shoreline development of more than 70 percent by the year 2020. Jim Fraser, a Virginia Tech professor, has created an admittedly crude computer model that shows the eagle population in the bay growing to as many as eight hundred pairs over the next five to twenty years. But Fraser's model predicts that, due to development, growth will be followed by a rapid crash to near-extinction by 2023.

While Byrd finds the current recovery gratifying, in the long run he also doesn't hold much hope for eagles, or for most other wildlife, in the Chesapeake Bay. "Two point six million people are projected to move into the bay area," he once told me. "Lawn runoff, septic systems, driveway runoff—you name it." Each day the flow of tainted groundwater into the bay approximates the volume of a major tributary larger than the Rappahannock. And half or more of the bay-choking inorganic nitrogen and phosphates that leach out of septic tanks are not agricultural, but urban or residential. "Coupled with the loss and fragmentation of suitable habitat," says Byrd, "one hundred years from now, unless eagles become more adapted to human beings than they are now . . ."

A quarter century ago, only 15 to 20 percent of ospreys nested on man-made structures such as channel markers and nest platforms; the rest nested in live or dead trees. Now 90 percent choose man-made nest sites, and those that do produce more offspring than those that don't.

But Mitchell Byrd believes bald eagles are different. Some of them are showing more tolerance than he once would have thought possible. He once had difficulty locating a nest along the Potomac because it never occurred to him to look up into the pines leaning over the property owners' house. Such nests are the exceptions, though, and he believes it will take a long time, if ever, before most eagles develop the ospreys' tolerance of human beings.

Along the north shore of the James River, the eagle action doesn't pick up again until we leave the homes and approach the entrance to Herring Creek, a vast green marshland edged with wild rice that lies directly across the river from the refuge and Henry Parker's tract. Here, for no apparent reason—no mutually coveted fish is involved—an osprey is chasing an adult bald eagle across the treetops. Another white-headed eagle flushes, then three immatures, then a trio of youngsters, an immature, two more immatures, an adult, two immatures. There are five—no, nine—in the air at one time, riding the morning breeze out of the west like kites suspended in midair. By morning's end, after patrolling a few miles upstream of Byrd's normal survey area, we have seen more than 150 bald eagles.

Two weeks later, taking advantage of the highest tides of the month, Byrd extended his survey area as far upstream as the Presquile National Wildlife Refuge, and as far downstream as Brandon Plantation. In that sixteen-mile stretch of river he counted 298 bald eagles. The nearer he came to the James River National Wildlife Refuge, the more eagles he saw.

"They're like cormorants," Byrd said the morning I was with him, enjoying—as we all were—the sight of eagles in the air above Herring Creek. In jest, he added: "Open [hunting] season is definitely called for."

ASKING FOR THE LIFE OF AN EAGLE

[Two tails, or about twenty-four feathers, were] esteemed by the Mandans, Minnetares, Ricares, &c as the full value of a good horse, or gun and accoutrements. . . . With the Great and Little Osages and those nations inhabiting countries where this bird is more rare, the price is even double of that mentioned.
—MERIWETHER LEWIS, *Original Journals*

First we set up an altar—a Mexican rug and on it a Lakota Bible in our own language. We use only the revelations of Saint John in our meetings. It's very Indian—full of visions, nature, earth, the stars. Something we understand very well, maybe better than you do.

Across the Bible we put an eagle feather—it stands for the Great Spirit, for the Holy Ghost. That holy spirit is like an eagle with sharp eyes. You can't fool him.
—LEONARD CROW DOG, IN *Lame Deer: Seeker of Visions*, BY JOHN (FIRE) LAME DEER AND RICHARD ERDOES, 1962

 The elders, in his mind, had spoken again, and Nathan Jim Jr. felt compelled to act. They had asked him to grant a last wish. They would soon be going on a journey to the place the white man called heaven but that he and the elders called home. Fearing death, one elder had told him that *her* elders had come to her in a sleep dream. They had an extra horse for her to ride, but she told them she wasn't ready. Among the items she needed for the journey were eagle feathers. She had asked Nathan Jim Jr. to bring her an eagle.

Jim's people, who lived on the Warm Springs Indian Reservation in north central Oregon, deeply revered the eagle. Flying the highest and remaining in the air the longest, it seemed to disappear into the sky with their prayers. As chief of all flying animals, it had great size and the world's sharpest eyes. As the Creator knows everything, is everywhere, and sees and hears all, so did the eagle. Even after its death, its spirit remained. When used in Native American religious ceremonies, the eagle feather was imbued with the same qualities the bird itself possessed.

During the services of the Washaat, or Seven Drums, religion in the longhouse on the reservation, participants would place one or more eagle feathers in their right hand and, to the beat of a drum, rhythmically wave them away from their heart so that the spirit of the eagle would transport their prayers to the Creator. Next to their right ear they would also place an eagle fluff feather. When the airy plume oscillated, it was thought that the Creator was speaking to them. In prayer and healing ceremonies, the large wing bones were transformed into sacred whistles. The dried head of an eagle was mounted on a staff and carried in honor of the bird's spirit. The talons, sometimes worn as necklaces, were amulets invoking the spirit and protection of the Creator. When young men and women had demonstrated the maturity to respect an eagle feather, they would be given one. One also might be given to a bride on her wedding day.

In addition, the feathers played a prominent role in healing the sick and burying the dead. After having their skin pierced with a needle, medicine singing healers had eagle feathers inserted into their backs. During a healing ceremony they would brush three eagle feathers over the person who was ill. To bury someone properly, an elder first would sew as many as five eagle feathers on the back of a man's buckskin jacket, or three feathers on the back of a woman's buckskin dress. One to three eagle feathers would be placed in the right hand of the deceased, another in the hair along with a plume. Depending on the person's stature, as many as five hundred mourners might crowd into the Washaat longhouse for the funeral. A hundred of the dancers and mourners, perhaps more, would clutch eagle feathers.

Bustles and headdresses adorned with eagle and hawk feathers also were often worn during dances, and at powwows.

To make all this possible, Nathan Jim Jr.—a Yakima Native American on his mother's side, and Colville, Umatilla, Warm Springs, Yakima, and Nez Percé on his father's side, a practitioner of the Washaat religion and the healing Was-lick-i, or Feather, religion, a former practitioner in the First Native American Church who believed the church was responsible for the disappearance of his diabetes a quarter century ago—four years ago was combing a remote section of southern Oregon for eagles. Shooting bald eagles violated the Migratory Bird Treaty Act of 1918, the Bald and Golden Eagle Protection Act of 1940 and 1962, and the Endangered Species Act.

Shooting golden eagles violated the first two statutes. But as Nathan Jim Jr. would later tell a federal judge, these were the white man's laws, not the laws of the Creator.

He knew the U.S. Fish and Wildlife Service maintained the National Eagle Repository, which until a recent move to Denver was located at the service's National Fish and Wildlife Forensics Laboratory in Ashland, Oregon. Three times Jim had applied for and received eagle parts from the repository: two bald eagle tails, two claws, and two wings in 1979; two bald eagle wings, a tail, and two claws in 1982; and fifty golden eagle feathers in 1988. Applicants had to be certified by a tribal religious leader. Then, after the request had been sent to the USFWS regional headquarters in Portland, the Bureau of Indian Affairs (BIA) had to certify that the applicant was an enrolled member in a recognized tribe. From there the application was sent to the Ashland repository, where the supply of feathers and birds sent in from around the country—victims of illness, roadkills, collisions, and electrocutions—was not keeping pace with the growing number of requests. The demand, in part, was fueled by a sincere though far from universal movement among Native Americans to reclaim their cultures, which for generations had been suppressed by the BIA and Christian missionaries.

This renewed interest was creating a quandary for those charged with enforcing federal law. What constituted traditional use of eagle feathers? Years ago they were awarded only to those who had performed great deeds, and this is still true among some tribes, where possession generally is limited to honorees such as elders and military veterans. But today in South Dakota, for example, federal agents receive requests from Native Americans who wish to present eagle feathers to college, high school, grade school, and even kindergarten graduates. There are requests for members of children's choirs and Lakota dance classes. On the Warm Springs reservation, eagle feathers embellish hats and dangle, depending on your point of view, like a rosary or Styrofoam dice, from car mirrors. One of the greatest, and most troubling, demands for feathers comes from Native Americans who travel the nationwide powwow circuit, dancing in elaborate headdresses, bustles, and other regalia that require large quantities of feathers, particularly eagle feathers. The Mashantucket Pequot, the small Connecticut tribe whose gambling casino generates $600 million in gross annual revenues, in 1994 sponsored a dance, song, and drum competition with a total prize purse of $500,000.

Finally there's the *Dances With Wolves* phenomenon. Two years ago at Bear Butte, South Dakota, USFWS law enforcement agents charged two white men from the Denver area with illegally possessing eagle feathers. The New Age Indian wanna-bes had been presented with the feathers by Native Americans who, for a fee, had led the duo on a Sioux vision quest at the sacred Lakota site.

Less than twenty years ago only about three hundred Native Americans a year were requesting eagles or eagle body parts from the federal repository. Recently the cabinets of repository director Jim Kniffen contained the color-coded waiting-list files of 2,500 natives, including 2,200 who wanted whole birds. The requests included those of Kathy Butler of Houston, Texas, and Mary Lou Petrullo of Stony Point, New York; Wayne Whiting Redhorse of Little Rock, Arkansas; Calvin Walks Over Ice of Billings, Montana; and Joe and Cynthia Feather of Cherokee, North Carolina. Requests came from small reservation towns and from the nation's largest cities, from Yakima, Washington; Pine Ridge, South Dakota; Bemidji, Minnesota; Hominy Indian Village, Oklahoma; Zuni, New Mexico; and the Penobscot Indian Nation, Maine; and from Milwaukee, Minneapolis, St. Louis, Jacksonville, Anchorage, Seattle, Phoenix, and Hollywood.

The wait for loose feathers ranged from a day to three months. Several times a week native volunteers such as Jolene Ajootian and her aunt, Bernie Stone, Ojibwe (or Chippewa) women from Minnesota now living in Oregon, would fill such requests at the repository. Encircled in a nimbus of floating eagle down, one afternoon Jolene knelt on the floor in a cramped work area. Pulling feather after feather out of a cardboard box, she pieced together the dozen tail feathers of an adult bald eagle for a grandfather in Apache, Oklahoma. First she found two straight, symmetrical center tail feathers, then two extremely asymmetrical outer edge feathers, and finally eight progressively more symmetrical ones. The women helped the repository ship more than twenty thousand feathers a year. Feathers are sent out immediately if an emergency, such as an illness or a funeral, arises. "For some people," Jolene said, "this is a matter of life or death."

But even though Kniffen attempted to empty his closet-sized walk-in freezer each week, generally eighteen months to two years passed before he could pack a whole frozen eagle in five pounds of dry ice and ship it overnight.

More than a decade ago Nathan Jim Jr. waited an average of six months for his first two requests to be filled and six weeks for fifty golden eagle feathers. His request for a whole golden eagle had neared the top of the waiting list when he was arrested in 1990 for the first of two series of eagle killings. He killed the eagles, he said, because the wait was too long and he never knew where the parts the USFWS sent him had come from or what had killed the birds. As a result, there was no "life" in them. The feathers could not carry prayers to the Creator unless they were "clean"; they could not come from birds that had been electrocuted or poisoned.

Nathan Jim Jr. believed that the eagle should be killed by someone who had first asked for its life. To give the elders a proper journey, the bird had to be taken by someone like him. Before he shot a bird, he would eat certain foods and conduct certain ceremonies—ceremonies he refused to describe in federal court—to prepare himself "for the taking of this bird, my brother and sister." The ceremonies and the Creator, he said, gave him the ability to discern whether an eagle was healthy or if it was diseased and full of chemicals, if it was old or if it had been disabled by a shotgun pellet or a collision with a power line. Only these would he take.

After he shot them he would engage in more rituals and prayers he said were taught to him by one of the Warm Spring elders, the late Andrew David, whom he informally referred to as his grandfather.

Late in 1990, near the Nevada state line, Jim shot seven golden eagles by moonlight as they slept perched atop power line poles. A woman who was with him later told federal investigators that Jim had instructed her to sprinkle sacred tobacco out their pickup truck window in propitiation whenever she heard his rifle fire.

Jim served three months in federal prison for that offense. Less than a year after his release he returned to the high desert country of southern Oregon in search of more eagles. About a thousand bald eagles, the largest concentration in the lower forty-eight states, winter in the Klamath Basin that straddles the Oregon-California border. Scattered across southern Oregon, many more bald and golden eagles spend the winter feeding upon jackrabbits and winter deer kills.

Shortly before sunset on December 12, 1992, Senior Trooper Paul Randall, an officer with the Fish and Wildlife Division of the Oregon State Police, was patrolling the remote rangelands of Lake County, Oregon, for mule deer poachers. The temperature had hovered below freezing all day, and three to four inches of snow covered federal Bureau of Land Management land just east of Fremont National Forest. Cruising along Route 31, Randall noticed a thin, ponytailed Native American in his early thirties slipping through a fence and moving toward an old Ford pickup truck. The man, whose upper front teeth were missing, explained that he was just relieving himself. A young boy, apparently the nephew of the truck's owner, accompanied him in the pickup. Curious, the trooper returned a few minutes later to find the man leaving the fenced area again. This time he sprinted to the truck and drove away.

After driving less than a mile, the man turned the pickup into the entrance of a closed road. Randall blocked his exit and asked for his identification. The man had none, but said his name was Nathan Jim Jr. The trooper soon learned that Jim was wanted for breaking a release agreement for a charge of driving under the influence in Jefferson County, which encompasses Warm Springs. After arresting Jim, at the suspect's request Randall started transferring items from the back of the pickup into the cab to secure them. A dark plastic garbage bag he picked up felt quite warm. Inside it Randall discovered two freshly killed rough-legged hawks. The next bag, which was even warmer, contained a dead adult bald eagle. The remaining three garbage bags held three more rough-legged hawks and the wings, tail, and feet of two golden eagles. Bright red sticky blood spattered the golden eagle parts. The hawks, according to the thermometer Randall plunged into their breasts, were still between 80°F. and 85°F.; the bald eagle, whose normal temperature is about 105°F., was still 98°F.

Back at the original site, a backup officer summoned by Randall followed footprints in the snow a short distance to a pine tree. Around its base lay blood and eagle feathers. Investigating further the next day, Randall found another garbage bag underneath sagebrush near the fence. Inside it was yet another dead bald eagle, an adult that presumably had been perching in the pine tree. Underneath the bag lay a .22 caliber semiautomatic rifle.

∼ For violating the probation terms of his first shooting conviction, Jim served an additional ten months. For the second offense he agreed to plead guilty to one count each of violating the Endangered Species Act and the Bald and Golden Eagle Protection Act. In return he received six months' home detention and the right to immediately appeal the conviction on the grounds that the two federal acts deprived him of his First Amendment rights to practice his religion. Shortly after Jim's guilty plea, the Religious Freedom Restoration Act of 1993 was enacted. The federal government, the law said, could substantially burden a person's exercise of religion only if it could demonstrate a compelling governmental interest. The government also had to show that it was employing "the least restrictive means of furthering that compelling governmental interest." In short, this meant that laws seemingly neutral to religion need not necessarily apply to everyone. For instance, as a matter of religious principle, Amish farmers can refuse to pay into the Social Security system or to put bright, reflective safety triangles on their black, horse-drawn buggies.

Citing the new statute and the bald eagle's improved status, Celeste Whitewolf, Jim's attorney, sought to overturn his latest conviction. She also was advocating a limited hunting season—for this country's two million Native Americans only—on bald and golden eagles.

Near Buena Vista Lake in California's southern San Joaquin Valley, anthropologists earlier in this century uncovered the skull of a bald eagle. Affixed with asphaltum, a round disk of abalone shell covered one of the bird's eye sockets. Nearby, the orbits of a human skeleton had been similarly sealed with rectangular abalone pendants. For at least four thousand years before the Spaniards traversed California's Central Valley, Native Americans ritualistically buried the eagles, condors, and falcons that filled their skies. Some of the birds' skulls, legs, and foot bones have been found buried with human remains in the lower Sacramento Valley, suggesting that the raptors' complete skins were interred as a type of regalia.

No people on earth have had a more complex relationship with the eagle than Native Americans. For millennia, eagles have played an integral role in the myths, beliefs, customs, religious regalia, and dress of the indigenous people of North America. At some point it's thought that nearly every native tribe in the United States that divided itself into clans had an eagle group. Some tribes engaged in elaborate eagle dances, and the birds appeared on pots, baskets, textiles, beadwork, quillwork, shields, crests, totem poles, house and grave posts, and pipes and rattles.

Perched vigilantly atop a pine, the bald eagle served as one of the great symbols of the Iroquois Nation. Many tribes esteemed the mythical thunderbird, an eaglelike bird whose flapping wings were believed to cause the thunder and whose eyes flashed forth lightning. Nowhere did the resurrection symbol of the phoenix burst more into life than on the Great Plains, where in some cases the dead were placed on scaffolds so that scavengers, including eagles, would return them to the elements from which they had come.

Eagles also figured prominently in some creation myths, including this tale of how the Sioux nation was born: A great flood drowned all the people on the prairie except one beautiful woman, who was rescued by a bald eagle that carried her to the top of a cliff. There she gave birth to twins fathered by the eagle. The twins founded a new tribe of strong, brave people. The flesh and blood of their ancestors, those who drowned, metamorphosed into pipestone, from which the new tribe fashioned pipes that they smoked as a sign of peace. The warriors of the tribe wore eagle feathers on their heads.

The eagle is also a seminal figure for the Anishinabe, or Chippewa, who pushed the Sioux out of the North Woods onto the Great Plains. Consider this legend told by the late Jimmy Jackson, an Anishinabe medicine man:

Long ago, when the earth was new, everything was going well according to the universal harmony that the Great Spirit had set in motion.

Then the Anishinabe did some disrespectful things, so the Creator sent a warning that all beings on earth would be destroyed. The eagle, a close friend of Anishinabe, heard the news and volunteered to fly to the Creator's world. This took much bravery, as the bird would have to fly close to the sun and could be destroyed by the heat.

So, on a given day, the eagle announced his departure and flew up, up, and away toward the sun. Soon the bird was just a speck in the sky.

The eagle flew around the sun onward toward the Creator. Finally it landed in the Creator's world.

"Who is walking in my world?" boomed the Creator.

"It is I, Mi-Ge-Zi," the eagle said in a trembling voice.

"What is it you wish?" the Creator asked.

"I have come because I love the Anishinabe and I ask that you consider something besides destroying them. Perhaps you could send teachers to instruct about the good life. Perhaps these teachers could teach about their old ways of respect and honor among all creatures large and small."

"You speak bravely and with great wisdom. Yes, I will send teachers. They will be called Elders. Some will be messengers; others will be teachers who have lived long, respectful, healthy lives. These will be the ones who have gained experience, the ones who live in harmony with all creatures and all earthly beings; the ones who remember our old ways when all creatures and beings lived and worked together like in the beginning.

"Mi-Ge-Zi, Eagle, you are a brave and courageous being. For your strong character and heroic act on behalf of Anishinabe, from this day forth, everything that is yours will be honored and revered as sacred.

Your image, your feathers, your claws, will be as symbols and messages of connections and communications to my world. From now
on, all those who respect and honor you will get special help from me.
Those whom your symbols protect, I will protect. Those who seek
refuge in your power will hear my message to all beings on earth.

"Go back then and remain with Anishinabe. You will also be a
messenger, a teacher, a symbol of courage and strength, respect,
sacredness, and honor."

This is why people must respect and honor the eagle.

As this tale indicates, the physical parts of the eagle were revered and
heavily utilized. Ceremonial whistles were fashioned from wing bones and
carried by warriors. Medicine men sucked away disease with the tubular
bones. The talons functioned as both amulets and ornaments.

Then there were the feathers: In the far Pacific Northwest, among some
Plains tribes and in the Southwest, eagle down was sprinkled on the hair, masks,
or dance costumes; attached to masks and rattles; or tossed or blown into the
air. Across the continent, feathers were worn in the hair and on bonnets;
attached to buckskin shirts, shields, lances, and pipes; and fashioned into fans.
A large eagle feather was a mark of honor. A Chippewa who had scalped an
enemy was permitted to wear two eagle feathers on his head; capturing a
wounded prisoner on the battlefield earned a warrior five eagle feathers.

To the Sioux, or Lakota, people, an eagle feather functioned as a badge
of courage and a complex emblem of utmost respect. It was awarded for
bravery in battle, for the audacious act of touching, but not killing, an enemy
with a hand, a bow, a lance, a rattle, or a whip. The first brave who scored
such a coup was given a golden eagle feather to wear upright at the back of
his head. The second brave to touch the same enemy wore a feather tilted
to the left; the third could wear a feather horizontally; the fourth, an upside-
down buzzard feather.

Braves were also granted coups for other courageous acts, including
killing a foe in hand-to-hand combat. Many coups elevated a man to great
social standing. Often, along with the coup feathers, such men received a
horse, yet another sign in Sioux society that, yes, here was a man of substance.

Selecting a site high on a treeless ridge, natives of the Great Plains
hunted eagles each autumn. A brave and his companions first inscribed into
the earth a rectangle six feet long by two feet wide, running north to south.

Slicing the sod into squares with their knives, they carefully set the turf aside. Then, again with their knives, they dug a pit. With spoons fashioned from the horns of mountain sheep, they scooped out the soil onto a robe, carted it away, and dumped it about the hillside in the shape of gopher hills.

When the pit was three feet deep, the brave placed a nest of sage at its south end. Then, except for the entrance at the north end, the pit was spanned with a series of pole beams. Roofed over with the replaced sod and camouflaged with other grasses around the opening, the pit was ready. Satisfied, the brave retired to a secluded nearby tepee. Inside, behind the fire pit, he placed an offering stick and ten small tobacco offerings hanging from small sticks, which remained undisturbed while he hunted.

Likewise, a Blackfoot would not eat rosebuds. If he did, the rosebuds in his stomach would make the eagle itch and scratch itself instead of eating the bait. He also did not use an awl in building the trap, for if he scratched himself with it, the eagle would scratch him. For the same reason, his wife and children, no matter how far distant, refrained from using an awl while he was hunting for fear of jeopardizing him.

Long before the sun rose the next morning, the brave purified himself by taking a sweat bath. Thus cleansed, to the pit he and a companion carried the bait—a dead jackrabbit or antelope, a squirming rodent, and perhaps a decoy such as a live crow, which they would tie down next to the bait. With the lure or lures secured atop the pit, the brave would slide into it and his aide would complete the camouflage.

All day he lay on his back without eating, drinking, or smoking. It was not a wait for the faint of heart. Attracted by the bait, a grizzly bear could, and did on occasion, crash through the roof and kill the prone man. Depending on tribal custom, some braves used a stick to make the bait move tantalizingly. A Blackfoot who had stretched a tanned coyote hide and raw meat across the top of the pit would continuously chant the coyote medicine song: "I want the eagles to eat my body."

Eventually, victimized by its keen eyesight, an eagle would swoop down for what looked like an easy meal. Two hands would suddenly be thrust up from the abyss, seizing the bird's legs above its rapierlike talons and yanking it downward. A Sioux would wring the startled bird's neck. A Blackfoot would break its back with his foot. A Hidatsa would spare the first bird he caught so that it could be tethered near the bait to entice more eagles. As modern-day eagle biologist Al Harmata has discovered, such eagles more successfully decoy younger birds, as adults are leery of a bird in distress.

In this manner Native Americans captured both bald and golden eagles. But at least among the Plains and Southwest Indians, the ideal (and more plentiful) prize was the immature golden eagle with its distinctive tail feathers: white with black tips. From the first paintings and sketches sent back by artists and ethnologists Karl Bodmer and George Catlin, our concept of what an Indian looks like has been inextricably intertwined with our image of the Native Americans of the Plains: a Sioux chief in an eagle headdress, with a staff and a sacred wheel trimmed in golden eagle feathers.

On the Plains black eagles, or mature golden eagles, were often ignored. As for bald eagles, "White Heads are very scarce, as well as dangerous," Brings-down-the-Sun, a Blackfoot, once said. "They are so strong they have almost lifted me out of the pit."

Once the brave had killed an eagle, he placed it on a bed of sage at the foot of the pit. On a good day a brave might seize two or three eagles. At sundown he would return with the birds to his purifying lodge. Laying the eagles in a row next to the fire pit, he again took a sweat bath in propitiation.

Most of the Plains tribes, as well as the Cherokee in the Southeast and the Apache, Hopi, and Navajo in the Southwest, used pits to capture eagles. The Cree, another Plains group, did not. They either shot eagles with a bow and arrow or allowed them to gorge themselves on so much bait that they could no longer fly. In the Pacific Northwest, Bellacoola natives hiding in blinds killed bald eagles by attracting them with a dead salmon and snaring them around the neck with a cord attached to a long pole.

Some other tribes caught eagles and kept them alive as a renewable source of feathers. Captured nestlings also were raised until their feathers were fully developed, at which point the natives plucked their tail feathers and released or killed the birds, depending on tribal custom. In the San Joaquin Valley a Miwok eagle hunter would scale a nest tree or cliff, bind the eaglets to cradles, and carry them down on his back like infants. Farther to the south, some eyries were considered the property of certain chiefs and their families.

Given its greater presence on the Plains, the golden eagle, particularly the immature with the black-tipped tail, played a greater role than the bald eagle in native ceremonial life. But both species were and continue to be revered equally by Native Americans throughout the country. In the 1950s and early 1960s, as dam construction, regrettably, transformed most of the Dakotas' magnificent Missouri River bottomland into several long lakes, anthropologists launched emergency excavations of prehistoric sites that had been inhabited by the Arikara people beginning in the fourteenth or fifteenth century. Of the thousands of bird bones salvaged, eagle bones, including cut bills and wing bones, were the most common. Of those, slightly more than half were the bones of bald eagles. In Oregon, eagle bones also were the most common bird remains found in one Indian midden.

No one can say whether such native American practices had any significant impact on eagle populations. However, the near-extinction of bald eagles in the Wichita Mountains of southwest Oklahoma by 1904 was attributed to Native Americans who killed them for ceremonial bonnets. As for golden eagles, one report claimed the Arapaho once caught fifty to one hundred eagles in just four days. It took at least sixty tail feathers—or the tails from five immature golden eagles—to make a full-train Great Plains headdress. Another four dozen were needed for a sacred wheel.

Currently only the Hopi tribe of Arizona receives a permit from the USFWS to take large raptors. Every spring a dozen golden eagle and a dozen red-tailed hawk nestlings are captured, raised to full size, and then ritualistically smothered for their feathers. Despite the historical precedent, however, among most tribes today it is strictly taboo, both spiritually and environmentally, to slay an eagle.

"You bet it's forbidden," said Larry Aitken, the administrator of the tribal college of the Leech Lake band of Anishinabe, or Chippewa/Ojibwe, in eagle-rich northern Minnesota.

"What would be the penalty?" I wondered.

"Excommunication, banishment from the tribe," he said. "But it hasn't happened in my lifetime. . . . You might steal from your mother or brother, but you wouldn't kill an eagle. It would be like killing God, or a messenger from God."

⁓ Sixteen years ago, along a deserted road on the edge of the vast Navajo reservation in northwestern New Mexico, a state livestock inspector, Rudy "Dude" Mauldin, stopped to offer a ride to a Navajo medicine man clutching a brown paper bag. As they neared Gallup, New Mexico, the medicine man extracted from the bag several hat feather bundles—a few small feathers, their shafts woven together with brightly colored nylon, to decorate a western hatband. Among them, Mauldin noticed, were eagle feathers. As a token of his gratitude, the medicine man wanted Mauldin to have a hat feather. Mauldin accepted and, for ten dollars, bought two more.

What, asked Mauldin, did he plan to do with the rest? Sell them in town, replied the medicine man.

Mauldin told him he knew of someone who might be interested in buying a sizable number of the hat feathers. He was thinking of his father, Nando Mauldin, a former state conservation officer who for the past seven years had been a U.S. Fish and Wildlife Service law enforcement agent. Now based in Salt Lake City, Nando previously had been the first to head the service's "special ops," or special operations unit: a half-dozen agents who worked full-time on large-scale undercover investigations.

That September the son introduced his father as a trader to the middle-aged medicine man at the latter's home in Crownpoint, New Mexico.

Saying he frequently made hat feathers, the Navajo also displayed some old golden eagle feathers. When asked where he had gotten the feathers, the medicine man produced a brochure and a tape recording entitled "Yankton Sioux Peyote Songo, Vol. 6," which Nando Mauldin bought as a "confidence buy." The Navajo identified the five medicine men pictured in the brochure as good friends of his who crafted peyote fans, feathered fans used in Native American Church ceremonies. All five men lived on the Yankton Sioux reservation, seven hundred miles away in South Dakota. The church, founded more than a century ago in Oklahoma, claimed Native American members throughout the West. During all-night ceremonies, practitioners sacramentally ingested psychedelic buttons of dried peyote, a small, spineless cactus from southern Texas and northern New Mexico. The ritual also involved the use of eagle-bone whistles to replicate the scream of an eagle, and feathered fans with beautifully crafted beadwork handles to circulate cedar incense, snare good songs out of the air, and dispense, in baptismal fashion, sacred water. Often the fans, particularly those of the leaders, were made of eagle feathers.

If Mauldin was interested in such fans, Miller encouraged him to contact the Sioux as a friend of his.

Thus began Operation Eagle, a landmark investigation that uncovered the killing and selling of more than fifty bald and golden eagles—including some that were shot or trapped inside a national wildlife refuge—by native Americans. The issues raised by the case ultimately were decided by the U.S. Supreme Court.

Established by an 1858 treaty with the U.S. government, the Yankton Sioux Reservation was located in southeast South Dakota, on the northeast side of the Missouri River near the Nebraska state line. The reservation was desolate, particularly in the winter. Many of its residents lived in mean frame houses cloaked in uninsulated weatherboard and rimmed, to the north and west, by shelter belts of leafless hardwoods vainly planted as a barrier against the relentless winds of the Great Plains. According to the 1980 census, the per capita income of the fewer than two thousand Yankton Sioux living on the reservation was less than $2,500, and more than half of them were living below the federal poverty level.

The high bluffs on the edge of the reservation below the Fort Randall Dam afforded an excellent view across the river of one of the last remaining stretches of rich, undammed, unflooded Missouri River bottomland: the 1,100-acre Karl E. Mundt National Wildlife Refuge. Through the sale of cups that featured endangered species, the Southland Corporation's 7-Eleven Food Stores had raised $250,000 to enable the National Wildlife Federation to purchase the land and transfer it to the USFWS. The main attraction: the cottonwood roosts and fish-rich open tail waters below the dam attracted what, at one time, was the largest population of wintering bald eagles in the lower forty-eight states.

In 1978, four years after the refuge was established, several bald eagles were found there clamped in traps. One bird had managed to pull up the spike that anchored its leghold trap. That eagle was discovered with the spike wedged into a cottonwood crotch. Hanging upside down in the tree, the bird had been dead for days.

The trapped birds remained a mystery until Nando Mauldin, posing as a southwest trader, wrote on his fictitious Night Hawk Trading Company letterhead to the five Yankton Sioux to whom he had been referred. One of them, Joseph Abdo Sr., soon phoned Mauldin with an offer to sell a $225 fan made from the beautiful tail feathers of the "waterbird," or anhinga, a diving, fish-eating bird from the Southeast. With their horizontal crinkles, the lustrous black-green tail feathers were prized for women's fans in the Native American Church. Abdo, in his mid-forties, also invited the undercover agent to South Dakota and offered to introduce him to others interested in selling feathered goods.

On February 25, 1981, Mauldin arrived at Abdo's home in Lake Andes, South Dakota, armed with fake business cards, some turquoise jewelry, and $2,700 in cash. Abdo had supposedly already traded the fan he had promised Mauldin for a .243 Remington rifle, but in exchange for a hundred-dollar bill Abdo sold Maudlin three sets of parrot wings, the tail of a red-tailed hawk, and forty-three scissortail flycatcher tail feathers—beautiful long, thin bluish and salmon-pink feathers from the state bird of Oklahoma. Another Sioux who lived with Abdo accepted Mauldin's offer of $75 for three partially completed anhinga- and hawk-feather fans. A third man accepted Mauldin's offer of $125 for a completed waterbird fan.

That afternoon Abdo and Mauldin moved on to the home of Dwight Dion, who some considered the reservation's best marksman. Several other eventual defendants, including Dwight's brother, Neulan, also were present. From Dwight Dion the agent purchased a bald eagle fan and a hawk-tail fan for $400. For another $400, from Neulan he bought a bald eagle tail fan, a small golden eagle fan, and some macaw feathers. After dinner it was more of the same at the home of Joseph Shields Sr. He sold Maudlin two hawk fans for $50; another suspect sold a scissortail fan, a hawk fan, and an anhinga fan for $500 in cash, jewelry, and a check; and Asa Primeux sold a ninety-feather scissortail fan, a large eagle fan, and a small eagle fan to Mauldin in return for a $700 check.

Mauldin, who was not wearing a body wire to tape the conversations, was having difficulty keeping track of all the transactions. In less than a day he had spent more than $2,500 and had declined to buy other items that would have more than doubled that total. Though he had bought illegal feathers throughout his career, he had never stumbled upon such a large cache. Members of at least eight or nine different families seemed to be involved, and Abdo wanted to introduce him to half a dozen more people.

The eagle feathers had apparently been obtained locally; Abdo confided that three bald eagles, including one that had been shot off a power-line pole, had been slain near his house. But Maudlin also was stunned by the apparent breadth of the feather-trading network: the scissortail flycatchers had come from Oklahoma; another Yankton Sioux was regularly traveling to Florida for the rare anhinga tails (ultimately a Seminole official would be implicated); and several of the suspects were leaving within the next two days to sell or trade their items in "Navajo land," in Arizona.

Several of the Sioux acknowledged it was illegal to sell protected feathers, but though Mauldin was a white man and a stranger, he sensed no hesitation in dealing with him. Neulan Dion also uttered a theme Mauldin would often hear: because he had procured a permit to receive feathers from the U.S. Fish and Wildlife Service's eagle repository, he erroneously stated he was authorized to keep and transport eagles and feathers.

During the summer of 1982, after Mauldin and another agent had journeyed several more times to South Dakota to purchase fans, Mauldin was joined by special ops agent Bob Standish, a former refuge manager from Illinois. In Atlanta, Standish recently had completed a storefront sting operation that had exposed a widespread illegal trade in turtles, lizards, snakes, and alligators; police officers, doctors, teachers, and zoo officials were involved. With Standish now posing as a wildlife and Indian art dealer from southern Georgia, the USFWS undercover agents had soon upped the stakes in South Dakota: they were buying whole eagles.

On December 6, 1982, Viola Dion told Mauldin by phone that her husband had been out the previous three nights, and would be going out again that night, to hunt eagles. They were strapped for money, she explained. "In fact, he's got some other orders that he's gotta fill, but he wanted to get you guys first because the other ones are Indians and . . . They more or less, you know, wanna pay him so much. But right now we wanna . . . our, uh, one of our cars is going on the blink and everything, so we kinda . . ."

"Uh-huh," Mauldin said.

"And then for Christmas coming up, so that's the reason why he told me to call."

The following day Dwight Dion called Standish, Mauldin's partner. His asking price was $750 to $1,000 for an adult bald eagle and $500 for a golden eagle. The reason: a single bird was worth a great deal if it was divided into parts. "Because I make about two-fifty, three hundred on the tail feathers alone, you know," Dion explained. "And about thirty-five dollars [each] for the [two whistle] bones. Sixty-five dollars for the feather, ah, ah, wing tips, you know."

"Yeah."

"And then, plus the claws. I can sell all that stuff."

Earlier that day, Dion added, he had shot an adult bald eagle with his .22 caliber rifle.

A week later Mauldin and Standish arrived in the early evening at the home of Viola and Dwight Dion Sr. outside of Lake Andes, South Dakota. Shortly afterward, three of the couple's sons—Isaac, Lyle, and Dwight Dion Jr.—joined them. Two adult and two immature American bald eagles soon were brought up from a basement freezer to the living room for the agents to inspect.

The father described to the agents how he drove down a road that terminated along the banks of the Missouri River below the dam and sat in his pickup, waiting for an eagle to cross the river from the refuge. When one did, he would get out of the truck and attempt to shoot it. He said that he and the others hunted at night, too, shooting the eagles out of roost trees with shotguns.

One of the adult eagles obviously had been soaked before it was frozen. The father explained he had to use his boat to retrieve it after it was shot. "Luckily," he said, "there was nobody on the river." He added: "The first one I got during the night, and the others I got during the day. I shot one with a shotgun using double-ought buckshot. You can't get them down with a twenty-two [caliber] rifle. I hit one with a twenty-two, a real nice one, a big baldy, kept going right across [the river]."

Lyle Dion, a twenty-two-year-old plumber's assistant in a federal CETA program at the Yankton Sioux tribal headquarters, showed the agents a set of fresh white bald eagle tail feathers he had plucked, he said, from a bird he killed the day before with a .223 caliber rifle as it flew overhead. He had given the body to his brother-in-law, but after Standish expressed continued interest in the rest of the bird, he left to retrieve it.

While they awaited his return, Dwight Dion Sr. told the agents, "If you find a place you want to sell those [eagles], just call up and let me know and I'll try to get you whatever you want. I'm after some black tips [immature golden eagles], but they just ain't around yet. I think when it gets cold they'll start coming in." He said he had other orders for an adult bald eagle and a black tip. He wanted to take some eagles out West, and a Minnesota man had offered to buy a new outboard motor for Dion's boat in exchange for an eagle.

Demand usually picked up each June, he said, when the Indian powwows started around the country. "A lot of people depend on me from all over—to get them eagles because their belief prohibits them from shooting eagles."

"Dwight has papers that [say] he can use these [eagles]," his wife, Viola, added. "We belong to the Native American Church."

Her husband then said, "You guys are going to have to keep it quiet if you have them mounted or stuffed. If it comes back to me, I'll probably do twenty-five to thirty years for it. The fine is ten thousand dollars and ten years right now for just killing one. Don't matter what kind it is, bald or golden."

Dion wanted $750 for each of the two adult bald eagles and $500 apiece for the immatures. "In Navajo country," he said, "you can get a thousand to fifteen hundred dollars for a whole bird, with no trouble."

Mauldin bought the two immature bald eagles for $700 in cash plus a $255 check he had previously mailed and $45 Dion's daughter owed him for turquoise jewelry. Standish, who had already forwarded Dion Sr. a $500 check to hold the birds, paid an additional $250 in cash for one of the adult bald eagles and negotiated the price of the other one down to $550, which

he paid in cash. Standish balked when Lyle returned, because the eagle carcass offered to him had a large flesh wound where it had been shot, so the
young man accepted Standish's lower offer of $250 cash.

One of the other sons, twenty-year-old Dwight Jr., had killed one of the
other four bald eagles. Standish asked the young man whether he had used
a rifle or a shotgun—a question often asked during the investigation in
order to get the suspects to confirm their guilt.

"Shotgun," Dwight Jr. replied.

"Dwight Jr.," his mother said proudly, "killed his first eagle when he was
fifteen or sixteen years old."

Later, as the agents were departing, Viola Dion said, "If you want any
more eagles, you call again."

Meanwhile the family of Asa Primeaux Sr., a heavyset Sioux in his
mid-fifties, was trapping and shooting bald eagles on and near the national
wildlife refuge. Today Primeaux—who was convicted on eight counts—
contends he sold but never killed eagles. "I didn't kill no eagles," he says.
"My grandparents raised me up not to be killing eagles." But in taped conversations with the federal agents, he indicated he was using deer illegally
killed at night as bait. He told them that trapping eagles was probably easier than shooting them because the only way to shoot them was to go out
on the river at night.

The eagle killings continued even after some of the suspects became
aware that authorities were investigating. "It's got risky somehow for us to
do this now," Primeaux told Standish by phone late in 1982. But he wasn't
concerned about himself. "I won't get in trouble . . . I know . . . as long as,
like, Nolan [Nando Mauldin's alias] told you about me, and we been doing
this for I don't know how many years now."

To shoot the birds, Primeaux explained, he and his family, armed with
shotguns, walked underneath the roosting trees when the moon came up.
"You can see 'em, but it's . . . have to kinda aim first and then shine the flashlight later, 'cause the minute that light shines, they going to take off. Shoot
the minute the light comes on. That's the way we get some."

The following morning—New Year's Eve—Primeaux placed a collect
call to Standish complaining that a $400 deposit for an eagle and a hawk
hadn't yet arrived at his bank via Western Union. Assured the money was
on its way, Primeaux confided that, in an effort to bag more eagles, he had
moved two sets of traps across the Missouri River onto the national wildlife

refuge. (Another suspect, Neulan Dion, later told agents some of the traps were set up in trees.)

"We moved 'em," Primeaux said of his traps. "They're roosting in another area, so we moved 'em across the river. It's kinda hard for us to get over. We're using a boat now."

"Is that the refuge area over there?" Standish asked.

"Yeah. Yeah, we have to kinda sneak in there."

A week later, in another collect call, Primeaux reported he had gotten two mature bald eagles and two "golden" eagles—probably immature bald eagles, since some of the Sioux involved in the investigation frequently misidentified bald and golden eagles; in some cases they seemed to have believed they were all one species going through different feather molts.

Primeaux told the agent the cost of the lone bird that wasn't sold yet, a trapped adult bald eagle, was $750. Standish told him he would wire him a $400 deposit later that day. The birds, Primeaux said, had been slain on the refuge.

"I was over there last night," he told Standish. "That's where they're comin' in now. About two or three years ago they were like that, ya know. After that, well, it was pretty slow, but all of a sudden they come back, a lot of 'em.

"But tonight I'll probably pick up about four more again. If there ain't nothin' in the traps, I'll probably shoot 'em. But they don't get shot up; we know where to hit 'em."

Standish cautioned Primeaux not to tell anyone about what they were doing, "or we'll both end up in jail." Primeaux said he shouldn't worry because Primeaux certified tribal members when they requested an eagle from the USFWS eagle repository, which at the time was located in Pocatello, Idaho. The following day the federal agents, Mauldin and Standish, visited Primeaux at his home outside of Lake Andes. One adult, which had been shot that week out of a roost tree at night, and one immature bald eagle were laid on the kitchen table: $1,250 worth of black-market eagles. Primeaux also brought out a frozen, shot ferruginous hawk. Sale price: $100.

As the agents were concluding their purchases, one of Primeaux's sons, Asa Primeaux Jr., returned with an adult bald eagle he had shot the previous night on the refuge—the same night, they said, that Dwight Dion had shot two eagles. The father asked if they would pay $800 for it. They said no, they would pay only $750.

"We're taking a chance to even shoot it for you, you know," the son said.

"We're even taking a risk on going where we get them; it's a rough place." Standish eventually peeled $775 out of his wallet for the bird.

How many eagles, he wondered, did Primeaux and his sons kill in a year?

"Oh, we get a few, about twenty-five or thirty," Primeaux said. "Yeah, that's year-round. There was a guy just came about an hour ago—he's a traditional man; he dances and all that. He wants one." Primeaux said eagles with black-tipped tail feathers—immature golden eagles—were worth $1,000 apiece.

"Those things," his son said, "are really hard to get."

"So we get them for the guy," his father said, "however he wants them."

When Operation Eagle was terminated in June 1983, charges were filed against more than forty men and women from eight different states from Florida to California. No one better illustrated the scope of the case than Neulan Dion, Dwight's brother. Neulan, who operated a tepee business that often took him out of South Dakota, was charged with selling the agents eight bald eagle carcasses for $3,200. When he sold them five eagles in January of that year, he said he was planning a trip to Wyoming and Arizona to deliver more.

"How many of these will you get in a year?" Mauldin asked him.

"Generally, sixteen," Neulan replied.

Two months later, while selling the agents three more, he indicated he had recently sold or bartered eight other eagles: four in Arizona, two to a gallery owner in Deadwood, South Dakota, and two in Oklahoma, where he expected them to go to two museums. Before his next trip to Arizona, he said, he planned to kill a dozen more.

To publicize the termination of case, James Watt, the controversial secretary of the interior, flew to Sioux Falls, South Dakota, for a press conference. Standing behind a table that held twenty-three frozen eagles, Watt said, "To appear in front of a table filled with the carcasses of our national emblem is a revolting and repulsive thing." Besides bald and golden eagles, the suspects were charged with the death or sale of seventeen other federally protected bird species. Eventually forty-one defendants, including thirty-three Native Americans, were sentenced.

Many of them maintained they had been entrapped, a common lament among targets of undercover operations. "I never did shoot eagles before in my life," Dwight Dion asserted in a late 1994 phone conversation with me. "The agents are the ones who asked me to get them birds and give me a thousand dollars apiece [it was actually less]. When you're having a hard time on the reservation, you make your living the best way you know how." Dion said he sold feathered fans to Mauldin one cold day only because he had run out of propane to heat his home and he was concerned about his three young grandchildren, who were living with him. But due to other evidence of predisposition, Dwight Dion and Asa Primeaux Sr. were unable to successfully assert that they had been entrapped simply because they were so poor they could not resist the opportunity to make some money.

The only two defendants to have their convictions overturned were Lyle Dion and Terry Fool Bull, Asa Primeaux Sr.'s son-in-law, both of whom did successfully claim entrapment. In trial testimony Dwight Dion Sr. contended that in July of 1982, Mauldin "asked my boy, Lyle, if he can go out and get him some birds." Lyle also testified that the agent had asked him to kill eagles for him. "That absolutely did not happen," counters Mauldin, who is now retired. "I never encouraged anyone to break the law." Nonetheless, the U.S. Eighth Circuit Court of Appeals ruled that Lyle Dion and Fool Bull had been tempted to sell single birds by offers of large sums of money near the end of the government undercover operation—a probe that, apparently to prevent the operation's unraveling in other states and to detect buyers of the protected eagle parts, the court felt had gone on too long.

Noting the desolate conditions of the impoverished reservation, the appeals court ruled that "The risk for the government in offering so much money to these individuals over a nearly two-and-one-half year period was that many who would never have shot a protected bird would be enticed into doing so. . . . [T]he longer and more involved the government became in buying protected birds and their parts, the greater the risk became that birds would be unnecessarily killed by individuals who would never have done so in the absence of the government's offers."

The court rejected most of the other defendants' appeals, including Dwight Dion's assertion that the convictions for taking and selling eagles violated his First Amendment right to religious freedom. Fashioning and selling Indian artwork from protected feathers, he declared, was part of his religious culture. The appeals court flatly rejected that argument. The justices agreed with federal prosecutors who contended Dion was killing eagles and hawks solely for commercial gain. Native American leaders had testified that killing eagles, at least for commercial purposes, was contrary to native beliefs and was generally unheard of on the South Dakota reservations. Douglas Long, president of the Native American Church of North

America, also testified that the church "looks with disfavor on the practice of the pawn and sale of religious prayer instruments."

Both a federal court and the federal appeals court agreed, however, that Dion could not be prosecuted for shooting a golden eagle on the reservation, because such hunting was protected by the 1858 treaty that established the Yankton Sioux reservation. Eleven years earlier the same appeals court had upheld the dismissal of charges against a Chippewa for killing a bald eagle because the bird had been taken on the Red Lake Reservation in Minnesota.

But in 1986, in a unanimous opinion written by Justice Thurgood Marshall, the U.S. Supreme Court ruled that Dion and other Native Americans do not have the right to shoot and kill bald eagles as a result of treaties granting them exclusive hunting and fishing rights on reservation lands. The question before the high court: Did the Bald and Golden Eagle Protection Act and the Endangered Species Act abrogate, or annul, those reservation hunting and fishing rights as they pertain to eagles?

The answer to that question, and the court's ruling, revolved around Congressional intent. To divine that, the court focused on the 1962 amendments to the Eagle Protection Act, which extended protection to golden eagles and authorized the secretary of the interior to issue permits to Native Americans for the "taking" of bald and golden eagles for religious purposes.

At that time, large numbers of golden eagles were being slaughtered for religious purposes by the Hopi, Zuni, and Pueblo tribes of the Southwest. Tourists were purchasing the feathers as souvenirs, and bounty hunters in Texas and elsewhere were gunning down golden eagles. "As a result of these activities," a House committee report concluded, "if steps are not taken as contemplated in this legislation, there is grave danger that the golden eagle will completely disappear." Bald eagles were also at risk, since at a distance it is extremely hard to distinguish between immature bald eagles and mature golden eagles.

After the Senate added an amendment allowing the secretary of the interior to authorize permits to kill golden eagles that were preying on livestock and game, the amended, newly christened Bald and Golden Eagle Protection Act became law.

"It seems plain to us," Justice Marshall concluded, ". . . that Congress in 1962 believed that it was abrogating the rights of Indians to take eagles. . . . Congress expressly chose to set in place a regime in which the Secretary of the Interior had control over Indian hunting, rather than one in which

Indian on-reservation hunting was unrestricted. Congress thus considered the special cultural and religious interests of Indians, balanced those needs against the conservation purposes of the statute, and provided a specific, narrow exception that delineated the extent to which Indians would be permitted to hunt the bald and golden eagle."

Overturning the federal appeals court, the Supreme Court ruled the Eagle Protection Act had nullified Dion's treaty right to hunt eagles on his reservation. Once that right was removed, the 1858 Yankton Sioux Treaty also could not shield Dion from the Endangered Species Act. And while the justices did not directly address the question of First Amendment religious rights, Marshall's opinion appeared to put the court firmly on the side of the eagles.

Dwight and Dion Neulan each served a year in Leavenworth. Asa Primeaux served a six-month prison term. Two years ago Neulan, at age sixty-one, suffered a fatal heart attack. Traditional Yankton Sioux, still embarrassed a decade later by the shame the eagle killings cast upon their people and their reservation, told each other that the spirits of the eagles were exacting their just revenge on Neulan for the disrespect he had shown. They believed that was also why Joseph Shields Sr. was dead. That was why Asa Primeaux, who had moved to Ohio, was blind. That was why Dwight Dion had suffered three slight strokes, why he had heart problems, why he was a diabetic with an amputated toe.

And that was why, they believed, last year at age sixty Dwight Dion pleaded guilty in federal court and was sentenced to more than nine years' incarceration for aggravated sexual abuse of a minor. Shortly before his guilty plea, by phone I asked him, "Has anyone from the reservation said the eagles are getting back at you?"

"Not really," he said, "but that's my opinion."

CHAPTER 11

THE CREATOR'S LAW

In an eagle there is all the wisdom of the world; that's why we have an eagle feather at the top of the pole during a yuwipi *ceremony. If you are planning to kill an eagle, the minute you think of that he knows it, knows what you are planning.*
—JOHN (FIRE) LAME DEER, *Lame Deer: Seeker of Visions* BY LAME DEER AND RICHARD ERDOES, 1972

My old war bonnet of eagle feathers would fetch a good price nowadays, but I won't sell it—even when I am broke.
—JOHN (FIRE) LAME DEER, *Lame Deer: Seeker of Visions* BY LAME DEER AND RICHARD ERDOES, 1972

 The eagle cases of Nathan Jim Jr. were not the first to involve a resident of the Warm Springs Reservation. In 1987 Joe Sandberg, a U.S. Fish and Wildlife Service law enforcement agent, paid a California woman five dollars for a barrette adorned with a fluffy: a small white eagle feather.

The woman led him to a non-Indian who claimed there were so many eagles that he was doing the birds a favor by thinning them out—and selling them. This man met Sandberg outside a Denny's restaurant and sold him three golden eagle carcasses for $875 plus $20 for gas. That sale, and the purchase of four golden eagle carcasses and the parts of two bald eagles from a Sheetrock worker in Klamath Falls, Oregon, eventually led Sandberg to the Warm Springs Reservation and Grant Clements. The name was familiar to Sandberg. Years earlier he had stopped at the tribal information center on the edge of the Warm Springs reservation and discovered a number of feathered craft objects for sale. Several, he recalled, had tags indicating they had been made by Clements.

At the time, Sandberg was engaged in his first major eagle investigation.

Originally with the game division of the Oregon State Police, Sandberg joined the USFWS in 1979 as an agent in its Bellevue, Washington, office. Shortly afterward, acting on a tip, he posed as a dealer in Native American arts and crafts and bought a half-dozen bald eagle feathers from a man at a Seattle flea market. That initial purchase evolved into an eighteen-month investigation in which he and other agents bought the bodies or parts of fifty-seven bald eagles.

Search warrants executed when the probe was terminated uncovered forty-three more, including some eagles and scores of feathers that had been stockpiled in Canada. Seventeen of the twenty-three persons charged were Native Americans, including a number who lived on the Lummi reservation near Bellingham, Washington. One of the Native American defendants told Sandberg he had killed thirty eagles that year. Another defendant, a thirty-three-year-old jewelry maker in a Native American store who claimed to have a network of hunters supplying her, matter-of-factly told Sandberg, "I do it [sell eagles and eagle parts] to make a living." Sandberg saw hundreds of eagle feathers at her home and the home of her mother, who told Sandberg she was "laughing all the way to the bank." The daughter, who was charged with selling Sandberg five bald eagles, received a two-year jail sentence; her mother served a six-month term.

One of the non-native defendants appeared to be so disabled that, during court appearances, he required crutches in order to walk. The Idaho man was convicted of selling Sandberg and Nando Mauldin just one immature bald eagle and some raptor feathers. But partly due to his past record, the man received what is believed to be the stiffest sentence ever imposed for dealing in bald eagles: five years in a federal penitentiary.

In dollar value, the worldwide black market in illegal wildlife items has now supplanted arms smuggling; it is second only to illegal drugs. In Sandberg's experience, though, the fields often intertwine. During wildlife probes he has purchased marijuana, machine guns, and rustled cattle and been offered cocaine. Like many USFWS agents, he has bought walrus ivory and dozens of bear gallbladders. In making cases against illegal hunting guides—some of whom have insisted he sign disclaimers verifying he isn't a game warden or law enforcement officer—he has shot black bears, mule deer, elk, desert big horn sheep, and mountain goats. He once was approached about hunting buffalo on federal lands in Utah. But, still stirred by the sight of an eagle, Joe Sandberg draws the line at shooting one or allowing anyone in his presence to kill one. He realizes the number of reported bald eagle shootings is declining and the birds are recovering. He knows golden eagles, whose numbers are not precisely known, are not even protected under the Endangered Species Act.

From his perspective, though, it is a wonder any eagles are still alive. He can, he claims, buy eagle feathers any day he wishes. The demand might have been suppressed by such highly publicized undercover operations as Operation Eagle and another large USFWS sting based in Gallup, New Mexico, in the mid-1980s, but the mania among some Americans and foreign collectors to own authentic Indian artifacts persists. While dyed turkey feathers are now being substituted for eagle feathers on modern reproductions, some buyers insist upon the real thing. Sandberg has heard of rodeo professionals buying eagle feathers to tuck into their hatbands. There are western clubs in Germany whose members dress up in authentic cowboy and Indian gear. To subvert the Bald Eagle Protection Act, which bans the sale but not the possession of eagle artifacts made prior to 1940, documents have been forged to predate reproductions fashioned from eagle feathers. To make what some illegal craftsmen mockingly call "artifakes" appear to be authentic nineteenth-century items, they put eagle feathers in an oven to brown them, soak them in tea or chemicals, or urinate on them to yellow them, and they cure skins the way Native Americans did, by rubbing them with animal brains.

Ten years ago Larry Keeney, another USFWS agent with whom Sandberg worked in Washington State, learned that a Tokyo dealer who supplied Japanese museums with mounted eagles had tendered a standing offer: $500 apiece for as many eagle skins as he could obtain. Secreting a radio transmitter inside a bald eagle skin, Keeney delivered it to a taxidermist who was acting as an intermediary. Eventually it was traced to a Seattle export warehouse. Keeney's eagle, as well as eight other bald and golden eagle skins like it, were hidden inside a fully-mounted black bear and a large elk head, ready to be shipped to Japan.

In May of 1988, after Clements's name again had surfaced, Sandberg drove north toward the Warm Springs reservation. Impersonating a California dealer in native arts and crafts, he was alone. He liked working by himself, particularly for initial contacts. To him, too many cops looked like cops, and it was easier for a duo to get "made"—suspected of being undercover agents. Except for a knife, Sandberg was unarmed. In the past he had been strip-searched, and several times he'd had guns pulled on him; reaching for a revolver, if he had carried one, might not have been wise. His number one defense was his ability to talk his way out of a tight situation. To be good at undercover work, you had to believe your own stories and aliases, and you better keep them straight because you never knew when you would encounter someone years later. There were times, though, when he wearied of the work: the sentences that were often too lenient simply because it was wildlife crime; the lengthy time spent away from his family; the duplicity that was such an integral part of the job. He usually perceived some good in his targets, no matter how corrupt or criminal their background. Some were personable, or they were kind to him, or their children would become so friendly they would call him "uncle." But there were few acts he despised more than the killing of an eagle.

According to Sandberg:

Sandberg arrived at Clements's home shortly before noon. Far removed from the Warm Springs village, Clements lived in a remote area where the high desert meets the ponderosa pines tumbling out of the Cascades foothills. Like Sandberg, Clements was in his mid-forties. But while Sandberg was a tall bear of a man, Clements was five feet seven and weighed about 250 pounds. A descendant of Wasco people from along the Columbia, Clements wore his wispy receding hair in a long ponytail, in contrast to his experience as a very young boy in the Bureau of Indian Affairs boarding school, when his hair was shorn and his clothes replaced, and he was forbidden to speak his native language.

When he was younger, Clements had been an alcoholic and a drug addict, but he claimed that the traditions of Native American culture had rescued him. The eagles warded off the evil that permeated the world, he believed, and because of his ability to craft high-quality feathered goods, the Creator had allowed him to become the caretaker of the birds. The businesses through which he now made his living included cutting Christmas trees and greens in the fall, performing seedling reforestation in the summer, and, Sandberg suspected, illegally selling feathered artifacts.

Arriving without advance notice, Sandberg was invited into Clements's home even though Clements said he was wary of selling eagle feathers to white men. Sandberg gained his confidence by mentioning a supposed mutual friend, a shaman dancer who Sandberg suspected had been an eagle killer. Though he had never met the shaman, Sandberg contended he had bought several eagle items from him. It was an airtight con: the shaman was dead. When Clements, who was caring for two of his four children, mentioned that he and his wife were experiencing marital difficulties, Sandberg commiserated by saying his marriage was also troubled. That wasn't true, at least at the time (since then Sandberg has divorced), but it struck a chord with Clements. That afternoon Clements—who indicated he was seeking other sales outlets because tribal police had forced the tribal information center to halt the sale of protected feathered items—sold Sandberg two fresh frozen golden eagle heads, two dance staffs, and two dance fans decorated with eagle parts and feathers for $450 and a ring worth $100.

Over the course of that year Sandberg visited Clements a number of times. One afternoon that summer he arrived with Kenner Harrington, the USFWS agent who would later transfer Nathan Jim Jr. into federal custody. Despite Sandberg's preference for working alone, he sometimes was accompanied by another agent. It was safer, and it helped to build a stronger case by corroborating future testimony. Harrington's cover: he was a taxidermist interested in obtaining eagle carcasses for mounting.

After Clements pulled Sandberg aside to explain that he wanted to deal only with him, the three discussed big game hunting and examined the contents of the footlocker in Sandberg's van. It was stuffed with cradleboards, dance fans, and the tusks and bacula—the prized penis bones—of walrus. Harrington blew his elk bugle for Clements and touted his taxidermy business.

Back in the house, Clements directed them to his kitchen table, where he had been working on a necklace for Sandberg. Eight bald eagle talons were strung along a leather thong. Stitched into it were the eagle's feet, and in the middle was an eagle carved out of a cross section of elk antler. The necklace wasn't complete, Clements said; he needed another hour to attach parallel rows of brass beads. At his request, Clements's daughter appeared in the kitchen wearing a similar necklace, this one made from eight golden eagle talons.

How much, Harrington wondered, did he want for the necklace? Clements allegedly said that he had been offered $1,000 for it at a fair in Portland, but he would sell it to them for $500.

Clements explained that he had obtained eagle parts from several different suppliers. One, whom he repeatedly referred to as "the Wild Man," previously had brought him eight whole eagles. The more Sandberg heard about the Wild Man, the more he was convinced he was Richard Rowe II. Back in the mid-1970s, while working as an Oregon state trooper out of The Dalles, Sandberg had heard allegations that Rowe, a Cherokee who had ties to the Warm Springs reservation, was killing and selling eagles. Rowe was eventually prosecuted in federal court. Following a mistrial, he was acquitted of selling golden eagle parts after he took over his own legal defense.

Six months later, in November 1975, Rowe was in Albuquerque, New Mexico, boasting about how he had got a handshake from the judge as he sold a merchant an Eagle Dancer costume with fifty-five golden eagle feathers. By prearrangement with the merchant, the entire transaction was overheard via an intercom by a USFWS law enforcement agent. Neither the jury nor the federal appeals court was impressed with Rowe's defense of himself in that case. He was fined $3,000 and sentenced to six months in federal prison.

Rowe had long since been released, and Clements was expecting fifteen more eagles the next time the Wild Man appeared. According to Clements, the man snared the eagles or shot them cleanly and traveled through Canada and the West selling whole birds and their body parts. Clements and the Wild Man, he once explained to Sandberg, were like brothers, had been ever since Clements focused his life on Indian religion and culture and the crafting of feathered objects.

From the kitchen Clements and the two agents moved to his garage where the dried, deteriorated heads of an immature bald eagle, an adult bald eagle, and a golden eagle lay on a workbench. They were useless, Clements complained, because his supplier had let the heads rot.

"How much do you want for them?" Sandberg asked. Clements accepted Sandberg's bid of $10 apiece.

Clements had driven nails into the garage wall on which to hang and dry raptor body parts. Nailed to the wall were the gray-and-black wings of a male American kestrel—a swift, jay-sized falcon. Also hanging there was what Clements referred to as his parts bag: a plastic bag that contained the feet (talons missing) of three golden eagles and one bald eagle.

Clements next asked Harrington about the possibility of inserting glass eyes into the eagle heads he used atop his dance sticks and staffs. No problem if the heads are fresh, Harrington said. To demonstrate, he offered to mount an eagle for Clements the next time the Wild Man brought Clements whole birds. Interested, Clements suggested that Harrington and Sandberg return to pick up some birds as soon they arrived.

Clements then led the agents back into his living room, where he offered to sell a medicine fan made from seven adult golden eagle primary feathers for $325. Momentarily retiring to his bedroom, where two golden eagle heads were mounted on elk antlers on the wall, he returned with a dance staff made from a golden eagle head, foot, and four feathers. Asking price: $400. He also displayed a smaller "lady's fan" made from four adult bald eagle feathers for which he wanted $200.

Sandberg offered him $470 for the dance staff, the lady's dance fan, and the three eagle heads. After declining an eagle bone whistle for another $30, Sandberg paid Clements $460 in cash. He would pay him the additional $10 later.

Clements later denied ever having offered anything to Sandberg for money. Although he ultimately reconciled with his wife, Clements says that at the time he was burdened with legal fees while in the throes of divorce proceedings and a custody battle for his children. "Every time he'd come he'd lay more and more money in front of me, and eventually I was gonna pick up the money and use it for my children," he said. "He claimed to be my brother, my friend, and used my personal tragedies against me."

Later, Clements also contended Sandberg had duped him into thinking he was an intermediary who resold eagle crafts exclusively to Native Americans. The afternoon that Sandberg and Harrington visited him, Clements said he didn't mind selling the items if they were going to the right people—Native Americans. No, Sandberg said, most would be sold to private collectors. Noting he didn't want to go to jail because he had a family to support, Clements supposedly said he could have easily sold the staff Sandberg had bought to an Oriental woman at a county fair in Portland for $1,000, and the talon necklace to a man for $1,000, but he was leery because he didn't know them.

Finally, before they left, Clements took the agents outside to his travel trailer and showed them a number of Native American craft items containing eagle feathers, including the following:

- Two hats with seventy golden eagle feathers and fifty smaller golden eagle feathers
- One medicine fan of adult golden eagle primary feathers, which Clements said his son used for dancing
- Two dance bustles, one each for Clements and his son, with a complete set of adult golden eagle wing and tail feathers
- One wedding bouquet with golden eagle feathers
- One dance ring with three golden eagle feathers
- Clements's dance staff with golden eagle head foot and feathers
- Clements's medicine fan, used for dancing, containing golden eagle feathers

As they drove back to the paved state road that cut through the reservation, the agents calculated in less than two hours that they had seen the parts of at least two dozen eagles.

Sandberg was stunned. Clements appeared to be one of the greatest processors of eagle parts he had ever encountered. Every time he visited Clements, Sandberg saw what appeared to be new dead eagles. Though Clements later denied all of it, in Sandberg's presence—and on the phone— he supposedly claimed to have several suppliers as well as other buyers. Items he had promised Sandberg or shown him, including fresh eagle heads, had already been sold.

Later that August, Clements called Sandberg to say his Canadian supplier had fifteen golden eagles and three eagle-feathered bonnets for sale. But the price would be steep: $600 for each dead bird, $2,500 apiece for two of the bonnets, and $4,000 for a bonnet with double trailers—two rows of feathers running down each side. "That'd be out of my ballpark," said Sandberg, who usually paid no more than $300 per eagle. Subsequently, Clements—echoing some of the South Dakota defendants—explained that he couldn't sell a whole eagle for $350 when he could earn $2,500 by incorporating the various feathers and parts from a whole eagle into different ceremonial items.

The undercover operation was terminated on February 13, 1989, when a dozen people in Oregon, Nevada, and California were arrested or charged. Clements maintains that he had so many eagle feathers and body parts in his home that day because many people "gifted" him with eagle feathers during a Lincoln's Birthday powwow in Warm Springs. He also says he was making several items as March birthday gifts for his son.

Upon his arrest, the following items were seized from Clements's property: five bags of loose eagle feathers, four brown bags containing eagle feathers, five boxes of assorted eagle feathers, a package of eagle feathers, a bundle of eagle feathers, a blue suitcase with eagle feathers, an eagle head, an eagle-headed dance stick, an eagle fan headdress, an eagle feather hat with a beak, two bald eagle feather fans, two eagle claw necklaces, an eagle bone whistle, two eagle feet, two eagle talons, a set of eagle wings, eagle bones, a bone fan, a dance fan, two hawk tails, hawk feet, and a string of hawk feathers.

~~~~⌐ That same morning Sandberg, still operating undercover as a trader, visited the Warm Springs home of Richard Rowe III. Three days earlier, during a visit with the younger Rowe, Sandberg had placed a twenty-dollar down payment on some eagles and body parts. When he pulled up, he noticed a red-and-white Ford pickup truck with a camper shell and an Alberta license plate. Standing at the back of the truck with another man was a powerfully built fifty-year-old wearing an eagle talon necklace around

his thick neck. Though he had never seen him before, Sandberg was certain it was the notorious Richard Rowe II.

"Aren't you a friend of Grant Clements?" Rowe supposedly asked.

After Sandberg said he was, according to the agent Rowe began using the pickup's tailgate to display some of his high-quality, custom-made knives. Clements had shown Sandberg some pictures of the knives carved by the Wild Man; on the blades were the initials "RR." The handle of one knife Rowe was offering for sale was fashioned from the jaw of a grizzly bear. While inspecting the knives, Sandberg noticed eagle fluffies stuck to fresh blood on the tailgate. After Sandberg called attention to Rowe's necklace, Rowe allegedly said he had killed the eagle in Canada and had a picture of himself with the eagle. Later recovered, that photo shows a barrel-chested Rowe, shirtless and wearing a fur hat and another eagle talon necklace. Half smiling, he holds the limp body of a dead golden eagle literally spread-eagled in his outstretched arms.

Sandberg then asked Rowe if he still had the double-trail eagle-feathered bonnet Clements had been offering. Rowe said it was in Canada, but offered to sell it to Sandberg for $2,500.

At that point, Rowe's son came out and ushered Sandberg inside to complete their own transactions. "Dad doesn't want me to sell eagle feathers," Sandberg says the younger Rowe told him. "It's illegal. He's been caught twice; he was set up."

Shortly afterward, after Sandberg had negotiated the sale of several eagle items for $260, other backup agents concerned about Sandberg's safety burst into the crowded home and arrested the younger Rowe.

Outside, although he stated he lived mostly in Alberta, agents say the elder Rowe showed them a Washington driver's license and other ID with a Warm Springs address. At Sandberg's suggestion, agents searching a cooler in the back of Rowe's pickup seized several golden eagle head skins, more than eighty coveted black-and-white tail feathers, two tails, and about two dozen golden eagle wings. Rowe claimed that Canadian officials had granted him a CITES (Convention on International Trade in Endangered Species) permit to bring the eagle body parts across the border, but no such permit was ever granted. He had transported the eagle parts, Rowe told the agents, so that they could be used in Warm Springs burial ceremonies.

Never charged with possession of the eagle parts because their source could not be determined, Rowe eventually pleaded guilty to offering Sandberg the $2,500 bonnet. Prior to his plea, however, he was a fugitive for three years.

Finally, in May of 1993, U.S. District Court Judge William L. Dwyer—the Seattle judge whose landmark spotted owl ruling curtailed timbering throughout parts of the Pacific Northwest—sentenced Rowe to two months in prison. Instead of reporting to prison, however, Rowe fled to Canada. Deputy U.S. Marshal Todd Kupferer tracked him for eleven months before Canadian officials apprehended him and put him on a flight to the United States. He was released to five months home detention after serving three months. Rowe's son, who also pleaded guilty, was sentenced to two months' incarceration, an imprisonment that was extended to six months after he also fled and was recaptured.

Clements, meanwhile, pleaded guilty to one of five felony counts of violating the Migratory Bird Treaty Act. In Portland he appeared before U.S. District Court Judge Owen Panner, a former Warm Springs tribal attorney who twice had represented Clements in civil matters. Clements's sentence: five years' probation and a $1,000 fine, about two-thirds the amount Sandberg allegedly paid Clements in federal funds.

Two evenings before Nathan Jim Jr.'s religious rights appeal was to be heard in federal court in Portland, I spoke with Clements at his home on the Warm Springs reservation. A short man with an enormous gut spilling over the waistband of his fleece shorts, he sat on his couch in a torn undershirt watching the once-brilliant boxer Roberto Duran in a meaningless cable TV fight. Clements was still bitter about Sandberg, a man he had considered a friend. He said he only agreed to take money from Sandberg after his young children begged him because they desperately needed money for food and electricity: "I'd tell him, 'I'll give you this, whatever you want. If you give something back to me, that's fine.'"

"His gift to me was always money," he said with a weak laugh. On a serving table behind Clements lay a beaded fan of golden eagle primary feathers.

"Are you making any more items now?" I asked.

"That I won't tell you," he said, adding, "I still practice my way of life. My way of life is the feather, the bone."

Yet when the conversation turned to Nathan Jim Jr.'s upcoming appeal, Clements echoed the view of wildlife law enforcement agents who believed that a legal, authorized hunt of eagles by Native Americans would be completely unmanageable and unenforceable. "Who distinguishes who's religious?" he wondered. "To be honest, we don't look at Little Eight-Ball [Jim's father] or Junior as being that kind of person. It's hard for us to say what Junior is doing is right. Who said he was a medicine man? Who gave him the right to go out and hunt birds?

"I can't say what he's doing is wrong, but I don't regard him as a medicine man. I don't even look at myself as being worthy of killing a bird. That's why I don't do it."

The first witness called by Nathan Jim Jr.'s attorney in federal court in Portland was Wilson Wewa Jr., a religious leader in the Washaat longhouse in Warm Springs and program coordinator of the reservation's senior center. A tall, dignified thirty-eight-year-old Paiute, Wewa wore his pigtails wrapped in red wool; a beaded bald eagle medallion adorned his chest. "Twenty years or more we used to have lots of eagles on the reservation in the Mutton Mountains and along the southern border in the Metolius River Canyon," he said on cross-examination by Joseph Perella, a U.S. Department of Justice wildlife attorney. "We used to have a lot of eagles wintering there, but today not that many eagles come back to our reservation. To me, that's sad." Wewa blamed commercial poachers. He said that when he was ten years old, he and his father were observing a golden eagle nest when they noticed a man using a cable attached to a winch on his pickup truck to lower himself over the edge of a cliff hundreds of feet above the Deschutes River in order to pilfer the nest's two young birds. That man, Wewa recalled, was Richard Rowe II. After Wewa's father scared Rowe off, he lectured his son: "Don't ever take eagles. They'll take care of you."

But decades after that incident and five years after the arrest of Clements and Rowe, Wewa believed a few people from Warm Springs were still killing eagles—for profit, not for religion. In the spring, as many as 130 bald eagles pause briefly during their northern migration to feed on the winter die-off of kokanee salmon along the Metolius arm of Lake Billy Chinook. The year before Wewa testified, during the springtime breeding season, someone cut down a ponderosa pine that held one of the reservation's three bald eagle nests. The crime was never solved. With a pair of eagles back in the area the following year, it is unclear if any birds were killed in the incident, but authorities suspect the tree was felled in order to retrieve an adult that had been shot in the nest. Three more bald eagle nests are located close to the reservation, and the deep basalt canyons of the Crooked and Deschutes rivers also harbor one of the country's densest concentrations of golden eagle breeding pairs. Yet on the reservation itself, there was only one such nest; after a decade of inactivity, two years ago the nest produced a young eagle, but then its father died, apparently due to a collision.

In the Washaat longhouse, from the time he was fourteen years old Wilson Wewa was a student of tribal elders Edna and Andrew David—the same Andrew David from whom Nathan Jim Jr. professed to have learned the ritual of killing eagles. But never, Wewa said, did he and Andrew David go out to kill eagles. In speaking with elders, Wewa had never heard of any religious ceremony that required the hunting, killing, or sacrificing of an eagle. Never had he heard of a Washaat or Feather religion doctrine stipulating that the power of a feather depended on the eagle having been hunted and killed by a Native American, or that prohibited the use of feathers received from the government. Never had he heard of anyone on the reservation being designated an eagle catcher.

Wilson Wewa believed it was wrong for Native Americans, the stewards of the land and all creation, to harm even one eagle. "When a person takes the number of eagles in this case, to me that's wanton destruction," he testified. "It's against the principles of the Creator." It was, he said, a violation of the same law that governed the taking of their foods—of the salmon that, before a Maginot line of hydroelectric dams blocked their passage, surged up the Columbia River and its tributaries; of the mule deer they took care never to overhunt; of the bitterroot and biscuitroot, of the huckleberry and chokecherries that they gathered and then held festivals of thanksgiving before consuming. "It is the same law, the Creator's law—many times people call it the unwritten law—which tells us we have to take care of these things. If we abuse what the Creator has given us, our resources will be lost."

As he was testifying, Wewa noticed that Nathan Jim Jr. refused to look at him. With his head bowed over the defense table and his eyes closed, Jim was alternately clenching and opening his fists. Apparently engaged in prayer, throughout the day Jim would sit up periodically and rapidly waved a golden eagle feather in his right hand before his forehead and shoulder.

When Nathan Jim Jr. was called to the witness stand by his attorney, he outlined his dilemma: "The elders that ask me these things, it's really hard on me as an individual because I have to deal with a government that tells me I have to have permission, but I end up breaking this government's laws for my religious rights as a human being. I did this for my love of elders and all creation, and they ask me, and I can't tell my elders no."

During cross-examination, Assistant U.S. Attorney Robert Ross attempted to assail Jim's credibility by pointing out that the eagle body parts he had received from the National Eagle Repository were delivered more quickly than Jim had claimed. As proof, Ross presented him with certified mail receipts signed by him, his father, and his sister.

"I believe in the Creator's way," Jim responded. "Not with a piece of paper. He didn't make that paper. Man made paper."

"Do you believe that the Creator requires you to tell the truth?"

"Depends if he calls me."

"Are you going to tell the truth today?" an exasperated Ross asked.

"Ummm . . . yes," Jim finally said. "I'm trying to get something accomplished here for all creation. Somehow stop you guys from destruction."

He said he had prayed over the feathers and eagle body parts he did receive from the USFWS. Then he had used them for ceremonies and for his personal dance regalia, and had given some away.

Jim told Ross that eighteen elders had passed away during a two-year period, and before they died, all of them, reluctant to petition the federal government and to wait, had asked him for eagle feathers. Pressed for names, he first offered that of Andrew David, who had passed away prior to 1992. He also named three current elders, including sixty-seven-year-old Prosanna Williams, who would follow him to the witness stand. Asked later by Ross if she had ever requested Nathan Jim to kill an eagle for her, she replied, "I have never asked Nathan, but he has given me two or three feathers as a gift, and I have seen him give feathers to other people who have no feathers."

Though it is doubtful the director of the USFWS would have granted it, Ross asked Jim why he had never applied for a permit to "take" an eagle. "I'm in a super bind all the time," Jim said. "I carry out my . . . our ways and try to deal with your destructional [*sic*] ways. You people kill how many millions a year? How many percentage of those eagles are hunted for sport, by sheep ranchers, by electrocution? What are *your* ceremonies?"

"Do the elders ask you to kill eagles or just for feathers?" Ross asked.

"They ask me for clean birds. They know I have their spirit when I kill them."

"Is there a ceremony to shoot an eagle?"

"Shooting an eagle *is* a ceremony," Jim said, gesturing sternly toward Ross with the long, thin fingers of his right hand. "I ask the Creator for respect, for knowledge, and how to get the bird. I have to hold the spirit of the eagle so I take care of it for burials, for healing ceremonies, whatever it is for."

"Did you tell Agent Harrington that the reason you killed eagles is because it took too long to get them from the government?"

"We always had rights before you guys came here," Jim replied. "We always had the right to do it. We didn't need a piece of paper. It's the Creator's way. We ask him, we give thanks to everything."

At the end of Jim's testimony, Chief U.S. District Court Judge James A. Redden asked him, "How many eagles is it necessary for you to take, or obtain, in any given year?"

"There's a limit . . ." Jim replied. "I can't go over twelve."

"Where's that limit from?" the judge asked.

"The Creator."

After several other Native American witnesses testified, Celeste Whitewolf, Jim's attorney, called to the stand several biologists who had devoted their careers to the comeback of the bald eagle. She asked them to discuss, at least hypothetically, the harvesting of the birds. Among those with whom she engaged in an increasingly surreal dialogue was Frank Isaacs, an Oregon State University researcher who supervises the annual survey of the state's 230 bald eagle nests.

"If there were a limited hunt of eagles, limited to Indian people, how would that affect the population?" she asked Isaacs.

"I think the hunting of adults would be difficult, since each pair that was impacted would impact the recovery process of the species," said Isaac, who estimates there once were six hundred bald eagle pairs in the state. "I don't know what to say about golden eagles because not enough is known about their numbers." If one member of a nesting pair of bald eagles were taken, he estimated it would take one to three years for them to find a new mate.

"If a limited take were authorized for Indian people, would there be a recommendation as to the time of year?" Whitewolf wondered.

Isaacs suggested that October, after the young had fledged, might be the best time, since that would give a widowed bird more time to find a mate. But he clearly found the concept absurd. "It wouldn't be appropriate," he said, "if you're interested in having them recover."

⟿ In March 1995, U.S. District Judge James Redden ruled against Nathan Jim Jr. The judge concluded that Jim had possessed the eagles for religious purposes, but he said the government had a compelling interest in prohibiting Native Americans from killing or possessing eagles. Redden also ruled that the eagle repository's system for disbursing eagles and feathers, while imperfect, was the least restrictive method possible. The Native Americans' growing demand for eagle feathers, not the government's procedure, had caused the delays.

Two weeks after Redden's ruling, Jim shot himself to death at his home on the Warm Springs Reservation. His father, Nathan Jim Sr., believed that the ruling had depressed his son. But others suggested that a dispute with his wife and the suicide of another young Warm Springs man a week earlier had compelled Nathan Jim Jr. to end his life. He was thirty-three years old. Hearing that there were no eagle feathers available for Jim's burial, Robert Ross, the assistant U.S. attorney who prosecuted Jim's case, obtained an emergency package of immature golden eagle feathers from the repository in Ashland. He drove them across the Cascades to Warm Springs, but arrived too late: the casket of Jim, who was hastily dressed with eagle feathers contributed by his attorney and other reservation members, had already been closed. Wilson Wewa Jr. told Ross he would use the feathers later that week. At the Tenino Cemetery in Warm Springs, there would be yet another sunrise funeral.

CHAPTER 12

"DAMN GOVERNMENT CROWS"

I don't give a goddamn what kind of birds they are. I shoot every one I see.
—ERNIE MOORE, WYOMING WOOL GROWERS ASSOCIATION OFFICIAL,
PUBLICLY DECLARING IN 1962 THAT HE DOESN'T DIFFERENTIATE
BETWEEN BALD AND GOLDEN EAGLES

 Shoot, shovel, and shut up." Doug McKenna heard it wherever he went: Utah, Colorado, Wyoming. It was the mantra of western sheep ranchers, their way of dealing with predators—coyotes, mountain lions, black bears, and even eagles, which some ranchers referred to as "those damn government crows." Don't tell your best friend. Don't confide in your wife; you don't want her to have something on you if she ever divorces you. And, the wool growers who schooled the undercover agent in illegal predator control might have added, make sure you pay your help.

In April 1989, Doug McKenna, a U.S. Fish and Wildlife Service law enforcement agent based in Salt Lake City, received a call from Dan Barnhurst, an investigator with the Utah State Division of Wildlife Resources. A Mexican-American sheepherder, angry that a rancher had not paid him, had led state officials to the carcasses of three dead eagles. They had been poisoned, the herder claimed, by the rancher, who had laced sheep carcasses with poison to kill coyotes. Two days later, speaking to McKenna, Barnhurst, and another Utah officer, the herder claimed that between November 1987 and April 1988 he had found at least ten dead eagles—all of them near carcasses that had been poisoned by his boss.

Leaving the herder behind in Vernal, Utah, the three officers spent the remainder of the day scouring the Book Cliffs, a remote expanse of weathered, bleached sandstone and shale benches rent by yawning canyons near the Utah-Colorado state line. Few humans venture here; aside from an occasional oil well or oil company track heading off into the outback, there is little sign of mankind. Each year wool growers from northwestern Colorado winter their sheep amidst the sagebrush, then shear them before driving them back across the state line and up into their summer ranges in Colorado. After retrieving the three eagle carcasses the herder had earlier identified—they were desiccated skeletons with feathers on their heads—the trio spent hours digging through the talus at the base of crumbling ledges, searching for more eagles.

As they were leaving Tabyago Canyon, though, they noticed a pickup truck with a horse trailer approaching: the rancher was driving, accompanied by two of his herders and a friend. For several hours the Colorado rancher, who was in his early fifties, denied the allegations. After McKenna showed him the three eagle carcasses, though, tears welled up in his eyes. He admitted he had found the eagles near a sheep carcass he had laced, the previous winter, with Temik, a lethal insecticide. It scared him so badly, he said, that he had stopped using it. Now, he conceded, he was using strychnine. He had no choice, he said; he had to eliminate coyotes in the vicinity of his sheep. At sundown he led the officers to the top of a mesa, to several small pieces of decomposing, strychnine-laced sheep meat that he recently had secreted under sagebrush, and gestured to another point a mile away, where more could be found. He disavowed, though, killing any more eagles.

Several days later, returning to the Book Cliffs, the herder led Barnhurst to another poisoned sheep carcass; within forty yards of it lay the remains of the rancher's dog and those of a fourth eagle. They also found the carcasses of a wild horse and a mule deer which, the herder claimed, the rancher had shot and packed with thallium and Temik. After dark, underneath a ledge where the wool grower supposedly told his herder he had buried two more eagles, Barnhurst's flashlight illuminated two eagle feathers and the parts of at least one other eagle, scattered throughout a wood rat's nest.

Nearly thirty-one, Doug McKenna did not look like a typical federal agent. Solidly built, nearly six feet tall, he drove a Harley-Davidson motorcycle, wore a beard, kept his brown hair long, and—to win the trust of sheep ranchers—soon would be wearing a diamond stud earring in his left earlobe. It all gave him the wild, slightly crazed look he believed appealed to his targets. Despite his blond Irish-American father's surname, McKenna owed his appearance to his mother, whose maiden name was Harriet Koutrelakos, a former teacher who was now the mayor of Helena, Montana.

"You look like the Greek priest who married your mother and me," his father, a civil engineer, often told him. One of three children raised in Lolo, Montana, a small town just west of the continental divide, McKenna as a youth trapped bobcats and lynx, fly-fished Lolo Creek, hunted elk and moose with his father, and won prizes at the county fair for the sheep he raised.

On his eighteenth birthday McKenna began fighting fires for the U.S. Forest Service. Until then he had envisioned a life working in a pulp mill or owning a logging truck, but that fall he entered the University of Montana after being informed he had to attend college in order to continue a career as a firefighter. After working as an elite smoke jumper during the summers, he graduated with a degree in wildlife management and was immediately hired as a Montana fish and game warden. His district encompassed the Blackfoot River, the locale of Norman Maclean's classic, *A River Runs Through It*. After assisting federal agents in several undercover operations, including probes of illegally traded live falcons and the slayings of trophy elk, deer, and sheep within Yellowstone National Park, McKenna joined the U.S. Fish and Wildlife Service in Denver in 1987. He had been stationed in the service's two-agent Salt Lake City office for a year when the poisoned eagles were found in the Book Cliffs.

As part of the rancher's plea agreement with federal prosecutors, early the following year the rancher agreed to talk with McKenna, Barnhurst, and another Utah wildlife officer. Each year, he estimated, wool growers along the Utah-Colorado border poisoned and killed a 100 to 150 eagles, primarily during the thirty days before and after the traditional April 20 lambing. He knew of a communal pit in Colorado where three sheep-ranching families had buried as many as 100 eagles with a bulldozer (McKenna later located the garbage pit, but could find no avian remains). Since the sheep-herders believed the coyotes stalked both their sheep and herds of wild animals, they killed deer, antelope, and elk on both public and private lands and laced them with poison. Sheep that died also became poisoned bait. The rancher said that he had bought a thirty-pound case of Temik, for $150, from some sheep ranchers who had purchased ten cases. Another rancher he knew obtained it from a farm supply store in Texas. The insecticide, also known as aldicarb, is legally used to control nematodes in such crops as cotton, potatoes, and sugar beets. It was so lethal, the rancher said, that some eagles were found dead atop the tainted carcasses from which they had eaten. He also claimed that Mexican sheepherders employed by another rancher were smuggling across the border sodium monofluoracetate, or Compound 1080. Banned by the Environmental Protection Agency in 1972, it was highly lethal: a drop smaller than a pinhead could kill a coyote, and it was equally effective in wiping out prairie dogs and ground squirrels. The compound was also partly responsible for the demise of the black-footed ferret, the California condor, and the red wolf.

The rancher agreed to report any eagle killings he learned of that spring; the indiscriminate poisonings, he said, were getting out of hand.

Less than two months later Barnhurst again phoned McKenna: While horseback riding and camping with his son on federal lands in the canyons that empty into the White River near the Utah-Colorado border, a man reported that two of his dogs had suffered violent convulsions, diarrhea, and vomiting. The veterinarian he consulted suspected the dogs had been poisoned, a suspicion their owner shared, since he had noticed a dead eagle along the bank of the White River and his dogs had sniffed around the scattered remains of a deer carcass.

The complainant had returned to the area with Barnhurst. They found the deer's meager remains—and five dead eagles. The first, a golden eagle, was at the mouth of Hells Hole Canyon, an aptly named declivity of high sandstone cliffs and washed-out arroyos that feeds into the White River. The other four, two bald and two golden eagles, were farther upstream, along the water's edge in a 400-yard stretch at the mouth of Weaver Canyon. Many sheep were grazing at the bottom of both canyons and on the slopes in-between—sheep that belonged, Barnhurst determined after checking Bureau of Land Management grazing allotment records, to rancher Nick Theos, of Meeker, Colorado. Theos was the Rio Blanco Country Republican Committee chairman, a former Colorado state representative, and a past president of the Colorado Wool Growers Association.

Five days later, McKenna and Barnhurst scoured Theos's grazing lease in all-terrain vehicles. Purely by chance, in a Weaver Canyon wash McKenna rode over the front half of a deer carcass. Someone had slit its throat, and made incisions between the front shoulders and rib cage, and into the shoulder muscles and back straps. Each incision was bluish-green: poison. Bite marks indicated that birds had eaten some of the meat. The following day, Barnhurst and McKenna took turns hovering along the edge of the river and its side canyons in a helicopter piloted by a Vietnam veteran who grew more outraged each time he dropped down to allow one of the officers to pick up another dead eagle. A mile east of Weaver Canyon, five bald eagles were spread-eagled underneath cottonwood perches; another golden eagle had died a mile and a half up Hells Hole. That same day at a sheep camp on Weaver Ridge, McKenna, posing as a trapper, spoke with two Hispanics who said they worked for Theos. One of them, a sheepherder, mentioned that he had noticed many coyotes, but had seen just a few eagles. At least a dozen of them, McKenna knew—eight bald and four golden eagles—recently had died.

On April 2, 1990, Doug McKenna alerted the U.S. Fish and Wildlife Service's National Wildlife Health Research Center in Madison, Wisconsin, that he was shipping five frozen eagles to be necropsied. He explained that the eagles had been found near the water, described the color of the deer carcass meat, and suggested that Temik or Compound 1080 might have been the culprit.

Eight days later the regional director of law enforcement in Denver, Terry Grosz, called the Madison lab to say that McKenna was sending more birds for analysis. Nancy Thomas, a veterinarian and wildlife pathologist who has necropsied as many as five hundred eagles a year, then called Grosz back for more information. Grosz told her that speed and confidentiality were high priorities because he did not want to jeopardize an agent (McKenna) who was working undercover. In addition to Temik or Compound 1080, Grosz indicated thallium could be a possibility since McKenna had learned that all three poisons had been cached in the area. Some previous eagle poisonings there also had involved strychnine. The eagles did not seem to be dying as fast as they normally would from Temik, Grosz noted, and the birds were gravitating toward water, as one would expect with a rodenticide, such as thallium sulfate, which had been banned in the U.S. as a predator control, and for most other purposes, in 1967. A fan of author Patricia Cornwall's medical-examiner mysteries, Nancy Thomas believed she had enough information to initiate her inquiry.

Using a scalpel, she first skinned the partially frozen heads. Peeling a flap from around the neck back over the closed eyes of each bird, with a small hand-held oscillating autopsy saw she cut a triangular area out of the back of each skull in order to remove the brains. The new generation of pesticides, the organophosphorus and carbamate compounds that have replaced banned organochlorines, have a profound immediate impact on the brain: depressing the activity of cholinesterases, the enzymes that regulate neurological system activity. A bird or other organism can die immediately, its beak still embedded in the tainted meat or, as McKenna has since seen in Utah, with its head and neck stretched grotesquely over its back. Available, with the proper applicator's license, at most farm supply stores, Temik and its like were creating what U.S. Fish and Wildlife Service law enforcement officials referred to as rings of death. On a New Mexico ranch the year before, investigators discovered a coyote that had been poisoned by meat bait laced with Furadan, a corn and alfalfa insecticide. Near the coyote was a dead golden eagle that had eaten the coyote; near the eagle lay magpies that had fed on the eagle; beyond them lay a golden eagle that had eaten a magpie. Within 250 yards of the coyote, another four golden eagles and a bald eagle had died. The previous September, 30 miles east of Meeker on a sheep-grazing allotment in the White River National Forest, Colorado game wardens found five poisoned black bears, including two cubs, three golden eagles, and a coyote within 150 yards of lamb carcasses permeated with aldicarb.

Although she did not believe aldicarb was a likely suspect, Dr. Thomas sent the brains to the research center's chemistry laboratory, where the tissue would be slurried and examined with an ultraviolet spectrophotometer to gauge the enzyme activity. By the time she began her first necropsy on April 11, the cholinesterase assays had been completed: normal.

Wearing latex gloves, the slight, wiry brunette laid the thawed bald eagle down on its back on a stainless-steel human autopsy table customized for smaller animals with a raised insert. Beside her lay the tools of her trade, all of which she had just sharpened: a kitchen knife, three scalpels, two forceps, three blunt- and sharp-pointed scissors, poultry shears, wire cutters, and drop-forged sheet metal shears, the only implement, in her view, capable of cutting bald eagle bones, which were much heavier and sturdier than golden eagle bones. Cutting through a bald eagle bone felt to her almost as if she were cutting through a tree.

First, she conducted a gross exterior examination. The bird appeared emaciated, an impression buttressed when she sliced down from the chin to the vent with her kitchen knife and, with small strokes of her scalpel, pulled away the skin to examine the yellow subcutaneous fat underneath. There was not much of it. After separating the esophagus with a quick snip of her scissors, she sheared open the chest cavity and, beginning with the heart, started removing, examining, and slicing all the internal organs into half-inch strips on a plastic cutting board. She noticed a lot of bile and staining of the liver and other internal organs; the gallbladder was engorged with bile, and the gastrointestinal tract was filled with green fluid. Along with emaciation, these were all signs she would have expected for poisoning from lead or some other heavy metal.

She noticed something different, though, from the many eagles that were once poisoned by lead bird shot: the kidneys had significantly more gout, or mineral deposits, caused by renal damage—a symptom of thallium poisoning. The other eagles she necropsied that day, and those she analyzed after receiving another shipment from McKenna, were similiar. Assays for lead in the birds' livers were normal. Not so for the kidneys.

The chemistry lab staff mixed the kidney tissue with nitric acid, microwaved the mixture into a solution, and aspirated it through an acetylene flame while an atomic absorption spectrophotometer measured its ability to aborb a beam of light. The results: the kidneys of the first bald eagle examined by Thomas contained 19 parts per million of thallium. Of the dozen birds she eventually necropsied, she was unable to determine the cause of death for one. With thallium levels ranging from 16.8 parts per million to 85.9 parts per million, the other seven bald eagles and all four golden eagles had perished of thallium poisoning.

Slightly altering his mother's maiden name, Doug McKenna quickly transformed himself into Nick Koutralakos, a contract trapper—the dated term for the government or private predator-control specialists who today rely more on rifles and poison than on traps. His Greek alias, he knew, couldn't hurt; like his mother's ancestors, many of the most prominent sheep-ranching families in the area were descendants of Greeks who immigrated at the turn of the century to work in eastern Utah coal mines, then took advantage of cheap land and federal leases to graze sheep. Among the first ranchers McKenna contacted was Theos, whom he met in mid-April on the rancher's lambing grounds fifteen miles east of Rangely, Colorado. According to McKenna, Theos allegedly said that the optimum time to use poisoned meat bait for coyotes was during the winter and early spring, before and after sheep are moved into an area. In warm weather, he said, the meat would rot too fast, the poison would leach out of the meat too quickly, and coyotes would be uninterested.

Another rancher admitted secreting two golden eagles he had inadvertently poisoned the previous year in a gopher hole. A third rancher asserted that both state and federal trappers were using poisoned bait on public grazing lands. One asked McKenna to trap inside the Dinosaur National Monument, which the wool growers believed was a coyote breeding ground. McKenna himself purchased an unidentified poison, believed to be a highly concentrated insecticide, from a Meeker feed store whose clerk confided that sheepmen were purchasing it in large quantities. McKenna, who also discovered a dead bald eagle on one grazing lease, was struck by the fact that, for these ranchers and sheepherders, poisoning seemed to be synonymous with predator control.

Several months before the dozen dead eagles were found along the White River, the U.S. Fish and Wildlife Service's regional office in Denver received an intriguing call from a student at the University of Wyoming in Laramie. Nearly thirty-four, Rex Shaddox had been a government trapper in the Texas Hill Country. At the university in Laramie, this father of three daughters was training to earn pesticide-application certification, and also was preparing to work in a research project supervised by the University of Wyoming and the Wyoming Department of Agriculture. The experiment involved placing inflatable rubber collars containing otherwise-banned Compound 1080 around the necks of sheep to kill marauding coyotes. The teacher of the training seminars and manager of the collar program was Randy Graham, the Wyoming Department of Agriculture's predator, or animal damage control, consultant. Shaddox said that, after a class one day, Graham started talking about all the dead bald and golden eagles his state employees were finding on Wyoming ranches. One employee, Graham said, had seen a 55-gallon drum full of eagles. Graham's supposed response—instructing one of the employees to warn the ranchers to be careful about how they got rid of eagles—irritated Shaddox. The Texas native believed it was one thing for a rancher to protect his property, but unquestionably improper for a state employee whose responsibilities included overseeing proper pesticide usage to condone eagle killings.

At a meeting with three FWS agents in a Laramie motel, Shaddox received $500 for the information he had supplied, and agreed to become a CPI, or paid cooperating private individual. Shaddox told them that: while he was installing the experimental Compound 1080 collars on sheep, ranchers repeatedly inquired about what had happened to all the Compound 1080 the state had collected after its use was prohibited in 1972. When Shaddox asked Graham about it, the state consultant acknowledged that Wyoming officials had secretly stockpiled Compound 1080 and other banned poisons that had been turned in to them. The officials had destroyed records and switched locks to a safe in Graham's office at the state Department of Agriculture Weights and Measures Laboratory building in Cheyenne. Not even the EPA, Graham claimed, knew the poison still existed. The laboratory director said that he could remove some of the Compound 1080 from the safe and, by switching labels and destroying other materials, make it appear that the 1080 had been properly discarded.

On May 19, 1990, after Shaddox told Graham he knew of a Wyoming rancher who wanted to buy Compound 1080 to poison coyotes and other predators, Graham escorted him to the lab building, a single-story brown cinder-block building on East Fifth Street in Cheyenne. Before giving Shaddox an eight-ounce can of 1080 and 150 strychnine capsules, he removed the 1080 label. He also asked Shaddox to test the market for 1080 among ranchers; Shaddox agreed to pay him half of whatever he was paid.

For more than half a year Shaddox worked under the supervision of U.S. Fish and Wildlife Service special agent Bob Prieksat, who simultaneously was involved in another investigation into misused pesticides, which resulted in the conviction of three Wyoming sheep ranchers for violating the Bald Eagle Protection Act and federal pesticide laws.

That fall, having decided to merge McKenna's Utah-Colorado investigation with the Wyoming probe Shaddox had initiated, the FWS moved McKenna to Laramie, Wyoming. Together, Rex Shaddox and "Nick Koutralakos" established a phony business called Wyoming Predator Control Service. Shaddox, a lanky man with long brown hair, a drooping mustache, and a nose tip bent in a childhood accident, inserted a diamond earring and teamed up with McKenna, whom he introduced as his divorced brother-in-law. Their business cards, which featured a helicopter, read, "PRIVATE PREDATOR CONTROL CONSULTANTS: THE PRIVATE APPROACH," a powerful attraction, they felt, to private ranchers and county predator boards in a state where ranchers prided themselves on their independence, who felt that the Department of Agriculture's Animal Damage Control trappers, hamstrung by federal regulations, were not doing enough to check coyotes and other predators. McKenna, who was called "Nick the Greek" by some ranchers, and Shaddox offered themselves as a full-service predator-control operation whose methods included calling, trapping, snares, M-44 cyanide canisters, and aerial hunting. Their rates: $1,500 a month salary and $500 a month for vehicle use, or $100 a day for their services and vehicle use.

According to government affidavits, late that October Shaddox—with McKenna, at Graham's request, waiting outside the state lab—paid Randy Graham his $300 share for the can of Compound 1080 Graham had given him in May. Graham gave Shaddox a can of 1080 from one of his desk drawers, then dialed the combination to a green safe in the lab's garage, removed another can of the banned poison, and scratched off the manufacturer's serial number with his pocketknife before handing the can to Shaddox.

Six weeks later he led Shaddox and McKenna to a pair of gray safes in the lab's garage. Reading a lock combination from a small appointment book he regularly carried in his front shirt pocket—he confided he had gotten a local locksmith to change the combinations so the EPA could not inspect the safes' contents—he opened one safe, removed a can of strychnine powder and some strychnine capsules, and put them into an ammunition box for his clients. The safe also contained a can of larvacide and a can of calcium cyanide, both, Graham explained, useful in killing prairie dogs. Again consulting his appointment book, Graham dialed the combination to the green safe, which was nearby, and removed two more cans of Compound 1080. There appeared to be about 130 cans of it in the safe, in addition to 100 one-ounce cans of strychnine, which Graham said was used to kill skunks. Graham removed the label from one of the cans of Compound 1080 and scratched the serial number off the other, then put the two cans into an ammunition box along with two cans of cyanide. In return, Shaddox paid Graham $700.

Graham was a small man in his thirties who often dressed in black. Above his desk was a plaque with a red circle and slash superimposed over a black-footed ferret, an endangered animal. The legend underneath read, "Pesticide Coordinator." McKenna and Shaddox were unnerved by what they perceived to be Graham's cavalier, perverse attitude toward poisons. According to them, he collected old, unknown poisons and test tubes of strychnine he found in nineteenth-century doctors' bags. There was a Gerber baby food jar filled with DDT in his top desk drawer. Graham would open containers of poison and urge them to smell it. "Several times both of us," says Shaddox, "went home feeling very strange and didn't know if it was from nerves or poison." They sometimes felt nauseated, and McKenna endured a throbbing headache for three days after Graham, he says, insisted they taste of pinch of strychnine. Graham also allegedly told the duo that when he incinerated the used Compound 1080 collars returned by ranchers—in violation of federal hazardous waste disposal regulations—he used copper tubing and a can to collect the resulting sludge, which still contained substantial amounts of Compound 1080.

Graham sold McKenna and Shaddox more sodium cyanide, strychnine, and Compound 1080 —once requesting $850 for eight items. He gave McKenna 200 sodium cyanide capsules, including one box marked "not in inventory," even though McKenna was not licensed to rig up the M-44 sodium cyanide coyote-getters. After Shaddox called Graham to say a rancher wanted 300 cube-sized drop baits, Graham instructed him to melt lard, lace it with poison, and let it cool in ice cube trays.

Two days later Graham said by phone that he was experimenting with drop baits containing Compound 1080. At the dose he was using, he told Shaddox, it would take animals that ate it several hours to die—enough time to allow them to distance themselves from the incriminating bait. Several days later, at the state lab, Graham handed McKenna a bag from a refrigerator containing about 320 lard–bacon fat–paraffin drop baits, for which McKenna two days later paid him $150 in cash. Barred from distributing the poison to the rancher, who was never charged, McKenna and Shaddox made 320 harmless duplicates laced with syrup of ipecac, which would cause an animal to vomit.

By the summer of 1991, Graham was suggesting that he, McKenna, and Shaddox could finance million-dollar retirement funds with the Compound 1080. On July 15, 1991, he discussed the possibilities with them. "Now, with seventy pounds and you got 454 grams to a pound, and there's a thousand milligrams to a—to a gram . . . and, ah, if you make 'em—divide that by four . . . or four milligram drop baits, you have $7.9 million dollars." Recalculating at a dollar per drop bait, Graham estimated they could actually generate $5.9 million from 5.9 million drop baits of Compound 1080. If they bundled them in 500-unit lots, Graham estimated they would need 15,000 customers.

"Fifteen thousand?" McKenna said.

Above the laughter, Graham said, "Hey, I did tell ya, it's gonna be simple." He said he could imagine them going door-to-door peddling the poison. "Well, the thing of it is," Graham continued, "is that, ah, I bet I could do it in six months. See, if you got in with the right people, and this is—this is unofficial . . . I think that they would probably be willing to work some deals with ya."

"Who do you think would do that, can I ask?" wondered McKenna. Graham replied that northern Wyoming ranchers with whom McKenna was dealing would probably know other interested ranchers in Montana. "Hell," Graham added, "those guys down in Colorado, if they got a chance, they'd do it . . . and there's guys over in southern Idaho."

Graham, who had previously warned them to avoid the two U.S. Fish and Wildlife Service special agents in the state, whom he accurately described, said that as long as they avoided killing eagles, FWS would not be interested in what they were doing. "The only people that you have to worry about other than that is, um, EPA."

"Well, that's who I'd be worried about," McKenna interjected.

"Shit, you know," assured Graham, "they only got one inspector in Wyoming."

While McKenna's secretary was typing his investigation notes one day, she recommended he read, *Slaughter the Animals, Poison the Earth,* a 1971 exploration of the ranching community's mania for exterminating coyotes and other predators by Jack Olsen, a Colorado writer. When McKenna read the book, the sense of déjà vu overwhelmed him: the FWS was pursuing some of the same sheep ranchers and families that Olsen had profiled two decades earlier. Olsen, once a staff writer for the *Rocky Mountain News* in Denver, had also reported in the spring of 1975 that more than a dozen bald and golden eagles had been found poisoned by thallium in northwestern Colorado.

History was repeating itself in Wyoming as well. In May 1971 more than fifty golden and bald eagles were found dead of thallium poisoning on the Casper-area property of third-generation Wyoming rancher Van Irvine, a former president of the Wyoming Stockgrowers Association. The rancher ultimately pleaded nolo contendere to state charges of killing twenty-nine eagles; he was fined $679, an average of $23.41 per eagle.

By late August 1971 environmental protesters had draped black cloth over the concrete eagles perched atop the chimney of Herman Werner's home in Casper, Wyoming. One of the state's most powerful sheep ranchers and land barons, Werner was one of thirteen men charged in the aerial killing of more than 550 bald and golden eagles the previous fall and winter. James O. Vogan, a Utah helicopter pilot, had testified before a stunned U.S. Senate subcommittee that he had flown more than twenty hunters over thirteen ranches in Colorado and Wyoming. Armed with shotguns, they had blasted eagles out of the air and their perch trees. Werner, he stated, had paid several of the gunmen $15,000—$35 for each dead eagle and $50 for each slain coyote. Contending he had only directed coyotes to be killed,

Werner pleaded not guilty to federal charges of killing 363 golden and three bald eagles. (He died before his case was adjudicated.)

During the mid-1970s in the Texas Hill Country, scores of eagles were shot from helicopters at the behest of sheep ranchers; some of those who fired upon the raptors were trappers with the federal Animal Damage Control, then an arm of the Fish and Wildlife Service. As a result of the uproar, ADC was transferred to the U.S. Agriculture Department.

Two decades later the poison culture still permeated the western rangelands. One of the most notorious trappers in the Texas case, McKenna soon learned, had been rehired by the ADC in Wyoming and was bragging about all the eagles he had slain in Texas (he was soon fired). It was apparent to McKenna and his superiors that supervisors and staff of the ADC, state and county predator control board officials, and local sheep ranchers were performing, promoting, or condoning the sale, distribution, and use of restricted or banned pesticides. One ADC supervisor allegedly admitted on tape that he poisoned eagles. Another ADC official asserted that it was safe to poison eagles on private, but not public, lands; he acknowledged that the ADC had covered up the illegal use of cyanide devices—a violation of EPA regulations—by an ADC trapper, and confided that he would not report anyone who killed eagles or endangered black-footed ferrets.

The president of one county predator control board allegedly used his own helicopter to illegally shoot predators and scatter Compound 1080 drop baits. He claimed the same ADC official had taught him how to make poison meat baits. Unconcerned, because his spread was so large, that he would ever be caught, he asked Shaddox "to harvest the black birds for me." The rancher said wool growers in the area would pay him to kill coyotes even if he was really eliminating eagles. He recommended burying dead eagles in fence-post holes. An ADC trapper talked about secreting poisoned eagles in gopher holes; another rancher favored badger burrows. Another suspect, a sheep rancher and outfitter, was said to have killed eaglets in their nests.

Interest in the fictitious Wyoming Predator Control Service heightened in the spring of 1991. McKenna and Shaddox placed ads in *Wyoming Wool Grower* magazine and distributed camouflage caps whose crowns carried the name "Wyoming Predator Control Service" above a howling coyote emblem. Their profile, and their credibility, was enhanced when their work with the experimental Compound 1080 collar was featured in several wool growers' trade publications. The articles included a photograph of Laramie rancher Dick Strom holding a lamb while Shaddox collared it.

The previous spring an ADC trapper had suggested to Shaddox that Strom might be willing to participate in the livestock collar research because he was plagued by coyotes. The trapper also confided that Strom set out poisoned meat baits. A former president of the Wyoming Wool Growers Association who served on both his county predator control board and the University of Wyoming Agriculture Advisory Board, Strom was a third-generation wool grower who raised a small flock of Rambouillet sheep on the edge of Laramie, less than two miles from a Holiday Inn. A lean man in his mid-sixties who smoked filtered cigarettes, Strom took a paternal interest in Shaddox and, later, McKenna. He was interested in helping anyone who wanted to tackle predator problems, of which, he claimed, he had many. Both Shaddox and McKenna believed Strom's chief predation problem, if he had any, was not coyotes but dogs emanating from the homes that surrounded him on lots he had subdivided from what was once his father's 2,500-acre ranch.

During Shaddox's first meeting with Strom, the rancher admitted he used a variety of illegal poisons. In July, Strom, who had collected poisons from other ranchers as they became illegal, sold Shaddox ten pounds of thallium sulfate, five pounds of sodium cyanide, two pounds of methomyl, eight grams of Compound 1080, five grams of pure strychnine, five hundred strychnine tablets, and five ounces of processed strychnine for $800 in cash. After McKenna arrived in the fall, Strom introduced him and Shaddox to other ranchers at a ram sale in Douglas, Wyoming. They began to help Strom clean out stalls and feed his sheep. The following February he informed them that he had tossed hot dogs laced with Temik around his ranch to kill dogs, coyotes, and foxes. In May, he told them he had laced a dead sheep with Temik; they later found the carcass and excised a sample. Shaddox also observed him give Ronald Heward, a sheep rancher from Shirley Basin, Wyoming, four ounces of methomyl, and he sold the two of them fifteen Temik capsules for $75. Finally, that August, Strom removed a jar of methomyl from a gray box in his den and gave it to Shaddox; but he said he would hold on to the Temik he had because it killed more quickly.

Meanwhile, Randy Graham led McKenna and Shaddox to two other suspects, Raymond V. Hall of Pueblo, Colorado, and Roy McBride of Alpine, Texas. Hall was the president and sole employee of Humane Coyote Getters, which manufactured .38 caliber shells that propelled cyanide into a coyote's mouth after it bit into a scent bait atop a metal tube embedded in the ground. Hall had legally continued selling the devices overseas after they were banned in the United States in 1972. Government trappers were also still using spring-loaded cyanide cartridges to control coyotes on sheep ranges. Hall sold McKenna and Shaddox six hundred cyanide cartridges and twenty coyote-getters and, with Shaddox acting as an intermediary, allegedly bought two hundred pounds of cyanide from Graham, who had stored it in a trailer outside of Cheyenne. McBride—a former ADC trapper, wildlife biologist, and legendary mountain lion hunter—had invented the Compound 1080 collar and was supplying them for the experimental Wyoming program. These transactions were legal until he shipped Shaddox some collars for northern Wyoming ranchers. In that shipment he included Furadan, a corn and alfalfa insecticide, and instructed Shaddox over the phone how to load it into the collar bladders.

McKenna first heard of Santiago "Junior" Curuchet Jr. while attending one of Graham's certification classes for M-44s, the spring-loaded cyanide devices. A ranch hand from Kaycee, Wyoming, named Ted Woodward confided that his boss had just shot an eagle out of a tree. He said Curuchet, a short, stocky fifty-two-year-old Basque, was angered when he saw two eagles ripping apart the womb of a live, pregnant, overturned ewe. Woodward claimed the incident was Curuchet's fault, that he'd knocked the ewe over with his pickup when it wouldn't move where he wanted it to. Denying Woodward's accusation—"I spend half my time trying to keep them alive"—Curuchet maintained he investigated the ewe after he saw a couple of eagles fly away from her. "Before shearing, they've got a lot of wool and they're heavy with lambs, and she had got off-balance and on her back in a little trail," he told me later. "The ewe was laying there, still alive, and they had ripped her open, and her dead lamb fetuses were laying beside her. They had ate their hearts and livers and were eating on that sheep." Curuchet claimed he shot the sheep, and two or three days later, "I seen an eagle sitting in that tree over there and I shot it. Makes you mad."

The next day, on Curuchet's Willow Creek Ranch along the Johnson-Natrona County line, Woodward, the ranch hand, fished a dead golden eagle out of a pond for McKenna, who pretended he wanted to sell it to Indians. By the time the agent returned weeks later, Curuchet had fired Woodward. After McKenna said he was interested in dealing in more eagles, though, Curuchet directed McKenna to a bald eagle carcass several miles from his ranch house. Curuchet said he had found the eagle in the middle of the road that December, about a quarter mile away from a sheep carcass he had impregnated with Temik. "I told him [McKenna] I wasn't in the eagle selling business," Curuchet later recalled. "If he wanted, he could take it, but I didn't want to know nothing about it." He also admitted telling McKenna that day that he had poisoned and shot forty eagles the previous winter, but said, "I was just trying to match stories with him" after he concluded McKenna was "a windbag."

"Then why'd he give me an eagle?" McKenna retorted.

For his work on the case, Doug McKenna was flown to Washington to receive an award from U.S. Attorney General Janet Reno, and Rex Shaddox was given $10,000 by the U.S. Fish and Wildlife Service. But the plaudits were earned at high personal cost. Often driving five hundred miles a day, McKenna was spending a week to ten days in Wyoming and just four days back home with his young family in Salt Lake City. Two weeks after being denied a request to have his family transferred with him to Wyoming, McKenna returned home to an empty house; his wife had left him. McKenna, now remarried and working as an FWS agent in El Paso, Texas, is convinced the sting cost him his marriage. Shaddox was so unnerved by what he perceived to be threats and intimidation that he fled Laramie with his family within a year after the undercover operation was terminated.

That occurred on September 5, 1991, when federal agents from both the U.S. Fish and Wildlife Service and the Environmental Protection Agency ended the probe with raids on Randy Graham's state laboratory, Dick Strom's ranch, and Raymond Hall's Humane Coyote Getter headquarters in Pueblo, Colorado. Galen Buterbaugh, regional USFWS director, said that during the raids in Laramie and Pueblo, "We found enough poison to kill every predator, man, woman, and child west of the Mississippi"— approximately 10 million doses of compound 1080, strychnine, and Temik. Estimating that 2,000 to 3,000 eagles were being killed each year from Texas to the Dakotas by various illegal or restricted poisons, USFWS officials stated that twenty-four ranches, including fifteen in Wyoming, five in northwest Colorado, and three in northeast Utah, had been targeted. Ultimately, however, just seven individuals pleaded guilty on behalf of themselves or their corporations and were assessed fines that totaled more than $90,000—rather stiff, federal prosecutors believed, considering the prevailing western attitude. They said they hoped the probe would deter others.

"We decided to go after known distributors [of poison] and cut off the source," adds McKenna. "We couldn't go after every rancher. It's not worth it, we would've gotten more five-hundred-dollar fines and requirements to write letters" to wool trade association newsletters—a reference to thirty-two-year-old John Maneotis, of Craig, Colorado. Maneotis later pleaded guilty to treating sheep carcasses on his ranch with aldicarb in March 1992, after federal and state agents, flying overhead in search of poisoned baits, marked the exact location of his laced carcasses for officers on the ground, using GPS signals relayed by global position satellites. Besides, McKenna says, officials were anxious to terminate the probe before another winter migration of eagles commenced.

Randy Graham received one of the lightest fines—only $5,000 —but was confined to his home for six months. During his guilty plea Graham, like Strom, contended that he sold poisons only because Shaddox had asked him repeatedly to do so. Asked by U.S. Magistrate William Beaman if he had profited from the sale of state lab poisons, Graham responded, "I have difficulty recalling. I had a problem with alcohol consumption at the time and do not remember dates or amounts involved." McKenna, however, said he never noticed Graham suffering from such a dependency.

Among the ranchers, Ronald G. Heward, who pleaded guilty to lacing a sheep carcass with methomyl (obtained from Strom) and Warbex (famphur), a cattle dip, received the stiffest fine: $30,000, and two years probation.

Public reaction to the probe was a matter of perception. Contending that no ranchers specifically target eagles and that few illegally use poisons, the Wyoming Wool Growers Association criticized the U.S. Fish and Wildlife Service for tarring wool growers with a broad brush. Others, noting the apparent involvement of Animal Damage Control personnel—none of whom were charged—felt the investigation hadn't gone nearly far enough. Feeling persecuted by environmentalists and government bureaucrats, wool growers like Nick Theos and Santiago Curuchet are hardworking individualists who love their sheep, love what they do for a living, and wonder where the country is headed if it cannot support that paragon of the western ideal, the rancher of the high plains. If they vanish, who will clothe and feed the nation? they ask, neglecting to mention the fact that few people eat lamb or mutton and that last year Pennsylvania and Florida each raised more cattle than Wyoming. To critics, they are welfare cowboys who for far too long have built a lifestyle and wealth based on subsidies from the federal government, which they so frequently claim to despise: heavily subsidized grazing leases, subsidized water, federal subsidized ADC trappers—the equivalent of having a federal exterminator come to your home at taxpayers' expense—and, until it was phased out this spring, a wool subsidy that, for example, in 1992 paid wool growers $1.97 for every dollar's worth of wool they sold the previous year. That phase-out aside, the sheep and cattle industry has a historic hold on the West's psyche and its legislators that far outweighs the industry's present economic import, the wool growers dwindling numbers, and even, considering the influx of professionals into the inter-mountain states, the true political will of the electorate. How else to explain the complete rebuff of Interior Secretary Bruce Babbitt's attempt to raise the severely undervalued monthly public land grazing fees?

Ranchers view themselves as stewards of a rugged land, the ultimate conservationists, convinced there would be no wildlife, no deer, elk or antelope on the range, if they didn't attempt to control coyotes and provide game animals with quality forage. Some ranchers, though, overgraze and degrade public range, regard it as their own private land, and, as decades of poisoning incidents indicate, have little esteem for any animals other than their sheep, which they graze there. Certainly coyotes prey upon sheep and lambs; they killed nearly a quarter-million in 1994 for an industry-wide loss of $11.5 million, according to the national Agricultural Statistics Board. That equals two-thirds of all reported losses to predators, which in turn account for 39 percent of all sheep and lamb losses; disease, weather, and thefts claimed the rest. These predator loss totals, however, are based upon reports from ranchers themselves. It is not hard to inflate such statistics, particularly if you see a coyote eating a sheep. Did it kill its prey, or was the sheep already dead?

Whatever the true losses to coyotes are—and ranchers will tell you such losses are accelerating—they are partially the result of this century's failed attempt to exterminate them. Bob Crabtree, who has studied coyote packs not stalked by man in Yellowstone National Park and Washington State, is convinced ranchers and government trappers have unwittingly bred an even wilier coyote, adept at avoiding man and more inclined to attack sheep. He asserts that if you indiscriminately kill adult coyotes, whether or not they are preying on livestock, coyotes respond by producing more surviving pups. To feed the rapidly growing canines, the surviving adults who otherwise might satisfy themselves with rodents seek out the largest meals they can find, such as lamb and sheep. Eliminating adults, particularly members of the alpha, or lead, pair, also disrupts their social structure, attracting transient coyotes into the area and further dispersing aggressive sub-adults that do not emerge as the leaders throughout the grazing lands. While certain management techniques might not prove economical for some ranchers, hiring more sheep herders and using specially bred guard dogs, lambing sheds, and "flerds"—sheep flocks integrated with protective herds of beef cattle—have all proven effective in reducing coyote predation. But they are not a total panacea, not when ranchers have created, in the words of USFWS law enforcement supervisor Terry Grosz, a supermarket for predators stocked with sheep that are inherently prone to mishaps.

Golden eagles and, to a lesser extent, bald eagles also prey on sheep, particularly lambs. Occasionally, goldens have zeroed in heavily on certain flocks. But even if you take the ASB's statistics at face value, two years ago eagles were responsible for just 1.5 percent of all sheep losses. That hardly justifies placing poisoned carcasses on the open range where they are clearly visible to sharp-eyed raptors.

This past spring, Gerald Bertagnole, a Salt Lake City rancher, pled guilty to supplying his sheepherder with Temik that was used to lace a mule deer carcass. The two were charged with the poisoning deaths of nine of the thirteen bald and golden eagles found in a canyon east of the city during an aerial traverse conducted by federal and state authorities in the spring of 1992. "What if a Boy Scout group went up there, what if they picked up a jar of the Temik and Compound 1080 that was stashed up there," McKenna said a year after the eagles were poisoned, pointing up toward a high bench, "or they found the dead eagles and picked them up to pose for pictures and came home and got sick?

"And this is just the tip of the iceberg. You're looking at remote areas. The only way it can be detected is if people wander into an area."

Nonetheless Mike Rosenthal, the Cheyenne attorney who represented Dick Strom and Roy McBride, questions whether it was sensible to have spent "the amount of money [the Federal government] spent undercover turning otherwise law-abiding people, hardworking tax-paying citizens, into criminals. There must be other ways to get the point across to people in the West who have been in the ranching business for generations."

Adds his client, Dick Strom: "We've got people in this country who don't want any animals killed—animal rights groups, the Humane Society, and environmentalists. They're more concerned about animal life than human life. They want to make the western states one big wildlife refuge, want to raise coyotes and wolves. We've got to have a balance between the whole of creation. We're here, too. I violated the law and I admit it, but in my own mind I figured I was justified in trying to protect myself."

That mind-set, says Jeremy F. Korzenik, an attorney with the Environmental Crimes Section of the U.S. Department of Justice, makes it difficult for wildlife investigators such as McKenna to interest prosecutors in pursuing wildlife cases, and presents a challenge for attorneys trying to convince judges that these crimes warrant significant sentences. Criminal conduct is usually considered morally wrong, he says. "You don't need a statute to tell you it's a crime if you hit or shoot someone, steal or smash their windshield. But environmental criminal prosecutions involve actions that only recently have been against the law. Juries and judges may have a hard time imposing criminal sanctions for conduct that has been perfectly legal."

At sundown, after spending a long day in a four-wheel ATV, tracking strays through the Utah hinterlands, Nick Theos—smelling of sheep, his Wranglers torn and his undershirt black with dirt—drives up a rutted one-lane path above the highway to his travel trailer and small corral, his lambing camp east of Rangely, Colorado. As he stops, a man in his thirties, in a denim jacket and jeans, pulls up in another pickup.

"Here's Glen, my trapper," says Theos, a robust man who looks nearly a decade younger than his seventy-two years. "See, that's a government trapper, that young boy. He helps me up at the ranch. He's kind of a neighbor who lives in Meeker."

"It froze up this morning, and they're knocking the piss out of 'em," Glen Papez calls to Theos enthusiastically. "They got seven or eight, and they were only up an hour and a half." A fresh snow had made it easy to track coyotes by air, enabling an ADC trapper to aerial-shoot that many coyotes up in the White River National Forest, in Theos's summer range leases.

"I just killed one over Fletcher," Papez says, referring to the edge of Theos's lambing lease two to three miles to the west. After helping Theos usher two woollies (unshorn sheep) out of the trailer and into a corral, Papez moves to the back of his pickup to show off his prize. The trapper, who had lured the coyote in by first howling and then using a call that sounds like a wounded rabbit, picks the coyote up by the right ear. "I shot him through the jaw, and [the bullet] came out here," he says, pointing to an exit hole in the animal's flank behind its right leg, "and [the coyote] ran clear to the top of the ridge," a half mile away. "Good thing I had him," he says of Goober, his large Airedale terrier, which is sniffing the coyote. "I would have never found him otherwise."

"Boy," says Theos, "a coyote (ki-oat) is a tough son of a bitch."

⌒ Shortly before the undercover operation in Wyoming was terminated, McKenna and another FWS special agent, Rick Branzell, met
covertly with Theos at his 6,000-acre ranch near Meeker, Colorado.
According to the agents, Theos admitted he was using both Compound 1080
and thallium; acknowledged he could obtain Temik, a black, granulated
insecticide, from Idaho potato farmers; and asked McKenna for illegal .38 caliber cyanide shells to use in coyote-getters. An eight-ounce can of Compound
1080, Theos said, cost $600; to fabricate drop baits for coyotes, he would dip
a toothpick into the poison and insert it into a mixture of fish meal and ham-
burger. His father, he told the agents, had bought a case of thallium years ago,
and he still had some—seventy pounds, McKenna inferred—stored on his
ranch. Theos told the agents how to slit an animal carcass and pack the bluish
poison into the slits, from where it would be dispersed through the meat. It
killed everything, he said, including coyotes and eagles, in a slow, agonizing
death. Other coyotes that ate the coyote vomit also died. It was inhumane,
Theos supposedly conceded, but he did not believe it was possible to be inhumane toward a coyote. Finally, Theos allegedly told McKenna that he would
ask other ranchers if they would be interested in having the "trapper" fly over
and kill coyotes on their winter ranges in Utah. Theos wanted it done, he said,
before he moved his sheep into that area.

Three weeks later McKenna was in Denver with Dan Marshall, his
senior resident agent, in the offices of the Immigration and Naturalization
Service, interviewing Jesus Garcia Rascon. The Mexican national, an INS
informant, had worked as a sheepherder for Theos between November 1989
and October 1990, the period during which the eagles were poisoned in
Hells Hole canyon. Rascon—he was not the herder McKenna met when
the dead eagles were discovered—alleged that early in 1990 Theos had
instructed him to kill a two-point mule deer buck, slit it down the back and
on the front shoulder, and inject it with a blue powder Theos handed to him
in a small bottle. This was not the same deer carcass McKenna had driven
over. Rascon said this deer was shot nearby in Colorado, less than a mile
from the Utah line. Rascon later retrieved the poison for federal agents from
underneath a tree; it was thallium. Rascon also contended he had seen
Theos cut dead sheep open and apply a black granular poison. Finally, he
charged that Theos had directed him to burn a dead eagle Rascon had found
next to a nearly stripped bone. Theos, he said, claimed that his brother-in-
law had killed it.

McKenna and state wildlife officers also interviewed a federal Animal

Damage Control trapper who asserted that, two winters earlier, one of Theos's herders had lost a dog because Theos had scattered drop baits along a road in Hells Hole. The previous winter, the trapper said, one of Theos's own dogs had died in the back of his pickup truck after eating some drop baits from a can.

With no witnesses, no physical evidence to link anyone to the thallium-laced deer that had killed the dozen eagles, no one was ever charged. McKenna believes these are among the hardest wildlife cases to solve. You must prove who placed the poison out on the range, and prove that that poison killed that eagle. "The only way to make a case is if some witness testifies or the person admits it," McKenna says. "And who wants to be known as an eagle poisoner?"

But Theos, the local GOP chairman, was charged in state court with willful destruction of wildlife, a felony in Colorado, based on Rascon's allegation about the mule deer buck. Tried in his hometown of Meeker, in the dark-paneled single courtroom in the Rio Blanco Country Courthouse, Theos and his attorney contended that Rascon lied about the deer to revenge his firing and encourage federal authorities to help him retain his visa. Two U.S. Fish and Wildlife Service special agents, John Griest and Gary Mowad, testified that Theos, eleven months later, had admitted to the crime and had turned over to them a can of Compound 1080, for which he signed a receipt. McKenna, who was not permitted by the judge to mention the eagle deaths, also testified that Theos had admitted to him that he used 1080.

After Theos first claimed he didn't recognize his signature on the receipts, his attorney, Ed Nugent, stipulated it was Theos's signature and that he had given the agents the 1080. But Theos denied all the other allegations: that he had instructed Rascon to poison the deer, that he had confessed to the federal agents, that he still used drop baits and other poisons. Vouching for his character during the three-day trial was former Colorado governor John VanDerhoof. During his closing argument, Nugent accused the federal agents of conspiring against Theos in order to make an example of the prominent rancher.

It was an argument, Nugent knew, that would resonate in a region that has bridled at federal authority ever since, early in this century, the U.S. Forest Service took control of federal lands and began to tell ranchers, miners, and loggers what they could and could not do on land that they had always treated as their own. "These people don't like [federal employees] and pretty much think they are a bunch of snakes," Nugent later told me. "I'd venture to say some people in the community would say, 'We don't care if he did exactly what they say he did. It shouldn't be against the law.' " The jury, after deliberating for six and a half hours, acquitted Theos, who afterward contended the government should be barred from targeting ranchers and farmers for undercover investigations.

With his wife, Lois, by his side inside their trailer at their lambing camp the following spring, Theos denied having coached McKenna on how and when to use poison. "I told him we used to do it when it was legal," he said. "I told him how we'd make these drop baits and we never killed anything indiscriminately. The trapper says you make these drop baits and just whatever you pick up with a match stick, that's all you put in there and it'll kill a coyote. He also told me it takes twenty times that much to kill an eagle. I explained this to this son of a bitch when he was acting like a Greek trapper.

"One thing we'd like to get out to the general population is we don't want to annihilate the coyote population, or any predator. We'd like to just control the ones in our area that are going to eat sheep or cattle. It's true that the drop baits were effective and did not kill eagles and did not kill anything that was over the ridge. It just killed the coyotes that came into your sheep."

I asked Theos about the dozen dead eagles found on his winter grazing lease. "Hell, I never did see any," he says. "This McKeena [*sic*], when he came off of my camp, by God, I don't even remember talking to him, but I must have. But I remember he left his card there at my camp, and this Jesus was at camp. But this Griest [an FWS agent] said that he [McKenna] came down the canyon and went on down and found all these dead eagles. But I never did see any, and my herders never did see any that I know of. And then they said they had a guy down there doing something and him and his boy went out and come down through Hells Hole, which is my private land, and he claims that his dog got sick and he rushed him to Vernal and they said that he was poisoned. . . . Whether it was true or not I don't know."

An hour later, on my way out, along the edge of the lane I jolted past a dead animal. A sheep just killed by a coyote? The clear, moonless night was so dark, I was uncertain until I turned my car around and trained my headlights on the coyote Papez had shot. The fur from its head back to its right flank was soaked in blood—a warning to any coyotes that might crave Theos's sheep.

Santiago Curuchet's paneled, double-width modular ranch home is situated in a draw beside Willow Creek, along a dirt road far from Interstate

25. His largest neighbor is the sprawling TTT Ranch once owned by sheep baron Herman Werner. Four miles to the northwest, clearly visible across the green prairie, stands the Hole-in-the-Wall, the narrow red sandstone box canyon where Butch Cassidy and the Sundance Kid felt immune from the long arm of the law during the Johnson County cattle wars. Five months earlier Curuchet had pleaded guilty to violating the Endangered Species Act by poisoning the bald eagle with Temik; to violating the Bald and Golden Eagle Protection Act by shooting the golden eagle; and to two counts of violating the Federal Insecticide, Fungicide and Rodenticide Act (FIFRA) by lacing the sheep carcass with Temik. He was fined $22,000 and placed on probation for two years. The Fish and Wildlife Service's unprecedented attempt to have his Bureau of Land Management lease revoked, under never-before-used provisions of the Bald Eagle Protection Act, was rejected by Interior Department attorneys because of the impracticality of fencing off BLM lands totally surrounded by Curuchet's private rangelands.

On a late April afternoon in 1993, after his flock had lambed, he and his wife—like Lois and Nick Theos, the Curuchets, who've lived here in splendid isolation since 1961, are clearly a team—sat with me at their dining room table. He, like Strom, was considering quitting and selling his sheep. Uncontrolled predators, depressed markets, and environmentalists dictating how other people should lead their lives, he contended, were killing this country's dwindling sheep industry. He also railed at his fine. "They kill babies every day in this country and they fine you that kind of money for killing a bird that's killing your livestock," he says disgustedly. "I always thought you had a right to protect what's yours." Putting on his silver wire-rimmed glasses, Curuchet read me a list of questions he was required to answer each month for his federal probation officer: Were you questioned by any law enforcement officer? Were you arrested or named as a defendant in any criminal case? Did you have any contacts with anyone having a criminal record? Did you possess or have access to a firearm? Did you possess or use any illegal drugs? "I don't feel like I'm a criminal," he said, his eyes widening. "I don't give a damn if they put me in jail, I still wouldn't."

After I left Willow Creek Ranch, as I approached the broken-up buttes that buffer the interstate, I noticed an immature golden eagle perched atop a rock outcropping, its attention riveted below to a group of ewes and bawling lambs. I pulled over, wondering if I was about to witness a kill, but several minutes later the bird flew off. Later, some three hundred miles away, I was describing my day to a woman tending the bar at the Rustic Pine Bar in Dubois, Wyoming. Small world, at least in the country's least populated state: in the early 1970s, both her parents had worked on the TTT Ranch, where she had lived while attending elementary school with the Curuchets' children. The TTT, she said, was then owned by Herman Werner, the principal figure in the 1971 Wyoming aerial shootings. Informed about the golden eagle I had seen eyeing the sheep, her response was matter-of-fact: "It's a wonder somebody didn't shoot it."

SINKHOLE

The haft of the arrow had been feathered with one of the eagle's own plumes. We often give our enemies the means of our own destruction.
—AESOP, FL. C. 580 B.C., "THE EAGLE AND THE ARROW"

So in the Libyan fable it is told
That once an eagle, stricken with a dart,
Said, when he saw the fashion of the shaft,
"With our own feathers, not by others' hands,
Are we now smitten."
—AESCHYLUS, 525–456 B.C., FRAGMENT 135

That eagle's fate and mine are one,
Which on the shaft that made him die
Espied a feather of his own,
Wherewith he was wont to soar so high.
—EDMUND WALLER, 1605–1687, "TO A LADY SINGING A SONG
OF HIS COMPOSING"

For a number of years, all that separated the two pairs of bald eagles was Charles W. Tippy Dam, a modest earthen bulwark plugging the narrow, steep-hilled valley of the Manistee River, thirty-one miles east of Lake Michigan. Built in 1918, the hydroelectric dam generates enough electricity for just six thousand Michigan homes. In a function no doubt totally unenvisioned by the engineers who designed it, the dam also serves as a Chinese wall between the pollution that still plagues the great lake to the west and the relatively clean upstream waters that have always fed it.

These sandy bottoms and glaciated hills of gravel and clay were once cloaked in white pine. Not for a long time, though, has the land been ever-green. By 1897 the sawmills of Michigan had processed 160 billion board feet, or more than 96 percent, of all the state's white pine. In their place, thanks to the suppression of wildfires, which the pines more readily resisted, now stand hardwoods which, this far north on Michigan's Lower Peninsula, acknowledge spring quite late. On a quiet Sunday morning in late May 1994, the oak leaves are unfurling. Distant hills shimmer with silver aspen buds. Above these pale gray woods relic pines, perfect platforms for bald eagles, sporadically tower in dark green relief.

Into this tranquil tableau Bill Bowerman and Rex Ennis launch a small flat-bottomed johnboat. Their purpose: to reconnoiter the nests on the Tippy Dam Pond, as these impoundments are called in Michigan, to deter-mine the optimum time to band the eaglets. Bowerman, who's in his early thirties, is an environmental toxicologist who recently earned his doctorate at Michigan State University. Fair-skinned and blond, with a broad build and a cherubic face, he has monitored the eagles here since 1989. A former Missouri farm boy, Ennis is half a generation older, a taciturn U.S. Forest Service wildlife biologist who came to the Manistee and Huron national forests a year before Bowerman. I am with them, as are two of Bowerman's volunteers: the boat's owner, Cheryl Portt, an office technician in the Wildlife Division of the state's Department of Natural Resources; and a friend of hers, Tracy Smith, who joined Bowerman's crew after Portt's hus-band died the previous spring.

"Where's the nest?" I ask shortly after we push off from the only boat ramp above the dam.

"Right where those boats are," Ennis says, pointing across a narrow arm of the dam pond to two small motorboats, each carrying two anglers, slowly working the shallows. Above them, in one of the pines scattered atop a red clay bluff, an adult bald eagle perches near its nest. Though no young are visible, Bowerman believes young are in the nest—a suspicion confirmed a couple of hours later on our return trip, when a small brown head pops up over the rim.

When Bowerman first studied this bald eagle pair in 1989 and 1990, their nest was just around a bend, in a open-crowned pine overlooking a pleasant cove and a small island. "After a storm blew their nest out," Bowerman says, "they tore what was left of the nest apart pretty good." Before then, he sus-pects this same pair nested in a maple below the dam. Feeding off what the Manistee provided, including spawning chinook and coho salmon, the pair produced no young. Even when the pair moved up above the dam, they continued to fish below it—with disconcerting results. In 1989 the PCB levels in the blood Bowerman drew from the pair's eaglet were nearly two and a half times greater than the levels he detected in a young eagle raised on the dam pond, less than two miles upstream. The first eaglet's DDE and DDD levels were, respectively, three and eight times greater.

A year earlier, Ennis had arrived from the Mark Twain National Forest in southern Missouri. At the time, there were seventeen bald eagle territories in the Manistee and Huron national forests. During Ennis's surveillance flights that first spring, every active nest he spotted was above the hydroelectric dams, and subsequently the greatest increase in nesting bald eagles (there are now twenty-seven pairs) has been upstream of the dams. Curious after those first flights, Ennis asked his predecessor, William George Irvine, if he knew of historic eagle nest locations. On topographical maps, Irvine penciled in nest locations—both above and below the dams. The two pondered why the eagles were now restricting themselves to the area above the dams.

One possible culprit was the tremendous increase in recreational use of the rivers downstream of the dams. As early as March and April, fishermen begin to line the rivers for runs of steelhead trout that continue into the summer. Each fall thousands of anglers are lured by the spawning runs of spectacular coho and chinook salmon. The big fish were introduced from the Pacific during the late 1960s to control alewives after lake trout were decimated by overharvesting and invading sea lampreys. The chance for fishermen to be out on an uncrowded river had even created an upsurge of use in late winter—the critical time when eagles begin their breeding cycle.

Ennis and Irvine wondered whether all the people drawn to the rivers by the spawning fish or, even more likely, the spawning runs of the contaminated fish themselves, were keeping the bald eagles away from the area below the dams. As early as 1969 longtime Michigan eagle expert Sergej Postupalsky had voiced fears that the spawning salmon would transport additional Great Lakes contaminants upstream, to the detriment of eagles. Recently Tim Kubiak and Dave Best, environmental toxicologists from the U.S. Fish and Wildlife Service's Contaminants Program in East Lansing, had also found a strong correlation between the contaminant load found in addled eagle eggs and productivity: the higher the contaminants, the fewer young eagles were fledged. Their data revealed a marked contrast above and below the first upstream dams.

When the Federal Energy Regulatory Commission's licenses for eleven hydroelectric dams on the Manistee, Muskegon, and Au Sable rivers came up for renewal in 1988, Kubiak and Best, Ennis, and the Michigan Department of Natural Resources all asked Consumers Power Company to evaluate the issue.

For more than a century we have flooded riverbeds to produce cheap electricity and, west of the 100th meridian, for cheap, government-subsidized irrigation water. We've upset natural water flows, altered water temperatures, and blocked fish runs. That's why environmentalists advocate removing dams and letting the rivers again run free. But environmental politics can make for strange bedfellows.

The multimillion-dollar Michigan sports fishery was slumping, in part due to a controversial National Wildlife Federation report, which concluded eating eleven meals of large Great Lakes lake trout over a lifetime increased a person's risk of contracting cancer from one in a million to one in ten thousand. That estimate was based on the combined effect of just four of the one hundred chemicals found in Lake Michigan fish: PCBs, DDT, dieldrin, and chlordane. Fishing had also ebbed because the glamour fish of the Great Lakes, stocked chinook salmon, were plagued by BKD, bacterial kidney disease. As part of the dam relicensing process, the Fisheries Division of the Michigan Department of Natural Resources indicated it would require Consumers Power to install fish ladders to increase the spawning areas for anadromous fish and increase the opportunities to fish for them. Charter boat captains lobbied for the ladders. With reservations, the Michigan United Conservation Clubs, ironically the state affiliate of the National Wildlife Federation, also supported upstream fish passage. Those opposed included the Michigan Audubon Society, the U.S. Forest Service and, most adamantly, Kubiak and Best, who were locked in an intra-agency conflict within their own U.S. Fish and Wildlife Service, which funded many of Michigan's fishery programs.

Besides producing aspen and red pine for paper products, and red pine for utility poles, the Manistee and Huron national forests, through which several of the dammed rivers flow, harbor 134 endangered, threatened, and sensitive species, including Kirtland's warbler, the third rarest bird in the United States. Under the U.S. Forest Service's multiple-use management plan, much of the land above the dams had been earmarked for semiprimitive, nonmotorized uses. The service had closed roads, limited boat launch ramps, and dispersed camping sites. It also had established different logging practices, such as longer tree-cutting rotations. Over future decades, it wanted to generate a richer mix of large old mature trees, young saplings, and underbrush. Dead trees remained standing, fallen trees were being allowed to decompose into the forest floor to create more diverse habitat for both the wildlife and the humans who ventured into the area.

Rex Ennis, the Forest Service biologist, feared that permitting anadromous fish, and anglers who covet them, to venture beyond the dams would drastically alter that vision. Already he was concerned that the increased numbers of fishermen, boaters, and canoeists were disturbing not only the bald eagle nest sites but also the edge of the water where the birds hunted. "If you've got eagles perched in a foraging area trying to exploit fish with people coming by the whole time," Ennis says, "they won't be successful, and that will affect their reproduction rate."

Allowing *contaminated* anadromous fish upstream was even more problematical. Ennis was concerned not only about bald eagles but about mink and river otters as well. There aren't many of either below the dams. Mink, in particular, are extremely sensitive to even low levels of contaminants. As little as one part per billion PCB in the liver of a female can impair reproduction; five parts per million can kill adult mink. Agreeing to fund a study—Consumers Power wanted to keep its dams up and did not want to erect expensive fish ladders—the utility hired the Michigan Audubon Society to study the issue. Among those Audubon turned to were Bowerman and John P. Giesy Jr., Bowerman's doctoral adviser at Michigan State University's Pesticide Research Center and Institute for Environmental Toxicology.

William Wesley Bowerman IV grew up in the North Woods, in Munising, Michigan, on the edge of the Upper Peninsula's Hiawatha National Forest. His mother, Barb, was, and still is, a legal receptionist. His father, Butch, has worked most of his life at Munising's Kimberly-Clark paper mill, where he is now the fire chief. Though he was raised on the shores of Lake Superior, a bald eagle was a rare sight for the young Bill Bowerman. While he was summering at the cabin his great-grandparents had built on a lake south of town, several times he looked up as he was swimming to see bald eagles soaring above him. But that was, and still is, quite an uncommon sight on the eastern Upper Peninsula. Between 1961, the year Bowerman was born, and 1973, the number of bald eagle pairs that bred in Hiawatha National Forest plummeted from about thirty-six to just five. The remaining trio in the western part of the forest were on inland lakes, not far from Bowerman's home. The Eagle Scout never saw an eagle nest until he went hunting for ruffed grouse with his uncle David when he was sixteen. To him the size of the nest, piled high in a yellow birch, seemed incomprehensible.

While he was in college, however, volunteer work he did for the U.S. Forest Service drew him to the big birds. To enhance sports fishing opportunities within the national forest, he cleared the lakes of so-called rough, or nongame, fish. Using fyke nets, which enabled him to pull up and sort his catch, he methodically eliminated suckers and bullheads to make the waters safe for walleye and muskellunge. He returned bass and panfish to the lake. The suckers and the bullheads became food for bears or for local Scandinavian-Americans, who liked to pickle them.

Several years later, during a senior-year ecology class at Western Michigan University, Bowerman was assigned to write a research proposal. He was struck by the fact that every scientific paper he reviewed indicated that bald eagles consumed suckers and bullheads—the very fish he had been eliminating with such great dispatch. He wondered if their removal was affecting the eagles' productivity. Said a professor: "I really think you can get this funded"—magical words for a nascent researcher. The U.S. Forest Service provided $200 and the use of a cabin. There was one caveat: the service was so protective of the only two inland pairs of bald eagles remaining in the forest that it forbade him to actually observe the nests during that first year.

Bowerman, who had just graduated, spent his days that summer of 1985 observing eagles. He also stocked some of the smaller lakes that were devoid of fish with rough fish that had been removed from other lakes. In one experiment, he tagged the gill covers of five hundred white suckers with orange disks. He recovered just one, months later, three miles from where he had released the fish, directly under an eagle's nest.

The next year Michigan's Nongame Wildlife Fund contributed several thousand dollars, enabling Bowerman and others he had enlisted to earn the grand sum of $10 to $25 a day. Few corporate or philanthropic sugar daddies clamor to fund basic wildlife research, particularly by a graduate student. Bowerman naively thought he could generate research funds simply by proposing a legitimate study. The National Geographic Society informed the master's candidate he would first need a Ph.D. Most research, Bowerman was made to understand, is funded through a professor, who metes out the work to his graduate underlings. To survive financially during the summer, Bowerman waited on tourists in Munising restaurants at night.

After the eaglets left their nests, each August for three years, Bowerman headed west to join U.S. Forest Service units battling fires in northern California and Oregon. He had never seen such large trees before, nor such flames. Quelling fires before the wisdom of fire suppression was widely challenged, Bowerman never questioned what he was doing. "I was there because there wasn't any other way I could make that much money in such a short amount of time," he recalls. "To me, twelve hundred dollars in ten or twelve days was a lot of money, and it was getting me into country I had never seen before."

Back in Michigan, Bowerman eventually concluded that, in areas where rough fish had been removed, bald eagles were producing fewer than half as many eaglets as were unaffected eagles. The most robust inland nest in the national forest was now barren. The production rate of .57 young per occupied nest was so low that he believed that in his native Upper Peninsula, the fish removals and contamination near the Great Lakes were retarding the bald eagles' recovery.

Dams, Bowerman points out as our group motors up Tippy Dam Pond in the johnboat, are good for eagles. "Leslie Brown credits the comeback of the African fish eagle to dams," he says. "There's more warm-water fish to eat." As opposed to a running river, the slower currents of a dam pond also probably make it easier for an eagle to detect and capture fish. Thanks to a number of dammed reservoirs in eastern Oklahoma, the Sooner state today has fourteen pairs of bald eagles, more than ever before. In Michigan, where longtime bander Sergej Postupalsky believes the impoundments served as refuges for bald eagles during their low point, dams obviously have helped as well. As we follow a shoreline rimmed darkly in hemlock and cedar, two miles beyond the first nest we pass a nest that didn't exist when Bowerman first came here: a three-year old structure with a large chocolate-brown nestling perched bolt-upright on the rim.

"There's a bird in Wilson's nest," Tracy Smith says. Her friend, boat owner Cheryl Portt, whose face is rimmed by a halo of tight brown curls, smiles approvingly. Not until Forest Service biologist Rex Ennis cuts off the engine do we notice one of the nestling's parents. Perched low in the morning shade on a log at the edge of the water, at our approach it flushes along the green bank to alight atop a broken-off birch.

Late the previous August, well after the adults and that season's eaglet had left the nest, Cheryl had strapped on climbing spikes and, with the aid of a tree climber, apprehensively scaled the nest tree clutching her husband's ashes. She and her husband, Wilson, a General Motors electrician and part-time freelance photographer, had purchased the johnboat in 1991, a year after they volunteered to help Bowerman trap and take blood samples of eagles. Ever since, its sides and carpeted bottom had been daubed with eagle whitewash. The day she climbed up to the nest, many of her family members and friends gathered below in the johnboat and four pontoon boats. As they played a tape of "Save the Eagle," a song by country musician Lee Greenwood, she poured Wilson Portt's ashes over the edge of the nest, a beautiful waterfall cascading out of the tree.

After we leave the nest, which is now known, in memory of Wilson, as the South Portt nest, a third nest appears a mile farther to the northeast, a ragged affair near the top of a large pine. Its bottom is so collapsed it looks like a long shock of Medusa's windblown snake-hair. Above it, like a sailor in a crow's nest or an ornament atop a flagpole, rides an adult bald eagle.

Several years ago this pair was nesting in a similar-sized pine about fifty yards to the right. No sign of that nest now remains, but Bowerman can still picture it, framed as it was by a couple of dead, upright limbs decorated with eagles. It was one of the most easily visible nests he had ever seen. Directly across a narrow arm of the pond was a shaded point. Concealed there from dawn to dusk inside a canvas blind camouflaged with evergreen boughs, Bowerman and his crew enjoyed an unimpeded view of nearly all of the eagles' foraging territory. Bowerman has worked with eagles in some rather spectacular country—Voyageurs National Park on the Minnesota-Ontario border, the Slate Islands on the north shore of Lake Superior, and the Baltic coast of Sweden—but his favorite is Tippy Dam Pond. He appreciates the way the broad hills step down to meet the water, the way the aspen, maple, and oak leaves paint themselves in the fall, the way relatively few people ever bother to experience the area.

From March till the eaglets had flown in July, Bowerman and his crew—over the three-year period, the group included MSU students, graduate students, and nearly a hundred different Earthwatch volunteers—observed six breeding pairs on the Manistee River and the Au Sable, which flows eastward and empties into Lake Huron. This pair's nest was one of them, and Bowerman and Ennis know these eagles' history well.

"This nesting territory had strong production even through the sixties," Bowerman says.

"It's one of the oldest territories on the Manistee," Ennis agrees. "Historically, the eagles had several nests up the oxbow a couple miles above here, but they've nested on this bay and around the point also."

"When we caught this female [in 1990], she was sixteen years old," Bowerman adds. The bird had been banded as a nestling in the western Upper Peninsula. "She was the oldest bird ever found in Michigan."

During the winter and spring of 1990, Bowerman's team caught both of the adults here and the two from the nest near where we had put in. After stuffing a fish with Styrofoam so it would float, Bowerman ran 25-pound test fishing line through staples in the fish and fashioned the line into a clover-leaf of loops with slipknot nooses. The line was then attached to 60-pound test line, which in turn was connected to a bungee cord attached to an 8-pound log.

The eagle would swoop down to retrieve the fish, then lift off, causing the nooses to tighten around its talons. Unable to overcome the resistance created by the bungee cord and log, the bird would drop back into the water. As Bowerman quickly approached in his boat, the bird would be swimming, surprisingly fast, dipping its wings into the water like a rower or an Olympic swimmer carving out a butterfly stroke. Ever wary of the bird's talons, Bowerman would take hold of one wing to divert the bird's attention while he grabbed underneath for the talons and brought the bird into the boat.

Bowerman had first attempted to trap the birds the previous fall, but there was so much food available that his stuffed fish bait did not interest them. He did have one nibble, though. "See that pine high up there?" he says pointing to a tree high atop the bluff to our left. Its crown rose more than 350 feet above the water. "The female from this nest was perched up there, and I had a sucker I was ready to set out as the float. I pumped it up and down in my hand a few times and then let it out into the water and backed off."

Bolting immediately out of the tree, the eagle swooped down on the proffered fish. But she was too wily for Bowerman's snare. "She nailed just the top of the head," he recounts. "The fishing line tightened as she pulled away, and all the Styrofoam popped out of the gullet as she took off."

The blood and feather samples Bowerman eventually obtained indicated the eagles had low contaminant levels. Since these bald eagles fished mostly above the dams, that was what he'd expected. He also fitted the birds with radio satellite transmitters which have since fallen off. The radio telemetry indicated they did not wander far, only to the shores of Lake Michigan, thirty-five to forty miles to the west. Nesting adult bald eagles usually remain on Michigan's Lower Peninsula year-round. Depending on the harshness of the weather, some of those that nest on the Upper Peninsula winter in Wisconsin and on the Mississippi River, as do some of the young from the Lower Peninsula. In the winter, fledglings from this nest have migrated across the lake and the state of Wisconsin to Prairie du Chien on the Wisconsin River, more than 250 miles to the southwest. Other young birds banded in Michigan have been found throughout the Gulf Coast and southern states.

Bowerman also wanted to figure out what the eagles were eating and delivering to their young. Not surprisingly, he and his researchers primarily saw the eagles haul fish to their nests. The prey remains they examined within and under the six nests he was studying, and under nearly three hundred other nests he visited in four Great Lakes states and Ontario, were also primarily fish. In early spring, the eagles might take an occasional bird or mammal. Bowerman's team found the remains of cottontails, muskrats, red squirrels, chipmunks, beavers and opossums as well as ducks, gulls, even a blue jay. They also observed three snakes and a turtle being carried aloft to two river nests.

As the water warms and fish become more active, however, the eagles nesting on the dam ponds concentrate on fish—and not just any fish. During the day trout and walleye in the dam ponds tend to lurk, off-limits, deep under the surface. Bald eagles, however, can see ten to twenty feet below the surface of this clear, sand-filtered water. The outline of a fish contrasted against a shallow sandy bottom is as obvious and easy a target for a bald eagle as a pompous politician is for a comedian. So much the better if the fish in question spawn in the shallows in early spring, like suckers. Or if, when the water warms a little more and aquatic plants sprout, the fish are benthic bottom feeders that have eyes oriented downward for that very purpose, and have no evasion reflex to aerial attacks—like the fish family Ictaluridae, or bullheads.

Based on what he found in the nests and what he observed being carried up to them, Bowerman calculated that 57 percent of the prey hauled to the nest were suckers—a simple case of the eagles opting for the easiest meal. While they tend to take fish near the surface, bald eagles can plunge up to a meter into the water to snare a fish. To determine the prey available to eagles, every two weeks another researcher plied the birds' foraging areas with an electroshocking boat that delivered 250 to 300 volts: enough to stun fish near the surface. Counting only the fish that rose from the water's top meter—within the reach of eagles—suckers again accounted for 57 percent of the fish. More than 315 were raised in the vicinity of just this one nest.

Talk of the fish reminds Rex Ennis of a day he spent with his brother here on the Tippy Dam Pond fishing for walleye and reeling in a sucker instead.

"Watch this," he told his brother, knocking the sucker's head on the boat's gunwale and tossing the fish into the water. They moved away from the fish, and ten minutes later they heard the call of an eagle. Soon an adult circled, swooped down, and carried off the sucker.

"Forget walleyes," Ennis's brother said. "Let's fish some more for eagles."

Now, as we study the nest, a large dark brown wing flaps up underneath the adult. "It's time," Bowerman says, "to band that one."

 Below the Tippy Dam, the Manistee River harbors two more bald eagle nests. More than an hour's drive south of the Manistee on the Muskegon River, where the dam ponds are flanked by houses instead of white cedar, and the waters churn each weekend with the buzz of power-boats, jet-skis, and water skiers, three more pairs of eagles nest. Another hour southward, on the Kalamazoo River near Lake Michigan, there are two eagle nests that never have produced any young.

Southward from the mouth of the Manistee the shores of the brilliant blue if somewhat sterile waters of Lake Michigan are barren of eagle nests all the way to Chicago, 250 miles away. The first two nests north of the Manistee are: one 30 miles to the north that consistently fails, and another 50 miles away, on an island in Sleeping Bear Dunes National Seashore. There are several more across the lake in Wisconsin's Green Bay. Along Minnesota's 150 -mile Lake Superior shoreline, not one pair of eagles can be found. That's also true of the entire shoreline of Lake Ontario. Eagles have never been very plentiful along these lakeshores, and this paucity of nests is partly due to habitat limitations; huge sand dunes are incompatible with good perch trees.

Nonetheless, in recent years bald eagle nests along the shores of the Great Lakes have multiplied much more rapidly than those located inland—a fact that has not gone unnoticed by critics who contend that Bowerman, Kubiak, and Best are crying wolf when they claim contaminated Great Lakes fish should not be permitted above the dams because of their negative impact on bald eagles.

Looking at the raw numbers, it initially is hard to understand what the trio is talking about. In Michigan, Wisconsin, and Minnesota, bald eagles have never been considered endangered, merely threatened. The three states harbor more than 1,400 adult pairs, more than 30 percent of all the occupied territories in the contiguous states. Bowerman, however, believes lakeshore nests are proliferating more quickly because suitable inland nesting territories have become harder to find, and increasingly crowded. In northern Minnesota's Chippewa National Forest, for example, several pairs of nests are uncommonly close together—less than a quarter mile from each other. (Such close proximity, and the resultant competition for food, is thought to have reduced the productivity in the Chippewa during the past fifteen years from 1.5 young to just 1 young per active nest.)

Crowded out, young adult birds fledged inland are dispersing to the lakeshores and anadromous streams in search of new nesting territories. For the first two years these young and inexperienced eagles don't produce as many offspring as older birds. But even later on, the pairs nesting along the lakes and their tributaries don't produce as well as inland eagles, and if they survive at all together as a pair, they experience a gradual reproductive decline. Bowerman and his colleagues surmise there is a much more rapid turnover rate along the lakeshores, with new, younger birds replacing older breeding eagles that die off prematurely. Between 1986 and 1988, for example, Bowerman noticed at least two, possibly three, different females in the same breeding area near Lake Michigan. He and his colleagues suspect the worst turnover is on Lakes Michigan and Huron, but they believe it is occurring on Erie as well. Large portions of the Great Lakes, they fear, are a bald eagle sinkhole.

These five great bodies of water contain 95 percent of our fresh water. Yet these sources of drinking water for almost a tenth of our population also contain nearly a thousand known chemical substances. Are the bald eagles along the Great Lakes primarily being negatively affected by the chemical-laden fish they are eating, or by the fish-eating colonial waterbirds, such as gulls, that the eagles also prey upon? Analyses of food remains found in and underneath bald eagle nests indicate that lakeshore eagles rely more heavily than inland ones on gulls, great blue herons, and mergansers. Bill Bowerman points out, however, that there is an inherent bias built into prey remains analysis: in an eagle's nest, bird bones and feathers, and mammal bones and fur, tend to last longer than fish remnants. He found that the ratio of fish to birds was higher when he sat in a blind observing what was being delivered to the nests. Nonetheless, bald eagles nesting along the lakeshores and anadromous streams probably prey upon a few more aquatic birds than do inland eagles—birds that, unquestionably, are more contaminated than the fish they and the eagles both eat.

It has been calculated that, from water laced with PCBs to the eggs of bald eagles, certain PCBs can concentrate, or biomagnify, 25 million to 100 million times. A composite of alewives collected in Lake Huron's Thunder Bay contained 11 parts per trillion of 2,3,7,8-TCDD equivalents—an environmental toxicologist's yardstick for measuring the relative impact of differing toxicities and combinations of dioxinlike PCBs, dioxins, and furans; 2,3,7,8-TCDD is the most toxic dioxin—the dioxin found in Agent Orange, the dioxin that closed the town of Times Beach, Missouri. A sample of northern pike taken from the same bay contained 57 parts per trillion TCDD equivalents, while a composite of herring gulls was carrying 469 parts per trillion. Atop the food chain, an addled bald eagle egg taken from Thunder Bay contained 1,065 parts per trillion.

Since the herring gull contained nearly half the contaminant load the eagle egg carried, one understandably might assume that the lakeshore eagles are deriving most of their contaminants from gulls. But as some contaminants, including PCBs and dioxins, ascend the food chain, they are biomagnified in great leaps. The contaminants carried by the gull were only half as concentrated as those found in the eagle egg; had gulls been a significant part of the parent eagles' diet, the egg would have contained ten or twelve times more contaminants. Kubiak and Best, the Fish and Wildlife Service toxicologists, concluded that the fish farther down on the biomagnification spectrum are more likely to be the major source of bald eagle contamination.

Looking exclusively at breeding bald eagles that were fledged after DDT was banned in 1972, Bowerman determined how many young were produced in ten different regions throughout the Great Lakes between 1977 and 1992. He found a direct correlation between the number of young eagles produced per occupied nest and the levels of PCBs, DDE, and dieldrin found in the eaglets' blood and addled eggs. As the levels of contaminants rose, productivity declined. The concentration of PCBs in the plasma of nestlings from Great Lakes breeding areas was eight times as great as that of nestlings from the interior; DDE concentrations were three times as great. The Lake Michigan eaglets had the highest PCB and DDE levels, the lowest productivity rate, and the lowest percentage of successful nests. The results from Lake Huron were nearly as bad. The PCB levels Bowerman found in nestlings along the Great Lakes equaled the PCB concentrations of adult eagles trapped in Missouri. They exceed the levels detected in nestlings from areas of Oregon and Washington where high levels of PCBs, DDE, and dioxins have been linked to poor nesting success along the lower Columbia River. Both the addled eggs analyzed by Kubiak and Best and the eaglet blood drawn by Bowerman contained some of the highest organochlorine residues ever encountered in bald eagles.

Today Bill Bowerman and his colleagues believe the principal threat to bald eagles in the Great Lakes is not DDT and its derivatives, but PCBs. One spring morning, driving toward nests along the Manistee River, he says, "The DDE levels have gone down to the point where they are right at the level for no discernible effects for eggshell thinning."

PCBs, or polychlorinated biphenyls, are not one chemical but 209 possible related congeners. Some are much more toxic than others. All, however, are relatively inflammable and chemically inert, making them ideal for a wide array of industrial applications.

First used in 1929 as electrical insulators, PCBs subsequently were utilized worldwide in coolants, cutting oils, lubricants, plasticizers, carbonless copy paper, and fluorescent lighting fixtures. Embedded in soils, transported through the water, and evaporated into the air, however, PCBs are, like DDT, highly persistent and omnipresent, found even in the snow and seawater of the Antarctic. In 1971, concerns about potential human health effects prompted the United States to restrict their use to closed electrical capacitators and transformers; in the late 1970s their use was totally banned in new products.

Yet two decades later nearly every one of us, including infants who drink breast milk containing PCBs, still carry the compounds in our fat tissue and blood. Stored in the fats of fish or animal flesh, PCBs cannot be removed by washing and are only partially removed by cooking. Even occasional consumption discernibly elevates the level of PCBs in the bloodstream. PCBs—again, like DDT—are organochlorines or chlorinated hydrocarbons—compounds in which at least one atom of chlorine is combined with organic matter containing carbon. At least 177 organochlorines—pesticides, herbicides, solvents, PCBs, dioxins—have been identified in the fat, breast milk, blood, semen, and breath of Americans and Canadians. Today we carry in our blood 40 to 60 parts per trillion of TCDD dioxin equivalents—four to five times more than the alewives swimming in Thunder Bay.

After infiltrating living tissue, a number of organochlorines and other synthetic compounds have the ability to mimic, enhance, or block hormones, significantly disrupting normal endocrine activity. Some organochlorines, for example, function as xenoestrogens—literally, foreign estrogens. Whether produced naturally or taken as postmenopausal therapy, estrogen increases the risk of breast cancer. In the industrialized world, the incidence of breast cancer has risen steadily since the 1940s. Could DDT be a factor? To date, there has been a handful of small, conflicting studies. The largest and most recent, reported two years ago, found no statistically significant link between the level of DDE in a woman's bloodstream and her risk of contracting breast cancer. But there were some intriguing results: both black women and white women (but not Asians) with higher levels of DDE in their serum had a slightly higher risk of developing breast cancer, a risk that, in most of the cases, increased as the bloodstream levels of DDE increased.

Nonetheless, no known definitive link between organochlorines and breast cancer has been established. There may, in fact, be none. But with the National Cancer Institute in the early stages of a series of long-range studies analyzing the relationship between environmental contaminants and breast cancer, the question is far from settled.

This specter of cancer, of potential carcinogenic effects, has long been the focal point of safety concerns regarding synthetic chemical compounds. PCBs and DDT produce liver cancer in rats and have been tied to human liver and lymphatic cancers. DDT has also caused lymphatic and lung cancer in rats and mice. Workers exposed to high levels of dioxin at chemical and pesticide plants have had higher cancer death rates. Today, though, there is a growing awareness that, for both wildlife and human beings, the hormonal ability of some organochlorines to compromise the immune system and to disrupt reproductive processes and behaviors, and embryonic sexual development might represent a threat as great or greater than any potential increased cancer risk, particularly since these effects might occur at exposure levels exponentially lower than those that might trigger cancer. These subtle, hard-to-decipher effects, not cancer, might be the true wildlife and human health "end point."

For example, in the laboratory the dioxin 2,3,7,8-TCDD is at least 100 times more effective in suppressing the immune system of laboratory mice than corticosterone, a hormone naturally produced by the adrenal glands. Exposing gull eggs to DDT has resulted in males with partly formed egg ducts and, in some cases, gulls with hermaphroditic sex glands. Researchers should not have been surprised; similiar results occurred as early as the mid-1940s when herring gull eggs were injected with diethylstilbestrol (DES), a synthetic estrogen. In rats, exposure to TCDD, in utero and as infants, appears to alter later patterns of sexual behavior involving the brain. Female sexual behavior increases; masculine sexual behavior decreases. Male rat offspring are uninterested in mounting females; their sperm production declines drastically.

The wild offers similar testimony. In Lake Huron's heavily contaminated Saginaw Bay, researchers several years ago found herring gulls and Caspian terns whose immune responses had been suppressed by 30 percent to 40 percent. Two decades ago, two-thirds of the male herring gull embryos and newly hatched chicks collected from a Lake Ontario island had feminized tissue in their testes; more than half of the females had enlarged oviducts. Both on the Great Lakes and off the coast of southern California, male gulls were ignoring breeding colonies and females were nesting with each other. Gulls were not incubating or defending their eggs with normal intensity.

In Florida, decades of ongoing agricultural pesticide and herbicide runoff have combined with a 1980 spill of dicofol pesticide components that included DDT and DDE to turn the state's fourth-largest freshwater lake, Lake Apopka, into a synthetic hormone stew. Wild animals at the top of the lake's food chain continue to have high levels of DDE in their tissue and eggs. Both female and male alligators and largemouth bass also have abnormally high levels of estrogen. Meanwhile, the testosterone levels in the males are identical to those of normal females.

Perhaps not coincidentally, during the past two decades the number of bass in Lake Apopka has dramatically declined. During the five years after the spill, the number of young alligators in the lake plunged 90 percent. Nearly half of the lake's newborn alligators die within their first two weeks, compared to 1 percent at another Florida lake. Of the alligators that do survive, the males have poorly developed testicles. The gonads of some of the lake's alligators and red-bellied slider turtles do not appear to be male or female; confounded researchers refer to them as "intersexed."

Replicating these results, University of Florida researchers painted alligator eggs with DDE in doses that approximated the levels in eggs found at Lake Apopka. The eggs were incubated at 34°C.—a temperature that should have produced all male alligators. Instead, just 40 percent were male, another 40 percent were female, and the remaining 20 percent were sexually unidentifiable. Somewhat similar results occurred with freshwater turtle eggs exposed to a number of different organochlorines, including DDE and atrazine, one of today's most commonly used herbicides. At least some PCBs also have the ability to reverse the sex of freshwater turtles.

What could be the mechanism for this demasculinization? The molecular structure of organochlorines and a number of other synthetic chemical compounds is so similar to that of many hormones that the organochlorines have the ability to attach themselves to the hormone receptors of glandular cells. They fit together as neatly as a docking lock on the space shuttle. Once attached, they can alter the messages that control the function of those cells. They can enhance the effect of the natural hormones they are mimicking, or make it impossible for such hormones to attach to their receptors.

The dioxin TCDD, for example, binds to the aryl hydrocarbon, or Ah receptor, a protein cluster inside most of the body's cells. It is unclear which hormone actually binds to the Ah receptor naturally. Yet when the infiltrating TCDD combines with at least two proteins, it can attach itself to DNA in the cell's nucleus and, like flipping a switch, turn genes on or off. Among the genes TCDD can manipulate is one that controls the production of P450 enzymes—enzymes that usually help the body rid itself of toxic substances but can also intensify the effects of other toxins. Besides dioxin, both DDT and PCBs accelerate the production of P450 enzymes.

Much of the research on this sort of synthetic endocrine disruption has concentrated on potential estrogenic effects. In its manufactured form, a 15 percent component of DDT was estrogenlike. But rather than mimicking and enhancing estrogen, DDE—the principal long-lasting metabolite of DDT—can interfere with androgens, the male sex hormones that include testosterone. Working with cell lines that replicate human tissue reactions and with laboratory rats, the Reproductive Toxicology Branch of the EPA's Health Effects Research Laboratory in Research Triangle Park, North Carolina, recently demonstrated that DDE is a potent antagonist, or blocker, of androgen receptors. At 63 parts per billion, the DDE that affected the cell lines was less than half the levels found in the blood of South Africans living in homes treated with DDT to ward off malaria. Those DDE levels were also far, far less than the levels found in the Lake Apopka alligator eggs (5,800 ppb) and in the tissues of infants stillborn in Atlanta, Georgia, in the mid-1960s, when DDT was still used in this country.

The EPA also found that male rats born of females exposed to DDE retained nipples and had phalluses located closer to the female position. DDE fed to male weanlings significantly delayed the onset of puberty by five days. And adult males that ingested DDE for just four days suffered significant reductions in the weight of their seminal vesicles and ventral prostate glands. These effects, EPA researchers stress, are not restricted to

DDE or organochlorines. The laboratory in North Carolina has identified approximately twenty other compounds, including some nonorganochlorines, that block androgen receptors.

So whether the effect is to enhance or mimic estrogen or to block androgen, or both, it is apparent that a wide array of synthetic compounds can wreak havoc with biological reproduction. The human implications are impossible to ignore. Indeed, some of these effects found in the wild and in the laboratory echo some of the effects of diethylstilbestrol, or DES, a synthetic estrogen prescribed to millions of women between the 1940s and the early 1970s to prevent miscarriages and premature births. DES, we now know, did nothing of the kind. But those women who took it have a slight increased risk of breast cancer; their daughters exposed to it in utero have an increased risk of developing malformed reproductive tracts, infertility, and a rare form of vaginal cancer—effects that, in many cases, evidence themselves only after the daughters reach sexual maturity.

Some evidence also suggests that, during the past half century, a substantial decline in the average man's sperm count and an increase in testicular cancer might have occurred. In Denmark, the lifetime risk of the latter has risen to nearly 1 percent. There is also a suspected increase in penis abnormalities and cryptorchidism, the failure of the male testes to descend out of the body cavity into the scrotum by the age of one.

As a teenager, one of my testicles was surgically lowered because it had failed to descend. My sperm count was so low that, prior to my marriage, a urologist estimated my chances of conceiving a child were a million to one. (My wife and I, thankfully, twice beat those odds.) It is impossible to know if my cryptorchidism was a random genetic quirk, a natural roll of the dice, or the result of a card deck stacked by the organochlorine contamination of my mother prior to my birth in 1952. When I was born, there was nothing to suggest anything was amiss. What makes these endocrine disrupters so insidious, and so difficult to ferret out, is that their effects on the embryonic development of a fetus might not manifest themselves until years later, when the person reaches puberty.

Formidable questions remain: questions of dosage, since different organisms, including human beings, react with varying sensitivity to various toxicants; questions concerning whether toxic hot spots such as Lake Apopka and Saginaw Bay are anomalies or are representative of widespread, persistent pollution; and the question of whether these endocrine-disrupting effects mirror current conditions or if, like the beam of a star fifty light-years away, they open a time-delayed window onto a more contaminated past. With each passing year, though, what becomes clearer is the profound ignorance and arrogance with which we loosed an army of synthetic compounds, now out of our control, that unimaginably can disrupt the very nature and source of new life.

⁓ The Great Lakes hint at potential effects of another kind as well. Babies born to women who regularly ate fish from Lake Michigan weighed less, had smaller head circumferences, and were born earlier than infants born to mothers who did not eat fish. By age four, they continued to weigh less. However, two researchers, Drs. Joseph and Sandra Jacobson of the Wayne State University Department of Psychology, did not consider these slight physical differences to be clinically or functionally significant. Rather, what intrigued them was that the newborns who had higher levels of PCBs in their umbilical cord serum exhibited poorer short-term memory during infancy. At age four these children did not perform as well in tests that assessed their visual, verbal, and quantatitive auditory memory. They couldn't remember words, sentences, or a story as well, for example, or repeat numbers dictated to them in sequence or in reverse order. Although there was no mental retardation or gross impairment, the Jacobsons, who are continuing to follow the Michigan children, fear the subtle memory deficits could affect the children's ability to master reading and arithmetic skills.

The Jacobsons' results with newborns were recently replicated with infants whose mothers had eaten Lake Ontario fish. These newborns had poorer reflexes, did not respond as well to stress and, while they slept, did not adapt as well to mild disturbances as other children. Those infants whose sleep was most bothered by a bell or a rattle were born to mothers who had eaten a lifetime equivalent of more than forty pounds of Lake Ontario salmon. The results did not surprise one of the study's researchers, Helen Daly, a psychologist at the State University of New York in Oswego. Rats to which she had earlier fed Lake Ontario salmon easily became frustrated, anxious, and less active than rats fed Pacific salmon or no salmon at all. Daly and the Jacobsons view the presence of PCBs in fish and in umbilical cord serum as merely a crude indicator of multiple chemical contamination. The effects, whatever they might be on humans, are likely the result of the additive and/or synergistic effect of this chemical brew.

Nonetheless, bans during the 1970s of some of the more toxic compounds, coupled with much stiffer water and air pollution regulations in the

United States and Canada, have made the Great Lakes cleaner than they have been in decades. Concentrations of DDT and PCBs in the breast milk of Canadian mothers have dropped sharply, as have the levels of PCBs found in lake trout and herring gull eggs. Double-crested cormorants, herring gulls, and nearly all other colonial waterbirds have staged a resounding comeback.

But countering the decline of PCBs in lake trout (from 23 parts per million to just three parts per million since 1974), between 1983 and 1993 the PCB levels in coho salmon taken from Lake Michigan increased from .3 parts per million to more than 1 part per million. Also, leaching from toxic hot spots in the Great Lakes sediments, transported by migrating birds and high-altitude atmospheric winds originating in countries where long-banned insecticides are still in use, such nemeses as DDT, aldrin, and dieldrin appear to have reached a plateau or actually may be rising. With DDE having a half-life of at least a hundred years, it is not likely to disappear any time soon.

Late in 1992, as part of its relicensing process, Consumers Power Company agreed to install fish ladders at its hydroelectric dams "upon approval of various federal and state agencies," when the agencies deem the waters and fish clean enough to allow anadromous fish above the dams. When will that be? It takes as long as a century for the water in Lake Michigan to recycle, and as much as three centuries for Lake Superior to renew itself. "*You,*" says Dave Best, the USFWS environmental toxicologist in East Lansing, "don't have to worry about it."

In the Great Lakes, crossed-bill birth defects in fish-eating birds are nothing new. So common are such deformities, embryonic problems, and wasting away of hatchlings that they've been given a name: Great Lakes embryo mortality, edema and deformities syndrome. It has been found in herring and ring-billed gulls; in common, Caspian, and Forster's terns; and in black-crowned night herons, great blue herons, double-crested cormorants, and Virginia rails.

Congenital defects in bald eagles, though, are quite rare. One crossed-bill eaglet was found in Florida; none are known to have been found anywhere else in the country—except the Great Lakes region, where six nestling bald eagles were found with deformed bills between 1968 and 1989. Then three years ago, researchers in Michigan found three eaglets, including two within little more than an hour, with crossed bills. A fourth had clubfeet. In Sweden, deformed toes and bill defects among white-tailed sea eagles have been linked to PCB contaminants in the Baltic Sea. PCBs consumed by the parents when they feed, then transferred to the egg where they are suspected of interfering with normal embryo development, also are a prime suspect in the Great Lakes. As the egg-thinning effects of DDT wane, the birth defects that never were apparent earlier, because of cracked shells and embryo mortality, are revealing themselves.

The first deformed eagle discovered three years ago was found in a nest along the western shore of Lake Erie, beyond the entry gates of the Ford Motor Company's Monroe Stamping Plant in Monroe, Michigan. For a half a century before the Great Depression, the vast marshes here at the mouth of the river Raisin were owned by the Insulheim Club, a waterfowl preserve to which Henry Ford came with Harvey Firestone and Thomas Edison to hunt ducks. The neat red brick plant, which now covers more than a million square feet, opened in 1929 as the Newton Steel Company. During World War II it was owned by the federal government. Alcoa, which forged aluminum aircraft parts here, operated it as a defense plant. After several years as a wheel stamping plant, the complex was bought by Ford in 1949. Today its two thousand auto workers stamp out auto body panels and fabricate catalytic converters for Ford vehicles. Before the advent of plastic car bumpers, the plant also electroplated chrome bumpers, mirrors, and trim. Prior to the 1970s all of the plant's wastewater was discharged directly into the river Raisin. To improve water quality, state and federal regulations then required Ford to settle out the heavy metals from the electroplating solutions in a processing canal and polishing lagoon just east of the plant. The resulting sludge was then dumped into lagoons between the plant and the edge of the marsh, just to the east, where the pair of bald eagles now nest.

Those lagoons now hold more than a million cubic yards of sludge, some of it as much as thirty feet deep, laced with cyanide and toxic heavy metals such as chromium, copper, nickel, zinc, cadmium—metals that also have migrated to a nearby marsh and a canal that draws water from Lake Erie. In one of the largest cleanups in the state, Ford has agreed to spend as much as $50 million to entomb the toxic metals in clay-walled vaults.

The heavy metals are not Ford's only environmental headache. Even though it closed off most of its storm and sanitary sewer drains to the river in the 1970s, samples of wastewater discharged later into the river continued to exceed allowable PCB levels. From the plant downstream to the lake, the river sediments contain high levels of PCBs. Near the mouth of one 48-inch storm sewer that has been shut since 1972, the PCB concentration is 42,167 parts per million: an astonishing 4 percent PCBs. The PCB involved is Aroclor (r) 1248, a type of PCB once used in high-temperature hydraulic fluids. Ford, which has operated the plant for nearly half a century, apparently never used such hydraulic fluid. It believes the plant and its storm sewers were contaminated by an earlier plant operator.

Nonetheless, while Ford seeks a previous owner to sue, the company has agreed to the EPA's plan to remove the contaminated river sediment from the underwater Superfund site at a cost of $5 million to $16 million.

The major source of human exposure to the submerged PCBs comes from eating PCB-contaminated fish, particularly bottom feeders. In its fish consumption advisory, the state recommends that no one eat carp or foot-long white bass taken from the river downstream of Monroe.

Eagles, of course, are not privy to such warnings. Situated in a large cottonwood, the bald eagle nest on the Ford property overlooks the diked east marsh where Ford, Firestone, and Edison once secreted themselves in duck blinds. Three years ago, none of the researchers who were banding and drawing blood from one of the nest's two eaglets initially realized anything was wrong. They were more concerned about its sibling, which had a fish-hook in its mouth.

But Lori Feyk, a Michigan State graduate student working for Bill Bowerman and John Giesy, was having difficulty closing the bird's beak. She wanted to measure its bill depth to determine its sex (the bills of females are larger). Dave Best, the red-bearded, wiry USFWS and environmental toxicologist, happened to be looking at the eaglet from above when he realized the problem: the bird's bill was crossed. It was subtle, but definitely defective.

Little more than an hour later, fifteen miles to the south at a nest on Woodtick Peninsula, there was no doubt about it. "We've got a major crossed bill up here," Bowerman's longtime climber, Al Bath, shouted down from the eyrie, which had been built on a plywood platform in a cottonwood. The platform had been erected eleven years earlier by members of the Michigan United Conservation Clubs, who commemorated the two-hundredth anniversary of the selection of the eagle as our national symbol by trying to lure the birds back.

Later that June another crossed bill was found far to the north on Michigan's Lower Peninsula, about twenty miles from Lake Huron's Thunder Bay. Near Manistique Lake on the Upper Peninsula, a fourth eaglet was discovered with clubfeet. With the rear and inner talons on both its feet half their normal length, the bird's claws spiraled around her talons, making it impossible for her to perch or catch her prey. Beside the deformed eaglet was an addled egg.

Unable to survive in the wild, all four of the deformed birds were taken to the wildlife rehabilitation center at Michigan State University's College of Veterinary Medicine in East Lansing. All four were females. Bowerman is not sure why. Deformed female eagles might survive better than male ones, but bald eagles also tend to lay female eggs first. Bowerman thinks it is possible that adult females—with the contaminants stored in their fat mobilized during the stress of breeding—unload much of their contaminant burden into their first egg. Ohio biologists similarly speculate that the stress of harsh winters prior to the 1991 and 1994 breeding seasons could have mobilized high contaminant concentrations from the fat of egg-laying females. The result, particularly in nests along the western Lake Erie shoreline, was a number of seemingly inexplicable deaths of eaglets shortly after they hatched.

Of the four deformed birds found three years ago in Michigan, all had high levels of PCBs in their bloodstreams. After being observed for several months, three of the four birds were euthanized. The eagle's necropsied brains, similar to the brains of herons in British Columbia thought to be affected by paper mill dioxins, were asymmetrical. Michigan State, however, saved one of the crossed-bill eagles for the Michigan United Conservation Club's wildlife encounters and wetlands public education programs. Ushering me through the MSU Wildlife Health Clinic one morning, Bowerman guided me past cages occupied by small, blinking owls and mourning doves on the mend to a ground-level cage dominated by a large brown bald eagle. "Meet Morrison," he said.

"Morrison?"

"They like to name their eagles here after dead rock stars," he explained. The other three deformed eaglets were named Elvis, Hendrix, and Joplin— rock luminaries who, like Jim Morrison, died of drug overdoses.

Bending down to peer into the dark cage, I saw that the bird's large dark beak was horribly twisted. Her top bill curved to the right, the lower bill to the left. Instead of a sharp-pointed eagle's beak, the top bill rounded and flattened like a small inverted spoon. Imagine unhinging and twisting a pair of pliers sideways, then flattening them with a hammer. This deformity is just as debilitating. "Stupid question: how is this a problem?" I asked.

"How can she tear her food?" Bowerman said. "She can fly and grab food, but she can't eat. Plus, in the wintertime with that big gap, her tongue and mouth could get frostbite."

The bird has to be fed bite-sized food, such as smelts or tiny hamsters. Because they wear down with use, the bills of raptors grow continually. Since she cannot use her bill, it and her little-used talons must be trimmed three or four times a year by Dr. James G. Sikarskie, the head of the wildlife veterinary clinic. The mere sight of him so upsets her that she must be physically restrained before he can proceed. When the bird was six months old, she caught her upper bill on the edge of her cage and pulled it off, as you would slip a claw off a cooked lobster, exposing her sensitive mandible tissue. Sikarskie had to pin her bill back on.

As I stood before the bird, she cocked her head to the right and stared at me inquisitively, reminding me of my grandmother's parakeet, Petey, which cocked its head in anticipation whenever I approached, as if I were going to feed it. In this bird there was none of the challenge, the completely remote otherness, I have sensed in the presence of wild bald eagles.

"She might have been wondering if you were bringing her food," Sikarskie later agreed. In order to prepare her for the nearly 100,000 people she now appears before in Michigan each year, her trainer, Dennis Laidler, sat with her for hours using food as a reward for interacting with him. That way, Sikarskie explained, when she appears before groups she is not nervous or excited.

"We don't want to hold her up like a circus thing, but she has to be well adjusted," he said. "Parakeets aren't afraid of people because most are bred in captivity, but this bird is a wild animal, so it takes some effort for her to be that well adjusted."

I learned later that a CAT scan indicated her brain, like those of the three deformed eagles that were euthanized, was asymmetric. Saved as a poster child for our tainted environment, in less than a year the malformed bird they now call Leuka had become something less than a bald eagle, an emblem far removed from what Congress originally intended more than two centuries ago.

Between 1994 and 1995, one or both of the adults at the bald eagle nest near the Ford Motor Company's Monroe plant changed. One or both of the parents of the crossed-bill eagle still found there in 1993 apparently had died or moved away. This past year, the white head of one of the pair—it was hard to tell whether it was the male or the female—was still streaked with brown. New to breeding, it was probably just four years old. When Dave Best walked into the pair's five-story-high nest from an adjacent fork in the cottonwood, he sensed nothing wrong. There were two eaglets, one with its back turned shyly toward Best. Only after he captured and lowered the first bird for banding and blood sampling did the other turn toward him—and he was face-to-face with another crossed-bill eagle.

Best was hardly surprised: it was the fifth deformed eagle he had encountered in three years. Never before, though, had the same nest produced a second crossed-bill eagle. Was this a genetic quirk, as some would suggest? With so many eagles in the Great Lakes, however, inbreeding was unlikely. Absent the machinations of some outside agent, Best knew the odds of the same pair of eagles producing deformed eaglets two out of three years were quite low. With one or both of the adults changing, the chances of a similar genetic breakdown reoccurring were all but incalculable.

No, the defect lay not in the eagles' DNA chains but in their food chain—in the fish they ate. In the fish that ate from the bottom of the river Raisin.

1,740 BALD EAGLES IN AN HOUR

Wheresoever the carcase is, there will the eagles be gathered together.
—MATT. 24:28

On my return [I] scarcely recognized my crew in their dress suits . . . while I, having nothing dressy in my bag, adorned my cap with an eagle's feather I found on the moraine, and thus arrayed we set forth to meet the noble Thlinkits.
—JOHN MUIR, *Travels in Alaska*

The young women from Fairbanks, the ones bundled up and asleep nearby in an extended-cab pickup, had assured me I would hear bald eagles calling to each other through the late night darkness. I hear no eagles, only the splash of salmon, the pop of newly formed ice, the whisper of sluicing slush. It is five-thirty in the morning in early November, and I stand alone on the banks of Alaska's Chilkat River. Behind me, the northern lights, gossamer bolts of green, pulsate above Iron Mountain. Across the river, the Big Dipper empties itself over Takhin Ridge. Upstream to my right, a bright three-quarter moon illuminates the snow-covered mountaintops, reflects off pinwheeling ice clots, and casts cottonwood shadows.

An hour later, the sky overhead blues ever so faintly. I can see salmon struggling up a shallow channel. Suddenly, sweeping across their path, an ephemeral shadow silently interrupts the rippling moonlight. I am not certain of what I have seen until a minute later, when another dark form, this one more clearly defined, breaks the light: a bald eagle. A third appears, noisily pouncing on a chum salmon, steadying itself with beating wings as it tries to land its very-much-alive catch. Out of their cottonwood roosts far across the Chilkat come more eagles. The brightening light reveals scores of them, already stationed on the broad gravel bars, erect, like somber jurors, atop driftwood logs and stumps. At the edge of the braided channels, eagles finally are talking, disputing last evening's leftovers. One breaks through the ice on a frozen pool, another skates haphazardly across it, both of them wrangling over a stiff salmon. Ten, twelve, fifteen, of them wheel about in a small kettle. An adult flies into a cottonwood twenty feet above my head. Its presence is enough to dissuade an immature eagle from doing the same. The adult peers down at me, curious but completely unconcerned. Moments later, though, a bolder immature flushes the adult, which swoops low over the green glacial water, scattering gulls. Then, no more than 20 yards across the channel before me, a mottled immature sinks both its talons into a live spawned-out salmon. Laboriously beating its wings, twice it lifts itself, and its prize, onto the edge of the frozen sandbar. Anchoring both of its talons in the fish's flank, it bows low, as if in thanks, and pulls up a strip of pink salmon meat. I hear the sound of ripping flesh.

"There's a good number of birds in here," Erv Boeker had said several days earlier as he panned the broad gravel bars of the Chilkat River with his binoculars. "I count six hundred." Moments earlier, two miles downstream off the Haines Highway, Boeker had scanned 350 eagles spread across the gray bars, and another hundred in the cottonwoods on the west side of the river. There are probably more, though. That morning, as we set off from the town of Haines, twenty miles downriver, the local public radio station weather forecast had predicted "Rain, followed by showers"—typical weather for southeast Alaska. Boeker, a retired U.S. Fish and Wildlife Service pilot and biologist who spent four autumns and winters studying the Chilkat bald eagles for the National Audubon Society, remembers some years when he did not see the sun between the first of October and Thanksgiving. Only a light, intermittent rain falls, but low clouds hug the mile-high mountains, obscuring all but a few ridges studded with Sitka spruce and western hemlock. "And it's a minimal count," adds Boeker, a large man in his early seventies with big hands, a broad, open face, ice-blue eyes, and wavy gray hair. "With this poor light, it's hard to pick out the subadults without a scope." No white heads, in other words, to distinguish the birds from the dark cottonwoods. Boeker is troubled, though, by the paucity of spawning salmon. "I've seen fish so thick in the channels here that everywhere I looked there were finning backs." Nonetheless, from just two vantage points, in less than half an hour he has spotted more than a thousand bald eagles. The continent's greatest congregation of bald eagles has convened.

The reason for this embarrassment of eagle riches is in plain sight, but not necessarily easy to perceive. Fed by a glacier grinding out of the Alsek ranges in British Columbia, the 25-mile-long Tsirku River has created a broad gravel, sand, and silt delta 2 1/2 miles wide and long, where it empties here into the Chilkat. Slightly upstream, the Tsirku broadens into another huge gravel fan. Boeker explains that the gravel overburden is 200 to 800 feet deep. "Water coming down the Tsirku goes under the gravel and then is warmed through friction as the solid substrate here [Iron Mountain] forces it to well up through these glacial silt aquifers. It stays four to five degrees centigrade [39–43°F.]—above freezing, warm enough to keep the river open here all winter long." Spawning in these oxygen-rich, spring-fed stretches of clear river water, an unusually late and large run of as many as 100,000 chum salmon, as well as sockeyes bound for Chilkat Lake, builds during the fall and often continues into December and January. This is not a stopover point for bald eagles migrating out of the north. Drawn by the promise of open water throbbing with spent salmon, bald eagles pour in from the south, funneling out of 100,000 square miles of southeast Alaska and British Columbia. Before their numbers rapidly decline in December and January—when frigid temperatures and shelf ice accumulating over shallow water make it harder to retrieve salmon—as many as 3,600 bald eagles have been counted from the air on the river, up in Chilkat Lake, and across the ridge to the east, along the Chilkoot River.

According to radio telemetry studies conducted by Boeker's Audubon-USFWS team, even more bald eagles than these unprecedented numbers depend upon the Chilkat. "We would track a bird with a radio transmitter for a week, then all of a sudden it was gone for a week or ten days, then it returned," recalls Boeker. "There's a constant turnover of birds coming in and out." The birds that arrive here are the largest bald eagles on the continent. Alaskan females weigh between ten and fourteen pounds and have wingspans approaching eight feet. The smaller males weigh between eight and ten pounds. Their greater size is an evolutionary adaption to the cold; larger bodies lose heat more slowly.

Today, as I accompany Boeker and Bill Zack, the state park ranger who patrols the Chilkat Bald Eagle Preserve, the eagle numbers pile up. In a pocket near Klukwan, the ancient native village that sits above what the Tlingits have long called the bald eagle council grounds, Boeker tallies 250 more eagles. From the bridge spanning the Klehini River, which empties into the Chilkat above Klukwan, we see another 32, including some perched in spruces filagreed with a dusting of snow. Skirting the Klehini, we follow a dirt road up the Dalton Trail, a former Tlingit route into the interior, where they became wealthy trading eulachon oil, which was extracted from tiny candlefish, for furs, hides, and copper nuggets from the Athabascans. Jack Dalton transformed the route, briefly, into a toll trail to the Klondike goldfields in 1898. That same year, nine miles upstream from here, the first of millions of dollars worth of placer gold was pulled out of Porcupine Creek, where tourists still pan for gold today. Along the Klehini we discover several hundred more eagles, primarily subadults, sitting on the flats and tucked into the cottonwoods.

At our last stop, three eagles maintain their perches as we exit Zack's truck. A mere 40 feet away, one adult cocks one eye toward us but never budges. "That's a good gauge of the harassment they experience," says Boeker. "In the Lower forty-eight, if you get out of your car, they flush."

In an hour we have counted 1,750 bald eagles.

The following day, I accompany Boeker and Zack up another dirt road that heads toward the Tsirku River on the west side of the preserve. "I always felt the worst thing would be if they built a road on this side beyond the Tsirku," Boeker confides. Along the way, a good number of eagles are camped on the council grounds; others are scattered throughout the preserve. "Normally, all these birds sitting here ought to be gobbling up fish," Boeker says. "My impression is that they are just sitting around waiting for fish, 'cause this time of day, eight-forty in the morning, is just about peak feeding time."

With the temperature slightly below freezing, the Tsirku's gravel bars and some isolated pools are freezing up. Seven sport utility vehicles are lined up on the gravel bar; heading for Lake Chilkat, which drains here into the river, a fisherman launches his small aluminum outboard into the main channel. Strolling out onto a gravel bar, Boeker and I inspect the frozen carcass of a chum salmon lying on the bank. It is about two and a half feet long, its fierce lower jaw bristling with canine teeth. "That's why they're also called dog salmon," says Boeker. "Some of the big ones grow absolutely grotesque, with their canine teeth way out and the top jaw longer. Andy [Hansen, his graduate assistant] and I weighed between two hundred and three hundred carcasses; they ranged from seven to nine pounds."

The first spawning channel we approach is only about ten yards wide and incredibly shallow, but it's boiling with salmon. The sleek green fish, their tail and dorsal fins extending far out of the water, shimmy and jolt their way up the cobbled bottom in great spasmodic splashes. Spawned-out salmon, their flesh paling and beginning to rot, float by the other way. Nearby, a first-year eagle quietly works on a carcass; an impassive adult perches in the weak sunlight.

"I'm surprised there aren't more birds up here," I say.

"Yeah, I am too," Boeker replies.

Looking around, though, Boeker says he doesn't believe he could design eagle habitat superior to the Chilkat Valley. "These cottonwood islands are optimum roosting, perching, and resting sites," he says, "and because there's human access on only one side, harassment is nil, and of course, normally a late big run of salmon provides food. Despite heavy winds downriver, the area here is pretty sheltered. On real cold days, they can go into the conifers to stay even more protected."

Framed by hanging glaciers and rugged snow-capped mountains, the small city of Haines, Alaska—population 1200—spectacularly straddles the Chilkat Peninsula at the head of Lynn Canal, North America's longest fjord. The town, eighty miles north of Juneau, was cofounded in 1879 by naturalist John Muir and the Reverend Samuel Hall Young as a site for a native Presbyterian mission. Muir was accompanying Young in order to explore the glaciers of southeast Alaska, particularly in Glacier Bay, which lies just over the ridges west of Haines. Traveling in a great red cedar canoe paddled by four Tlingit guides, Muir had long anticipated meeting the most influential of all Tlingit tribes. As they approached Yin-des-Tuk-ki, a long, low-built village on the Chilkat River, one of the natives called out to Young and Muir's party: "Who are you? What do you want? What have you come for?"

"A great preacher-chief and a great ice-chief have come to bring you a good message," their guide replied. Satisfied, the natives delivered an odd salute, firing their muskets over the canoe. "A swarm of musket-bullets, flying scarce high enough for comfort, pinged over our heads," Muir wrote of that November 1, 1879, encounter. When he and Young landed at the village, slaves of the Tlingits captured far south in the Pacific Northwest shouldered their provisions and bedding, and they were ushered into the large wooden house of the chief, Don-na-wuk, who greeted them warmly and staged a banquet feast in their honor: heaping bowls of dried salmon, deer back fat, small potatoes, and wild rose apples, all with seal grease dressing. Afterward Muir and Young were granted an audience with Chief Shathitch (Hard-to-Kill), the supreme chief of the Chilkat Tlingits, who had come from Klukwan, twenty-five miles upstream. Shathitch was wrapped in an elegant chinchilla blanket which, to the surprise of his guests, bore this inscription: "To Chief Shathitch, from his friend, William H. Seward!" The following year the mission, and what ultimately became the town of Haines, was established overlooking Portage Cove, the spot along the Chilkoot Inlet where the Tlingits beached their canoes and portaged across the Chilkat Peninsula to the Chilkat River.

When Boeker first came to Haines and the Chilkat Valley in the fall of 1978, the greeting he received was not nearly as warm as the one accorded Muir and Young a century earlier. "People were hostile and suspicious of our motives," recalls Boeker. "They didn't want anything to do with any biologist, and they didn't want anything to do with eagles. Talk of federal control of the valley was like waving a red flag at these people. It was a grim scene."

Invited to speak during a chamber of commerce luncheon at the Hotel Halsingland in the Fort William H. Seward historic district, Boeker was asked: "What in hell good are those eagles?"

"The eagles are just an artifact of this valley," Boeker responded. "It's the fish you've got to be concerned with." (Commercial fishing is the largest employer in Haines, and in the state.) Boeker pointed out that extensive timbering could interfere with fish spawning and feeding. "If the fishing community goes down, where's your community going to be?" he asked.

Boeker, then age fifty-eight, had recently retired from the U.S. Fish and Wildlife Service. A former World War II navy pilot, he had spent much of his career flying for the USFWS, working first with endangered whooping cranes, then with golden eagles. The National Audubon Society had just hired him to head a study of bald eagles in the Chilkat Valley. Environmentalists were concerned that a state Department of Natural Resources land use plan for Haines, and the nearby town of Skagway, favored timber and mineral interests more than protection of the eagles and the salmon upon which they, and Haines's large commercial fishing fleet, depended. With one of the town's two sawmills dismantled and the other idle, others just as adamantly believed that the valley's natural resources needed to be utilized. To bolster Haines's chronic boom-bust economy, in August of 1979 the state signed a contract with the Schnabel Lumber Company of Haines, permitting it to clear-cut 10.2 million board feet from the valley's state-owned forests—including some of the cottonwoods in which the eagles perched—each year for the next fifteen to twenty-five years.

The impending timber cut was not the first threat to the bald eagles. In the late 1950s Columbia Iron Mining was the first of three companies (followed by U.S. Steel and Mitsubishi) to consider mining low-grade magnetite, an iron ore, just above the bald eagle council grounds, at the present village of Klukwan. Working first through the alluvial plain and then into Iron Mountain itself, the operation would have diverted the river and annually dumped millions of tons of tainted mine tailings over six square miles of floodplain. Ultimately, the proposal was deemed economically infeasible. Then, at the urging of Fred Robards, a Juneau-based USFWS eagle biologist who had monitored the Chilkat eagles since the Columbia mine threat, the Alaska state legislature in 1972 established the 4,800-acre Chilkat River Critical Habitat Area. Encompassing the bald eagle council grounds, the unfunded area included less than a quarter of the habitat Robards had originally recommended. Simultaneously, the Fish and Wildlife Service's plan to create a Chilkat National Bald Eagle Refuge faltered over conflicts with private and state land holdings. Five years later the state dropped its proposal to set up a park for the eagles along the river in the face of intense opposition from local residents, who feared the park would impede traditional recreational pursuits, such as fishing and hunting, and jeopardize planned timber and mining development. Recalled a bewildered Robert LeResche, the state commissioner of natural resources. "The people screamed out against it like gut-shot rhinos,"

～◯ In Alaska, particularly southeast Alaska, bald eagles are not an uncommon sight. Were you to lift an overlay of bald eagle nest locations off a map of Admiralty Island, you would still detect the outline of the entire island southwest of Juneau, which comprises 860 miles of shoreline and 901 bald eagle nests. Alaska's eagle numbers—a stable, gradually increasing population of 40,000 to 45,000 bald eagles—dwarf those of the lower forty-eight states. Earlier in this century, however, their numbers had dwindled precipitously in Alaska as well. Fox farmers contended eagles were preying upon young foxes, and fishermen believed the birds were competing with them for live salmon. Between 1917 and 1952, more than 128,000 bald eagles were killed in Alaska for bounties ranging from fifty cents to two dollars. "Eagle-shooting, of all forms of rifle shooting, is . . . most attractive to the finished rifleman," asserted a 1935 article in the *American Rifleman*. That author's one-day take: thirty-one pairs of eagle talons. Some bounty hunters ran traplines. By 1941 the slaughter had depressed eagle numbers to half the population they had regained by the 1970s.

Although Haines was one of the epicenters of that pogrom, today it's hard to find anyone who shot an eagle. The wary birds flushed as soon as you got out of your car, one longtime resident recalled. "I shot at one eagle, but I didn't kill it. It was a long way off," says another, John Schnabel, the owner of the closed lumber mill.

"But shooting eagles was a big business," Schnabel recalls. "I had friends that made five, six hundred dollars a year. For two dollars each they were killing two, three hundred birds apiece."

Ross Hevel, who operated a barbershop—fifty cents for a hair cut, twenty-five cents for a shower—also served as a federal commissioner for the territory of Alaska. To prove they had earned a bounty, hunters presented Hevel with two eagle talons; Hevel authorized a voucher and dumped the talons in a 55-gallon drum that sat outside of his shop. "By springtime it was full of eagle feet," Schnabel remembers. "He'd haul it up to the garbage dump and throw them away."

Anxious to reopen its idle mill, the Schnabel Lumber Company, which had cut its first logs in Haines in 1939, successfully lobbied the state legislature in 1978 to authorize negotiated timber sales in areas of high unemployment—in other words, in Haines. The state pegged the town's unemployment rate at 29 percent; the chamber of commerce asserted it was nearly 70 percent. During the 1960s, Schnabel's mill and another squared off logs into "cants" for shipment to Japan. After improving market conditions led to mill expansions, by 1975 all the available state stumpage had been cut and one mill had been dismantled. Schnabel's mill operated part-time until it closed in 1977.

In September 1979, a month after the state completed its timber sale to Schnabel, the Southeast Alaska Conservation Council, a coalition of fifteen local conservation groups, including Lynn Canal Conservation, sued the state and Schnabel to block the clear-cutting. The suit, filed for the council by the Sierra Club Legal Defense Fund, contended the state was jeopardizing salmon spawning grounds and essential bald eagle habitat, including some of the eagles' cottonwood perches. Supported by the Haines Coalition, a group of businessmen, sportsmen, miners, commercial fishermen, natives, and timber interests who had helped modify the area land use plan, the Haines City Council voted to a join in the suit as a codefendant with the state and Schnabel.

Haines, a melting pot of passionate loggers, miners, potters, and professionals, of second-generation Alaskan individualists and California dropouts, was a town divided. "We felt our lifestyles were being challenged and dictated by people who didn't live here in the valley, under pressure of the media and preservationists in America," recalls Dave Olerud, the owner of a sporting goods store who later broke his back putting up the walls of his American Bald Eagle Foundation building, now a popular tourist attraction. "People were afraid, afraid all the timber would be shut down, the economy would be destroyed, we wouldn't be able to make a living, and we'd lose our homes."

"It was an ugly war, as only it can be in a small town," remembers Dick Folta, an attorney, engineer, and surveyor who opposed the clear-cutting. "Half on one side, half on the other, and no in-between." The anonymous phone calls Folta received were so threatening—"I'm going to mutilate your daughter"—that Folta moved his family to Micronesia for six years. The wife and daughter of David Nanney, a planner who was the borough's administrative secretary, also received obscene calls. Nanney, who with his wife now operates a bed-and-breakfast, resorted to commercial fishing when he lost his borough job. Twice all the wheels on his car fell off while he was driving because the lug nuts had been loosened; the windows of his car also were smashed. Logging opponents' businesses were boycotted. At their target ranges, residents shot at silhouettes of President Jimmy Carter and his interior secretary, Cecil D. Andrus. The last car bearing a faded "Sierra Club, Kiss My Axe" bumper sticker drove out of Haines just a few years ago. "These eagles were just a surrogate for other things," John Schnabel, the owner of the lumber company, claimed. "They wanted to make the whole damn valley an eagle preserve because they didn't want no logging."

Southeast Alaska Conservation Council's lawsuit failed. Its request for a preliminary injunction to halt the logging was denied, and at the end of 1980, the state superior court ruled against the council and ordered it to pay Schnabel $25,000 in court costs.

While environmentalists were not faring well in court, they were gaining the interest of national newspapers, magazines, and television networks, and they were developing support in Washington, D.C. In 1979, Representative Stewart "Mo" Udall of Arizona introduced a bill calling for a federal-state study aimed at protecting the eagles. The following summer, as the U.S. Senate commenced debate on the massive Alaska National Interest Lands Conservation Act, Senator Gary Hart of Colorado believed that only a national wildlife refuge could permanently protect the Chilkat bald eagles.

Conservationists suggested that the federal government, in exchange for 175,000 acres of state land in the valley, could cede other lands elsewhere of equal value to the state. In a state that refers to the rest of the distant country as "outside," the thought of federal control of Chilkat Valley was anathema. That May the state senate, at the urging of the borough and city of Haines, unanimously resolved that "it is essential to the social and economic well-being of our communities that the land adjacent to them be available under state and local law for the use and enjoyment of their citizens and not under the domination and control of federal agencies under federal law."

Anticipating correctly that Hart's maneuver to add the refuge to the lands bill would fail—it was blocked in a parliamentary move by Senator Mike Gravel of Alaska—Hart's staff, along with state officials and the National Audubon Society, crafted a fallback position: on July 21, 1980, Governor Jay Hammond declared a moratorium on logging in any areas that Audubon and the USFWS deemed essential for eagles, until studies, including Boeker's work, could be completed. The moratorium was almost moot: that month Schnabel announced it was slashing its workforce from fifty to twelve due to an inexplicable inability to fell and haul enough logs out of the state forests. Of the 10.2 million board foot allotment, only 1.5 million board feet of timber had been cut.

Establishing an advisory committee that included representatives of most factions in the dispute, Governor Hammond also contributed a quarter-million dollars in state funds to help fund complementary ecology studies—in hydrology, fisheries, big game—through 1981. One ironic finding: though today one of the big draws for the burgeoning cruise ship trade is a summer raft trip through the preserve, the ninety bald eagle breeding territories in the Chilkat and Chilkoot valleys experience one of the lowest success rates in North America—little more than a third are occupied each year, and of those, only a third successfully fledge young. Throughout southeast Alaska, as few as 14 percent of the adults in pristine areas breed each year. "It's a function of the summer water levels and the number of fish in the river," explains Boeker. "If a cold spring slows the glacial melt, the river gets real low and there's not any food in it for eagles at the time when they most need it, when the chicks first hatch and then fledge."

As the scientific pieces of the puzzle crystallized Boeker and Andy Hansen seemed to be making inroads with the people of Haines as well. Boeker was a widower and former military man whose most common rejoinder was "You bet!"—an enthusiastic, genuine affirmation of what others said. "It was hard to find someone we could trust," said Bill Thomas, then the chairman and CEO of Klukwan, Inc., the native village's corporation. "Erv's honest and really laid back. Some of the others were working on emotion, but Erv came in and worked on real needs." Hansen, a University of Tennessee graduate student and a rock climber, enjoyed speaking with the schoolchildren who came out to the council grounds to observe their work. Hansen's wife worked as a substitute teacher. The first two seasons he spent in Haines, Boeker did not receive one invitation for Thanksgiving Day dinner; the third year he fielded a dozen.

After the Southeast Alaska Conservation Council lawsuit was filed, Boeker advised Dave Cline, Audubon's regional vice president in Alaska, against joining as a plaintiff. "If you do that, we're dead in the water," said Boeker, who had been laboring to portray Audubon as a conservation organization interested in local residents as well as bald eagles. "Heck," he said recently, "I could see that logging wasn't all bad, but on the scale that was proposed, I thought it would be disastrous." Part of the Chilkat Valley's appeal is that, lying at the extreme northern range of North America's temperate rain forest, it is drier than the rest of southeast Alaska—60 inches of precipitation a year, compared with 90 inches in Juneau and more than 200 inches farther south on the panhandle. He felt that rotating timber here on an eighty-year cycle, as was done on the wetter islands in the Tongass National Forest, was absurd. Walking through forty-five-year-old clear-cuts farther up the Chilkat, he found alders and willows just three feet high, with a few sparse spruce seedlings struggling up among them.

The eagle-versus-timber conflict remained unresolved until January 28, 1982, when negotiations of the governor's Haines-Klukwan Cooperative Resource Study Advisory Committee again reached a stalemate—until a snowstorm cancelled the last flight out of Haines. With four more hours to wait for the Juneau ferry to arrive, the combatants reconvened in the Haines municipal building, in a room where maps and wish lists were pinned to the walls. There the years of controversy melted away into a consensus. Badly needing some sort of bill to lift the moratorium imposed by Governor Hammond, Schnabel decided to discuss a permanent preserve once he became convinced Audubon was not interested in grabbing land "based on politics and emotions rather than facts." Instead of the originally proposed 500-foot-above-sea-level contour boundaries—everything below that elevation was to be part of the preserve, everything above it would not be protected—Erv Boeker, Dave Cline, Jack Hodges, Schnabel, and state fish, wildlife, and forestry officials negotiated boundaries that protected almost all of the habitat that the eagle, salmon, and hydrology studies indicated were critical: a thirty-five-mile stretch of the Chilkat, extending nearly to its headwaters south of the Canadian border; cottonwood and evergreen perches southwest of the council grounds; and stretches of the Tsirku, the Klehini and, on the other side of the Takshanuk Mountains, a section of the Chilkoot above Chilkoot Lake.

Schnabel liked the fact the eagles' area would be called a preserve, not a sanctuary. With the exception of landing airplanes, residents and natives would continue to have complete access to the preserve: to hunt, fish, float the river, pick berries, cut wood for personal use, or even drive all-terrain vehicles or snowmobiles through the area, provided such activities did not disturb the eagles. All agreed that the legislation creating the preserve and adjacent state forest must be one bill, not two separate ones. "We aren't losing a damn thing, and we'll have more flexibility than we have now," Schnabel explained afterward to the *Chilkat Valley News.* "My so-called abandonment of the valley's stand against any bill is really no abandonment at all, for now instead of a blank map with nobody being able to do anything, we have a very specific plan."

State and federal officials began drawing up the bill during the ferry trip back to Juneau. After more marathon sessions in the state capital, the principal parties in the dispute signed a consensus document calling for a state bill to establish both a 48,000-acre Alaska Chilkat Bald Eagle Preserve and a Haines State Forest and Resource Management Area about five times as large. Among those signing were the mayors of the city and borough of Haines; members of the National Audubon Society, the Southeast Alaska Conservation Council, and Lynn Canal Conservation; and representatives of the U.S. Fish and Wildlife Service, the Schnabel Lumber Company, and the Haines branch of the Alaska Miners Association. Governor Hammond signed the legislation later that summer.

Fifteen years ago you could not find the image of a bald eagle on Main Street in Haines. Now such images seem as ubiquitous as the real thing along the Chilkat: pictures of eagles adorn hotel flyers and tourist brochures, including the Haines Visitor Center booklet, which touts the town as "The Valley of the Eagles." River trips through the preserve, albeit before the fall gathering, are among the more popular options for the growing number of cruise-ship tourists who dock each summer; sixteen thousand visitors rafted or jet boated there last year.

"Everybody admits right now the eagle preserve is a good thing," says retired teacher Ray Menaker, the founder and former editor of the weekly *Chilkat Valley News,* whose wife, Vivian, was the first to alert the National Audubon Society to threats to the eagles in the early 1970s. "It's helped eagles and also helped the economy of the area while not really hurting the timber or mineral industry." The state, after investing $1.8 million in the Schnabel mill to become a half-owner, did foreclose on the mill in 1983, however. It was subsequently sold and closed again. "The preserve is one of the things people around here are reasonably proud of," Menaker continues. "Some things didn't satisfy anyone, but we could all live with it. When you stop using hype and pejorative terms like 'locking up the valley' and 'cutting every last tree' and instead talk about what's real, where can you log or where do eagles need protection, what do you do about the fish, it makes a tremendous difference." Along with his wife, another retired teacher, Menaker is a Haines fixture. A former borough chairman and acting mayor, he is also an amateur actor who had a brief speaking part in the locally filmed Disney production of *White Fang.* Each Saturday the World War II naval officer and graduate of Columbia and Stanford reads short stories on KHNS-FM, the energetic public radio station that has a mere three thousand people within the sound of its signal.

Some animosities, though, die hard. Four years ago Governor Wally Hickel replaced Menaker on the bald eagle preserve advisory council, a seat Menaker had held representing Lynn Canal Conservation since the committee's inception in 1982.

Explaining Menaker's removal, Brenda Wilcox, an administration aide and former Haines resident, erroneously told the *Chilkat Valley News,* "He's probably the only person I've ever known to be a member of the Communist party." Three weeks later, the state parks director lauded the Democrat and independent for his instrumental role in helping "the many separate voices become one in support of both the eagles and their habitat."

⌒ The only significant constituency that did not sign the agreement was the Chilkat Tlingits of Klukwan, the native village overlooking the bald eagle council grounds. They had always opposed a preserve. "The eagle is valuable, but people are more valuable," Joe Hotch, the sixty-three-year-old longtime president of the village tribal council, explained to me one afternoon. "The eagles can very well take care of themselves." The 125 to 150 residents of Klukwan—about a quarter to a fifth of the population that lived here a century ago—feared a preserve would jeopardize private land allotments granted to some village members as a result of the Alaska Natives Claims Settlement Act. They feared it would draw more gawking tourists to the village. And they feared they would be restricted from trapping, fishing, hunting rabbits and ducks, and picking berries—the subsistence lifestyle that both sustained them and served as a communion with their environment.

Long before Europeans reached southeast Alaska, the Chilkat and Chilkoot Tlingits had zealously guarded their euchalon "grease" trails into the interior. For nearly a century, beginning with the Russian occupation in the late 1700s, this monopoly enabled them to grow wealthier and more powerful serving as intermediaries between Russian, Spanish, British, and American traders and the Athabascans. They hauled in both native and European commodities, such as Hudson Bay Company muskets, for which they demanded four to five times the amount of beaver, lynx, and fox furs they had originally exchanged for the goods. In 1852, to protect their franchise, they routed the occupants and burned Fort Selkirk, which the Hudson Bay Company had erected on the Upper Yukon River. During the 1880s, though, canneries on the Chilkat Peninsula tremendously depleted their salmon stocks, and the discovery of gold soon reduced the Tlingits to the role of hired packers. Whites then quashed much of their culture and appropriated some of their land during the construction of the Haines Highway, built in 1943 to provide an alternative military supply route to the Alaska Highway. The Tlingits lost more land in 1955 to the laying of a jet fuel pipeline to the Eielson Air Force Base used by the Strategic Air Command in Fairbanks. "We've always been resistant to change," explains Lonnie Strong Hotch, the thirty-seven-year-old secretary of the village council. "We pretty much want to be left alone by the outside world."

The Chilkat Tlingits were divided into two clans, the Ganaxtedih Ravens and the Daklawedih Eagles-Wolves; at birth, one became a member of one's mother's clan, and marriage within that group, or moiety, was forbidden. The Tlingits hunted bald eagles: their wings were used as brooms, their feathers fletched arrows, and according to some anthropologists, the Tlingits ate the flesh of eagles. During certain ceremonial dances, eagle down still is shaken out of headdresses as a sign of peace. Unlike the highly revered raven, however, anthropologists who visited the Tlingits early in this century did not sense the eagle was considered sacred. "No one ever instructed me on what the eagle means to Tlingit people," Lonnie

Strong Hotch told me one afternoon as eagles flew past the window of her modern kitchen. "All I know is it's the crest in our family."

Joe Hotch, whose warm, round face is trimmed in long gray sideburns, sits at a folding table in the village council offices and explains the relationship this way: "The eagle is sitting in a tree and looking out into the water. He's looking for food. We have to talk to the eagle. 'Give us something to eat. Give us something to eat.' We say it also to the other birds and the fish. We believe all the birds and animals can understand us. We always believe they respond to us." Hotch has never heard of Tlingits eating eagle flesh, but he recalls the days of the eagle bounty quite well. "That was an income for many, and for many, if you didn't own a boat, it was the only source of income," he says. "I wasn't a good shooter. I probably got ten. Maybe they were proud of me . . . for not eating them."

From a distance, from the bald eagle council grounds, Klukwan doesn't look much different from the scattering of frame buildings visible in century-old photographs, or from many other native Alaskan villages. Woodsmoke curls up from pipes pushed through tin roofs. Fishing gear and nets, hoses and rusty chain saws, clutter front yards. Next to the tribal homes boarded up with plywood, satellite dishes pull in television signals. A number of the homes, though, are quite modern, and in front of many are new four-wheel drive Toyotas, Chevrolet Luminas, and S-10 pickups: Klukwan, though it is not apparent to the casual visitor, is ground zero for Klukwan, Inc., one of Alaska's fifteen largest corporations.

As part of the Alaskan Native Claims Settlement Act, in exchange for native lands all native Alaskans were given shares in both regional and village corporations. In 1976, Klukwan, Inc., the village corporation, was granted 23,000 acres on Long Island, far south in the southwest Alaska archipelago, the land of the Tlingits' former enemies, the Haida. During the 1980s, Klukwan, Inc., clear-cut Long Island in a manner that appalled conservationists but generated considerable dividends for shareholders, many of whom live outside of the village.

Bill Thomas, the middle-aged board member and former CEO of Klukwan, Inc., makes no apologies for clear-cutting Long Island. Sitting in his handsome Haines home overlooking Lynn Canal in a *Northern Exposure* T-shirt, the stocky Klukwan vice president explains that Klukwan needed to accelerate the cut because interest rate increases were causing the value of the timber to plunge. Klukwan cut as much as 60 million board feet a year. Sustained-yield forestry was impossible, he says, without the subsidies the U.S.

Forest Service provides in Tongass National Forest. "We found out we couldn't build a 1.5 million-dollar road to log 160 acres unless Big Daddy was paying for it," he says. Also a commercial fisherman, he shows me two painted totem poles his brother carved for Thomas's dining room. On each pole, he explains, are the money signs: salmon swimming up the side of the pole, a halibut in the middle of one pole, and a Sitka spruce centered on the other. "That's Long Island," he says. Several years ago Klukwan, Inc., which maintains offices in Juneau and Haines, grossed $97 million and paid each of its 253 native shareholders $35,000 in dividends. Though its timber resources are now depleted, Klukwan, Inc., has diversified into logging, plywood, road building, stevedore operations and, in Japan, fuel barges; only one-eighth of its 400 employees are natives. Earlier this year the corporation made a one-time, annual distribution of $65,000 to each of its shareholders or their heirs. Thomas views the company's success as a natural extension of the riches enjoyed by the Chilkat Tlingits, true capitalists whose celebratory potlatch ceremony was, he believes, a show of wealth. "You can't live fifty years in the past if you [have] electricity and a car," he says.

Lonnie Strong Hotch isn't so sure. "The reservation system hasn't worked, and I don't know if this will work," she says. "The whole thrust to assimilate native people into mainstream America, none of it's worked." Dividends from Klukwan, Inc., she says, have "been a blessing and a curse. There's an element of alcohol and drug abuse, and a lot of younger people spend [the money] carelessly on frivolous things like new cars and stereos."

Until shortly before my 1993 visit, a Klukwan, Inc., subsidiary was also a 51 percent partner with Geddes Resources, Ltd., in a venture to develop Haines's port to handle the ore from the proposed Windy Craggy copper mine. Geddes, a Toronto company, had proposed a vast open-pit operation to mine the continent's largest known deposit of copper ore, along the Tatshenshini River north of Haines in British Columbia. Those who have rafted the river into the U.S. and Gulf of Alaska say that the stream, which increases its volume fifty times in a span of five miles, is North America's wildest. Besides altering the grand, untouched Tatshenshini wilderness, some feared that the Windy Craggy mine could significantly affect the Chilkat bald eagles. Originally the mine would have sent an ore truck down the Haines Highway past the Chilkat foraging grounds every twenty minutes for the next thirty years. Geddes then proposed a 150-mile-long pipeline to carry the slurried copper to Haines. Treated slurry water would be dumped into an arm of the Lynn Canal.

This time the opposition was led in Haines by Peter Enticknap, a tall, comfortable investment broker and real estate agent in his mid-forties from southern California who in 1988 retreated to a home on the same hillside as Bill Thomas. Enticknap was appalled to learn that in addition to the potential threat to the eagles, the salmon, and the water quality of the Lynn Canal, the mine operation would require a mammoth impoundment of acidic mine tailings high in the mountains in the most seismically active region of the world. He teamed up with Ric Careless, a British Columbia environmentalist, and the two men orchestrated a five-year campaign to stop Windy Craggy. One key: a National Park Service staffer alerted Enticknap to the Boundary Waters Treaty of 1906, which prohibits Canada and the United States from allowing polluted streams to harm each others' drainage areas. During the 1970s, Enticknap learned, a mine proposed on a creek that flows into Glacier National Park was scuttled because the plan violated the treaty. "It was like somebody had handed me a road map of how to kill this thing," he recalls. Aware that the United States and Canada also had agreements not to affect each other's World Heritage Sites, he also lobbied to have Glacier Bay declared a World Heritage Site by the United Nations Educational Scientific and Cultural Organization.

While he understandably made no progress with the Tlingits of Klukwan, Inc., Enticknap succeeded in alarming the people of Yakutat, a village north of the mouth of the Tatshenshini and Alsek rivers whose residents eat an average of 600 to 700 pounds of fish each year. Carolyn Powell, the former chair of the Yak-Tak Kwaan Native Corporation, called Windy Craggy "an act of genocide against the Yakutat Tlingit people." Klukwan's tribal council leader, Joe Hotch, also opposed the copper mine. "We had the position that it would harm wildlife and the river if there was a spill by one of the ore trucks," he said.

The debate continued, as it always does, in Haines, but the Alaska congressional delegation was deaf to Enticknap's concerns. In concert, though, with the American Rivers conservation group, which declared the Tatshenshini one of the continent's ten most endangered rivers for four consecutive years, the opponents of the mine enlisted the support of Senator Al Gore. The political winds began to shift against Windy Craggy. With the late 1991 election of the progressive New Democratic Party in British Columbia, the province's new premier, Mike Harcourt, ordered a freeze on all new mining claims in the Windy Craggy area and established an independent review panel which concluded, a year later, that the mine posed a real risk for acid mine drainage and the permanent destruction of fish and bear habitat. Gore, who by then was vice president of the United States, insisted that the Canadian government honor its international agreement not to degrade U.S. waters. By the time the fight was over, even Klukwan Inc.'s Bill Thomas, unwilling to risk damaging Lynn Canal water, had drawn the line at the slurry pipeline. "I told Geddes they could pipe it," he said, "if they took it back and dumped it in their Yukon tundra holes."

The Windy Craggy mine proposal was canceled, and the Tatshenshini-Alsek Wilderness is now a World Heritage Site, as are its neighbors—Glacier Bay National Park, the trans-boundary Wrangell–St. Elias National Park, and Canada's Kluane National Park. Haines and the bald eagles of the Chilkat are now surrounded by the globe's largest area of world-class preserves.

⌇◦ Driving by myself from Haines to the council grounds one day, I first notice bald eagles above the airport at Mile 8. They perch in trees along the road and on low stumps out on the gravel bars. At Mile 15 an eagle flies by at eye level, like a gull on the Chesapeake Bay Bridge-Tunnel. The first broad pullover overlooking the eagle flats is at Mile 19. Formally tuxedoed on this gray day, before me about three hundred bald eagles caucus in twos and threes on low stumps and gravel bars. A few of the eagles cruise low over the channel, their reflections dazzling in the cold gray water. Rocking forward like a seesaw, an adult rips into a salmon and gulps it down like a kid sucking up a strand of spaghetti. Alighting nearby, two gulls wait at a respectful distance, but finally give up. The flats here are a peaceable kingdom: while adult eagles flying low over a slough might lift up gulls, scavenging gulls and magpies coexist with their larger neighbors. "In the lower forty-eight during the winter, about half the eagle's diet is composed of other birds," Boeker had told me, "but up here we never saw an eagle make a determined pass at another [avian] species."

Twenty minutes later the same eagle is still eating, but another adult thrusts its chest against the glutton's right flank, displacing it. "They're opportunistic," Boeker had explained. "It's a lot easier to displace a bird that's already eating than to catch a fish on your own. It's a communal effect"—a strategy that ensures all eagles are adequately fed and that also conserves energy.

A hundred yards upstream an adult flies in at the feet of another that has perched on a snag to dine on a beached salmon; a third, approaching in a long glide, quickly replaces the second bird. All three arch their backs, calling to each other. As they do, two brazen magpies appear; the third eagle is so unfazed it doesn't even pick at them. The magpies quickly retreat. Back at the first group I am observing, a third adult alights nearby, then quickly reverses direction and lunges into the air toward the bird that has just commenced feeding. Backing off, the second bird bobs its head in the water to wash its bill, and itself, of the entire matter.

As the day wears on, I can see more white heads salting the cottonwoods upstream, along the road, and across the river. At one stop I count more than a hundred, their white heads as gaudy as Christmas ornaments, decorating a handful of trees, as many as four birds on a single branch. In the days that followed, more birds would arrive. A week later a U.S. Fish and Wildlife Service aerial survey of the entire preserve counted 2,890 eagles; in early December, the second aerial count climbed to 3,284—one of the higher totals in recent years.

More salmon would come too, but not as many as chum or sockeyes that used to spawn in the Chilkat. "The fish," Erv Boeker says, "are the major question." His concerns are well founded. For more than half a century kokanee salmon spawning in a 2.4-mile-long stretch of Glacier National Park's McDonald Creek attracted the densest autumn concentration of bald eagles south of Canada. In 1981, 100,000 spawning salmon drew 639 eagles in one day. But that same year, opossum shrimp introduced during the 1960s and '70s into the Flathead River basin migrated into Flathead Lake, where the landlocked salmon spent most of their lives. Instead of supplementing the salmon's diet—the purpose of the shrimp introduction—the shrimp preyed upon zoo plankton, the principal food source for both juvenile and adult salmon. Between 1987 and 1989, the salmon population completely crashed. As a result, bald eagles no longer pause along the creek to forage during their southward migration. Seven years ago researchers there counted just twenty-five bald eagles.

Meanwhile, theories abound regarding the recent sporadic salmon runs on Alaska's Chilkat River: overfishing on the high seas; problems with the smolt leaving fresh water for salt water; inadequate food supplies in the Pacific; a slight temperature increase in the Pacific caused by El Niño. But it is all simply speculation. According to Mike Jacobsen, a USFWS raptor biologist in Juneau, "Nobody knows what's going on."

⌒ Leaving Klukwan on my next-to-last day on the Chilkat, I was driving along the Haines Highway when I observed a small squad of amateur photographers with long lenses trained high in the air, up toward the tree-less ridge of the Takshanuk Mountains. The group included a young bearded man from Sheridan, Wyoming; two young Japanese men; an American expatriot living on British Columbia's Victoria Island; and the two women from Fairbanks. Taking advantage of a rare sunny day, the eagles—the expatriot explained—at one o'clock had left the gravel bars to the gulls. Two hours later, with the river cloaked in shadow, they are still cavorting in the sun. I count nine eagles wheeling about in one of my binoc-ulars' view fields, then seventeen, piling up above the top of the mountain, soaring into view from beyond the ridge, above the Chilkoot River Valley.

I focus on two birds, one an adult, one an immature, synchronizing their long glides against the face of the mountain. Banking and veering abruptly, high against the blue sky and a white snow saddle, they lock talons and tum-ble once, twice, before splitting apart like trapeze artists a mile above my head. During the breeding season, the talon lock is a courtship ritual; it can also be an aggressive death spiral. This, though, is sheer play, the joie de vivre of frolicking bald eagles. Other duos, exquisite aerialists all, swerve wing to wing. Within half an hour, though, as the mountain blushes with alpenglow and the river draws pale yellow light from the sky, the birds descend earth-ward, some to the cottonwoods, some to a meal. Thirty salmon are strug-gling up one narrow side channel; at the head of the gauntlet await eight bald eagles.

Forty yards across deeper water a straining eagle tugs a large fish out of the river. Another adult, tail flared, quickly arrives, tilting its head back in a threatening cry; the air is so cold I can see the bird's exhaled breath. The dis-play earns the eagle a single bite of salmon. Retreating, the aggressor picks, without much conviction, at one of the five large fish heads scattered across the sand. Across the council grounds, bald eagles chastise each other. Those perched in the cottonwoods above me answer. More birds still are in the air. Emerging out of the north, a pair of adult bald eagles veers again and again in unison against a dark snow massif and a thin nimbus of radiant, flaming yellow clouds. One flies upside down underneath the other, their talons nearly clamped together; then they cant to the left and glide to the right until they disappear, far across the river, into their dark cottonwood roosts for the night.

CHAPTER 15

IN THEIR
RIGHTFUL PLACE

That which is not useful is vicious.
—COTTON MATHER

Nature and books belong to the eyes that see them.
—RALPH WALDO EMERSON

An elegant osprey, Ben Franklin's fish hawk, flushes from a snag along the river's edge and veers up a narrow gut that drains the marsh. In search of one of New Jersey's newest pairs of bald eagles, Larry Niles and I follow it, his small aluminum motorboat cutting up through a canyon of tall phragmite reeds deepened by a three-foot tidal drop.

The eagles' nest had been discovered the previous winter, on the wild, wooded edge of a sand mine, yards away from where the sandy soil of southern New Jersey dissolves into tidal marsh. The pair's two eaglets, which Niles had banded two months earlier, probably had been airborne for three to four weeks. The chances of seeing them soar, though, or even locating them perched, long past feeding time in the middle of a hot, muggy July day, are slim. After passing Mauricetown, once a Victorian sea captains' hamlet, our odds diminish further as the serpentine Maurice River swerves away from its west bank. Off to our right, we can see the ninety-foot towers of the sand mine plant. The nest is in a pitch pine a thousand feet to the south. But how to reach it, separated as we are from the tree line by at least a half mile of impenetrable phragmites?

Then, before disappearing westward, the osprey shows us the way. As we enter the tidal gut, waves of tiny fiddler crabs scramble up the slick, exposed banks to flee our noisy approach. Soon we are striking submerged tree trunks, so many that Larry is forced to cut the motor and raise the propeller.

Armed with oars, we pole our way, zigzagging past ancient trunks of Atlantic white cedar, glazed with mud, polished twice a day for generations by the brown tides. Their size—many are much wider than dinner plates—and their enduring presence seem inexplicable. "The marsh was probably diked and flooded a hundred or more years ago by salt hay farmers," Larry speculates.

Several hundred yards later the cedar stumps are impassable. We are fortunate, though. Just beyond where we clamber up the slippery silt bank, the tall phragmite reeds give way to waist-high *Spartina patens*, yellow-green cordgrass that affords us an unobstructed view of the bald eagle nest, 300 yards away. On the other side of the gut, our osprey guide perches in a snag above its nest. The remainder of the marsh is as still as a watercolor. With my binoculars, I scan the tree line. Nothing. Planting a tripod in the muck sucking at our sneakers, Larry Niles trains his spotting scope on the nest tree itself. Slowly, like the pattern embedded in a three-dimensional puzzle, the eagles reveal themselves.

"There's a bird," Larry reports.

"One of the immatures?" I ask.

"Yep. It's definitely a bird," which in his parlance means an "eagle." "I can see its mouth open, panting."

I take a one-eyed look through the scope. Barely perceptible through the pine boughs, the fledgling is perched in a limb fork about 25 feet below the nest. Surrounded by a gray penumbra in the noonday light, the brown silhouette is staring directly at us. "But," Larry says, "we're too far from it to represent any threat."

Workers at the Morie Company's sand plant first saw the eagles, both adults and young, two summers earlier. They spotted them again the following year, particularly at the pond where the adults taught the young to fish. As the employees spent more time on the plant grounds as part of the company's new wildlife monitoring program, the sightings increased. Finally, assistant plant manager Nick Carapelli, a lean ruddy man in his late forties, stumbled upon the nest early one February morning while checking on a wood duck box he had erected. He noticed fur balls, pieces of bone, and white splash at the base of the nest tree.

When Jim Zadorozny, the company's manager of environmental affairs, learned of Carapelli's find, he briefly wondered how involved state zoologists would become at the plant. Fortunately, he realized, the nest was at the edge of the plant property, where federal and state wetlands regulations had long forbade further expansion of the sand-mining operation. The company had also already developed a relationship with Larry Niles and his staff. For years the sand industry had been at loggerheads with the Pinelands Commission, which regulated land use within the New Jersey Pine Barrens. The presence of state-threatened barred owls had precluded some of Morie's expansion plans at another plant. It was only a matter of time, company officials believed, before another rare species issue would disrupt its operations.

Adopting a proactive approach, Morie joined the Wildlife Habitat Enhancement Council, a Maryland-based nonprofit organization that assists corporations in upgrading wildlife habitat on their property. Morie's employees, many of whom hunt, embraced the council's recommendations. They surveyed and monitored wildlife, established deer and wild turkey feeding stations, constructed an underground hibernaculum for wintering snakes, and created a park where the public could enjoy wildlife. Several miles upstream, at its Port Elizabeth plant, Morie also was working with Niles's office, WHEC biologists, and local conservation groups to innovatively reclaim one of its abandoned sand ponds.

"Instead of having adversarial relationships, we wanted to see if we could find some common ground with the environmental community," explains Bob Cook, Morie's president. "Understanding their point of view, and trying to have them understand ours, is essential to our business's long-term viability." Rather than leave a sterile, steep-sloped pond, the company was excavating a shallow ledge 50 to 100 feet wide and planting it with pickerel weed, cattails, and woolgrass bluestem, the kind of aquatic plants that draw fish—and ultimately fish eaters such as herons, ospreys, and eagles.

Zadorozny's phone conversation with Niles about the new eagle nest marked the second time in two months the Morie company had called Niles about eagles. While deer hunting near the Port Elizabeth plant the previous December, Ron Johnson, Morie's chief executive officer, noticed an emaciated eagle by a sand pond. Summoned by Johnson, Niles crawled over a berm and nabbed the listless bird by hand. It wasn't his first encounter with the eagle. Nearly three years earlier, Niles and Kathy Clark had needed a deer carcass bait and a cannon-fired net to trap it, even though it had been flying for days with a five-pound otter trap clamped to its right leg. Its toes were decayed and dead, but, reluctant to sentence the bird to a life of zoo captivity, Niles and wildlife rehabilitator Don Bonica, of Toms River, New Jersey, ultimately decided to release the bird. Despite a foot bottom that flared out into a club, the remarkable eagle had fended for itself for thirty-four more months. This time, though, it couldn't be saved, and died at Bonica's facility.

The day Carapelli discovered the eagles' nest, Niles scaled one of the plant's tall towers hoping to observe the birds, but trees obstructed his view. Looking around, though, he was impressed by how much of their former South Jersey stronghold the eagles had reclaimed. Just a month earlier, seventeen eagles—half the entire count for the Delaware Bay region and 20 percent of New Jersey's total—had been spotted along or near the Maurice. Now, from the tower, Niles could see upstream to the water towers and industrial plants of Millville, to the north. Past it, on dammed Union Lake, a pair soon would be incubating three eggs in a nest he had built two years earlier to lure them away from an island where they were too exposed to fishing disturbance. Turning westward, Niles could see the Unamin sand operation. Just beyond it, he knew, stood the Bear Swamp nest tree, the sole remaining breeding territory in the state when he had come to New Jersey more than a decade ago, the first nest he himself had fashioned. Across the river to the east, Belleplain State Forest had long harbored a nest. Now another one had been constructed on the river.

Below Niles's feet were dunelike piles of silica quartz sand, so pure it was used for foundry castings and moldings, swimming pool filters, and playbox sand. The irony was not lost on Niles. It was the same high-quality South Jersey sand that prompted the failed sand barge proposal on the Cohansey River, the same sand that, more than a decade ago, had forced the state to invoke eminent domain in order to save the Bear Swamp nest from another company's sand mine expansion.

Peering again from the marsh through his spotting scope, to the right of the first bird Larry Niles discerns a tail and a drooping wing: the other fledgling.

"They can fly now, right?" I ask.

"Oh, yeah," he says, "but they're just taking it easy. The first couple weeks can be rough. If they've been poorly fed, it takes longer for them to fly. And physical condition is not the only [requirement] for flying. It takes guts, too. When we were hacking birds, some of the best-conditioned ones wouldn't fly, but they were so aggressive they made everyone else fly."

Niles is surprised, though, that the fledglings are still lingering so close to the nest. There is no sign of the adults. They could be anywhere along the river, or over the horizon, perched above the fifty-acre sand-mining pond where they occasionally fish. "At this point, the adults want nothing to do with this nest," Niles says. "They'll feed them, but they don't want to be near them."

꩜ With minimal fanfare, a week earlier the Fish and Wildlife Service had officially upgraded the bald eagle's status from endangered to threatened throughout the contiguous United States. Though the protections for threatened eagles are essentially the same, a few biologists privately groused that the reclassification was based more on politics than on science, an attempt to prove to congressional critics that the Endangered Species Act wasn't a one-way street: once listed for protection, a species could recover enough to warrant reclassification. Yet, in terms of numbers and geographic spread, bald eagles clearly had risen far above the predicament of the still endangered California condor, for example, or the whooping crane or Florida panther. In the contiguous states there were nearly 4,500 occupied bald eagle breeding territories, with at least one in every state except Rhode Island, Vermont, and Nevada. The breeding population had been doubling every six or seven years since the late 1970s, and those pairs were producing more than 1.1 young per nest—a sign of a healthy population, and far better than the anemic .59 per nest rate of 1963. In Florida alone last year, 831 occupied territories fledged 982 eaglets, including a nearly unprecedented four from a single nest apparently tended by three adults.

In less than a decade, New Jersey's one remaining nest had multiplied to eleven, nine of which had fledged young. For the fourth time in the past five years the nest, suspended in a sycamore above Stow Creek, had yielded an eagle rarity—triplets. So had the Union Lake nest. Each of the remaining eyries fledged two young eagles, for a statewide total of twenty—the state's most productive spring in at least three decades. Besides the nests clustered along Delaware Bay and its tributaries, one was hidden near a cranberry bog in the Pine Barrens not far from the Atlantic Coast, and yet another on a central New Jersey reservoir. There also were intriguing, albeit unsubstantiated, reports of other breeding pairs—up the Great Egg Harbor River, along the Atlantic Coast; on the Wanaque Reservoir near the New York State border; on a series of lakes west of there; and far up the Delaware near the Pennsylvania–New Jersey–New York border.

Larry Niles knew that the 1973 ban on DDT was the principal factor in the bald eagles' recovery here in New Jersey and across the nation. Pulsing out of the Chesapeake Bay, bald eagles eventually would have reclaimed southern New Jersey—with or without the Endangered Species Act. But he also knew that, were it not for that act and similar state legislation that it inspired, the comeback would have taken much longer. A year after the enactment of the earlier Endangered Species Protection Act of 1966, bald eagles residing below the fortieth parallel—roughly, from northern California to the Mason-Dixon line—were declared endangered; in 1978 all bald eagles in the lower forty-eight states were protected.

As a result, over the past decade public and private agencies spent as much as $4 million a year to restore and protect the bald eagle. In New Jersey, as throughout the country, declaring the bald eagle endangered mobilized public support. Private citizens donated funds to "adopt" nests. In Haddon Heights, New Jersey, schoolchildren raised a thousand dollars from bake sales. The Save the Bald Eagle Foundation, based in Tennessee, funneled corporate donations to New Jersey's bald eagle recovery efforts, which were also supported by state residents who credited overpayments on their state income tax returns to the state's endangered wildlife fund.

Like other states from New York to California, New Jersey filled in some of the eagle gaps on its map with its hacking program, releasing, over a six-year span, fifty-six first-year Canadian eagles into the South Jersey marshes. Some of the chicks placed in the sole remaining New Jersey nest were produced by captive eagles cared for at the U.S. Fish and Wildlife Service's Patuxent Wildlife Research Center in Maryland—by far the largest of the captive breeding programs conducted by zoos and foundations. The Southeast was repopulated, in part, through a cooperative effort of Florida wildlife officials and the George Miksch Sutton Avian Research Center in Bartlesville, Oklahoma. Eggs were removed from Florida nests shortly after they were laid, forcing the parents to "double-clutch"—lay another set of eggs. Artificially incubated, the eaglets hatched from the removed eggs were placed in hacking towers and released throughout the Southeast. Nesting bald eagles might have eventually spread into these areas, but because of the extraordinary recovery efforts, these jump-started eagles were protecting essential habitat that otherwise might have been lost. Combined with the Bald and Golden Eagle Protection Act, the Endangered Species Act's penalties also had helped curtail illegal shooting. The ESA also led the government to ban lead shot for waterfowl hunting, a significant cause of fatal lead poisoning in bald eagles.

Less than a month before Niles and I stood in the Maurice River marsh last summer, the act had scored a major environmental victory as well. The

U.S. Supreme Court had ruled that, under the ESA, the Interior Department had the right to protect not only endangered and threatened species but also their essential habitat, on both federal and private land. The case had been brought by the Sweet Home Chapter of Communities for a Great Oregon, a group of small landowners, logging companies and families dependent upon the forest products industries in the Pacific Northwest. They alleged that the Clinton administration's plan to save the northern spotted owl, a threatened species that relies upon old-growth forests, had injured them economically. The ESA, they argued, was powerless to prevent the destruction of such an organism's habitat.

The lawsuit, which had been upheld by a federal appeals court, revolved around the language of the Endangered Species Act and the subsequent regulations implemented by the secretary of the interior. Under the act, it is unlawful to "take" any protected species—"take" meaning "to harass, harm, pursue, hunt, shoot, wound, kill, trap, capture, or collect, or to attempt to engage in such conduct." Since 1981 the Interior Department further has defined "harm" as "an act which actually kills or injures wildlife. Such act may include significant habitat modification or degradation where it actually kills or injures wildlife by significantly impairing essential behavioral patterns, including breeding, feeding, or sheltering."

Justice John Paul Stevens's majority opinion found three reasons to conclude that the Interior Department had reasonably interpreted the intent of Congress. The first: an ordinary understanding of the word "harm." "The dictionary definition of the verb form of 'harm' is 'to cause hurt or damage to; injure,' " Stevens wrote. "In the context of the ESA, that definition naturally encompasses habitat modification that results in actual injury or death to members of an endangered or threatened species." Writing for a three-judge minority that included himself, Chief Justice William H. Rehnquist, and Justice Clarence Thomas, Justice Antonin Scalia objected to the Interior Department's interpretation. "Impairment of breeding does not 'injure' living creatures; it prevents them from propagating, thus 'injuring' a population that otherwise would have maintained or increased its numbers." Scalia also articulated well the mood of many members of the Republican Congress. "The Court's holding that the hunting and killing prohibition incidentally preserves habitat on private land imposes unfairness to the point of financial ruin—not just upon the rich, but upon the simplest farmer who finds his land conscripted to national zoological use."

Section 7 of the ESA requires all federal agencies to ensure that any action it authorizes, funds, or carries out is not likely to jeopardize the existence of any listed species. Headline-grabbing "train wrecks," such as the controversy surrounding the Tellico Dam and the snail darter—which Congress ultimately decided we could do without, though it still lives—and the northern spotted owl, have been few. Between 1987 and 1991, only 19 of 74,000 such consultations resulted in total denial of the proposed projects. On private land, however, the impact of the act has been much more nettlesome and less easy to quantify. This dilemma must be resolved. An estimated 50 percent of endangered species occur almost exclusively on private lands; another 20 percent have at least half their occurrences on private property.

That certainly includes bald eagles, the majority of which nest, perch, and feed on private property. Twenty-five years ago Carey Lightsey, a sixth-generation cattle rancher in central Florida, rarely saw a bald eagle. On his ranch now are fourteen nests. When he guts the wild boars his paying guests hunt, nearly five dozen eagles perch expectantly on nearby fence posts. He says, "People ask me, 'My God, there are eagles everywhere. How do you even operate?' But it's never affected us. If there's one thing I learned being raised on the ranch, it's that we can live with eagles."

There are those in Congress, however, who have their doubts, who believe environmental protection is an impractical luxury we can no longer afford. Despite real progress in improving air and water quality over the past twenty-five years, by the time Larry Niles and I stood in that Maurice River marsh, Congress had declared war on the environment. Through odious bills, back-door legislative legerdemain, and grossly underfunded appropriations, western Republicans in particular were intent upon dismantling a generation of progressive environmental policies. Clearly out of step with the American public, this Congress was, in effect, voting to pump more raw sewage into the nation's waterways, to compromise wilderness, to destroy wetlands, and to open up more federal lands for logging, mining, and grazing at the expense of U.S. taxpayers. Before the year was over the Environmental Protection Agency, its budget slashed, would drastically cut its inspections of toxic-waste disposal, asbestos removal, industrial air emissions, sewage treatment plants, and drinking-water supplies. Seventy-three words embedded in an $80 billion appropriations bill, if enacted, would prevent the EPA from vetoing U.S. Army Corps of Engineers' approval of wetland projects.

In this atmosphere of antiregulatory, private property rights fervor, no statute was more under siege than the Endangered Species Act. Out West, someone fired shots at a U.S. Forest Service biologist in California. Last year two bombs destroyed the Carson City, Nevada, office, the family van, and part of the home of a Forest Service ranger; he had cancelled public land grazing leases in order to protect the riparian habitat of threatened Lahontan cutthroat trout. Back in Washington, since the spring of 1995 a congressionally imposed moratorium had prevented the Interior and Commerce departments from adding new species to the endangered and threatened lists—a moratorium that would continue until the ESA was either reauthorized or dismantled. In the forthcoming budget, funds would be available only for removing species from the endangered list.

Meanwhile, the Endangered Species Act reauthorization bills sponsored by western legislators—written, in some cases, not with the assistance of industry representatives but by attorneys and lobbyists representing timber, mining, and development interests—would effectively repeal the act. Overturning the Supreme Court's recent ruling, bills introduced by Representatives Don Young of Alaska and Richard Pombo of California and Senators Slade Gorton of Washington and Dirk Kempthorne of Idaho would limit restrictions against harming a member of an endangered species to injuring or killing such a member—while exempting destruction of its habitat, generally the principal cause of endangerment. Recovery would no longer be the ultimate goal for all species. The reauthorization bills placed great faith in captive breeding, a highly expensive and, in the case of many animals, an extremely difficult and dubious method of perpetuating a species—as if preserving a narrow gene pool, but not the habitat upon which it depends, constitutes preserving that species. After advocating a more scientific approach to the ESA process, the bills would require the secretary of interior to determine whether it is in the "national interest" to continue to protect distinct populations, even if the species exists outside of the United States. Congress would then vote on the secretary's decision. Under this provision, gray wolves, grizzly bears, and, were it not for the Bald and Golden Eagle Protection Act, even bald eagles could not be protected without explicit congressional approval.

Finally, after creating a process involving costly, time-consuming red tape, the bills would compensate any private landowner if the ESA depreciated the value of any portion of his or her property by 20 percent. Should that value be diminished by more than 50 percent, private landowners could compel the federal government to buy, at fair market value, that property.

Taxpayers also would finance half of anyone's cost to comply. The cost of such compensation would be deducted directly from the annual appropriation of the agency, such as the meagerly funded U.S. Fish and Wildlife Service, whose regulation was responsible for the real or imagined decline in market value. These takings provisions would cost the federal government billions of dollars annually—a blank invitation for abuse. Whether or not a farmer had any intention of developing a protected wetland, he could claim he wanted to build a shopping center there and file a claim for the ensuing business losses. Under the ESA, listing a species, designating critical habitat for such a species, or denying permission for an incidental "take" could generate claims against the federal government. The effect on the implementation and enforcement of federal law would be chilling.

~~~◗ Judged by its ultimate goal—to enable species to recover so well that they no longer need the Endangered Species Act's protection—the ESA, at first glance, appears to be an abject failure. Since its enactment in late 1973, only twenty-one species have been removed from the list. Seven of those, including four fish, two sparrows, and a mussel, were declared extinct. Eight were removed from the list after the FWS determined that the organisms were more plentiful than original data indicated. The status of nearly twenty other species, including most recently the bald eagle, has been upgraded from endangered to threatened.

These numbers pale in comparison to the total number of plants and animals listed under the ESA: 759 endangered species, 204 threatened. In addition, the USFWS has proposed listing another 242 species, and is considering another 182 species as potential candidates for the ESA's protection.

Yet, given the complex nature of plant and animal populations, it is unrealistic to expect one underfunded law to reverse, in the span of one human generation, the ill effects of fifteen or more human generations upon the American landscape. The seven organisms, however, that have been declared extinct since 1968 represent just about 1 percent of all the species listed as endangered. Those that were listed earliest, between 1968 and 1973, also have the highest percentage that are considered stable or improving: 58 percent, with 30 percent still in decline and another 12 percent whose status is unknown. For those species granted protection between 1989 and 1993, less than a quarter are stable or improving. However one analyzes those numbers, however, the need for the Endangered Species Act, or something like it, is incontrovertible. There is little question that the world is in the midst of the latest of five great mass extinctions that have occurred during the past 500 million years. What makes the current extinction unique is its broad impact on both plants and animals, and its cause: man.

~~~ Attempting to demonstrate that the Endangered Species Act is more practical and flexible than its critics claim, last year Interior Secretary Bruce Babbitt announced a ten-point administrative and legislative reform plan. Echoing some proposed reauthorization bills, it mandates scientific peer review of listing decisions, expands the role of state and local agencies, and promotes both multispecies conservation plans and efforts to save candidate species before they become basket cases. To tap nontraditional expertise, build local support, and develop alternatives that have the least socioeconomic impact, Babbitt has diversified the makeup of species-recovery teams, which often were composed of just biologists, to include such persons as water developers, ranchers, county extension agents, and timber and range specialists. One of Babbitt's most progressive reforms has been the increased use of safe-harbor protections extended to private landowners who agree to habitat conservation plans. For example, a number of timber companies and a golf resort in the Southeast have reached long-term agreements to protect or increase habitat for the red-cockaded woodpecker. Having done that, they can operate confident they will not be asked to do more if, in part because of their efforts, more woodpeckers, or other listed species, subsequently appear. It's a necessary reform: after creating a lake on his Oregon ranch that attracted bald eagles, one founder of an Oregon wildlife preservation group was forbidden to drive a truck onto his property because he might disturb the eagles.

Besides Babbitt's suggestions, more incentives, both within and outside the act, are needed to encourage private landowners to treasure rather than fear the presence of rare species, to overcome the mistrust of the sort of governmental intrusion that prompts property owners in New Jersey to keep an eagle's nest secret and spurs developers in Florida to encourage workers to disturb or destroy eagle eyries. While stopping short of outright compensation for real or imagined lost opportunities, the incentives could include:

- Federal tax credits to offset local and state property taxes for landowners who agree to long-term habitat protection plans, and partial tax credits for the cost of complying with the ESA. For example, the Maurice River marsh was owned by the Natural Lands Trust, a suburban Philadelphia conservation group which was exempted from paying local property taxes by New Jersey's Green Acres program. (Without state reimbursement, however, such programs place an undue burden on rural townships.)

- Income tax deductions for revenue earned from lands managed to support endangered species, such as substantially modified timber or grazing programs; lands privately managed for wildlife viewing, recreation, and hunting; and housing developments designed to incorporate and retain sensitive habitats.

- Eliminating perverse federal incentives, such as price supports for crops and commodities, like sugarcane, and below-market prices for water, energy, minerals, timber, and grazing rights, which encourage the overuse of federal lands and accelerate the loss of habitat. Federal leases also should be open to all bidders: if a timber company can be granted a lease to fell ancient forests, concerned citizens should be permitted to outbid the loggers to preserve the same woods. Babbitt estimated last year that he had given away minerals worth $15 billion and more than $1 billion in royalties as a result of the antiquated 1872 Mining Law. Under that law, hard rock mining companies may claim land and mineral rights on federal land for $2.50 to $5 an acre. At a cost of $10,000 one Canadian company secured an estimated $10 billion in gold deposits, for which it will pay no royalties.

   Similar perverse incentives promote sprawling residential development. Automobile travel is so heavily subsidized that, since 1960, new development acreage has been increasing four to eight times faster than the population in metropolitan areas such as Chicago, New York, and Washington-Baltimore. Also, the farther beyond the city limits you go, the cheaper it is to build a house, when in fact the land under the bulldozer blade in more rural areas could be the most valuable in terms of open space and biodiversity. One solution would be to impose impact fees similar to those imposed on developers whose operations have a negative impact on schools and transportation arteries; the more rare and crucial the habitat, the higher the fee.

   Mortgage interest deductions for second homes should also be eliminated.

- User impact fees. A percentage of revenues generated by users of public lands who affect wildlife habitat through logging, grazing, or recreation could be dedicated to a biodiversity trust fund.

- Increased funding for habitat conservation. Biodiversity trust funds, financed both publicly and privately, could buy conservation easements from private landowners or could purchase, as does the Nature Conservancy and Conservation Fund, endangered species habitat at fair market value.

- Innovative approaches. Defenders of Wildlife has paid $5,000 bounties to several western ranchers who have had wolves breed on their properties, and compensated ranchers who have lost livestock to wolves. If the government were to pay an extremely high bounty of say, $10,000 for each of the estimated 350 pairs of spotted owls that mate on private property in the Pacific Northwest, the cost would be $3.5 million—far less than the $9.7 million spent on the bird in 1990.
- Conservation contracts or subsidies, such as the Conservation Reserve Program, which, in inducing farmers to allow native vegetation to return to some of their acreage, has fueled a stunning recovery of ducks on the prairies of the upper Midwest.
- Tradable developments or conservation credits, which would allow owners of significant habitat to trade or sell their development rights to owners of less sensitive property, or to trade, buy, or sell the right to degrade or destroy habitat in exchange for protection or improvement of habitat elsewhere.
- Reduction or elimination of inheritance taxes for landowners who agree to protect or enhance wildlife habitat. This would discourage the sale and breakup of large tracts of rural land. Landowners should be able to deduct donations of land to the federal and state governments.
- Greater public financial involvement. Each year the sale of federal duck stamps generates $15 million for the acquisition of national wildlife refuges. Federal excise taxes on the sale of firearms, shells, cartridges, and archery and fishing equipment have poured more than a billion dollars into state fish and game departments. The International Association of Fish and Wildlife Agencies and a coalition of conservation groups are now spearheading the Wildlife Diversity Funding Initiative, an attempt, for the first time, to generate reliable funding for state non-game and endangered species programs. The proposal involves assessing a user fee, or surcharge—excise taxes have become verboten—on outdoor products and supplies such as camping equipment, canoes, binoculars, and bird seed. A modest fee would generate a minimum of $350 million a year for state wildlife conservation, recreation, and education programs.

〰️ At the heart of the endangered species conundrum is the value that different human beings place upon a piece of land, a plant, or an animal. For many of us, for far too long, the sole value of land or of a species has been the timber or minerals or food that can be extracted from it, the revenue or sustenance it can produce. This narrow view ignores other values that species provide: maintaining fertile soil and water, controlling the composition of the atmosphere, regulating climate, and controlling floods and pests. One must not ignore the recreational value of wilderness and wildlife or the importance of preserving these resources for the enjoyment of future generations. There also is value in knowing that bald eagles exist, even for those who have never seen one. "We need wilderness whether or not we ever set foot in it," the late Edward Abbey once explained. "We need the possibility of escape as surely as we need hope; without it the life of the cities would drive all men into crime or drugs or psychoanalysis."

Subjective though these concepts might be, it is possible, if one is so inclined, to place dollar figures on some of them. Nationwide, the USFWS estimates that bird-watchers annually spend $5.2 billion on their passion. (By comparison, $5.8 billion is spent on movie tickets and $5.9 billion on admission to sporting events.) In just one of many examples of the eagles' economic clout, the Wisconsin River's Sauk-Prairie Wintering Ground draws approximately 125 bald eagles each year. They, in turn, attract thousands of tourists who, according to estimates, pump more than $600,000 — in excess of $4,800 per bird—into the rural economy.

Supporters of the Endangered Species Act also have literally made poster children out of the beneficiaries of plant-derived pharmaceuticals. Next to the picture of a cute six-year-old named Jackie Buckley and a five-petaled rosy periwinkle, an Endangered Species Coalition poster reads: "She's alive today because of this flower." The rosy periwinkle, a Madagascar flower, has produced vincristine and vinblastine, two alkaloids that preclude cancer cells from dividing. The two chemicals have been credited with achieving 80 percent remission in those who suffer from Hodgkin's disease, and 99 percent remission in patients with acute lymphocytic leukemia, a deadly childhood cancer. The rosy periwinkle also contains seventy-five other alkaloids. Alkaloids from other organic sources have produced hundreds of products that include anticancer agents, painkillers, heart drugs, muscle relaxants, and respiratory stimulants.

A number of women also have stepped forward to declare they would not be alive today were it not for taxol, an extract from the bark of a former "trash tree," the Pacific yew. Taxol treats ovarian, breast, and non–small cell lung cancers. While synthetic taxol has now replaced the natural extract for most treatments, it is doubtful that it could have been created in a laboratory: in both its chemical structure and its therapeutic action, the compound was totally unanticipated.

Only 5 percent of the world's 25,000 known flowering plants have been analyzed for medicinal properties. Nonetheless, nearly 80 percent of the 150 drugs most often prescribed in the United States originate from natural sources. Acetylsalicylic acid, the wonder drug better known as aspirin, initially was derived from the European white willow. From molds have come penicillin and immunosuppressants used in organ transplants. Ergot, a wheat fungus, has yielded antihistamines used to treat allergies and motion sickness. The Cameroon vine tree in Malaysia has produced a compound that, in the laboratory, shows promising activity against the AIDS virus. Indian snakeroot has given us tranquilizers. Quinine prevents and treats malaria. Numerous compounds derived from sources as diverse as foxglove, the opium poppy, and the venom of toads and snakes are used to combat congestive heart failure, angina, blood clots, high blood pressure, and high cholesterol. The economic impact amounts to $80 billion annually; the manufacture and sale of vincristine alone generates $180 million a year.

Endangered species, in particular, have yet another value. "The bald eagle was trying to tell us that there was something terribly wrong in the ecosystem," Mollie Beatty, the director of the U.S. Fish and Wildlife Service, said June 30, 1994 as she announced that the status of the bald eagle would be upgraded to threatened. "In this case, it was DDT. Any reform that guts the [Endangered Species] act is the equivalent of unplugging the fire alarm to make the fire go away, a way of sticking your head in the sand and not paying attention to the very life of the system that supports us all. At our own peril do we ignore endangered species and the human activities that place species on the list."

Nonetheless, bald eagles will never cure cancer or AIDS. Perhaps only one in 10,000 species might yield any true economic value. To say that we must save rare and endangered species because of their potential economic or pharmaceutical benefit ensnares us in the same anthropocentric trap of those who see no value in anything unless it has some palpable human use. "Nothing is down here," Larry Niles is saying as we stand out in the Maurice River marsh, in view of one of New Jersey's newest eagles' nests as greenhead flies probe for our blood. "People have been raping this area—no, utilizing it—for a long time, and you can see why. It's such a hostile land. Whenever it's hostile, people don't value it. They just get whatever they can out of it."

His comment reminded me of Gerald Harper, president of the Canadian company that failed in its bid to develop the Windy Craggy mine above the Chilkat valley. "As defined by the more extreme persons, the environment is devoid of Homo sapiens," Harper once complained to me. "Homo sapiens is a perfectly legitimate, rightful part of the ecosystem." He is correct, of course, but our rightful place, and that of the eagles, is a matter of balance. Blessed with opposable thumbs and a large brain, for centuries we have ensured that the scales have tipped much too far in our direction, without regard for the long-term consequences—even for our own health or the future of our children. This immoral fixation on short-term gains without regard to their long-term consequences is evident throughout our society, whether it be business's focus on quarterly shareholder dividends, the depletion of the Social Security Trust Fund, or, until recently, the disregard of the federal budget deficit. Despite recent declarations that our two-decades-long embrace of the environment is a passing fancy we can no longer afford, economic growth and a sound environment are not mutually exclusive. A study two years ago by MacArthur Fellow Bob Hall concluded that nine states rank among the top twelve in terms of economic performance and quality jobs, and a healthy environment; another dozen were among the worst fourteen in both categories.

Perhaps it is a simple matter of not appreciating what we have until it's gone. This past fall and winter a growing coalition of moderate eastern Republicans, bolstered by strong public support, began to thwart the efforts of congressmen from the vast western states to dismantle environmental protection laws. At least on a national basis, to wage such attacks was viewed as political suicide, an untouchable "third rail." Emboldened by the polls, President Clinton adopted some of the strongest pro-environment stands of his administration, and House Speaker Newt Gingrich buried the Young-Pombo assault on the Endangered Species Act bill. A more moderate proposal was expected to be introduced this year. Laws, however, are constructs of man and, as such, can easily be dismantled, circumvented, or ignored. Congress considered a bill for ten years before it passed the Bald Eagle Protection Act in 1940, and it could not halt the bird's already precipitous decline. Laws cannot protect wildlife if people do not support such laws or the tenets upon which they are based. Writes Colorado State University philosophy professor Holmes Rolston III, "The only landowners who really possess and enjoy their land, in a deeper philosophical sense, are those who respect the life that is native there."

Those are wealthy men.

∽ Midway between Larry Niles and I and the bald eagle nest, on the other side of the gut, an osprey—possibly the one that led us to this sanctuary—perches, a handsome sentinel. Erected in a short dead tree, or snag, the osprey nest is the only one in the entire Delaware Bay not built on a man-made platform. Another osprey soon flies in to an adjacent snag. A young head pops up above the rim as a just-fledged bird hovers in from the river— an entire osprey family. "What a scene," Larry Niles says, beaming. "Eagles, ospreys—you can't beat it."

With eleven nests this year, he thinks perhaps as many as twenty pairs of bald eagles might ultimately nest in New Jersey—the same number that graced the state before DDT was introduced. Given a reprieve from the pesticide, the birds' resiliency has been remarkable. This being New Jersey, though, the nation's most densely populated state, their hold will always require some assistance. Niles likens them to the beach nesters, the piping plovers, least terns, and black skimmers, that lay their eggs on the same beaches on which the state's multibillion-dollar tourist industry depends each summer. The conflicts between people and the beach nesters and the eagles require constant vigilance. Whatever Congress ultimately decides about the habitat provisions of the Endangered Species Act, Niles knows that minimizing disturbances wherever eagles forage, roost, and nest, whether on the edge of a remote marsh or in a farmer's field, is essential to ensure their long-term survival. I have told him about some of the nests I have seen in Florida, in backyards and on the edge of golf courses. One nest there is a hundred feet from a four-lane highway; only a very small percentage are located in completely pristine environments. Florida biologists were debating whether, as the amount of prime habitat decreased, a growing percentage of bald eagles were becoming urbanized, adapting, like ospreys, to man's presence. "If it starts going in that direction here, it would make everything easier," Niles says, "but that's not the way it is. Right now our experience is that our species has almost unending responsibility for taking care of them."

Niles's other chief concern remains persistent pollution. "I'm still worried about contaminants," he says, because of their effect on both ospreys and eagles. While the osprey nests here along the Maurice and out on the

Atlantic coast are doing well, those farther west on the Delaware Bay suffer 10 percent eggshell thinning and 50 percent nest failure. All of the plasma drawn from a dozen Delaware Bay eaglets over the past several years contained DDE and mercury, and almost all of it contained levels of PCBs that, while not as high as those found in Maine and along the shorelines of the Great Lakes, exceed the levels found in inland Michigan eaglets and young birds from the Columbia River estuary. The addled egg from the Raccoon Creek nest that blew up in Kathy Clark's face three years ago also contained elevated levels of DDD, DDE, and PCBs—all of which may have contributed to its demise.

"The contamination seems," Niles says, "particularly poisonous because of the Mannington pair"—one of the two New Jersey pairs that for years has failed to produce young. "We think the females switched last year, so this year would have been the first year for the new female, but she didn't lay, or she laid but the eggs failed." She could have been too young, but Niles suspects otherwise.

He has no such concerns, though, for most of the state's burgeoning population, and certainly not for the Maurice River pair. Looking south from Mauricetown as far as he can see, he surveys the river's wooded banks. The bald eagles, he concludes, selected the best possible tree for their nest. A few other pines to the south are as tall, but they're farther inland. "This really is a fine nest," he says, one nest builder complimenting two others. Well past noon, a slight breeze rustles the phragmites behind us. A marsh wren, its tail bobbed forward over its back, alights on a slender strand of *Spartina* thirty feet in front of us, serenading us with its sweet, bell-clear song.

We must go. Before we do, though, I take one last look through Niles's spotting scope. The dark brown fledglings are as still as stone griffins guarding a Gothic cathedral. Along this waterway bald eagles like them have perched inscrutably for longer than they or we can ever fathom. They, of course, know nothing of how, in the blink of an eye in geological time, their kind all but disappeared from our rivers, lakes, and bays. It is both a triumph, and a pity, that we find their renewed presence so remarkable. We need them, these bald eagles, more than they need us.

Collapsing the tripod and shouldering the scope, Larry Niles slogs back toward the boat. I follow. "This is so peaceful here," he says. "I hate to leave."

EPILOGUE

Once again the bald eagles have returned to their nests. In late February, standing in the spongy yard of a small home at the edge of a remote New Jersey tidal marsh, I train a spotting scope far across the salt hay meadows, to a bald eagle nest that was first discovered a year earlier. With the naked eye the eyrie, a deep conical structure that resembles an ice cream cone wedged into the three-pronged crotch of a tall gum tree, appears empty.

The home's tenant, a man in his thirties whose boots are polished with the manure of the thoroughbred race horses he handles, tells Larry Niles, "I've seen them perched and flying around a lot, but they haven't been on the nest yet."

Peering through the telescope, however, I spot something white just above the nest rim—the unmistakable head of an adult bald eagle. With the rest of her body hunkered low over her eggs and her eyes and bill shyly hidden behind a small branch, the incubating female is barely visible. Fifteen minutes later, she bails out of the back of the nest, her white tail in retreat as she wings rapidly westward behind a tree line. In a moment she returns accompanied by her mate, who alights on the nest while she perches on the stub of a thick, broken-off branch twenty yards away. Raising her head and arching her back, she emits a high-pitched call, and he responds in kind, their duet—a love song? a couple squabbling over household duties?— reverberates across the still marsh. Gazing down at the eggs beneath him, the male gingerly rearranges the nest cup grass around the eggs with first his left foot, then his right, before gently settling over them.

Much bolder than his mate, he peers right at us.

∼ I spent one December afternoon with three volunteers who were helping rehabilitate sick and injured bald eagles by flying them on a 100-yard-long tether in a public park in St. Paul, Minnesota. The eagles were among the 80 to 125 bald eagles cared for each year by the University of

Minnesota's Gabbort Raptor Center in St. Paul. George Clarke, an industrial education student at the university, and Ernie Olsen, a residential and commercial building remodeler, alternated playing out a reel of parachute cord attached to the eagles' legs and clapping their hands and running toward the birds in order to flush them into the air. Linda Wadsworth, a flute musician, also chased the birds and observed their flight: Were they getting good wing extension? Were their wing beats, glides and banked turns symmetrical? Were they achieving decent altitude?

One eagle, a veteran of such flights, flew so well that Clarke had to rein in the bird and ground it before it cleared the road at the edge of the park. "The coolest kite around," he marveled.

The first bald eagle they exercised, however, a small adult, had not flown for months. It had been found, anemic and emaciated, in northern Minnesota the previous July; unable to fly, it kept beating its wings into the ground. Its left wing tip had a small laceration, and the wrist joint of its right wing was swollen and bruised. On its first retraining flight in the park, the eagle covered a mere 25 yards before skittering to a stop on the snow. But he briefly willed himself into the air again, and several more times as he was pursued by Olsen and Wadsworth.

The bird's second series of flights were equally brief. Head erect, it panted heavily as Clarke approached to retrieve it. Moments later, though, Linda whooped as the bird, pointed into the wind, flew much longer and higher.

"That's good," says Clarke. "He's still not getting full extension with his left wing, but I think he's gonna be good."

Trailing the path of the bird's flight, I come upon the spot where the bald eagle took a running start and flapped its wings several times before it became airborne. Inscribed in the snow, as delicate as the brush strokes on a Chinese scroll, were the impressions of the bird's outstretched primary feathers. I have never seen a finer snow angel.

Several days earlier I had viewed a confiscated home video of a February family outing on the Crow Reservation in Montana. The sound track was provided by the murmur of the high plains wind and a saccharine sixties pop song blaring from a pickup truck radio. The lens quickly zoomed in on a bald eagle whose right leg was caught in the jaws of a leg-hold trap. Beyond the eagle lay a mule deer that had been shot for bait.

As a little boy approached the bird, it flared its wings and lunged at the toddler with its beak flared wide, but the trap pulled the bird up short.

"Get away!" yelled the toddler's father, off-camera.

After the boy obeyed, a rifle barrel slowly protruded into view from the upper left-hand corner of the frame. Fired at point-blank range into the eagle's chest, the first shot of the .22 caliber rifle briefly stunned the bird, but it resumed its aggressive stance. The second shot further staggered the eagle, but it remained standing. Subsequent slugs drove it onto its back, but it continued struggling. The execution—there is no other word for what I witnessed—required six bullets.

In mid-April of last year, at least two weeks after the Gibbstown pair had begun incubating, Larry Niles removed two eggs from their nest. The pair had not fledged an eaglet since 1991, and he was concerned contaminants were preventing the birds from reproducing. Placing plaster egg replicas in the nest to keep the adults occupied, he held out faint hopes that the eggs could be artificially incubated.

Before driving the eggs to a Pennsylvania falconer who would artificially incubate them, he allowed me to briefly hold one of the eggs. Off-white, with no luster, the surface of the egg felt course and rough. It was rather large for an egg, but—considering the immense potential it embodied—it was shockingly small, fitting easily into my small hand, and it weighed just several ounces. When the falconer, Alan Pollard, candled the eggs, both embryos were alive; they also wobbled when he set them on a counter top. Over the course of the next couple weeks first one egg, then another stopped moving and died. When he opened up the eggs, one was a rotting mess, the other a nearly completely formed bald eagle chick.

Nearly five weeks after he visited that Gibbstown nest, Larry Niles lowered triplets from another eagle eyrie, one that my father and I had helped him build. After I assisted in holding the largest of the birds so a blood sample could be taken and it could be banded, zoologist Kathy Clark handed the female to me. Standing up, I held her with her back against my chest, with her silently hissing, polished black beak inches from my face and my hands firmly gripping her legs just above her talons. Holding a bald eagle, even one just seven weeks old that already is as long as your torso, it is hard to figure whether you or the bird is more in awe of the other. "I've handled a lot of different birds, and often that diminishes them," Phil Schempf, the head of the U.S. Fish and Wildlife Service's raptor project in Alaska, once told me. "But with an eagle, I've never gotten the feeling that I've had this bird really under control. You have the feeling that unless you're paying the utmost attention, this bird is capable of causing you problems."

Despite her open beak, the eagle seemed relatively calm to me; there was not a lot of tension in her legs. Occassionally, though, I could feel her trying to unfold her wings, pushing against my biceps with a force that in a matter of weeks would begin to rival the strength of a man. I had no doubt that, had I relaxed my grip, she would have readily sunk her talons into me.

It is late the same February day that we witnessed the pair of bald eagles incubating their eggs. Standing along a fog-enshrouded creek four miles from Delaware Bay, Larry Niles, my father and I hear and feel the deep throbbing foghorn of an oil tanker or a cargo container ship moving up the bay. In 1687 a six year-old boy from Lancashire named William Baines and his older sister, Eleanor, made their way in a wooden ship up the same bay, a bay that, I have no doubt, was haunted by bald eagles. Since their parents and siblings died during the crossing, the two were raised by Quakers in Chester, Pennsylvania. When he reached his majority, William settled in Southampton, Bucks County. There, he fathered ten children, all but one of whom inexplicably changed their surname to Beans. On a farm in Southampton, my grandfather, Horace Beans, was born in 1905.

"Have you ever seen a bald eagle?" I asked him last summer, shortly after his ninetieth birthday.

"No," he said with a resigned shake of his head, as if such an event was beyond the realm of possibility. No one should live for nearly a century near one of this nation's great rivers without setting eyes upon our national symbol. If we grant the birds enough space, if we allow at least a portion of their wonderfully mysterious world to remain, most Americans will happily not be able to make such a claim.

The same fog blanketing the distant bay lifts off the frozen marsh before us, revealing the Stow Creek pair. The male perches five hundred yards away, low in a tree overhanging the marsh. Somewhat closer, the female— her white head and yellow bill remarkably visible even in the dim fog-filtered light—sits nearly a hundred feet high on a sycamore branch a couple feet away from her nest. They remain in their positions, unmoving, for an hour, till daylight fails us. Most years, the female is already incubating her eggs by now. Clearly, though, the first egg is forming inside of her. The long, laborious task of raising bald eagles lies ahead.

Bucks County, Pennsylvania
February 29, 1996

NOTES

Chapter 1: To See an Eagle Fly

16 More than 90 percent of the day is spent simply perching: Mark V. Stalmaster, *The Bald Eagle* (New York: Universe Books, 1987), p. 125.

18 To say because an eagle does a flyover: Jeff Gammage, *Philadelphia Inquirer,* "DEP Rebuffs Plan for a Port in Bridgeton," Oct. 1, 1991.

24 Naomi Dower-LaBastille: Decision, "In the Matter of Bridgeton Bulk Materials Handling Facility," April 30, 1993.

Chapter 2: Shell Game

30 Corralling fish: John James Audubon, *Ornithological Biography,* vol. 1 (Philadelphia: Judah Dobson, 1831), p. 163.

30 Elk, the wolf, the bison: Peter Matthiessen, *Wildlife in America,* rev. ed. (New York: Viking Penguin, 1987), p. 62.

Chapter 3: An Eagle Eyrie

36 Sound of chalk: Witmer Stone, *Bird Studies at Old Cape May* (Philadelphia: Delaware Valley Ornithological Club at Academy of Natural Sciences, 1937), p. 296.

36 It felt . . . baseball bat: Teryl G. Grubb, "Nesting Bald Eagle Attacks Researcher," *The Auk* 93, 4 (Oct. 1976): 842–43.

37 In this great wooden maw: Calculations based on Hal H. Harrison, *Birds' Nests,* Petersen Field Guides (Boston: Houghton Mifflin, 1975), pp. 38, 156, 246.

37 A bald eagle nest . . . half century later: Francis Hobart Herrick, *The American Eagle: A Study in Natural and Civil History* (New York: Appleton-Century, 1934), p. 24.

37 Two metric tons: Ibid., p. 9.

37 The largest nest . . . 20 feet high. Charles L. Broley, "Migration and Nesting of Florida Bald Eagles," *Wilson Bulletin* 59, 1 (March 1947): 3–21.

48 No bird in North America . . . 160 thousand calories: Stalmaster, *Bald Eagle,* p. 69; John B. Dunning, Jr., *Handbook of Avian Body Masses* (Boca Raton: CRC Press, 1993), p. 31.

49 Years ago in Ontario . . . in one nest: Myrtle Jean Broley, *Eagle Man: Charles L. Broley's Field Adventures with American Eagles* (New York: Pellegrini and Cudahy, 1952), p. 60.

49 In visits to hundreds of Florida nests . . . crane leg bones: Charles Broley, "Migration," p. 11; Jon M. Gerrard and Gary R. Bortolotti, *The Bald Eagle: Haunts and Habitats of a Wilderness Monarch* (Washington, D.C.: Smithsonian Institution Press, 1988), p. 43; Petra Bohall Wood, Stephen A. Nesbitt, and Anthony Steffer, "Bald Eagles Prey on Sandhill Cranes in Florida," *Journal of Raptor Research,* 27, 3 (Sept. 1993): 164–65.

49 Outnumber white pine there three to one: John Mathisen, "A Band for an Eagle," *The Loon,* September 1970: 84.

49 160 thousand calories: Stalmaster, *Bald Eagle,* pp. 60, 68–69, 114.

Chapter 4: Omnipresent, Omnivorous

57 25,000 to 75,000 bald eagles: Dan James, U.S. Fish and Wildlife Service, phone conversation with author.

57 250,000 or a half million: Gerrard and Bortolotti, *Monarch,* p. 3.

57 Search for a national emblem: Richard S. Patterson and Richardson Dougall, *The Eagle and the Shield: A History of the Great Seal of the United States,* Publication 8900, U.S. Department of State, 1976; also Philip M. Isaacson, *The American Eagle* (Boston: New York Graphic Society Books, 1975); and Clarence P. Hornung, *The American Eagle in Art and Design* (New York: Dover Publications, 1978), Introduction, pp. V–X.

60 Earliest fossils: Stalmaster, *Bald Eagle,* p. 5.

60 Etana myth: Herrick, *American Eagle,* p. 187.

60 Eagle's long association . . . bird of fire: Herrick, *American Eagle,* pp. 179–183.

60 Astrologers . . . the engagement: Myrtle Jean Broley, *Eagle Man,* p. 197.

60 Walking sticks and seals: Herrick, *American Eagle,* p. 188.

60 Ganymede: Michael Stapleton, *A Dictionary of Greek and Roman Mythology* (New York: Bell Publishing, 1978), pp. 84–85.

60 Some linguists . . . 250 years: Herrick, *American Eagle,* p. 184. Pliny: Herrick, Ibid., p. 215.

61 Hopewell culture: Deborah Wood, phone conversation with author.

61 Christian symbol: Isaakson, *American Eagle,* foreword, pp. viii, 17.

62 Franklin letter: Patterson, *Shield,* pp. 30–31.

63 Franklin's history . . . quarter-billion turkeys: Stephen W. Eaton, "Wild Turkey," in A. Poole, P. Stettenheim, and F. Gill, eds., *The Birds of North America,* no. 22 (Philadelphia: The Academy of Natural Sciences; Washington, DC: The American Ornithologists' Union, 1992), p. 1.

63 Audubon seal: David Iams, "Book Sale Features Items Linked to 3 Famous Men," *Philadelphia Inquirer,* March 19, 1994.

63 Suffer me: Audubon, *Ornithological Biography,* vol. 1, p. 168.

63 He was brave: Audubon, *Ornithological Biography,* vol. 1, p.61

63 Unknown . . . weaker updrafts: Gerrard and Bortolotti, *Bald Eagle* pp. 14, 22–23, and Stalmaster, *Bald Eagle,* p. 27–28.

64 Delaware trapper tale: Stone, *Old Cape May,* p. 287.

64 Apparently more than ospreys . . . single bald eagle: Stalmaster, *Bald Eagle,* p. 98. Range Bayer, "Bald Eagle-Great Blue Heron Interactions," *The Murrelet* 60 (1979): 32–33; Dennis G. Jorde and Gary R. Lingle, "Kleptoparasitism by Bald Eagles Wintering in South-Central Nebraska," *Journal of Field Ornithology* 59, 2 (1988): 183–88; Charles. F. Batchelder, "The Bald Eagle as a Hunter," *Bulletin of the Nuttall Ornithological Club* 6, 1 (1881): 58–60; Michael C. Wells and Mark Bekoff, "Coyote–Bald Eagle Interactions at Carrion," *Journal of Mammalogy* 59, 4 (1978): 886–887.

64 Audubon's vulture chase: Audubon, *Ornithological Biography,* vol. 1, p. 163; Stalmaster, *Bald Eagle,* pp. 97–98.

65 Keen vision: Hugh McIsaac, phone conversation with author. Twenty-three fish: Myrtle Jean Broley, *Eagle Man,* p. 17.

66 Eagle's menu: prey lists from: Stalmaster, *Bald Eagle,* pp. 93–96, 182–83 and Ralph S. Palmer, ed. *Handbook of North American Birds,* vol. 4 (New Haven: Yale University Press, 1987), pp. 232–36.

66 Some biologists have speculated: Gerrard and Bortolotti, *Bald Eagle,* p. 4.

67 Sperm whale: Palmer, *North American Birds,* p. 233; and USFWS special agent Jerry Cegelske, phone conversation with author.

67 Dead for a month: Jerry Olsen, "An Unusual Incident with the Bald Eagle," *Journal of Raptor Research* 20, 1 (Spring 1986): 41.

67 First used on a document: Patterson and Dougall, *Shield,* p. 128–30.

67 Indian Peace Medals: Isaacson, *American Eagle,* pp. 194–200.

68 "Old Abe": George Laycock, *Autumn of the Eagle* (New York: Scribner's, 1973), pp. 49–51.

68 Massachusetts copper: Patterson and Dougall, *Shield,* p. 529.

68 The Great Seal . . . grandly eagle-like: Patterson and Dougall, Ibid., pp. 230–278.

69 Newspapers will print anything: W. Bryant Tyrrell, "Report of Eagle Survey," report to National Audubon Society, 1936.

69 Near Great Egg Harbor: Alexander Wilson, *American Ornithology, or the Natural History of the Birds of the United States,* vol. 4 (Philadelphia: Bradford and Inskeep, 1811), p. 93.

69 Petersburg, Georgia: Thomas Nuttall, *A Manual of the Ornithology of the United States and Canada* (Cambridge, Massachusetts: Hilliard and Brown, 1832), p. 76.

69 North Carolina . . . lamb gripped in its talons: J. E. West, tale recounted in A. K. Fisher, *The Hawks and Owls of the United States,* U.S. Department of Agriculture, Division of Ornithology and Mammalogy, Bulletin No. 3, 1893, p. 99.

69 McGuffey's Readers: Rosalie Edge, *Eagles in Wonderland, Including a Brief Description of the McGuffey Eagle,* Publication No. 10, Hawk Mountain Sanctuary Association, October, 1945, unpaginated; and Ellen Roney Hughes, Smithsonian Institution, phone conversation with author.

70 Hollywood producer: Edge, *Wonderland.*

70 *New York Herald Tribune* story: Emergency Conservation Committee, pamphlet, "Save the Bald Eagle!" 1935.

70 *Literary Digest* story: *Literary Digest,* Nov. 9, 1929, as quoted in Daniel P. Mannix, "Did Eagles Really Carry Off Babies?" *True,* Feb. 1970, p. 74.

71 One falconer . . . recommendation: Mannix, "Did Eagles," pp. 96–97.

Chapter 5: "In at the Death"

72 Broley background: Myrtle Jean Broley, *Eagle Man;* and Jon Gerrard, *Charles Broley: An Extraordinary Naturalist* (Headingley, Manitoba: White Horse Plains, 1983).

75 In three months . . . the same journey: Myrtle Jean Broley, Ibid. p 81–86; Gerrard, Ibid. pp 43–44; and Charles Broley, "Migration," pp. 3–7.

76 Recent research: Petra Bohall Wood and Mitchell A. Byrd, conversations with author.

76 newscast . . . Prince Edward Island: Charles Broley, "Migration," p. 4.

77 90 percent: Charles L. Broley, "Plight of the Florida Bald Eagle," *Audubon,* Jan.–Feb. 1950, p. 45.

77 In North Carolina: Myrtle Jean Broley, *Eagle Man.,* p. 119.

77 Tyrrell: W. Bryant Tyrrell, "Report of Eagle Survey," report to National Audubon Society, 1936.

78 Cantwell: George C. Cantwell, "Nesting of the Alaska Bald Eagle," *The Osprey* 3, 5 (1899): 66–67.

78 Forty-seven eggs: Egbert Bagg, "A Series of Florida Eggs of the Bald Eagle," *Ornithologist and Oölogist* 14, 5 (May 1889): 73.

78 Horse-and-buggy egging expedition: Willard Eliot, "A Day's Trip for Bald Eagle Nests in Florida," *The Oölogist* 9, 2 (1892): 40.

79 Nearly half century later . . . underground: Myrtle Jean Broley, *Eagle Man,* p. 130–31.

79 Toppling every nest tree: Stone, *Old Cape May,* p. 290, 296.

79 One Florida rancher . . . eagles took pigs: Myrtle Jean Broley, *Eagle Man*, pp. 55–56.

80 Pine Island: Charles L. Broley, "Plight," Jan.–Feb. p. 45.

80 Two sawmills: Charles L. Broley, "Plight of the Florida Bald Eagle Worsens," *Audubon*, March–April 1951, pp. 72, 136.

80 In just a decade: Charles L. Broley, "Plight," p. 43.

80 Casco Bay: U.S. Fish and Wildlife Service, "Northern States Bald Eagle Recovery Plan," July 1983, p. 14.

80 Manhattan parks: G. B. Grinnell, "Recollections of Audubon Park," *The Auk*, July 1920.

80 Long Island: U.S. Fish and Wildlife Service, "Northern States," p. 17.

81 Sacramento: Phillip J. Detrich, "The Status and Distribution of the Bald Eagle in California (master's thesis, California State University, Chico, spring 1986), p. 29.

81 California aerial shootings: F. H. Dale, "Eagle 'Control' in Northern California," *The Condor* 38, 5 (Sept. 1936): 208–10.

81 St. Johns River: Audubon, *Ornithological Biography*, vol. 2 (Edinburgh: Adam and Charles Black, 1834), p. 160–61.

82 1950 list: Charles L. Broley, letter in *Audubon*, May–June 1950, p. 139.

83 In both 1951 and 1952: Charles L. Broley, *Audubon*, March–April, 1951, pp. 72, 136; and Charles L. Broley, "Broley Reports on Eagles," *Audubon*, March–April, 1952, pp. 71–72.

83 Banding list: Gerrard, *Extraordinary Naturalist*, p. 50, with 1950–1952 results added from Charles L. Broley, "Broley Reports," *Audubon*, March–April 1952, pp. 71–72.

83 By 1955 his nests: Charles L. Broley, "Plight of the American Bald Eagle," *Audubon*, July–August, 1958, pp. 162–63.

84 Franklin's gulls: Gerrard, *Extraordinary Naturalist*, p. 37–38.

CHAPTER 6: "THE DDT MAN IS COMING"

85 Radioactive fallout: Charles L. Broley, "The Bald Eagle in Florida," *Atlantic Naturalist* 12, 5 (1957): 230–31.

86 Howell: Joseph C. Howell, comment, *Audubon*, July–Aug. 1958, pp. 163, 171.

86 even Howell's numbers . . . Merritt Island: Alexander Sprunt IV, "Population Trends of the Bald Eagle in North America," in *Peregrine Falcon Populations: Their Biology and Decline*, edited by Joseph J. Hickey (Madison: University of Wisconsin Press, 1969), p. 348.

86 Continental Bald Eagle Survey: Statistics in subsequent paragraphs from: Sprunt, "Population Trends," pp. 347–50, Sprunt and Frank J. Ligas, "Continental Bald Eagle Project: Progress Report No. III," proceedings of the 59th annual National Audubon Society convention, Miami, Florida, November 9, 1963; and Sprunt and Ligas, "Audubon Bald Eagle Studies-1960–1966," presented at the 62nd annual convention of the National Audubon Society, Sacramento, Calif., Nov. 12, 1966.

87 So pervasive . . . three failed eggs: Lucille Stickel, "Wildlife Studies, Patuxent Wildlife Research Center," in *Pesticide-Wildlife Studies, 1963*, U.S. Fish and Wildlife Service circular, Aug. 1964, p. 80; and Stanley N. Wiemeyer, Christine M. Bunck, and Charles J. Stafford, "Environmental Contaminants in Bald Eagle Eggs, 1980–84, and Further Interpretations of Relationships to Productivity and Shell Thickness," *Archives of Environmental Contamination and Toxicology* 24 (1993): 213–27.

87 Late in 1961 . . . residues of DDE: L. F. Stickel, N. J. Chura, P. A. Steward, C. M. Menzie, R. M. Prouty, and W. L. Reichel, "Bald Eagle Pesticide Relations," reprint from transactions of the Thirty-First North American Wildlife and Natural Resources Conference, March 14–16, 1966, (Washington, D.C.: Wildlife Management Institute, 1966).

88 Sperm activity: Louis N. Locke, Nicholas J. Chura, and Paul A. Stewart, "Spermato-

genesis in Bald Eagles Experimentally Fed a Diet Containing DDT," *The Condor,* 68 (1966): 497–502; and Locke, phone conversation with author.

88 Joe Jacobs: *Journals of Joe Jacobs,* unpublished.

88 Paul Hermann Müller: *Modern Scientists and Engineers,* vol. 2 (New York: McGraw-Hill, 1980), pp. 336–37; and *Notable Twentieth-Century Scientists,* vol. 3 pp. 1439–40, (New York: Gale Research, 1995).

89 Cheap, easy to apply: Details of the growing use of DDT and its effects gleaned from Thomas R. Dunlap, *DDT: Scientists, Citizens and Public Policy* (Princeton, N.J.: Princeton University Press, 1981); and Rachel Carson, *Silent Spring* (1962; reprint, Boston: Houghton Mifflin, 1987).

89 Naples: Dunlap, *DDT,* pp. 61–62.

89 Atomic bomb of pesticides: Ibid., p. 17.

90 Kitchen shelf paper: Carson, *Spring,* pp. 174–75.

90 DDT in human fat and breast milk: Nancy Krieger, Mary S. Wolff, Robert A. Hiatt, Marilyn Rivera, Joseph Vogelman, and Norman Orentreich, "Breast Cancer and Serum Organocholorines: A Prospective Study among White, Black, and Asian Women," *Journal of the National Cancer Institute* 86, 8 (April 20, 1994): 589–99.

90 Fatty degeneration: Dunlap, *DDT,* p. 64.

90 British researchers: V. D. Wigglesworth, "A Case of DDT Poisoning in Man," *British Medical Journal* 1 (April 14, 1945): 517; and R. A. M. Case, "Toxic Effects of 2,2bis (p-chlorophenyl) 1,1,1, trichlorethane (DDT) in Man," *British Medical Journal* 2 (Dec. 15, 1945): 842–45.

90 Food and Drug Administration . . . AMA and Beech-Nut: Dunlap, *DDT,* pp. 65–6

90 Every restaurant meal: Carson, *Spring,* p. 178.

91 Tolerance levels: Dunlap, *DDT,* p. 64.

91 Wayland J. Hayes: Wayland J. Hayes Jr., "The Effect of Known Repeated Oral Doses of Chlorophenothane (DDT) in Man," *Journal of the American Medical Association* 162, 9 (1956): 890–97; and Hayes, et al., "Storage of DDT and DDE in People with Different Degrees of Exposure to DDT," *AMA Archives of Industrial Health,* 18 (Nov. 1958): 398–406.

91 Use peaked in the late 1950s: U.S. Environmental Protection Agency, "DDT: A Review of Scientific and Economic Aspects of the Decision to Ban Its Use as a Pesticide," prepared for the Committee on Appropriations, U.S. House of Representatives, July 1975.

92 As early as 1946: Clarence Cottam and Elmer Higgins, "DDT and Its Effect on Fish and Wildlife," *Journal of Economic Entomology,* 39 (Feb. 1946): 44–52.

93 Wallace complained: Dunlap, *DDT,* pp. 83–84.

94 Trout in Lake George: Joel Carl Welty, *The Life of Birds,* 3d ed. (1962; reprint, Philadelphia: Saunders College, 1982), p. 641.

94 How could intelligent beings . . . and man himself: Carson, *Spring,* pp. 8, 13.

95 The detective work began: Joseph J. Hickey, "Some Recollections about Eastern North America's Peregrine Falcon Population Crash," and Derek A. Ratcliffe, "The Madison Conference and Research on Peregrines," in Tom J. Cade, James H. Enderson, Carl G. Thelander, and Clayton M. White, eds., *Peregrine Falcon Populations: Their Management and Recovery* (Boise, Idaho: Peregrine Fund, 1988) pp. 9–16, 17–20; also Ratcliffe, *The Peregrine Falcon,* second edition, (London: T & A D Poyser, 1993) and Ratcliffe, phone conversation with author.

96 Told author Thomas R. Dunlap: Dunlap, *DDT,* p. 85.

96 Hickey recruited: Daniel Berger and Chuck Sindelar, phone conversations with author.

97 Clear Lake: Carson, *Spring,* pp. 46–50; Dunlap, *DDT,* pp. 94–96; and EPA, "A Review," pp 26–27.

98 Senator Abraham Ribicoff: Dunlap, *DDT,* p. 124.

98 Tom Cade: Phone conversation with author.

99 Daniel Anderson: Phone conversation with author.

99 North American birds . . . auks in the Arctic: EPA, "A Review," p. 30, 35–36, 49–63.

100 Mallard ducks: R. G. Heath, J. W. Spann, and J. F. Kreitzer, "Marked DDE Impairment of Mallard Reproduction in Controlled Studies," *Nature,* Vol. 47, No. 5214, October 4, 1969, pp. 47–48.

100 American kestrels: Stanley N. Wiemeyer and Richard D. Porter, "DDE Thins Eggshells of Captive American Kestrels," *Nature,* Vol. 227, No. 5259, August 15, 1970, pp. 737–38.

101 Jeffrey Lincer: Jeffrey L. Lincer, "A Suggestion of Synergistic Effects of DDE and Aroclor 1254 on Reproduction of the American Kestrel," in *Raptor Conservation Today,* proceedings of the IV World Conference on Birds of Prey and Owls, Berlin, May 10–17, 1992 (Berlin: Pica Press, 1994).

101 Wiemeyer's later analysis: Wiemeyer, "Environmental Contaminants," p. 213.

102 Calcium ATPase: EPA, "A Review," p. 67.

102 David Peakall: EPA, Ibid. p. 67; and David Peakall, phone conversation with author.

103 Edmund M. Sweeney: Dunlap, *DDT,* p. 212–34; and UPI, "U.S. Urged to Drop Proposed DDT Ban," *New York Times,* April 26, 1972.

104 Ruckelshaus . . . factual findings: EPA, "A Review"; "EPA Consolidated DDT Hearings: Opinion and Order of the Administrator," June 14, 1972, in *Federal Register,* 37, 131 (July 7, 1972): 13369–76; and William Ruckelshaus, phone conversation with author.

106 Myrtle and Charles Broley: Jon Gerrard, *Extraordinary Naturalist* pp. 53–54; and Jean Broley Patric, phone conversations with author.

106 Montrose Chemical: *United States et al. v. Montrose Chemical Corporation et al.,* second amended complaint for natural resource damages, response costs and declaratory relief, filed April 3, 1992, by U.S. Department of Justice; "Injury Determination Plan, Damage Assessment; Los Angeles/Long Beach Harbors, Palos Verdes Shelf, and Ocean Dump Sites," draft prepared for National Oceanic and Atmospheric Administration, U.S. Department of Commerce; U.S. Dept. of Interior; and the State of California, March 8, 1991; and David K. Garcelon, "Effects of Organochlorine Contaminants on Bald Eagle Reproduction at Santa Catalina Island," report prepared Sept. 27, 1994, for U.S. Department of Justice.

108 Risebrough and Garcelon theorize: Robert Risebrough and David Garcelon, phone conversations with author.

108 Do-gooders and pointy-heads: Marla Cone, "In Surprise, Lawsuit over DDT is Dismissed," *Los Angeles Times,* March 23, 1995.

CHAPTER 7: TAKING CARE OF AN EAGLE'S NEST

109 This chapter is based on testimony at civil trial in January 1993 in Bradenton, Florida, before Circuit Court Judge Scott M. Brownell, and on author's interviews of principals, and the following:

121 Two months later . . . Fetters admitted . . . : Plea agreement, *United States of America v. Stephen Fetters and Flotilla, Inc.,* Nov. 2, 1988. Testimony at sentencing, *United States of America v. Stephen Fetters and Flotilla, Inc.,* Jan. 5, 1989.

121 South Carolina developer: *David H. Lucas v. South Carolina Coastal Council,* cite 112, S.Ct 2886 1992.

122 Circuit Court Judge Scott M. Brownell: Order, in the Circuit Court in and for Manatee County, Florida, *Flotilla, Inc., vs. State of Florida, Florida Game and Fresh Water Fish Commission, and the City of Bradenton, Florida,* Feb. 2, 1993.

124 Second District Court of Appeal: *Florida Game and Fresh Water Fish Commission v. Flotilla, Inc.*, Second District Court of Appeal, Case No. 93-00554, opinion, March 16, 1994.

CHAPTER 8: SEMINOLE WIND

126 This chapter is based on author's interviews of principals and *Florida Raptor News* 10, 4 (Winter 1993), published by Florida Audubon's Society's Madalyn Baldwin Center for Birds of Prey; and *Seminole Wind: The Egg-cellent Adventure,* a video produced by the Florida Audubon Society.

129 Sixteen of the thirty-seven eagles: Memo, Jan. 22, 1992, from Resee Collins, Center for Birds of Prey, *Bald Eagle Report 1991.*

132 More than seven hundred names: Fact sheet, suggested names for Florida Audubon Society's Baby Eaglet, Jan. 12, 1993.

CHAPTER 9: AS THICK AS FLIES

140 Seven thousand one hundred eighty-two: P. Brodkorb, "Number of Feathers and Weights of Various Systems in the Bald Eagle," *Wilson Bulletin* 67 (1955): 142.

142 A half-billion-dollar project by Q Corporation: Besides interviews with principals on both sides of the issue, details about Q Corporation plans are derived from Mark Di Vincenzo, *Newport News–Hampton (Va.) Daily Press,* "Company Proposes $400 Million Project," May 12, 1994, and "Q Corp. Tactics Prompt Reaction," Aug. 22; Jon Pope, *Richmond Times-Dispatch,* "Firm Eyes Area near Refuge for Site," May 13, and "Q Corp. Presses Steps to Make Site Eagle-Friendly," July 21; and Rebecca Isom, *Hopewell (Va.) News,* "30,000 Want Job at Q," Sept. 26, 1994.

143 Expenditure of nearly $7 million: Details of real estate transactions that led to establishment of the James River National Wildlife Refuge confirmed by USFWS officials, including Gibb Chase of the service's Region 5 realty division, assistant refuge manager Oscar Reed, and Nature Conservancy personnel, including George Fenwick.

146 Globally rare prairie senna . . . striped bass: U.S. Fish and Wildlife Service, "Final Environmental Assessment: Proposal to Protect Endangered Bald Eagle Habitat, Prince George County, Virginia," Feb. 1989, pp. 16–17.

146 Kepone pesticide: Associated Press "Pesticide Studied in Chesapeake Fish," *New York Times,* Dec. 29, 1975.

146 USFWS report. . . . suffocate: USFWS, "Final Assessment," pp. 14–15; and Nancy J. Morse, David A. Stilwell, and Donald Kane, "The Potential for Contaminant Exposure to Bald Eagles of the James River, Virginia: Prey Contaminant Studies," USFWS report, 1993, p. 3.

148 Longest pontoon bridge: James M. McPherson, *Battle Cry of Freedom: The Civil War Era* (New York: Oxford University Press, 1988), p. 740.

149 Thank God I have lived . . .: Shelby Foote, *Civil War: A Narrative,* vol. 3 (New York: Vintage Books, 1986), p. 896.

149 But long before the North and South . . . afterlife: USFWS, "Final Assessment," pp. 20–21; Tony Opperman and Lefty Gregory, phone conversation with author.

150 Kiewit Industries: Jim Okell, spokesman, Kiewit Industries, phone conversation with author.

150 Nature Conservancy finances: Linda Kanamine and Paul Overberg, "Green Crusade at Crossroads," *USA Today,* Oct. 19, 1994.

159 FWS would "continue to deny any access": Letter from Robert E. Lambertson, USFWS regional director, to Robert T. Barbera, Aug. 4, 1994.

159 one-minute phone call from Barbera: Cindy Schulz, phone conversation with author.
160 Radio telemetry sightings: David A. Buehler, Timothy J. Mersmann, James D. Fraser, and Janis K. Seegar, "Effects of Human Activity on Bald Eagle Distribution on the Northern Chesapeake Bay," *Journal of Wildlife Management* 55, 2 1991:282–90.
160 Increase in shoreline development . . . 2023: James D. Fraser, Sheri K. Chandler, David A. Buehler, and Janis K.D. Seegar, "The Decline, Recovery and Future of the Bald Eagle Population of the Chesapeake Bay, U.S.A.," in B. U. Meyburg and R. D. Chancellor, eds., *Eagle Studies* (World Working Group on Birds of Prey, Berlin, in press).
160 Tainted groundwater . . . urban or residential: George M. Simmons, Virginia Tech, phone conversation with author.

CHAPTER 10: ASKING FOR THE LIFE OF AN EAGLE

162 Nathan Jim Jr.: Material based on author's interviews with principals; court briefs filed by Celeste Whitewolf and Assistant U.S. Attorney Robert B. Ross; depositions of Nathan Jim Jr. and Wilson Wewa Jr.; testimony during an evidentiary hearing before U.S. District Judge James Redden, Portland, Oregon, Oct. 20–21, 1994; and Judge Redden's March 10, 1995, opinion.
164 Today in South Dakota: Former USFWS special agent John Cooper, interview with author, Dec. 1993.
164 Bear Butte, South Dakota: John Cooper, phone conversation with author.
165 Color-coded waiting-list files: Jim Kniffen testimony at evidentiary hearing, interview with author, October 1993, and phone conversation with author.
166 Shortly before sunset: Senior Trooper Paul Randall, phone conversation with author.
168 For at least four thousand years . . . abalone pendants: Robert F. Heizer and Gordon W. Hewes, "Animal Ceremonialism in Central California in the Light of Archaeology," *American Anthropologist* 42, 4 (1940): 587–603; William J. Wallace and Donald Lathrap, "Ceremonial Bird Burials in San Francisco Bay Shellmounds," *American Antiquity* 25, 2 (1959): 262–64.
168 No people on earth . . . pipes and rattles: Frederick W. Hodge, ed., *Handbook of American Indians North of Mexico*, part 1 (New York: Pageant Books, 1959), pp. 409–10.
168 Symbols of the Iroquois Nation: Iroquois Indian Museum, Howes Cave, New York.
168 The dead were placed on scaffolds: Barry Holstrum Lopez, *Of Wolves and Men* (New York: Scribner's, 1978), p. 119.
168 Sioux creation myth: William K. Powers, *Oglala Religion* (Lincoln: University of Nebraska Press, 1975), pp. 84–85.
169 Ashinabe legend: Jimmy Jackson, in John Mathisen, ed., *Bald Eagles: A Comprehensive Look at Bald Eagles,* Cass Lake, Minn.; Chippewa National Forest, USDA Forest Service, copyright Lake States Interpretive Association, International Falls, Minn. (undated), pp. 1–2.
170 Ceremonial whistles . . . five eagle feathers: Hodge, *Handbook*, p. 409.
170 Badge of courage . . . man of substance: James R. Walker, *Lakota Belief and Ritual* (1980; reprint, Lincoln: University of Nebraska Press, 1991), pp. 270–72.
170 Hunted eagles . . . in propitiation: Royal B. Hassrick, *The Sioux: Life and Customs of a Warrior Society* (Norman: University of Oklahoma Press, 1964) pp. 171–72; and Walter McClintock, *The Old North Trial, or Life, Legends and Religion of the Blackfeet Indians* (1910; reprint, Lincoln: University of Nebraska Press, 1968), pp. 427–29.
171 Blackfoot would not eat rosebuds: James George Frazer, *The Golden Bough: A Study in Magic and Religion* abridged ed. (New York: Macmillan, 1960), p. 24.
171 Harmata: Palmer, *North American Birds*, vol. 5, 1988, p. 222.

172 Bellacoola natives: Harlan I. Smith, "Eagle Snaring among the Bellacoola Indians," *Canadian Field-Naturalist* 38 (1924): 167–68.

172 Miwok eagle hunter: Edward W. Gifford, "Miwok Cults," *University of California Publications in American Archaeology and Ethnology* 18, 3 (May 8, 1926): 395.

172 Emergency excavations . . . bones of bald eagles: Paul W. Parmalee, "The Avifauna from Prehistoric Arikara Sites in South Dakota," *Plains Anthropologist* 22, 77 (1977): 189–222.

173 In Oregon, eagle bones: Loye Miller, "Bird Remains from an Oregon Indian Midden," *The Condor* 59, 1 (Jan., 1957): 59–63.

173 Near-extinction . . . Wichita Mountains: Palmer, *North American Birds*, vol. 4, p. 229.

173 At least sixty tail feathers: Ibid., vol. 5, p. 224.

173 Sixteen years ago: Details of Operation Eagle based on USFWS investigative reports and transcriptions of covertly recorded conversations; federal appeals court opinions; and author's interviews with a number of the principals.

174 Native American Church ceremonies: Omer C. Stewart, *Peyote Religion: A History* (Norman: University of Oklahoma Press, 1987), pp 36–39.

174 1858 treaty . . . below the federal poverty level: *United States v. Dwight Dion, Sr., et al.*, U.S. Court of Appeals, Eighth Circuit, May 20, 1985, 762 F.2d 674 (1985).

175 Clamped in traps: John Cooper, interview with author, Dec. 1993.

181 James Watt quote: Dale Russakoff, "Ring Killing Bald Eagles Broken," *Washington Post*, June 16, 1983.

182 Due to other evidence of predisposition . . . such hunting was protected by the 1858 treaty: U.S. Court of Appeals, Eighth Circuit, *U.S. v. Dion*.

183 Eleven years earlier . . . on the Red Lake Reservation: *United States v. Jackie White*, U.S. Court of Appeals, Eighth Circuit, Dec. 9, 1974, 508 F.2d 453 (1974).

183 Justice Thurgood Marshall . . . put the court firmly on the side of the eagles: *United States v. Dwight Dion Sr.*, U.S. Supreme Court, June 11, 1986, 106 S.Ct. 2216 (1986).

CHAPTER 11: THE CREATOR'S LAW

187 Ten years ago . . . elk head: Larry Keeney, phone conversation with author.

187 Grant Clements: Peter S. Nylander, special agent, USFWS, search warrant affidavit, Feb. 10, 1989; *USA v. Grant Clements, Sr.*, indictment, Feb. 23, 1989; interviews with Clements and Sandberg.

190 Six months later . . . in federal prison: *United States v. Rowe*, U.S. Court of Appeals, Tenth Circuit, opinion decided Nov. 10, 1977, 565 F.2d 635 (1977).

192 That same morning . . . burial ceremonies: USFWS investigative reports.

193 Never charged . . . and was recaptured: U.S. District Court Judge William L. Dwyer's staff, U.S. Marshal Todd Kupferer, and Joseph Sandberg, personal communications.

194 Clements, meanwhile, pleaded guilty . . . in federal funds: Clements and Sandberg, interviews with author; letter to author from U.S. District Court Judge Owen Panner, Oct. 25, 1995.

194 Nathan Jim Jr.'s religious rights appeal: Material based on author's interviews with principals; court briefs filed by Celeste Whitewolf and Assistant U.S. Attorney Robert B. Ross; depositions of Nathan Jim Jr. and Wilson Wewa Jr.; testimony during an evidentiary hearing before U.S. District Judge James Redden, Portland, Oregon, Oct. 20–21, 1994; and Judge Redden's March 10, 1995, opinion.

198 Ruled against Nathan Jim Jr.: U.S. District Judge James Redden, opinion, *United States of America v. Nathan S. Jim, Jr.*, March 10, 1995.

CHAPTER 12: "DAMN GOVERNMENT CROWS"

200 In April 1989 . . . : First eagle poisoning incident based on investigative report of Dan Barnhurst: on the author's interviews with Agent Doug McKenna; and on McKenna's investigative reports.

202 The rancher agreed to talk: USFWS investigative reports, including those of McKenna.

203 Compound 1080 . . . red wolf: Jessica Speart, "War on the Range," *Wildlife Conservation,* Sept.–Oct. 1992, pp. 60–61, 82.

203 Barnhurst again phoned McKenna: Investigative reports of Barnhurst and McKenna; author's interview with McKenna.

204 National Wildlife Health Research Center: Nancy J. Thomas and Terry Grosz, phone conversations with author.

204 cholinesterases: U.S. Department of Interior, Fish and Wildlife Service, "New Generation Pesticides Cause Deaths of Bald Eagles," *Research Information Bulletin,* no. 28, 1993.

205 Rings of death: Dan Marshall, U.S. Fish and Wildlife Service senior resident agent, phone conversations with author; Ted Williams, "Who's Poisoning the West?" *Audubon,* March–April 1992, p. 26.

205 Five poisoned black bears: Dan Marshall, phone conversation with author; Williams, "Who's Poisoning," p. 26; Gary Gerhardt, "High Tech Helps Spot Carcasses," *Rocky Mountain News,* March 21, 1992.

206 Slightly altering his mother's maiden name: McKenna, USFWS investigative report and interview with author, April 1993.

207 Several months before the dozen dead eagles: Wyoming phase of investigation based on author's interviews with Rex Shaddox and Doug McKenna; U.S. Department of Justice press release and USFWS fact sheet, Nov. 20, 1992; USFWS investigative reports.

207 Randy Graham: Michael J. Bergin, special agent, criminal investigation division, U.S. Environmental Protection Agency, search warrant affidavit, Sept. 4, 1991; *U.S.A. v. Randy L. Graham,* criminal information and plea agreement, Nov. 20, 1992.

210 July 15, 1991, conversation: Transcript of covertly recorded conversation.

210 Mania for exterminating coyotes: Jack Olsen, *Slaughter the Animals, Poison the Earth* (New York Simon & Schuster, 1971).

211 Spring of 1975: Jack Olsen, "Eagle Poisoning Difficult to Prosecute," *Rocky Mountain News,* June 8, 1975.

211 Wyoming rancher Van Irvine: Ed Christopherson, "The Massacre of Jackson's Canyon," *Outdoor Life,* February 1972, p. 39.

212 Herman Werner . . . killing 363 golden and three bald eagles: Kirk Knox, *Christian Science Monitor,* Aug. 13, 1971; Michael Frome, "The Eagle Killings And Their End Result," *Field & Stream,* December 1971, pp. 44, 79–81.

212 Texas Hill Country: Donald G. Schueler, *Incident at Eagle Ranch,* 2d ed. (1980; reprint, Tucson: University of Arizona Press, 1991), pp. 2–74.

212 Poison culture still permeated the western rangelands: McKenna and Shaddox, interviews with author, April 1993; USFWS investigative reports; and Nov. 11, 1990, USFWS request to continue the covert operation.

213 Dick Strom: Author's interviews with Strom, Rex Shaddox, and Doug McKenna; U.S. Department of Justice press release and USFWS fact sheet, Nov. 20, 1992; USFWS investigative reports; Lori A. Hanson, special agent, criminal investigation division, U.S. Environmental Protection Agency, search warrant affidavit, Sept. 4, 1991; and *U.S.A. v. Richard E. Strom,* criminal information and plea agreement, Nov. 20, 1992.

213 Ronald Heward: U.S. Department of Justice press release and USFWS fact sheet, Nov. 20, 1992; *U.S.A. v. Ronald Heward,* criminal information and plea agreement, signed Nov. 19, 1992.

213 Raymond V. Hall and Roy McBride: U.S. Department of Justice press release and USFWS fact sheet, Nov. 20, 1992; Jim Carrier, "Pueblan Must Wear Monitor for Selling Cyanide Pellets," *Denver Post,* March 24, 1992.

214 Santiago "Junior" Curuchet Jr.: Author's interviews with Curuchet and Doug McKenna; U.S. Department of Justice press release and USFWS fact sheet, Nov. 20, 1992; *U.S.A. v. Santiago Curuchet, Jr.,* criminal information and plea agreement, Nov. 19, 1992.

215 We found enough poison . . . targeted: Speart, "War,"; and Gerhardt, "High Tech," and Gerhart, "Poison Sales Probed in 3 States," *Rocky Mountain News,* Sept. 25, 1991.

216 John Maneotis: Letters from J. Clayton Bedell, U.S. probation officer, and John Maneotis published in *Fence Post,* Jan. 4, 1993.

216 "I have difficulty recalling": Charles Pelkey, "Former State Ag Employee, Laramie Rancher Plead Guilty," *Casper Star-Tribune,* Nov. 21, 1992.

217 Predator losses: U.S. Agricultural Statistics Board, "Sheep and Goats Predator Loss," report, April 27, 1995; and Todd Wilkinson, *Track of the Coyote* (Minocqua, Wisconsin: NorthWord Press, 1995), pp. 103–124; Bob Crabtree, phone conversation with author.

219 Nick Theos . . . drives up: April 1993 interview with author near Rangely, Colorado.

220 McKenna . . . met covertly with Theos: USFWS investigative reports; McKenna, interview with author, April 1993; trial testimony of Rascon, according to Peter Michaelson, special prosecutor, state of Colorado.

221 Theos trial: Theos and McKenna, interviews with author, April 1993; Michaelson, John Griest, Gary Mowad, Ed Nugent, phone conversations with author; Associated Press, "VanDerhoof Testimony Helps Get Rancher Acquitted," *Glenwood Post,* Nov. 6, 1992.

222 Santiago Curuchet's paneled . . . home: Interview with author, April 1993.

CHAPTER 13: SINKHOLE

226 By 1897 the sawmills of Michigan: Wallace Stegner, *Where the Bluebird Sings* (New York: Random House, 1992), p. 124.

226 When Bowerman first . . . three and eight times greater: Bowerman, interview with author, May 1994.

227 A year earlier, Ennis . . . mink and river otters: Rex Ennis, interview with author, May, 1994.

228 eating eleven meals: National Wildlife Federation report, Barbara S. Glenn, project manager, "Lake Michigan Sport Fish: Should You Eat Your Catch?" 1989; and NWF and the Canadian Institute for Environmental Law and Policy, "A Prescription for Healthy Great Lakes," Report of the Program for Zero Discharge, February 1991, p. 5.

229 Mink . . . are extremely sensitive: Timothy J. Kubiak and David A. Best, "Wildlife Risks Associated with Passage of Contaminated, Anadromous Fish at Federal Energy Regulatory Commission Licensed Dams in Michigan," USFWS report, June 21, 1991, pp. 5, 17–18; and Best, phone conversation with author.

229 Between 1961 . . . and 1973, the number of bald eagle pairs: Bowerman, phone conversation with author.

231 Bowerman eventually concluded: William W. Bowerman IV, *Factors Influencing Breeding Success of Bald Eagles in Upper Michigan,* master's thesis, School of Graduate Studies, Northern Michigan University, April, 1991, p. iv.

233 The oldest bird ever found: Bowerman, interview with author, May 1994, and Postupalsky, phone interview with author.

233 The radio telemetry indicated: Bowerman, interview with author, May 1994, and Postupalsky, personal communications.

234 Eating and delivering . . . of just this one nest: Bowerman, *Regulation of Bald Eagle Productivity in the Great Lakes Basin: An Ecological and Toxicological Approach,* doctoral dissertation, Michigan State University, 1993, pp. 18–34; and Bowerman and John P. Giesy Jr., "Ecology of Bald Eagles on the Au Sable, Manistee and Muskegon Rivers," final report to Consumer Power Company, May 15, 1991, Chapter 7, pp. 1–10.

235 Below the Tippy Dam . . . good perch trees: Bowerman, Dave Best, Postupalsky, phone conversations with author.

236 Chippewa National Forest: John Mathisen, interview with author, December 1993, and phone conversation with author.

236 Crowded out . . . sinkhole: Kubiak and Best, "Wildlife Risks," pp. 2–3; and William W. Bowerman, John P. Giesy, David A. Best, and Vincent J. Kramer, "A Review of Factors Affecting Productivity of Bald Eagles in the Great Lakes Region: Implications for Recovery," *Environmental Health Perspectives* 103, suppl. 4 (May 1995): 51–59.

236 Nearly a thousand known chemical substances: Harold E.B. Humphrey, "Chemical Contaminants in the Great Lakes: The Human Health Aspect," in M.S. Evans, ed., *Toxic Contaminants and Ecosystem Health; a Great Lakes Focus* (New York: John Wiley and Sons, 1988), p. 154.

237 Biomagnification factor . . . major source of bald eagle contamination: Kubiak and Best, "Wildlife Risks," pp. 12–17.

237 Certain PCBs can concentrate: James P. Ludwig, John P. Giesy, Cheryl L. Summer, William Bowerman, Richard Aulerich, Steven Bursian, Heidi J. Auman, Paul D. Jones, Lisa L. Williams, Donald E. Tillitt, and Michael Gilbertson, "A Comparison of Water Quality Criteria for the Great Lakes Based on Human and Wildlife Health," *Journal of Great Lakes Research* 19, 4 (1993): 799.

237 Ten different regions: Bowerman, *Regulation of Bald Eagle Productivity,* pp. 219–84.

238 PCBs cannot be removed . . . the bloodstream: Humphrey, "Human Health," pp. 155–56.

238 We carry . . . 40 to 60 parts per trillion; Linda Birnbaum, director, Environmental Toxicology Division, U.S. EPA, phone conversation with author.

239 Xenoestrogens: Devra Lee Davis, H. Leon Bradlow, Mary Wolff, Tracey Woodruff, David G. Hoel, and Hoda Anton-Culver, "Medical Hypothesis: Xenoestrogens as Preventable Causes of Breast Cancer," *Environmental Health Perspectives* 101, 5 (Oct. 1993): 372–77.

239 With higher levels of DDE . . . DDE increased: Mary S. Wolff, Paolo G. Toniolo, Eric W. Lee, Marilyn Rivera, Neil Dubin et al., "Blood Levels of Organochlorine Residues and Risk of Breast Cancer," *Journal of the National Cancer Institute* 85, 8 (April 21, 1993): 648–52; Nancy Krieger, Mary S. Wolff, Robert A. Hiatt, Marilyn Rivera, Joseph Vogelman, and Norman Orentreich, "Breast Cancer and Serum Organocholorines: A Prospective Study among White, Black, and Asian Women," *Journal of the National Cancer Institute* 86, 8 (April 20, 1994): 589–99; and Brian MacMahon, "Pesticide Residues and Breast Cancer?" *JNCI* 86, 8 (April 20, 1994): 572–73.

239 PCBs and DDT produce . . . in rats and mice: Krieger, "Serum," p. 590.

239 Workers exposed: Karen F. Schmidt, "Dioxin's Other Face," *Science News,* Jan. 11, 1992, pp. 24–25.

239 Suppressing the immune system: Schmidt, "Dioxin," p. 24.

239 Exposing gull eggs to DDT . . . defending them: Jon R. Luoma, "New Effect of Pollutants: Hormone Mayhem," *New York Times,* March 24, 1992; National Wildlife Federation and the Canadian Institute for Environmental Law and Policy, Glen Fox, Cana-

dian Wildlife Service, phone conversation with author; and Timothy J. Kubiak, letter to author, Feb. 12, 1996.

240 In Florida, decades . . . most commonly used herbicides: Timothy S. Gross, Louis J. Guillette Jr., Greg R. Masson, John M. Matter, H. Franklin Percival, and Allan R. Woodward, "Contaminant-Induced Reproductive Anomalies in Florida, *Comparative Pathology Bulletin* 26, 4 (Nov., 1994) 1, 2, 6, 8; Guillette, Gross, Masson, Matter, Percival, and Woodward, "Developmental Abnormalities of the Gonad and Abnormal Sex Hormone Concentrations in Juvenile Alligators from Contaminated and Control Lakes in Florida," *Environmental Health Perspectives* 102, 8 (August, 1994) 680–88; Guillette, Gross, Denise A. Gross, Andrew A. Rooney, and Percival, "Gonadal Steroidogenisis in Vitro from Juvenile Alligators Obtained from Contaminated or Control Lakes," *Environmental Health Perspectives* 103, suppl. 4 (May 1995) 31–36; and Gross and Percival, phone conversations with author.

240 At least some PCBs . . . freshwater turtles: Judith M. Bergeron, David Crews, and John A. McLachian, "PCBs as Environmental Estrogens: Turtle Sex Determination as a Biomark of Environmental Contamination," *Environmental Health Perspectives* 102, 9 (Sept. 1994): 780–81.

241 The dioxin TCDD . . . P450 enzymes: Schmidt, "Dioxin," p. 27.

241 Synthetic endocrine disruption . . . block androgen receptors: William R. Kelce, Christy R. Stone, Susan C. Laws, L. Earl Gray, Jon A. Kemppainen, and Elizabeth M. Wilson, "Persistent DDT Metabolite p,p'-DDE Is a Potent Androgen Receptor Antagonist," *Nature*, Vol. 375 (June 15, 1995) 581–85; "Masculinity at Risk," *Nature*, Vol. 375 (June 15, 1995) 522; and Richard M. Sharpe, "Another DDT Connection," *Nature*, Vol. 375 (June 15, 1995) 538–39; and Kelce and Gray, phone conversations with author.

242 DES: Susan M. Love with Karen Lindsey, *Dr. Susan Love's Breast Book*, 2d ed. (New York: Addison Wesley, 1995), p. 208; and Donald F. Tapley, ed., et al., *The Columbia University College of Physicians and Surgeons Complete Home Medical Guide*, rev. ed. (New York: Crown Publishers, 1989), p. 789.

242 Sperm count . . . cryptorchidism: Sharpe, "Another," p. 538.

243 Babies born . . . arithmetic skills: Joseph L. Jacobson, Sandra W. Jacobson, and Harold E. B. Humphrey, "Effects of In Utero Exposure to Polychlorinated Biphenyls and Related Contaminants on Cognitive Functioning in Young Children," *Journal of Pediatrics* 116, 1 (Jan., 1990): 38–45; Jacobson and Jacobson, "A Four-year Follow-up Study of Children Born to Consumers of Lake Michigan Fish," *Journal of Great Lakes Research* 19, 4 (1993): 776–83.

243 One of the study's researchers: Helen Daly, "Laboratory Rat Experiments Show Consumption of Lake Ontario Salmon Causes Behavioral Changes: Support for Wildlife and Human Research Results," Cause-Effect Linkages II Symposium Abstracts conference, Michigan Audubon Society, Sept. 27–28, 1991, pp. 35–37; and Helen Daly, phone conversations with author.

243 Bans during the 1970s . . . any time soon: Keith Schneider, "Progress, Not Victory, on Great Lakes Pollution," *New York Times*, May 7, 1994.

244 Water in Lake Michigan to recycle: William K. Stevens, "Pesticides May Leave Legacy of Hormonal Chaos," *New York Times*, Aug. 23, 1994.

244 Congenital defects in bald eagles: Bowerman, *Regulation of Bald Eagle Productivity*, pp. 203–17; USFWS briefing statement, "Bald Eaglets with Deformities Discovered during 1993 Banding Operation; USFWS fact sheet, "Biologists Discover Eaglets with Deformities," July 8, 1993.

245 Ford plant: EPA bulletin, "U.S. EPA Proposes Cleanup of Ford Outfall Site," January 1995; Charles Slat, "Ford Cleanup Expands to Marsh," *Evening News*, Monroe, Michi-

gan, September 6, 1994; Karen Holtschneider, Ford spokesperson and Steve Sliver, environmental engineer, Michigan Department of Natural Resources, phone conversations with author.

247 Tend to lay female eggs first: Stalmaster, *Bald Eagle*, p. 70; Gary R. Bortolotti, "Evolution of Growth Rate and Nestling Sex Ratio in Bald Eagles," doctoral dissertation, University of Toronto, 1984.

248 Between 1994 and 1995 . . . bottom of the River Raisin: Best, phone conversation with author.

CHAPTER 14: 1,740 BALD EAGLES IN AN HOUR

252 Embarrassment of eagle riches: My principal source of scientific information for this chapter is Andrew J. Hansen, Erwin L. Boeker, John I. Hodges, and David R. Cline, "Bald Eagles of the Chilkat Valley, Alaska: Ecology, Behavior and Management," final report of the Chilkat River Cooperative Bald Eagle Study, National Audubon Society and U.S. Fish and Wildlife Service, March 1984. Largest bald eagles: Gerrard and Bortolotti, p. 14.

252 Their size is an evolutionary adaptation: Gerrard and Bortolotti, *Monarch*, p. 16, and Stalmaster, *Bald Eagle*, pp. 16, 109.

253 Dalton Trail: Lee Gorsuch, Steve Colt, Charles W. Smythe, and Bart K. Garber, "A Study of Five Southeast Alaska Communities," prepared for the U.S. Forest Service, Bureau of Land Management and Bureau of Indian Affairs, Feb. 1994; and Maureen Milburn, "Louis Shotridge and the Objects of Everlasting Esteem," essay in Susan A. Kaplan and Kristin Barnsness, co-authors, *Raven's Journey*, (Philadelphia: University Museum, University of Pennsylvania, 1986), pp. 54–56.

254 John Muir and the Reverend Samuel Hall Young: John Muir, *Travels in Alaska*, 1915 (Reprint, New York: Penguin, 1993) pp. 126–33; and S. Hall Young, *The Alaska Days with John Muir* (New York: Fleming H. Revell, 1915), pp. 83–92.

255 Land use plan for Haines . . . fifteen to twenty-five years: Hansen et al., "Eagles of the Chilkat," p. 8; Jim Reardon, "The Chilkat Miracle," *Audubon*, January 1984, pp. 49–50; David R. Cline, "Citizen Action to Protect the Chilkat Bald Eagles," Audubon paper, 1982; Michael Frome, "Logging Where the Eagles Nest," *Los Angeles Times*, Sept. 16, 1979; Mike Macy and Leonard Steinberg, "A Feast of Eagles: Chainsaws vs. the Food Chain," *Sierra* magazine, July–August 1980, pp. 26, 28; and *Chilkat News*, March 15, April 12, and Aug. 16, 1979.

256 Magnetite, an iron ore: Hansen, "Eagles of the Chilkat," p. 8; Cline, "Citizen Action," pp. 85–86; Raymond Menaker, interview with author, November 1993.

256 People screamed like gut-shot rhinos: Vic Banks, *Smithsonian* magazine, 1979 p. 56.

256 Admiralty Island . . . 40,000 to 45,000 bald eagles: Phil Schempf and Mike Jacobsen, U.S. Fish and Wildlife Service, phone conversations with author.

256 More than 128,000 bald eagles: Fred C. Robards and John G. King, "Nesting Productivity of Bald Eagles in Southeast Alaska," Bureau of Sport Fisheries and Wildlife, 1966.

256 American Rifleman: As quoted in "Eagle Shooting in Alaska," *Nature*, vol. 28, 21, 1936, p. 106.

257 Anxious to reopen its idle mill . . . Hammond signed: Sources for the events that lead to the creation of the eagle preserve include Reardon, "Miracle," pp 40–54; Cline, "Citizen Action," pp. 83–97; and Macy, "Chainsaws," pp. 26, 28.

258 Target ranges: Erwin Boeker, phone conversation with author.

259 State senate: "Haines Seeks Support Against Land Exchange," *Lynn Canal News*, May 15, 1980.

259 Slashing its workforce: Sharon Resnick and Ray Menaker, "Schnabel Mill Will Slash Work Force," *Lynn Canal News*, July 31, 1980.

259 One of the lowest success rates . . . breed each year: Hansen, "Eagles of the Chilkat," pp. 20–21; and Andrew J. Hansen and John I. Hodges, "High Rates of Nonbreeding Adult Bald Eagles in Southeastern Alaska," *Journal of Wildlife Management* 49, 2 (1985): 454–58.

261 Schnabel explained afterward: Sharon Resnick, "Local Folks Draft New Bill For Eagle Home," *Chilkat Valley News*, Feb. 4, 1982.

262 Brenda Wilcox: Angus Durocher, "Eagle Preserve Choice Political, Wilcox Says," *Chilkat Valley News*, Oct. 22, 1992.

263 Tlingits had zealously guarded . . . role of hired packers: Milburn, "Raven's Journey," p. 56; Gorsuch et al., "Five Communities," Appendix A, pp. 5–6; and Wallace M. Olson, *The Tlingit: An Introduction to Their Culture and History* (second edition, Auke Bay, Alaska: Heritage Research, 1991), p. 41.

263 Divided into two clans . . . sacred: George T. Emmons, *The Tlingit Indians*, ed. Frederica de Laguna (Seattle: University of Washington Press–American Museum of Natural History, 1991) p. 138; and Aldona Jonaitis, *Art of the Northern Tlingit* (Seattle: University of Washington Press, 1986), pp. 80, 86–87.

264 Ground zero for Klukwan, Inc.: Thomas R. Berger, *Village Journey* (New York: Hill and Wang, 1985), p. 142; Bill Thomas, personal communication.

265 Annual distribution of $65,000: Bill Thomas, phone conversation with author.

265 Windy Craggy copper mine: Peter Enticknap and interview with author, November, 1993; Bill Thomas, phone conversation with author; Gerald Harper, Geddes Resources Limited president; phone coversation with author; David Darlington, "Windy Craggy and the Rover Big as the Ocean," *Wilderness*, winter 1990, pp. 50–51; "Alsek/Tatshenshini Rivers Wilderness Area Saved," *American Rivers* newsletter, Summer 1993; Peter Enticknap, "Tatshenshini Wild, Forever," *Ravencall*, Southeast Alaska Conservation Council newsletter, Autumn 1993; Carolyne Powell, phone conversation with author; and Geddes Resources 1990 annual report.

265 McDonald Creek: Craig N. Spencer, B. Riley McClelland, and Jack A. Stanford, "Shrimp Stocking, Salmon Collapse, and Eagle Displacement," *BioScience*, vol. 41, 1, January 1991, pp. 14–21; and McClelland, phone conversation with the author.

Chapter 15: In Their Rightful Place

274 Federal listing of bald eagle as threatened, and accompanying data: *Federal Register*, July 12, 1995, pp. 36000–10; and related U.S. Fish and Wildlife Service releases.

274 1995 Florida information: Don Wood and John White, Florida Game and Fresh Water Fish Commission biologists, phone conversations with author.

274 1995 New Jersey information: Larry Niles and New Jersey Endangered and Nongame Species Program, conversations with author.

275 Hacking program: Fact sheet, New Jersey Endangered and Nongame Species Program, May 26, 1992.

276 A small group of landowners: *Babbitt v. Sweet Home Chapter of Communities for a Great Oregon*, June 29, 1995, Supreme Court Reporter, vol. 115 S.CT., p. 2407.

277 Only 19 of 74,000 such consultations: Walter V. Reid, "Creating Incentives for Conserving Biodiversity," essay in "Building Economic Incentives into the Endangered Species Act," a special report from Defenders of Wildlife, Third Edition, May 1994, p. 43.

277 An estimated 50 percent of endangered species: Jim McKinney, Mark Shaffer, Jeff Olson, the Wilderness Society, "Economic Incentives to Preserve Endangered Species

Habitat and Biodiversity on Private Lands," Defenders of Wildlife, "Economic Incentives," p. 1.

277 Seventy-three words: John H. Cushman Jr., "Brief Clause in Bill Would Curb U.S. Power to Protect Wetlands," *New York Times,* Dec. 12, 1995.

278 Out West: Eric Larson, "Unrest in the West," *Time,* Oct. 23, 1995, p. 54; and Ted Williams, "Defense of the Realm, *Audubon,* January–February 1966, pp. 34–36.

278 Pombo and Young bill and Gorton bill: H.R. 2275 and S. 768 and S. 1364; and testimony of George T. Frampton Jr., assistant secretary for fish and wildlife and parks, before the House Resources Committee regarding H.R. 2275, Sept. 20, 1995.

279 Whether or not a farmer: Testimony of Alice Rivlin, director, Office of Management and Budget, before the Senate Environment and Public Works Committee, July 12, 1995.

279 Since its enactment: U.S. Fish and Wildlife Service data, including *Endangered Species Bulletin* 20, 6 (Nov.–Dec. 1995); "Report to Congress: Recovery Program, Endangered and Threatened Species," U.S. Department of the Interior and U.S. Fish and Wildlife Service, 1994.

280 Babbitt's ten-point plan: "The Administration's Ten-Point Plan for the Endangered Species Act," Interior Department paper, Oct. 31, 1995.

280 After creating a lake: John A. Baden and Tim O'Brien, "Toward a true ESA: An Ecological Stewardship Act," Defenders of Wildlife, "Economic Incentives," p. 96.

280 Short of outright compensation: Defenders of Wildlife, "Economic Incentives," including essays by McKinney, Shaffer and Olson; Michael J. Bean; Todd G. Olson, Dennis D. Murphy and Robert D. Thornton; Jane O. Yager; Reid; John H. Goldstein and H. Theodore Heintz Jr.; Patrick Graham; Larry McKinney; Ralph O. Morgenweck; Baden and O'Brien; and Randal O'Toole.

281 Babbitt estimated: Jack Anderson, "Babbitt Battles over Mining Rights," *Doylestown (Pa.) Intelligencer,* Oct. 27, 1995.

282 Wildlife Diversity Funding: *Conserve Wildlife,* newsletter of NJ Endangered and Nongame Species Program, spring-summer 1995.

283 We need wilderness: Edward Abbey, *Desert Solitaire: A Season in the Wilderness* (New York: Ballantine Books, 1968), pp. 148–49.

283 Bird-watchers spend $5.2 billion: FWS study.

283 Sauk-Prairie Wintering Ground: Richard Van Konigsveld, "Eagle Watchers along the Wisconsin River: Survey Results from the Winter of 1993–1994," Report of the Ferry Bluff Eagle Council and the University of Wisconsin—Extension, August 1994. Plant-derived pharmaceuticals: Thomas Eisner, Gordon Cragg, phone conversations with author.

284 Only one in 10,000 species: "Science and the Endangered Species Act," National Research Council, 1995, p. 149.

285 Bob Hall: Bob Hall, "Green and Gold" study produced by Institute for Southern Studies, October 1994.

286 The only landowners . . .: Holmes Rolston III, "Life in Jeopardy on Private Property," in Kathryn A. Kohm, ed., *Balancing on the Brink of Extinction* (Washington: Island Press, 1991), p. 58.

286 Chief concern is persistent pollution: Osprey data, Kathy Clark, personal communication; eagle data, Mark R. Roberts and Kathy Clark, "Evaluation of Contaminant Residues in Delaware Bay Bald Eagle Nestlings," NJ Endangered and Nongame Species Program, October 1995.

SELECTED BIBLIOGRAPHY

For readers interested in delving deeper into the natural history of the bald eagle, two books in particular warrant serious review: Mark V. Stalmaster, *The Bald Eagle* (New York: Universe Books, 1987); and Jon M. Gerrard and Gary R. Bortolotti, *The Bald Eagle: Haunts and Habitats of a Wilderness Monarch* (Washington, D.C.: Smithsonian Institution Press, 1988). For an earlier, classic take on the subject, consult Francis Hobart Herrick, *The American Eagle: A Study in Natural and Civil History* (New York: Appleton-Century, 1934).

For briefer authoritative species accounts, the most recent is contained in volume 4 of the *Handbook of North American Birds,* edited by Ralph S. Palmer (New Haven: Yale University Press, 1987). Palmer's handbook was launched, in part, to replace Arthur Cleveland Bent's *Life Histories of North American Birds of Prey: Order Falconiformes* (Part 1), which contains accounts of both the southern and northern bald eagle. Bent's work was originally published in 1937 as *The Smithsonian Institution United States National Museum Bulletin 167.* Dover Publications reprinted both parts in one volume in 1961. For sheer reading pleasure, I also recommend these classic works of American ornithology: John James Audubon, *The Birds of America* (London, 1827) and *Ornithological Biography* (1834); Thomas Nuttall, *A Manual of the Ornithology of the United States and Canada* (1832); and Alexander Wilson, *American Ornithology or the Natural History of the Birds of the United States,* vol. 4, (Bradford and Inskeep, 1811).

George Laycock's *Autumn of the Eagle* (New York: Scribner's, 1973), presents the finest book-length account of the bald eagle at its nadir. His work includes details on the poisoning and shooting of eagles by wool growers in Wyoming and elsewhere in the early 1970s. The ranchers' war on predators, including eagles, is also the focus of two other outstanding volumes: Jack Olsen's *Slaughter the Animals, Poison the Earth* (New York: Simon & Schuster, 1971); and Donald G. Schueler, *Incident at Eagle Ranch: Predators as Prey in the American West,* 2d ed. (Tucson: University of Arizona Press, 1991).

For a comprehensive understanding of how the eagle became our national symbol, read Richard S. Patterson and Richardson Dougall, *The Eagle and the Shield: A History of the Great Seal of the United States,* Publication 8900, U.S. Department of State, 1976. Philip M. Isaacson, *The American Eagle* (New York: Graphic Society Books, 1975), offers an expansive review of the eagle in art and design; photographically, so does Clarence P. Hornung in his aptly titled work, *The American Eagle in Art and Design* (New York: Dover Publications, 1978).

For more details on the life and work of Charles Broley, I refer you to the biography written by his wife, Myrtle Jean Broley, *Eagle Man: Charles L. Broley's Field Adventures with American Eagles* (New York: Pellegrini and Cudahy, 1952); and Jon Gerrard's brief but sweet *Charles Broley: An Extraordinary Naturalist* (Headingley, Manitoba: White Horse Plains, 1983).

For a greater understanding of the effects of DDT and the process that led to its being banned in the United States, I recommend Thomas R. Dunlap's thorough *DDT: Scientists, Citizens and Public Policy* (Princeton, N.J.: Princeton University Press, 1981). To understand the genesis of the movement that culminated in the prohibition of DDT and its ilk, you may want to reread Rachel Carson, *Silent Spring* (1962; reprint, Boston: Houghton Mifflin, 1987).

Readers interested in wildlife law should seek out Michael J. Bean, *The Evolution of National Wildlife Law,* rev. ed. (New York: Environmental Defense Fund, Praeger, 1983).

Finally, for those interested in researching bald eagles or other raptors, a seminal source is the Raptor Information System, part of the U.S. Department of Interior's Raptor Research and Technical Assistance Center in Boise, Idaho. The system is based, in part, on *Working Bibliography of the Bald Eagle,* by Jeffrey L. Lincer, William S. Clark, and Maurice N. LeFranc Jr. (Washington, D.C.: National Wildlife Federation, 1979), a comprehensive compilation of articles and publications to that date on the bald eagle.

INDEX